D1594696

# The Fighting 69th

## A History

by

Richard Demeter

*Cranford Press • Pasadena, California*

# The Fighting 69th
## A History

Published by
Cranford Press
500 Cliff Drive, Pasadena, California 91107
Tel: 626-351-9263 • Fax: 626-568-0152
Email: DemeterR45@aol.com

First Edition

Printed in the United States of America

ISBN: 0-9648253-5-X

### Copyright Acknowledgments

For permission to use the copyrighted material included in this volume, the publisher is indebted to:

Ted Savas for excerpts from *My Life in the Irish Brigade: The Civil War Memoirs of Private William McCarter*, edited by Kevin E. O'Brien and published by Savas Publishing Company, 1996.

Victor Olney for "The New 69th Veteran" by Victor Olney. Copyright © 2001.

### Other works by Richard Demeter

*Primer, Presses, and Composing Sticks: Women Printers of the Colonial Period*
*Irish America: The Historical Travel Guide (Volumes 1 and 2)*
*Irish Americans: A Versified Company*

# Contents

# Introduction

One of the most recognized and most honored military units in American history is the 69th New York Regiment, known since the Civil War as the "Fighting 69th." Originally an amalgamation of militia companies composed almost entirely of Irish immigrants, it was first known as the 69th New York State Militia Regiment, a designation it officially received on October 12, 1851.

It was as a militia regiment that the 69th and its famous commander, Colonel Michael Corcoran, answered President Lincoln's call for volunteers to defend the Union in April 1861. During the Union rout at Bull Run the following July, the regiment suffered heavy losses, including the capture of Corcoran. Although the 69th was soon mustered out of federal service, more than 500 of the men decided to offer their services to the federal government once again. Formed into a newly recruited regiment now known as the 69th New York State Volunteers, they were commanded by Lieutenant Colonel Robert Nugent. The 69th was one of three New York regiments which later joined the Irish Brigade, organized and led by Thomas Francis Meagher, the famous Irish patriot and orator. The 69th participated with the Brigade in some of the war's most hard-fought battles, including Antietam, its bloodiest, and Fredericksburg, its most desperate. At Antietam the 69th suffered a casualty rate of 61 percent, while at Fredericksburg three months later the regiment lost 128 men killed and wounded, fully 68 percent of its strength. Of the 2,000 regiments that fought for the Union, the 69th New York was ranked sixth in the number of men killed or mortally wounded. (Its fatality rate was higher than that of any other regiment from New York State.) Of the regiment's total enrollment of 1,513 men, 259 soldiers were killed or mortally wounded, an additional 535 suffered less serious wounds, 148 were described as missing, eighty-six died of disease or accidents, and fifty-six perished in Confederate prisons.

When the United States declared war on Spain in the spring of 1898, the 69th New York National Guard displayed the same readiness to serve which earlier members of the regiment had shown at the commencement of the Civil War. After being mustered into the service of the United States, the regiment first underwent training in Chickamauga, Georgia, and then was transferred to Tampa, Florida, and Huntsville, Alabama. (The 69th made such an impressive showing during a review of the troops at Huntsville that the secretary of war mistook the men for regulars rather than volunteers.) Because the men of the 69th were eager to participate in the fighting against Spain, when it appeared that they might be assigned merely to garrison duty in Cuba or Puerto Rico, more than 700 of them signed a petition in protest. In the end, the 69th New York was never sent to the front during the war, although it remained in the service of the United States until January 31, 1899.

Seventeen years later the 69th New York was one of the National Guard units called into service to combat Mexican marauders along the border with Mexico. Although most of the Guardsmen had expected to see military action, they instead spent most of their time drilling, improving their marksmanship, and "hiking." A potentially disastrous incident occurred, however, near the pumping station in Mission, Texas, along the Rio Grande, when a squad from the 69th returned fire against what was thought to be a band of Mexicans crossing the river in a boat. In the end, the experience along the border was disappointing because the 69th participated in no significant military engagements. Nevertheless, the regiment's officers and men gained valuable experience for what was soon in store for them in France.

When the United States declared war on Germany in April 1917, almost all the men who had served with the 69th New York along the Mexican border accompanied the regiment on its famous expedition to France. Redesignated as the 165th Infantry, the regiment logged 180 days of actual contact with the enemy and suffered 3,501 casualties (644 killed and 2,857 wounded). The unit's most illustrious exploit during the war occurred in the battle on the Ourcq River in July 1918 — what Colonel Frank McCoy correctly predicted would always be the "proudest remembrance" of every man in the regiment. After the war the 165th adorned its famous battle flag with nine new furls for action in the following sectors or campaigns: Lunéville, Baccarat, Esperance-Souain, Champagne-Marne, Aisne-Marne, St. Mihiel, Essey and Pannes, and Argonne-Meuse (first and second phases). In addition, the regiment boasted three winners of the Congressional Medal of Honor and 160 recipients of seven other major honors, including the French War Cross (62 men) and the Distinguished Service Cross (60).

During World War II the 165th Infantry served in the Pacific with the 27th Division. By then about 70 percent of the men in the regiment — which still bore the title "Fighting Irish" — were of Irish ancestry, a decrease of about 10 percent since 1917. When the 165th sailed from San Francisco for Hawaii, the regiment was part of the first combat infantry division to be deployed overseas during the conflict. (In addition, the regiment's wartime overseas service would become the longest of any National Guard division in the United States Army.) In Hawaii the 165th commenced training for the first American offensive in the Pacific — an invasion of Makin, a small atoll 2,000 miles southwest of Oahu in the Gilbert Islands. When Makin was finally taken in November 1943, its capture was the first of a Japanese-held island by U.S. army troops. Seven months later, in June 1944, the 165th Infantry was part of a force that wrested control of Saipan, an island in the Marianas, from an enemy force of 30,000 troops. The 165th captured the island's airfield and suffered heavy casualties while helping clear off Purple Heart Ridge. (During the Saipan campaign the 27th Division, which went into action with 16,404 men, suffered 3,566 casualties — 1,034 killed and missing and 2,532 wounded.) The following spring the 165th was again part of the 27th Division as it played a major role in the capture of Okinawa off the Japanese mainland. In advancing toward Machinato Airfield, the 165th was forced to overcome a formidable system of Japanese defenses. The three main obstacles in this network came to be known as Ryan's Ridge (for the captain of F Company, which captured it), Charlie Ridge (for C Company, which tried for several days to take it), and Potter's Ridge (for the captain of I Company, which eventually occupied it). For their remarkable endurance during this campaign, Company F and Captain Bernard Ryan later received a Distinguished Unit Citation.

After World War II the 165th Infantry returned to its earlier designation as the 69th New York, a unit in the New York National Guard. Although the famous command is still called the "Fighting 69th," today it is a mechanized one officially known as the First Battalion, 69th Infantry, and is part of the 42nd Infantry Division (Mechanized).

* * * * * * * * * * * * * *

The members of the 69th New York were preparing to celebrate the famous unit's 150th anniversary when terrorists attacked the World Trade Center in New York City on September 11, 2001. The "Fighting 69th" was activated immediately, and at about 9 p.m. on that fateful day eight city buses arrived at the 69th's armory to transport men from the 105th Infantry and from Company E of the 69th to assist in rescue and recovery efforts. The 69th was thus one of the first military units on duty at what quickly became known as "Ground Zero." About half the soldiers in the 69th were later sent to provide security at the U.S. military academy at West Point, while the other half helped protect New York City's bridges and tunnels.[1]

On Tuesday and Wednesday after the attack on the World Trade Center, the 69th served with other search and rescue teams on the site. Beginning on Thursday, however, the unit was deployed as a guard around "Ground Zero" until ordered to stand down on September 17. On that same Thursday troops from the 69th were dispatched to the rooftops of neighboring buildings, where they discovered the grizzly remains of victims who had desperately jumped from the Twin Towers. Besides recovering the bodies of these unfortunates, troops from the 69th guarded the temporary morgue set up at 1 Liberty Plaza — the old Merrill Lynch building.[2]

One of the soldiers who spent three days searching the roofs of the buildings near the attack site was Sergeant Norberto Berrios. For twelve years he had been an engine mechanic with the First Battalion, 69th Infantry, until he joined the battalion's Scout Platoon on September 11. "Nothing can prepare you for what we've seen during the past week," said Berrios, who in civilian life is a security officer for a real estate firm. "These terrorists have woken a giant that has been asleep since World War II." On September 18, however, Berrios suffered a broken ankle, an accident which led to his medical release from duty the next day. Despite his injury, Berrios came away from the week-long experience with a positive point of view: "This has made me more of a people-oriented person because I've seen New York come together as one people. This has made me cherish my wife and my three kids even more."[3]

In the meantime, the 69th's armory on Lexington Avenue had become the bereavement and support center for the families of the World Trade Center victims. Although the facility takes up about three-quarters of a city block and the drill shed is six stories high, it was too small to handle the situation. As a result, the information center and emergency operations were transferred to the Passenger Terminal Pier along the Hudson River at 54th Street. Within days of the terrorist attack, the armory and the area around it were enveloped with thousands of posters containing information about the missing victims. In addition, thousands of grieving family members gathered at the armory to give DNA samples and scan lists for the names of identified bodies. At night the hundreds of lighted candles which surrounded the armory created a religious atmosphere. Victor Olney, a former sergeant in the 69th Infantry, described the scene to his friends and acquaintances: "[T]his beautiful 1906 Beaux Arts Building stands like a Cathedral with all the flickering lights of love and tribute and remembrance."[4]

The enormity of the catastrophe that had hit New York City came home to the 69th Infantry in a special way when it was learned that Gerard Baptiste was among the more than 300 firefighters reported missing. Baptiste, a fireman with Ladder 9 in the SoHo district of lower Manhattan, was also an officer in the 69th — first lieutenant of Company A, First Battalion. A memorial service for the native of Santo Domingo was held at Riverside Church in Manhattan on November 16. A profile of Gerard in the *New York Times* three weeks later noted that he routinely carried dog biscuits in his pockets to give to the pets that walked past his fire station. "I always found crumbs in his pockets," reported his girlfriend.[5]

Although New York City was still reeling from the attack on the Twin Towers, a handful of soldiers from the First Battalion, 69th Infantry, gathered in Battery Park in lower Manhattan on October 12 to mark the 150th anniversary of the "Fighting 69th." At 12:30 p.m. a color detail marched into Castle Clinton, where Corporal Lazar proceeded to read a proclamation in honor of the occasion. The document noted that the 69th traced its roots to a militia regiment formed in 1851 by a group of immigrants desirous of protecting their homes and their families. The proclamation went on to point out the regiment's subsequent service in the Civil War, in France during World War I, in the Pacific during the Second World War, and in the aftermath of the attack on the World Trade Center — "their nation's darkest hour." For the next 150 minutes the regimental colors flew proudly above Castle Clinton.[6]

During the brief ceremony one of the chaplains attached to the 69th Infantry, First Lieutenant Scott Kovalcik, gave the invocation:

"Dear Heavenly Father: We come before you today to ask your further blessing and protection upon our unit. We are soldiers forever dedicated to the idea that all peoples have the right to worship you in freedom. Freedoms that include the inalienable right to be liberated from all physical, radical, and spiritual oppression. From our humble beginnings in 1851, the 69th has fought against the forces of evil that would limit an American's God-given right to live in peace, to worship you, and to prosper as a people [sic].

"These men and women today represent immigrant peoples from all over the world who have come to New York to find rest, freedom, and peace from all sorts of oppression and violence. We desire, like our Irish comrades before us, to finally lay to rest the divisions in our society like nationality, race, gender, and slavery. Our comrades before us died to make all of mankind free in places called *Bull Run, Antietam, and Fredericksburg! Their fighting selfless spirit and bravery under fire even brought them the respect and admiration of our enemy's commanding general [Robert E. Lee], who gave us our title — 'The Fighting Sixty-Ninth.'

"We were called on again to fight oppression and world imperialism in the fields and woods of France in places named *Somme, Meuse, and the Argonne, where scores of Irish immigrants paid the ultimate price to be able to worship you in freedom and live their lives in liberty.

"Only a few years later, we were called by our great nation to oppose the forces of evil and genocide under the banners of a pagan, twisted cross and an effigy of the rising sun! The 69th again answered our nation's call in places named *Saipan, Makin, and [Okinawa]. It was the darkest moment of World War II when the fate of our country hung in the balance that we bled and died 'til Old Glory waved once more over *Mount Surabachi [sic].

"Today we stand our ground where we once were formed a hundred and fifty years ago, on the streets of Manhattan, where Old Glory was again raised by immigrant firemen over the sacred ground where our loved ones paid their last full measure of devotion to our God and country! Most gracious and ever-loving father of us all, we stand here today recalling your blessing and grace upon us. We, the soldiers of the 69th, ask you again to make us your strong, ready, and holy people. Make us an instrument of your justice, ever willing to sacrifice our very lives in the cause of our founding fathers and mothers. A holy and righteous cause, to defend our people and to grant to them our blessing of life, liberty, justice, and the pursuit of peace in the land of the free and the home of the brave."[7]

Early the following month Victor Olney versified the thoughts that had been forming in his mind as he witnessed firsthand the aftermath of the attack on the World Trade Center. His mention of West Street in the poem below is an allusion to the western boundary of the World Trade Center area.

*"The New 69th Veteran" by Victor Olney

I stroll along these hallowed halls
And hear the Regiment's story,
The saga of old Veterans
And their tales of Honor and Glory.

I hear of Erin's Pride
And I am quite moved,
As their stories have left me
A soldier with deeds unproved.

I follow in their footfalls
And am proud to do just that,
For they have shown me the way,
The path to Hell and Back.

Now it is my time —
For me alone to shine,
And make the 69th more Hallowed.
'Tis our Unit — yours and mine.

Enemies of our Country
Attack one bright fall day,
Not just like Pearl Harbor,
But it hurts us the same way.

I join my Comrades seeking
To save lives that can't be found,
As we scratch and crawl among the rubble
Of this most sacred ground.

I can't tell you what I saw
This most horrible of days.
It can't have been as bad as this

In the Regiment's historic forays.

Gettysburg, Fredericksburg,
These names echo true.
None can be worse than West Street.
This 69th soldier was there for us and for you.

You may speak of Makin, Okinawa and Saipan;
I was there on West Street and I grew to be a man.
Like you I served with honor
And served my Country in its darkest dawn.

The next time that you see me
Let us exchange a salute.
The 69th is yours and mine,
That is something no one can refute.

You may recall Pearl Harbor
And I Baptiste's sacrifice.
In the end we are one and all
69th brothers — one universe.

I am now the new Veteran!
Ready to serve, fight and die like you.
I am the Fighting 69th!
My color? Red, White and Blue!

I salute you, my 69th brother,
And ask that you stand with me.
Raise the Colors; share a Toast;
Praise our common home — the Land of Liberty.[8]

* * * * * * * * * * * * * * *

*Arma virosque poesemque cano.*

The *Fighting 69th: A History* is a survey of the illustrious military career of the 69th New York. This work focuses less on such topics as tactics
and strategy, however, than on the personalities who emblazon the pages
of the famous regiment's history. In addition to its well-known officers —
men like Michael Corcoran, Thomas Meagher, Robert Nugent, William
Donovan, Gardiner Conroy, Gerald Kelley, and Bernard Ryan — the 69th
boasted hundreds of other "sons of Mars" who, though little heralded,
contributed to its glorious reputation.

In composing this tale of "Arms and the Men," I have included thirty-five poems and songs related directly or indirectly to the saga of the 69th New York. Some of these works of verse were written by journalists or other scribes who were attached to the renowned regiment for various periods of time. "Requiem for the Dead of the Irish Brigade," for example, was penned by John Savage, a journalist who acted as a volunteer aide to Colonel Corcoran soon after the 69th New York State Militia Regiment offered to serve in the Union cause. This plaintive yet hopeful poem honors the soldiers of the Irish Brigade who made the supreme sacrifice, including those 69th New York Volunteers slaughtered at Fredericksburg. As a similar tribute Charles G. Halpine, a reporter for the *New York Times*, composed "On Raising a Monument to the Irish Legion" several years after serving briefly as a private in the 69th New York. Rupert Hughes, a third professional author who soldiered in the 69th, wrote a humorous magazine article about the rigorous training which the regiment endured along the Mexican border in 1916. (When a slight hearing impairment later prevented Hughes from accompanying the 69th overseas to France, he dedicated a volume of his Irish short stories to the famous regiment "with homage and with envy.") The most renowned versifier in the Fighting 69th, though, was Joyce Kilmer, who, like Halpine, had been a member of the *New York Times* staff before enlisting in the American Expeditionary Force sent to France during World War I. To memorialize the men of the regiment who were killed in an enemy attack on their dugout in March 1918, Kilmer wrote a moving poem entitled "Rouge Bouquet." Another poet of sorts in the 69th New York — though of a decidedly unprofessional calibre — was John O'Keefe. His poem "Blaustein of the Irish" — a piece of doggerel about a Jewish soldier in the regiment — reminded the world that not all the men in the famous 69th were of Irish ancestry.

Of the many sources used in the composition of this history, eleven deserve special mention because their authors were members of the 69th New York. The lengthiest of the five Civil War sources is an autobiographical account of Colonel Michael Corcoran's thirteen-month-long captivity in Southern prisons after the battle of First Bull Run. Two of the other Civil War memoirs give details of the battle of Fredericksburg. The first — a letter from First Lieutenant John Donovan of Company D — was written while he was recuperating from wounds sustained during the devastating battle. The second contains recollections and statistics from the battle compiled by Colonel Robert Nugent, who commanded the 69th New York on that dreadful day in December 1862.

The final two Civil War chronicles were written by men who shared a common Irish ancestry but whose contemporary reputations were decidedly different. The more famous author — Thomas Francis Meagher — wrote about the last days of the 69th in Virginia, while William O'Meagher was the little-known co-author of *The Irish Brigade and Its Campaigns*.

O'Meagher, a surgeon with the 69th New York, completed this latter work on behalf of his friend, David Power Conyngham, the book's better-known co-author. Because Conyngham had spent the last two years of the war covering General William Sherman's campaign through the South, he was unfamiliar with the final months of the Irish Brigade's history. As a result, Conyngham entrusted what he called the "pleasing task" of writing the Brigade's history for 1864 and 1865 to O'Meagher.

Four other members of the 69th New York chronicled the exploits of the regiment during World War I. The most lively — and at times the most earthy — of the accounts is *A Doughboy with the Fighting 69th*, coauthored by Albert Ettinger. This book contains numerous anecdotes, as does *Father Duffy's Story: A Tale of Humor and Heroism, of Life and Death with the Fighting Sixty-Ninth*. These two memoirs differ distinctly in tone, however, since the latter work was written by the 69th's beloved chaplain. In its published form Father Duffy's memoir is followed by a historical appendix by Joyce Kilmer surveying the history of the 69th in France until the poet's untimely death at the front. Kilmer's account is notable for its portrayal of French domestic scenes. Of the four World War I accounts, Martin Hogan's — *The Shamrock Battalion of the Rainbow: A Story of the "Fighting Sixty-Ninth"* — is the most martial, recording at length military tactics and the horrors of the battlefield. After describing the welcome which the 69th received on its return to New York City, Hogan concluded his memoir with characteristic pride: "This parade closed the latest chapter of the regiment's service, and throughout that chapter the old organization was true to its proud tradition, a tradition that reaches back to the founding of the Sixty-ninth in 1851, and that was maintained in fifty battles of the Civil War and forty-four battles of the World War — 'It never disobeyed an order; it never lost a flag!'"[9]

Throughout the following chapters, the reader will occasionally notice words or allusions preceded by an asterisk. This marker alerts the reader to a corresponding note of explanation in the chapter notes at the end of the book. An asterisk preceding the title of a poem indicates that allusions within the verse are explained in the chapter notes also. Because the 69th New York is mentioned so frequently throughout the text, references to it are not noted in the index.

Richard Demeter
March 17, 2002

# Illustrations

191.  Thomas Francis Meagher equestrian statue
      *State Capitol grounds, Helena, Montana*

192.  Thomas Francis Meagher equestrian statue
      *State Capitol grounds, Helena, Montana*

208.  Memorial to the men of the 69th New York
      who died during the Spanish-American War
      *Calvary Cemetery, Woodside, Queens, Long Island, New York*

210.  Armory of the 69th New York National Guard Regiment
      *Lexington Avenue and 25th Street, Manhattan, New York City*

245.  Birthplace of Joyce Kilmer
      *17 Joyce Kilmer Avenue, New Brunswick, New Jersey*

282.  Statue of Father Francis Duffy
      *Father Duffy Square, Broadway and West 47th Street,*
      *Midtown Manhattan, New York City*

301.  Memorial to the 69th New York Regiment
      *Calvary Cemetery, Woodside, Queens, Long Island, New York*

# Poems and Songs

# Chapter 1

## Michael Corcoran, the 69th New York State Militia Regiment, and Corcoran's Irish Legion

According to the U.S. Sanitary Commission's report of 1869, 144,221 Irish-born soldiers and officers served on the Union side during the Civil War. Estimates run higher, to 170,000 Irish soldiers, and a case has been made for 300,000 based on casualty figures. Of the Irish-born soldiers officially recorded, New York had the largest number (51,206), followed by Pennsylvania (17,418), Illinois (12,041), Massachusetts (10,007), Ohio (8,129), Missouri (4,362), and Wisconsin (3,621).[1]

One of the most famous of the predominantly Irish units in the war was the 69th New York State Militia Regiment, commanded initially by Colonel Michael Corcoran. Born in 1827 at Carrowkeel, County Sligo, Ireland, Corcoran claimed descent from Patrick Sarsfield, a leader in the Irish Catholic resistance to King William III at the end of the seventeenth century. At the age of nineteen and perhaps because of the influence of his father, a retired officer in the British army, the younger Corcoran accepted an appointment as a member of Her Majesty's revenue police. For three years he carried out his duties tracking down and arresting outlaw distillers from his base at Creeslough in County Donegal.[2]

As Corcoran enforced the revenue laws, though, he could not help but be affected by the misery, starvation, and poverty which accompanied those high-water days of the "Great Hunger" then ravaging Ireland. Incensed by centuries of English oppression in Ireland and by landlords who callously evicted their tenants rather than provide relief for them, the young man joined a company of rural guerillas known as the Ribbonmen. Before long he found himself leading an ironic double life: pursuing lawbreakers during the day and harassing and terrorizing ruthless landlords by killing their livestock and burning their barns at night. Because his six-foot-two-inch frame made him easily recognizable on his nocturnal raids, he came under suspicion for seditious activity. Wisely, he sailed for America in the fall of 1849.[3]

Soon after his arrival in New York City that October, the young exile found employment at the Hibernian House, a tavern at 42 Prince Street, very close to St. Patrick's Old Cathedral. At the tavern he not only kept the books for the owner but also controlled rowdiness at the dances and organized the various social and political events held there. When the proprietor fell ill and died in 1853, Corcoran assumed the management of the well-known public house. His reliability, good looks (blue eyes and light auburn to brown hair), and personal contacts made him a useful client of the city's Tammany Hall political machine. His principled loyalty to St.

Tammany led to his appointment to a well-paying patronage job in the post office.[4]

It may have been through the urging of acquaintances at the Hibernian House that Corcoran joined one of the many companies of "minutemen" which recent immigrants to the city had formed. In April 1850 the first regiment of Irish-Americans — the Irish Volunteer Regiment — had been mustered into the New York State Militia. By June of the following year, eight new companies had been organized in response to the desire to form another regiment of Irishmen or men of Irish parentage. In August another unit — Company I, the "Irish Rifles" — was added, numbering among its thirty members Private Michael Corcoran. Known as the Second Regiment of Irish Volunteers, this militia unit was officially accepted as part of the New York State Militia on October 12, 1851. Following its redesignation as the 69th New York State Militia Regiment, this unit was placed in the hands of its first commander, Colonel Charles S. Roe. At its first regimental inspection, the 69th New York was composed of eight companies numbering 643 men, but in its second year the 69th grew to its full complement of 1,000 men in ten companies. Colonel Roe was succeeded in command of the 69th by Colonel Michael Phelan and Colonel Michael Doheny, and in 1855 Colonel James Ryan was elected to lead the regiment. Two years later two other Irish units — the Ninth and the 75th New York militia regiments — were added to the ranks of the 69th New York.[5]

As of 1853, of the 6,000 uniformed militiamen in New York State, 2,600 were Irish born. Numbered among the more well-known of these part-time soldiers was *Michael Doheny, who had enjoyed a notable career in Ireland as a writer, a barrister, and a revolutionary before his escape to America in 1848. The forty-three-year-old emigrant was naturally drawn to the Celtic military companies that abounded in New York City, and by 1853 he was a lieutenant colonel in the newly formed 69th New York State Militia Regiment. On St. Patrick's Day that year he delivered an eloquent oration detailing the struggle between James II and William III on Irish soil at the end of the seventeenth century. With William's victory, Doheny said, the Irish patriot *Patrick Sarsfield fled with his followers to France, where they formed the fabled Irish Brigade in the service of France. The account of Doheny's speech in the *New York Times* indulged in the litany of the Brigade's victories on the Continent: "Frequently was Irish bravery the means of humbling the English flag. On the plains of *Landen Sarsfield fell — the green flag of his brigade floating victorious, that of England lowered before him. When the City of *Cremona was surprised in the dead of night, by Prince Eugene, who had gained secret access to the city with seven thousand of his forces, the Po gate was defended by an intrepid band of thirty-five Irish soldiers; and thus preventing Prince Eugene's junction with his other forces, the French had time to recover from their surprise, and the city was saved. Once again, on the plains of *Fontenoy, the

Irish Brigade met their old enemy, the English. *One hundred and eigthy thousand men had met upon that field. After ten hours fighting, little impression had been made, when *Lord Edward Hay led a body of eight thousand English, and forced the French from a hill. Victory now seemed with the English. It was then that the Irish Brigade, led on by *Sir Arthur Dillon, who gave the watchword, 'Remember Limerick and the treachery of the *Sassenach,' rushed on the victorious English, and in one fierce charge decided the day. Of the eight thousand English who had ascended the hill, but four thousand returned." Doheny concluded his remarks by reminding his audience that Irishmen had helped win American independence and that 20,000 Irish-American militiamen stood ready to fight for the interests of America, "this Land of Freedom."[6]

In the meantime, Michael Corcoran had risen up the ranks of the 69th New York State Militia Regiment. First elected orderly sergeant and then first lieutenant of Company I, the young Irishman was commissioned captain of the Irish Rifles (now known as Company A) in 1853. In August 1859 he succeeded Colonel Ryan in command of the regiment. Just over a year later, however, Corcoran and the 69th New York found themselves at the center of a minor international incident. The political, commercial, and social elites of New York City had planned a glorious welcome for the Prince of Wales when the nineteen-year-old future King Edward VII vis-

*The grave of Michael Doheny, organizer of the 69th New York Regiment, in Calvary Cemetery in Woodside, Queens, Long Island, New York. (Location: Section 4, Range 23, Plot R, Grave 11/14)*

ited the city in October 1860. When the local militia regiments were called upon to participate in a grand military parade in Prince Albert Edward's honor on October 11, the 69th New York voted to boycott the event in protest against British imperialism in Ireland. In its resolution the regiment proclaimed the duty of Americans to aid the struggle for freedom in other lands as well as "the spread of republican principles throughout the globe." Accordingly — so the resolution went on — it would be beneath the dignity of the American people "to pay court in any form to monarchs, or give public honors to the representative of a system which they believe to be antagonistic to the great fundamental principles of human liberty" and whom they hold responsible for "the wrongs afflicted upon Ireland — for the banishment and proscription of her people, the destruction of her homes and the suppression of her ancient nationality." Corcoran accepted his men's decision and issued a statement that he could not in good conscience order out a regiment of Irish-born citizens to honor the son of Queen Victoria, "under whose reign Ireland was made a desert and her sons forced into exile."[7]

Although Colonel Corcoran was subsequently vilified by most of the New York press — one newspaper demanded that he be tried for treason and shot — his principled defiance made him the darling of Irish-America. From all across the country came gifts in his honor, among them a one-pound gold medal from San Francisco, a gold-headed cane from South Carolina, and a gold-ornamented sword from New York. The most historically significant gift, however, was a banner known ever since as the Prince of Wales Color, presented to the 69th by Irish citizens of New York City. The banner's green field contained a sunburst (a Fenian symbol) surrounded by two scrolls containing the memorial words "Presented to the 69th Regiment in Commemoration of the 11th Oct. 1860." Corcoran's moment of glory quickly faded, however, when he was arrested and court-martialed for his defiance.[8]

The country's long-simmering sectional conflicts finally reached a climax when Confederates fired on Fort Sumter in Charleston, South Carolina, on April 12, 1861. After President Abraham Lincoln called for 75,000 volunteers for the defense of the nation's capital, Father Michael Creedon of Holy Family Church in Auburn, New York, expressed a sentiment prevalent among the Irish immigrants in the North. In his sermon the Sunday after the president's proclamation, the priest reminded his Irish parishioners that they were indebted to the United States for giving them refuge. In gratitude they should come to her defense: "This is the first country the Irishman ever had that he could call his own country. The flag of the Stars and Stripes is the only flag that he can fight under and defend as his own flag. Now, in the time of the nation's peril, let every Irishman show that he is worthy to be part of a great and glorious nationality. Now, when the American flag is bombarded and struck down by traitors, let every

Irishman show that he is true to the flag which always protects him. I want every Irishman who hears me to enlist, if he can."[9]

In response to President Lincoln's call for volunteers, the 69th New York Regiment voted to offer its services. Corcoran's court-martial was quickly dissolved and the charges dismissed, and the grateful colonel helped recruit men to answer the president's call. Although Corcoran's authorization was for only 1,500 men, almost 5,000 volunteered to enlist, more than 1,800 recruits applying in person and almost 3,000 more submitting letters or making oral requests to join. Despite the success of Corcoran's call for volunteers, the Irishman realized the dilemma which faced him. As one of the founders of the Fenian Brotherhood in the United States, he valued militia training and its use in the American civil war as useful experience for that future day when Fenians from America would launch a war against British rule in Ireland. The possibility of success in this future venture would be diminished, however, if too many Fenians responded to the call for Union volunteers. With this consideration in mind, Corcoran urged his Fenian followers to stay out of the war if they had not already enlisted so as to be available to fight for Irish independence. But if you *must* join the Union army, he conceded, join an Irish unit.[10]

Corcoran's hope that the successful outcome of the American civil war — the restoration of the Union — would herald the day when Ireland's "union" with Great Britain would be forever severed found expression in the following verse:

*"The Two Unions" by F. D. B.

When concord and peace to this land are restored,
And the Union's established forever,
Brave sons of Hibernia, oh, sheathe not the sword: —
You will then have a Union *to sever*.

The flags of two nations appear on the field; —
You have vow'd to defend them forever;
Your duty to one, is the Union to shield; —
To the other, the Union *to sever!*

Though the "Star-Spangled Banner" proclaim o'er the sea
Success crown'd each noble endeavor,
Will any acknowledge Hibernians are free,
While the Sunburst's in exile? No! never.

On Erin's green soil (and on Erin's alone)
You can purchase your freedom forever,
When, joined with your patriot brothers at home,
The foul Union of tyrants you sever.[11]

On April 23 the 69th New York was among the units which gathered in front of Hibernian Hall preparatory to setting sail for Annapolis, Maryland. Besides Colonel Corcoran, Lieutenant Colonel Robert Nugent, and fourteen other men on the general staff, the regiment numbered twenty-seven company officers and 996 enlistees (in nine companies). At 3 o'clock that afternoon, after forming ranks in Great Jones Street, the 69th Regiment received a silk American flag from the wife of Judge Charles Daly. In accepting it, Colonel Corcoran promised on behalf of his men that the flag would never suffer a stain of dishonor while one of them remained alive to defend it. After proceeding into Broadway, the troops received the blessing of Archbishop John Hughes, who was sitting in the editorial rooms of the old *Metropolitan Record*, near Houston Street. At the head of the line was a horse-drawn wagon bearing banners with the inscriptions "No North, no South, no East, no West" and "Sixty-ninth, *Remember Fontenoy." Finally, by 7 p.m. — eight hours behind schedule — the 69th Regiment was aboard the *James Adger* at Pier 4 along the North (Hudson) River. Two days later Corcoran's men arrived at Annapolis and were assigned the task of guarding the railroad line to Washington, D.C.[12]

At the beginning of May the regiment was transferred to the nation's capital and was quartered at Georgetown College, a Catholic institution known for its pro-Southern sympathies. There all but seventeen men were sworn into federal service, the nonjuring soldiers being turned out amid the hisses of their former comrades. Then began in earnest the regiment's grueling regimen of drilling and training for more than seven hours a day. Some comfort must have been afforded the men, however, by the presence of their unofficial chaplain, *Father Thomas Mooney, the pastor of St. Bridget Church in New York City. While quartered on the campus, the men of the 69th acquired the reputation for cleanliness which followed them — and Irish soldiers generally — throughout the war. In fact, a professor at Georgetown, himself an Irishman, noted that the school's three wells were in danger of running dry due to the "incessant ablutions" of the 69th. After the war the author John Maguire penned an apt metaphor for the Irish soldier's grooming habits: "No cat that ever polished her fur into velvety softness was more careful of her coat than the Irish soldiers — Federal or Confederate — were of the cleanliness of their persons and their clothing."[13]

On May 23 the 69th New York was reinforced by 300 recruits — including a company of "Irish Zouaves" — under Captain Thomas Francis Meagher. These Zouaves, who became Company K in the 69th, were remarkable for their colorful uniforms: blue jackets and vests, caps adorned with a wreath of shamrocks, and grey pants lined with crimson and gold stripes. Thus reinforced, the 69th New York was among the 13,000 Union troops who advanced into northern Virginia to protect Washington, D.C., from an expected Confederate attack. After occupying Arlington Heights, the regiment proceeded to build a ring of defenses around the nation's capital. Although it had been estimated that construction would take 3,000 men a month to complete, Corcoran's much smaller number of men finished the job in a week. Named Fort Corcoran, these fortifications measured 650 feet by 450 feet, boasted walls fourteen feet high, and trained their sixteen cannon on the approaches to Aqueduct Bridge spanning the Potomac River.[14]

In a letter written on May 28 to Captain Patrick Phelan of the Phoenix Brigade, Private James McKay Rorty of the 69th New York tried to dispel rumors that the regiment suffered severe privations and severity at the hands of the officers. While admitting that the men of the regiment had been doing "considerable fasting, watching and other penitential exercises," he stressed that tales of privation had in many respects been "greatly exaggerated." (He expressed thanks for the viands which a benefactor had graciously provided the regiment but lamented that enjoyment of the meal was marred by "the grief of the boys over a broken bottle of Jamieson's [sic], the contents of which were unfortunately spilled.") As to charges that the officers were treating the men with "arrogance and severity," Rorty called the accusations completely false and calumnious. In fact, about some of the officers he had special praise: "The calm[,] steady bearing and faultless judgment of [Colonel] Corcoran, the chivalrous and somewhat impetuous air of [Robert] Nugent . . . who is to my mind the *beau ideal* of a soldier, and whose ubiquitous movements and eagle eyes are on us everywhere — the veteran and marshal air of [Captain James] Haggerty, with the enthusiastic energy which pervades every subaltern . . . ." And as to the false rumor that the 69th had been defeated, Rorty gave the witty advice that none of the "widows" should remarry and that the girls should remain constant, "as both lovers and husbands may return."[15]

One of the other prominent figures in the 69th's camp was *Charles Graham Halpine, a staff member of the *New York Times*. This Irish native had accompanied the regiment from New York not as a journalist but rather as a civilian commissary while he awaited a commission as a second lieutenant. On the night of his arrival, the would-be officer was seized by secessionist members of the Maryland militia as he attempted to reach Washington, D.C., with important dispatches. He escaped being hanged as a spy when his captors failed to find the papers in his boots and accepted his claim that he was a newspaperman. By the end of May, Halpine had received his commission and was busy carrying out his duties as Colonel Corcoran's assistant adjutant — writing orders, distributing passes, and questioning prisoners. On May 29, though, Halpine gave up his position with the 69th New York to become an aide-de-camp to Colonel David Hunter, the regiment's brigade commander. Because Hunter made his headquarters with the 69th, however, Halpine was able to remain with his former comrades. It was probably from this experience that the journalist acquired the inspiration for "Miles O'Reilly," his literary mouthpiece, through whose persona he wrote numerous poetic and prose pieces. Like his fictional character, Halpine was motivated by the thought "that he was earning a title, which no foul tongue or niggardly heart would dare to dispute, to the full equality and fraternity of an American citizen."[16]

The day after Halpine's promotion, the 69th New York Regiment conducted its first flag-raising ceremony. According to Henry Watterson, a writer for the *Philadelphia Press* who witnessed the scene, Captain Meagher made "a brief but high-toned and patriotic address, showing the devotion Irishmen should bear to that flag which brought succor to them in Ireland, and to which, upon landing in this country, they swore undivided allegiance." Meagher concluded with the wish that "the 69th would stand by the flag until the banner of the entire Union had been replaced on every fort and arsenal from which it had been improperly, illegally and nefariously torn down." The event was then enlivened by the singing of "The Starry Flag," a song composed by *John Savage, a journalist and a volunteer aide to Colonel Corcoran. The Dublin-born Savage had been inspired to write the song — to the tune of "Dixie's Land"— by an incident which had occurred in May as he sailed up the Potomac aboard the transport *Marion*. It seems that during the night the crew of a rebel boat had silently maneuvered its craft alongside the *Marion* with the intention of hauling down its American flag. After seeing that the transport was guarded by Union troops, though, the Confederates sailed away, one of them exclaiming, "Damn that rag! We cannot pull it down to-night."[17]

"The Starry Flag"

I

Oh, the starry flag is the flag for me!
'Tis the flag of life! the flag of the free!
Then hurrah! hurrah!
For the flag of the Union!

Oh, the starry flag, etc.

We'll raise that starry banner, boys,
Hurrah! Hurrah!
We'll raise that starry banner, boys,
Where no power in wrath can face it!
On town and field,
The people's shield,
No treason can erase it!
O'er the land
That flag must stand,

Where the people's might shall place it.

### II
That flag was won through gloom and woe!
It has blessed the brave and awed the foe!
Then hurrah! hurrah!
For the flag of the Union!

That flag was won, etc.

We'll raise that starry banner, boys,
Hurrah! hurrah!
We'll raise that starry banner, boys,
Where the stripes no hand can sever!
On fort and mast,
We'll nail it fast,
To balk all base endeavor!
O'er roof and spire
A living fire
The Stars shall blaze forever!

### III
'Tis the people's will, both great and small,
The rights of the States, the union of all!
Then hurrah! hurrah!
For the flag of the Union!

'Tis the people's will, etc.

We'll raise that starry banner, boys,
Hurrah! hurrah!
We'll raise that starry banner, boys,
Till it is the world's wonder!
On fort and crag
We'll plant the flag
With the people's voice of thunder!
We'll plant that flag
Where none can drag
Its immortal folds asunder!

### IV
We must keep that flag where it e'er has stood,
In front of the free, the wise, and the good!
Then hurrah! hurrah!

For the flag of the Union!

We must keep that flag, etc.

We'll raise that starry banner, boys,
Hurrah! hurrah!
We'll raise that starry banner, boys,
On field, fort, mast, and steeple!
And fight and fall
At our country's call,
By the glorious flag of the people!
In God, the just,
We place our trust,
To defend the flag of the people![18]

Watterson, the Philadelphia journalist, described as "electrical" the effect which this song had on the regiment. With obvious emotion of his own, he painted a poignant picture of the scene as it unfolded at sunset: "There stood the author himself by the side of Meagher, both symbols of Irish patriotism; there stood those dauntless men, their brothers in arms and exile; and there, above all — the stripes vying with the red streaks of the west, and its stars [vying] with the silver globes that already began to break through the sky — waved the banner which had come to them when starving, which had protected them when flying, and for whose preservation and perpetuation they now marched to the roll of the national reveille! Well might it awaken those grateful hearts; and no wonder that when the last thunders of the final verse, roaring like distant artillery, were rising up like vigils around the flag, they broke from their places and surrounded their chief [Corcoran], their orator [Meagher], their priest [Mooney], and their poet [Savage] in a general Irish 'hullabaloo,' as inspiring as a camp-meeting."[19]

On June 12, when a number of heavy guns arrived, Colonel Corcoran asked Father Mooney to bless one of the cannon. The priest exceeded the colonel's request, however, and actually *baptized* the piece of artillery after making the following remarks: "It is with more than ordinary pleasure that I come forward to perform a ceremony which is not only pleasing to us all, but highly honorable . . . the christening of the noble gun on Fort Corcoran. In the kind providence of God, it has been for me, as a priest, during the last nine years, to baptize many a fine blue-eyed babe; but never had I brought before me such a large, quiet, healthy, and promising fellow as the one now before me. Indeed, I may remark, it has often occurred, when pouring the baptismal water on the child's head, he opened his little eyes, and got a little more of the baptismal water than he wished; but, on this occasion, this noble son of a great father has his mouth open, evidently indicating that he is anxious to speak, which I have no doubt he soon will, in a thundering voice, to the joy of his friends and terror of his enemies. I need not tell you that a most appropriate name has been selected by our esteemed Colonel, and one that will be welcomed by you all; and that is the honorable name of the gallant commander of our brigade, Colonel [David] Hunter. Therefore, the great gun shall hereafter answer to its name — the Hunter Gun. Now, parents anxiously listen to the first lispings of the infant's lips, and the mother's heart swells with joy when she catches the first utterance of her cherished babe, in the words 'mamma, mamma!' but here I shall guarantee to you that this promising boy will speak for the first time, in loud, clear accents, those endearing words, 'papa, papa, papa!' — *patria mia, patria mia!'* [my fatherland] and, in name as in effect, he will hunt traitors from this fort, while the echo of his voice will be as sweet music, inviting the children of Columbia [the United States] to share the comforts of the father's home; and thus may he soon speak, to the glory of the Stars and Stripes, honor to the name that he bears, and lasting credit to the Sixty-ninth New York."[20]

During the Irish regiment's celebration of its first Independence Day in the field, Captain Meagher conducted a public reading of the Declaration of Independence. The next day, though, Colonel Corcoran had to put down an incipient mutiny when he was reminded that the regiment's three-month term of enlistment would end on July 20 and that the men had not been paid since leaving New York. (The men were told that their term of service actually dated from May 9, the day on which they were mustered in at Georgetown.) After the soldiers were finally paid on July 12, they turned over most of their wages — about $25,000 — to *Father Bernard O'Reilly, the regiment's new chaplain, who in turn delivered the money to the men's families in New York.[21]

On July 16, 1861, the 69th New York marched out of Fort Corcoran as part of an advance by General Irwin McDowell's army toward Centreville, Virginia. McDowell's objective was to destroy a Confederate force there under General Pierre Beauregard before that rebel officer could be joined by troops under General Joseph Johnston coming from the west. As the federal troops advanced toward Centreville, the Confederates abandoned their positions. During that retreat the 69th suffered its first casualty when Captain John Breslin of Company F was wounded after a musket fell to the ground and fired in his direction.[22]

On July 18 McDowell's army faced Beauregard from across a creek known as Bull Run. Reconnaissance efforts by Union troops led to a minor battle at Blackburn's Ford that day. Although Corcoran's men — now part of Colonel William Sherman's brigade — were called into action, their advance was met by retreating soldiers. When the Irish regiment came upon the retreating 13th New York, they mistook the gray-clad militiamen for Confederates and prepared to charge with bayonets. After realizing that the retreating troops were Union men, Captain James Haggerty of the 69th New York prevented a disaster by dashing along the Irishmen's line and knocking their bayonets upwards with his sword. In the end, though, McDowell ordered a withdrawal to Centreville. His subsequent decision to await supplies allowed Johnston to arrive from the west and to reinforce Beauregard's troops.[23]

Typically, Meagher's description of the 69th's rush onto the battlefield that day emphasized the honor of the Celtic race. "Of those thousand men, sweeping on to battle, through choking clouds of dust and under that smiting sun," he wrote, "there was not one but carried himself right gallantly — not one who did not feel that the honor of his race and its military character was [sic] staked that hour upon the conduct of the 69th, and who, feeling this and lifting his eye in rapture to the *Green Flag as it danced above the rushing column, did not swear to meet the thrusts of battle with a fearless heart."[24]

When Father Thomas Scully, the chaplain of the Irish Ninth Massachusetts, heard of the fight at Blackburn's Ford, he rushed from Washington, D.C., to Captain Meagher's camp thirty-five miles away. There he stayed long enough to relieve Father O'Reilly of his duties in the confessional. "There were few of the 69th who failed to confess and ask forgiveness on that day," wrote Meagher. "Every one, officers as well as privates, prepared for death. Sincerely and devoutly they made their peace with God. This is the secret of their courage, and the high, bright spirit with which they bore all the hardships, the privations, the terrors, and the chastisement of the battle. It was, in truth, an affecting sight — that of strong, stalwart, rugged men — all upon their knees, all with heads uncovered, all with hands clasped in prayer and eyes cast down, approaching, one by one, the good dear priest, who, seated at the foot of an old bare tree, against which some of our boys had spread for him an awning of green branches, heard the confessions of the poor fellows, and bid them be at ease and fearless."[25]

In the epic struggle which ensued on July 21, a Confederate force of 40,000 men bested McDowell's 35,000 troops. Before the battle of Bull Run was joined, however, Henry Villard, a correspondent for the *Cincinnati Commercial*, noticed Captain Meagher mounted on his steed and holding with his right hand a cocked revolver on his hip. In answer to Villard's question about whether he was ready for the contest, the captain replied that "there is nothing like being always ready for the 'damned rebs.'" Villard suspected that Meagher had taken a swig of the "crater" in preparing himself for the ensuing clash: "The leer from his [Meagher's] eyes and a certain unsteadiness in the saddle indicated plainly that he had braced himself up internally for the fight." During the battle Corcoran's regiment successfully crossed Bull Run, at first chasing the retreating Confederates but then coming under fire from the Louisiana Zouaves. The 69th replied with two devastating volleys, but the Louisiana "Tigers" recovered and began to fight back. In the ensuing counterattack, James Haggerty, now the acting lieutenant colonel, was shot and fell dead from his horse. His men took savage revenge, though, firing as many as fifty times into the rebel who had killed him. (Recruitment efforts in New York later that month featured a flyer urging the city's Irishmen to enlist in order to avenge Haggerty, whose throat, the circular erroneously claimed, had been cut "from ear to ear" by a cowardly rebel.)[26]

In an attempt to capture the Confederate guns which dominated Henry House Hill on the battlefield that day, Colonel Sherman sent in three regiments in successive waves. When the Second Wisconsin and the 79th New York were both repulsed, however, he turned to the 69th. After the Irishmen's chaplain, Father O'Reilly, blessed them, Captain Meagher exhorted the men: "Come on, boys, you've got your chance at last!" With a cry that was described as half-English and half-Gaelic, the regiment charged the hill, many of the men without shirts and some without shoes. Three times the Irishmen charged, but each time they were cut down by Confederate riflemen. While leading one of the attacks, Colonel Corcoran was wounded in the leg. Although Meagher's horse was shot from under him, he jumped up, waved his sword, and cried out, "Boys! Look at that flag — remember Ireland and Fontenoy!" But when the regiment's green flag began to attract heavy fire, Corcoran ordered the conspicuous ensign lowered. "I'll never lower it," protested the color-bearer, just before falling dead from a bullet through the heart. When another man took up the flag, he too was killed. John Keefe, one of Meagher's "Irish Zouaves," then dashed into the fray with the banner, until it was snatched from his hands by a Confederate. Keefe shot the man and recaptured the colors. Although Keefe again lost the banner when he was overpowered and taken prisoner, he regained the green prize after shooting his two captors with a revolver which he conveniently pulled from his shirt.[27]

In the rout which followed the arrival of Confederate reinforcements, Meagher was knocked down and lay senseless on the ground until Joseph McCoy, a mounted Union soldier, saved the famous Irishman by pulling him up from the ground by the back of the neck and carrying him to safety. Meagher eventually climbed aboard a passing artillery wagon but was hurled into Bull Run when one of the horses pulling the caisson was shot by Confederate cavalry. As other Union troops retreated across Bull Run, the wounded Corcoran was able to gather his men into a hollow square formation designed to protect them from an expected cavalry attack. When Colonel Sherman told the men to flee, Corcoran, two of his officers, and nine privates were cut off from the regiment and were forced to surrender. A member of Meagher's "Irish Zouaves" summed up the frustrating day: "We were taken to the shambles to be slaughtered; we got no chance to fight, but we stood until we were half thinned; all we have saved is our

honor. We have lost our principle [*sic*] officers, and have made the bravest
stand of the day." In all, the regiment lost thirty-eight killed, fifty-nine
wounded, and ninety-five missing, a total of 192, about 16 percent of its
strength. The number killed was the highest mortality rate suffered by
any unit in Sherman's brigade that day. According to the diarist Maria
Lydig Daly, the wife of Judge Charles Daly, Father O'Reilly was mistaken
for an officer and a bullet struck his hat and "turned it round a little on his
head." The chaplain, she continued, "was indefatigable in his attention to
the wounded and dying. When parties of the enemy came up in search of
prisoners, he lay down upon the ground and feigned death until they
passed, and then continued his charitable work. Behold, indeed, an Apostle
of Christ, a follower of his self-denying Master!"[28]

Despite the disaster which befell the 69th New York at Bull Run, the
regiment's heroism became the subject of numerous songs, many of ques-
tionable quality. In a mournful lyric entitled *"Our Brave Irish Champions," Thomas Walsh recounted the battlefield events, apparently for an
audience in Ireland. Although he dispelled the rumor that Captain Meagher
had been killed, he erroneously reported that Father O'Reilly and Lieutenant Colonel Nugent had been mortally struck during the fighting.

> You feeling-hearted Christians of high & low degree,
> I hope you'll pay attention and listen unto me.
> The great battle in America to you I will explain:
> On the 21st day of July, there was [*sic*] 20,000 slain.
>
> By the dawn on Sunday morning, that battle did take place.
> 'Till Six o'Clock that Evening, the firing did not cease.
> No sooner on the battery, than put to flight again,
> And many a valiant Irishman lay bleeding on the plain.
>
> For the Rev. Fr. O'Riely [*sic*] let every [C]hristian pray,
> While giving absolution his life was snatched away.
> The dreadful slaughter on that day was awful to behold[.]
> The moans of dying and wounded, would make your blood run cold.
>
> The great report of Meagher's death is false we understand,
> Who was exiled in '48, far from his native land,
> But gallant Captain Hagerty [*sic*], we need expect no more,
> And Nugent fell dead off his horse, all bleeding in his gore.
> The fighting in America, is to us a woful [*sic*] day.
> Our Friends will write no more[,] I fear[,] in haste across the sea;
> There is nothing there but open War, as we can understand.
> God help our Irish strangers on that far & distant land.

There are numbers of our Countrymen upon that foreign shore,
And many of them we will never see nor hear from any more.
Poor Granu grieves unto herself, for those who lie far away,
And numbered with the dead, alas! all in America.

A sense of horid [*sic*] slaughter was the battlefield that day.
The 69th brave Irishmen were all near cut away.
Far from their friends and country, they're in a silent grave,
But I hope the King of Glory will their precious souls receive.[29]

Even less partisan voices joined in acknowledging the bravery of the 69th New York. A Memphis newspaper praised the regiment for maintaining the tradition of "Irish valor" and predicted — somewhat arrogantly — that the Irishmen in the regiment would "range their fearless hearts in line with their brethren of the South" once they understood the principle at issue in the war. A Confederate officer admitted that the "Irish fought like heroes," and when President Lincoln visited Fort Corcoran four days after the battle, he congratulated the men for their fighting spirit, bravery, and devotion, adding that the defeat at Bull Run had been a misfortune but not a disgrace. The *New York Illustrated News* of August 5 joined the chorus of adulation: "Our men fought bravely and suffered severely before they turned their backs on those accursed batteries; and nobly they purchased, with drops of bloody sweat, the welcome that warm hearts, fair hands and beaming eyes gave them on their return to New York. The 69th left New York 1,500 strong. They returned with about 1,000. The loss is heart-stirring. All honor to the brave!" Judge Holt of Kentucky even went so far as to say that *Leonidas "would have been proud of the leadership of such men."[30]

With his usual eloquence, Captain Meagher eulogized the men of the 69th who had fallen at Bull Run, saving particular praise for Lieutenant Colonel Haggerty, a native of Glenswilly, County Donegal. "On the silent fields which these noble mountains overlook and these deep graves shadow," Meagher declaimed, "I see many a strong and gallant soldier of the Sixty-ninth, whom I knew and loved; and they lie there in the rich sunshine, discolored and cold in death. All of them were from Ireland, and as the tide of life rushed out, the last thought that left their hearts was for the liberty of Ireland. Prominent among them, strikingly noticeable by reason of his large iron frame and the boldly chiselled features, on which the impress of great strength of will and intellect was softened by a constant play of humor and the goodness and grand simplicity of his heart — wrapped in his rough old overcoat, with his sword crossed upon his breast, his brow boldly uplifted as though he were still in command, and the consciousness of having done his duty sternly to the last animating the Roman face — there lies James Haggerty — a braver soldier than whom

*The grave of Captain James Haggerty in Calvary Cemetery in Woodside, Queens, Long Island, New York. (Location: Section 1W, Avenue A, Grave 4/11)*

the *land of Sarsfield and Shields has not produced, and whose name, worked in gold, upon the colors of the Sixty-ninth, should be henceforth guarded with all the jealousy and pride which inspires [*sic*] a regiment whenever its honor is at stake and its standards are in peril."[31]

A large Celtic cross marks the grave of Captain James Haggerty in Calvary Cemetery in Woodside, Queens, Long Island. The base of the memorial cross bears the inscription:

> James Haggerty
> Captain (acting Lieutenant Colonel),
> 69th Regiment, New York State Militia.
> Fenian comrade of Michael Corcoran.
> Killed in action at the age of 45
> leading a charge, battle of Bull Run,
> 21 July 1861. Native of Glenswilly,
> County Donegal, Ireland.[32]

Meanwhile, because the captured Colonel Corcoran refused to agree never again to take up arms against the Confederacy, he was imprisoned in various places throughout the South during the next thirteen months. He and his Union fellow prisoners — now numbering almost fifty — were first held captive in a warehouse in Richmond, Virginia. Early in his account of his lengthy imprisonment, Corcoran wrote of his love both for his native land and for his adopted country: "One half of my heart is Erin's, and the other half is America's. God bless America, and ever preserve her the asylum of all the oppressed of the earth, is the sincere prayer of my heart."[33]

The imprisoned officers soon formed themselves into the Richmond Prison Association for the "improvement and entertainment of the members." To keep up their spirits — and no doubt to annoy their captors — the members of the association occasionally sang "The Star-Spangled Banner," doing so with as much gusto as they could muster. Corcoran again expressed his love for America when he described the effect which the anthem had on him: "Oh, America! Could you in those moments only have looked within my breast, you would have seen my heart beating, with all its Irish fervor, for your welfare and success." The colonel was less sentimental, though, when he challenged the prison commandant over an incident in which a guard shot and wounded one of the prisoners merely for looking out his unbarred window.[34]

One of Corcoran's fellow prisoners was Alfred Ely, a member of Congress from New York who had been a spectator at the battle of Bull Run before being captured in the general Union rout. Ely, who kept a detailed journal of his imprisonment, left a pithy description of the Irish officer: "In personal appearance, Colonel Corcoran is tall and slender, has a remarkably fine complexion; and though apparently of a delicate constitution, he is susceptible of enduring great fatigue. In his deportment, he is silent without being indifferent; reserved, but hospitable; earnest, firm, laborious, and always animated by a feeling of the loftiest integrity."[35]

By the end of August a rumor was claiming that Corcoran had been transferred to Fort Sumter in Charleston, South Carolina. Lieutenant John Mitchel Jr., a Confederate and the oldest son of the famous Irish patriot, reported from his post at Fort Sumter that Corcoran was still in Richmond. Apparently reacting to reports that Corcoran was being treated cruelly, Mitchel claimed that the Irish prisoner "is treated only to cocktails, mint juleps and other like beverages, such as only Richmond can produce to perfection, and he will be returned to you doubtless soon, in health and spirits, except in so far as said cocktails, etc., may have proved too much for him. In fact, he is treated like an honorable gentleman, taken prisoner while fighting on the side he conscientiously believed to be right. If he should be sent to our post, I shall be very happy to see him, and as Adjutant of the post, I will have our band play *'Patrick's Day'* and *'Garry Owen'* on his especial behoof."[36]

In September Corcoran and the other Union prisoners were transferred by train to Castle Pinckney, a fort in the harbor at Charleston, South Carolina. As the train approached Gaston, North Carolina, an axle on the car in which the prisoners sat suddenly broke, although there were no injuries. After the Yankee captives had reassembled along the tracks, they were verbally abused by a local partisan orator. As a crowd of locals looked on and cheered, the orator hurled a string of epithets against the Northern prisoners — "blinded fools of the Lincoln tyranny," "gallow-birds," and "Yankee scum of the earth." The orator suddenly turned his ire on Corcoran, singling him out as one of the first to volunteer with his "hireling soldiers" to invade the South and asking, "Where is your boasted Sixty Ninth now?" Throwing caution to the wind, Corcoran replied, "You'll see the Sixty Ninth very likely before long, with standards waving victoriously in this very place." Just then a "murderous-looking ruffian," fingering a knife in his belt, confronted Corcoran. The colonel was saved from possible assassination when a "beautiful young lady" rushed forward and interposed herself between Corcoran and his would-be assailant. "Will you dare shed the blood of a helpless, unarmed prisoner?" the female rescuer asked Corcoran's challenger.[37]

In a diary entry for October 13, Corcoran noted a visit from Patrick Lynch, the city's Irish-born Catholic bishop, whose "benignant smile and kind word" often drove the "gloom and despondency from the hearts of the captives immured within these frowning walls." On another occasion, the colonel recorded the courtesy with which the people of Charleston treated him and his men: "not a single offensive word was spoken or act committed" by any of the large crowds which met their arrival and departure. This civility, he noted, was in contrast to the inhospitality accorded the prisoners in Virginia, where they were not allowed fresh air or exercise during the fifty days of their detention. Corcoran did speak highly, however, of a group of nuns in Richmond who ministered to the wounded. "[O]ur officers and men who were there, and who represent all classes of religion," he wrote, "are unanimous in their praise of the care and attention bestowed in dressing and cleaning the wounded, and many attribute their recovery to their [the nuns'] untiring exertions." In a typical expression of concern for his fellow soldiers, Corcoran added: "The poor fellows . . . are suffering much from want of proper clothing or any changes of under garments. Many are without shoes, coats or bed covering, which is a cheerless prospect with the near approach of cold weather. . . ."[38]

In the middle of November, the prisoners were installed in Charleston's city jail. It was there that Corcoran explained to a Confederate visitor why he had not requested or accepted parole: "I believe that honor and patriotism alike forbid my doing so." The colonel went on in more detail: "When I started from New York for the seat of war, I did so with the intention of doing your bad cause all the harm I could; and nothing would have given me greater pleasure than to have planted the Stars and Stripes over this very castle. As fortune had it, however, after doing a little, I fell into your hands. Then I was called upon to *suffer* for my cause. Previously I had been called upon to *act*, to fight. And, if it would be honorable for me to escape the suffering by any means, I am sure it would be equally so for me to have avoided the fighting. Besides, here I have an opportunity of doing at least a little good to those about me, whom the fortunes of war have placed in a worse predicament than myself."[39]

Soon after giving this apologia, Corcoran learned that he was now at the center of a diplomatic crisis preoccupying the North and the South. A man by the name of Smith — a crew member on the Confederate privateer *Savannah* — had recently been condemned to death as a pirate by a court in Philadelphia. In response, the Confederate secretary of war ordered that lots be drawn from among the names of the Union prisoners in the Charleston jail to see who would be hanged in retaliation for the expected execution of Smith. Six slips — one for each of the imprisoned officers — were readied. When the "death slip" was selected, it bore the name of Corcoran. Thirteen more Yankee prisoners of war were selected by lot to serve as hostages if Lincoln's government hanged the thirteen other privateers in its possession. Now under virtual threat of death, Corcoran feared that he would have "to suffer the ignominious doom of a convicted felon upon the scaffold." He also wrote that he despaired of freeing his native land "from the galling yoke of oppression under which she has been suffering for centuries." In the same letter he consoled himself with the thought that "there could be no possible other cause for which I could be more content to freely offer up my life than in the endeavor to maintain the Glorious Flag which has afforded a home and protection to me and my oppressed countrymen."[40]

At the beginning of 1862, Colonel Corcoran, now afflicted with typhoid fever, was transferred with the other hostages to a jail in Columbia, South Carolina. In short order they were packed off again, first to Salisbury, North Carolina, and then back to Richmond. In May, when Union forces approached within eight miles of the Confederate capital, the hostages were again transferred to North Carolina. By the end of that same month, however, an exchange had been arranged, and the Confederate officer for whom Corcoran was to be exchanged was brought from Fortress Monroe in Virginia. The Irishman's captors refused to give him up, though, until mid August, when he and the other hostages were returned to Richmond for the last time. After his long-awaited exchange, Corcoran recorded his feelings at seeing the American flag for the first time in more than a year: ". . . as my eyes fell upon its bright stars and stripes, my soul thrilled to its centre, and my Irish heart welled up with emotion such as it had never experienced before. And in the wild shout of delight that went up from the prisoners, I joined to the full extent of my voice."[41]

Upon his release Colonel Corcoran was feted in Washington, D.C., Baltimore, Philadelphia, and Jersey City en route to New York. In the nation's capital he dined with President Lincoln, who commissioned him a brigadier general, and he informed the secretary of war that he would like to recruit and command a regiment of his own. On August 18 Corcoran and the other principal prisoners were warmly welcomed in front of their hotel by the 69th New York Regiment and between 10,000 and 15,000 wellwishers. Before presenting Corcoran to the adoring crowd, Congressman Ely, the general's companion in prison, praised the endurance and heroic spirit with which the Irishman had met "the taunts and jeers of an insolent and barbarous enemy." To his praise for Corcoran, Ely added that "in all our victories for the Union the dauntless daring of the Irish volunteer has added lustre to the triumph of our arms."[42]

In his response Corcoran, as usual, preferred to view his tumultuous welcome as a sign of the public's "signal devotion to the glorious institutions under which we have the blessing to live." Claiming that the North had finally become aware of the importance of its struggle with the South, Corcoran said that the Union was willing to give a million men to put down "this wicked rebellion and preserve our glorious institutions as they were handed down by our forefathers." In special words to the 69th, its former commander said he rejoiced to see again "that good old Green Flag," which had been saved from the battle of Bull Run. He then expressed his hope that he would soon be at the head of the 69th New York, "again to take the field with more of my countrymen to endeavor to preserve this country for our people." Later, in reply to the praise of the Washington, D.C., city council, Corcoran said he was ready to peril his life in defense of the Star-Spangled Banner, which he called "the emblem of freedom and banner of human rights."[43]

Three days later throngs of citizens greeted Corcoran as he was escorted through the streets of Philadelphia. At the "Volunteer Refreshment Saloon" — where soldiers passing through the city were freely fed by patriotic volunteers — Corcoran promised never to sheathe his sword "until the last vestige of rebellion should be swept away." He hoped that the Irishmen in the city would flock to the ranks of the Union cause and do all they could for a country which had done so much for them. Later in the day, at Independence Hall, he lamented that the "degenerate sons" of the men who had adopted the Declaration of Independence should "endeavor to drag down this edifice which they gave their lives to erect." Recalling that the framers of the Constitution had been willing to concede "everything but their honor" to form the Union, he prayed that "we can well enter into bonds for its preservation." In remarks at the Continental Hotel, Corcoran urged his listeners to allow no infringements on the Constitution "unless such as are essentially necessary." Though a Democrat, he expressed his support for President Lincoln, even going so far as to say that if the president "encroaches at all and makes a tear in" the Constitution, he (Corcoran) would not say a word *now* but would wait until after the war and "then put a patch on it." He expressed his regret at not having "entered into a contract to have it [the rebellion] put down by the Irish alone," claiming that he would have had enough Irishmen to end the war with a victory at Bull Run.[44]

From the City of Brotherly Love, Corcoran progressed by train across New Jersey en route to his home in New York City. At Trenton, when the "delicate" platform at the rear of his car began to crack under his weight as he addressed the crowd, he assured his listeners that as far as the war was concerned he stood on the "broad platform of the Constitution." That platform, he said, was "strong enough to hold me and all my brother Irishmen and protect them from tyranny and oppression." At Princeton Corcoran donned his new uniform as a brigadier general, while at Rahway he struck a theme that he would repeat along the way: that the thunderous reception he received was not for him personally but for the government and the Constitution of the United States. During the stop in Jersey City, where he was literally mobbed, he told the crowds that when the war was over he could forget what the rebels had done to him, but he could never forget "the insults offered to our flag" until those insults were wiped out in the enemy's blood. Finally the general and his party — by now "red-faced and fagged out" but "with unbroken limbs and untorn vestments" — boarded a ferry to cross over to New York.[45]

Corcoran's welcome in the Empire City later that August 22 included a reception in Battery Park, a triumphal parade up Broadway, and speeches at City Hall. Mayor George Opdyke commended the general for the nobility with which he had endured his imprisonment and warned that such a wrong had intensified every Irishman's hatred of treason and whetted his desire to punish the "perfidious cruelty" of the general's captors. The mayor assured Corcoran that thousands of his countrymen were ready — under his leadership — to avenge the insults. Then began a parade of various military units and members of civic organizations that was fully two miles in length and took forty-five minutes to pass in front of City Hall. Maria Lydig Daly wrote in her diary that during his welcome Corcoran "stood in the carriage bowing to the crowd right and left, but in his face was none of the consciousness or conceit which a small man would evince. . . . His manner was full of dignified humility." Five weeks later she noted that Corcoran "is a plain, unpretending man, without a shadow of personal vanity; he is really of the *heroic* stamp — most disinterested, tender-hearted, and a man of very few words."[46]

On the first night of Corcoran's return to New York City, a noisily insistent crowd in the streets near his hotel demanded to see and honor him. From a balcony the general said that the 600,000 voices which had cheered him along Broadway that day were 600,000 hearts ready to support the Constitution and preserve the Union. Then he expressed his gratitude to see regiment after regiment rushing to the defense of the national capital and commended the people of New York for having done their duty "nobly and patriotically." Toward the end of his remarks, he expressed his confidence that Irish New Yorkers would come to the defense of the Union, "for I believe they have ever been first in their allegiance, and first with the American citizens themselves by never being otherwise than loyal to the land of their adoption." One of the well-wishers who responded to Corcoran that night was John O'Mahony, his friend and fellow Irishman and the cofounder of the Fenian movement to secure Ireland's independence by force. In his comments O'Mahony praised America's "democratic republicanism" and expressed his happiness at seeing that his countrymen were among the Union's foremost defenders and that they appreciated the blessings which they enjoyed in the United States. "I trust that they will defend it until the American Republic is again restored as it has been, and until it stands forth as the beacon light of liberty throughout the world," he concluded.[47]

Corcoran's exploits and the thunderous welcome which he received from the people of New York became the topic of a song by William Ferris entitled *"Return of Gen. Corcoran, of the Glorious 69th":

The Southerners in fierce array against the Northmen bold,
When Irish voices rung [*sic*] on high, as in the days of old;

And in one loud, united voice that rent the very sky,
They swore they'd put base traitors down, and conquer them or die.

'Twas then the Gallant Sixty-Ninth with spirits light and gay,
Cheered by the ones they dearly loved, when [went?] marching down
Broadway;
Went forth to meet the Rebel foe, who would destroy the land
That gave them birth and nurtured them, the dastard rebel band.

'Twas not to subjugate the South, those Irish braves went forth,
Nor emancipate their negroes to satisfy the North —
But bring them back unto the laws, their noble sires had made,
And place again, beneath our Flag, each Southern renegade.

'Twas at the battle of Bull Run, when first they met the foe,
They charged the rebels with cold steel, and laid their columns low:
And while the Northern ranks were broke, mid showers of shot and
shell
The Gallant Sixty-Ninth still stood, nor flinched, but nobly fell.

God bless the noble CORCORAN, who led them on the field,
Against the odds of two to one he fought, but could not yield,
For CORCORAN, valiant CORCORAN, the bravest of the brave[,]
Would fight to death, but ne'er retreat before a rebel knave.

God bless the Gallant Sixty-Ninth, God bless each manly heart —
They done their duty faithfully, they acted well their part —
For on the bloody battle-field, where lay their martyr dead,
Was heard their wild and fierce hurrah, when Southern traitors fled.

As at the charge of "Fontenoy," our brave men of to-day,
With gallant Meagher, drove the foe, in terror and dismay —
For at the battle of "Fair Oaks," as at the "Seven Pines,"
The Irish charge, with one wild yell, broke through the rebel lines.

A CEAD MAILLE FAILTHE we give to thee[,] brave man,
Thou hero of the Sixty-Ninth who nobly led the van, —
With a hundred thousand welcomes we grasp thee by the hand,
And proudly claim thee, Corcoran, brave son of Erin's land.

Hurrah! Hurrah! for the Sixty-Ninth[,] how brave they look to-day,
With gallant Corcoran at their head, as if to meet the fray —
God bless our Irish soldiers, in our hearts we shall entwine,
The name of Michael Corcoran, and the Gallant Sixty-Ninth![48]

That the New York press was just as effusive about Corcoran stood in contrast to its attitude almost two years earlier when the Fourth Estate branded him a traitor for his insult to the Prince of Wales. At the head of its lead news article about the Irishman's return, the *New York Times* opined that "on no previous occasion has the City of New York tendered to an individual, be he President or Prince, such an apparently heartfelt ovation, such an outpouring of its people, such a rousing, unstinted, undiluted specimen of enthusiastic greeting." The *Times* editorial page praised Corcoran for nobly enduring his captivity and consistently upholding republican principles. When he was under sentence of death, the paper reminded its readers, the Irishman expressed his willingness to die in the service of his country rather than betray it. The *Times* also noted that, after New York State had conferred "an office of honor" upon the penniless prisoner, he refused the salary, on the grounds that he was unable to perform the office and therefore was not entitled to the public's money. "Thus it is," concluded the editorial, "that by his unselfishness, his modesty, his courage in battle, his fortitude in a long protracted bondage, his civic virtue, and his final triumph over every trial, Col. Corcoran has taken captive the American people, and they have honored him as men are seldom honored."[49]

The day after his return to New York City, Corcoran proceeded to take steps to form the regiment which he had promised to raise. Despite his weakened physical condition, he traveled to Washington, D.C., Boston, Worcester, Poughkeepsie, and Albany to encourage recruitment. About 700 officers and men from Corcoran's Old 69th New York State Militia enlisted immediately, while another 1,800 men signed up for Corcoran's "Irish Legion" within the space of only three weeks. In mid October 1861, Maria Lydig Daly visited General Corcoran and his troops at Camp Winfield Scott on Staten Island. There the general pointed out to his visitor a small boy by the name of Michael Corcoran, formerly a sailor on a Baltimore vessel until he ran away to join the elder Corcoran's new military unit. After that encounter in camp, Mrs. Daly again described Corcoran in the most flattering terms: "The General attaches everyone to him[self] by his great manliness and tenderness of character, his utter disregard of self. He treated me as if I had been a princess. One must feel complimented by such marks of attention from anyone so sincere."[50]

General Corcoran had originally hoped to enroll eight regiments, but transfers, desertions, consolidations, and organizational mismanagement doomed his expectation. The 116th Pennsylvania, for instance, though originally offered to Corcoran by Colonel Dennis Heenan, was sent to defend Washington, D.C., after the second battle of Bull Run, while the 55th Massachusetts failed to recruit enough men. In the end, the Irish Legion was composed of only four regiments, all from New York State: the 69th (under Colonel Mathew Murphy), the 155th (under Colonel William

McEvily), the 164th (under Colonel John McMahon), and the 170th (under Colonel Peter McDermott). The first of these regiments was officially known as the 69th New York National Guard Artillery, so called to distinguish it from the Old 69th, at the time known as the 69th New York Volunteers. Because both regiments were usually referred to as the "Sixty-Ninth" — a practice that caused confusion — the name of the more recently formed unit was eventually changed to the 182nd New York Volunteers. Corcoran's Legion was at first assigned to the Seventh Corps of the Department of Virginia and was in active service for almost three years, participating in many of the bloodiest battles of the war, including Suffolk, Spotsylvania, Cold Harbor, and Reams' Station.[51]

While Corcoran was still a prisoner in the South, Thomas Meagher had organized an Irish Brigade consisting of three New York regiments, and other Irish units had been created by the various states. These developments contributed to another difficulty which Corcoran encountered in his recruitments efforts — a diminished supply of available and suitable manpower. As a result, men who aspired to command by recruiting a company of their own often resorted to bribery and promises of whiskey to enlist recruits. John Winterbotham, for example, though only nineteen and a sometimes vicious critic of the Irish, hoped to organize a company for the 155th New York Infantry, a regiment in Corcoran's newly formed legion. To do so, though, the ambitious young man had to scour the prisons in New York City and offer bribes to their inhabitants. A more experienced officer was James McIvor, a native of Ireland and a veteran of life as a captain with the 69th New York State Militia. After assuming the lieutenant colonelcy of Corcoran's 170th New York, he found the problem of alcohol abuse in the regiment so serious that he requested the sutlers not to sell whiskey to the officers except by leave of a field officer.[52]

By mid autumn General Corcoran and his Irish Legion were ready for service at the front. At the end of October they presented themselves for a blessing by Archbishop Hughes and ten assistant priests. Among the recruits was the archbishop's nephew, Tracy Hughes, a member of Corcoran's staff. A newspaper correspondent reported that it was a "most impressive sight to see over four thousand men kneeling, in reverence, under the bright sky." In November they finally headed south, at first garrisoning Fort Slocum in Washington, D.C., and then reporting to General John Dix near Newport News, Virginia. The following month the Legion was ordered to Suffolk, Virginia, where it constructed large fortifications and picketed the Dismal Swamp. Despite reservations about future prospects for the Union cause, Corcoran wrote confidently to Judge Charles Daly about the men under his charge: "The Irish Legion is now everything its most ardent friends could desire, and I am fully confident that when the great hour of trial arrives they will do honor to their race and their name." The general added that the 155th and the 164th had been on a three-day reconnaissance mission that netted a few prisoners without suffering any losses. With obvious relief Corcoran noted that Colonel Peter McDermott of the 170th had submitted his resignation, the result of his being charged with four instances of drunkenness on duty.[53]

The Irish Legion spent its first Christmas Eve under General Corcoran encamped near Newport News, Virginia. The men were allowed to decorate their camp with what one correspondent described as "arches of evergreens, some as high as thirty feet; [and] stars made out of the time-honored holly." *Father James Dillon, the Irish-born chaplain of the Legion's 69th New York National Guard Artillery, celebrated midnight mass in Corcoran's headquarters, after which the general presented each of his staff officers with a glass of "genuine Irish whiskey." At 10:30 in the morning, the men of the Legion assembled by regiments and marched off to a mass celebrated by *Father Paul Gillen of the 170th New York. The rest of the holiday was given over to feasting and a variety of races. The men of the 155th New York, for example, dined well that day, as each company in the regiment received ten geese and a dozen turkeys. The horse racing, which prompted considerable betting, resulted in an upset. Although "Blue Bird," the horse belonging to Lieutenant Colonel James McMahon of the 155th New York, was the clear favorite, the winner of two of the three heats was "Old Bull Run," Corcoran's white steed at the battle of Bull Run. About the pig race one observer wrote: "[A]s the 'animal' was let loose, just imagine the whole Brigade running and shouting after Mr. Porkey, and he too commenced to squeal as hard as he could, and kept up the running as fast as a pig can go. . . . [A]fter sundry upsets and knock-downs he was finally captured and placed *hors de combat* [out of commission]."[54]

At the end of January 1863, the Legion had its first taste of battle when Corcoran led his men and other troops against a Confederate force commanded by General Roger Pryor. The battle took place at Deserted House, about ten miles from Suffolk, and resulted in a tremendous victory for Corcoran and his men (even though the Union side lost 150 killed and wounded to the Confederates' twenty-four). In the middle of February, Corcoran attended a social event at the home of Francis Cutting, a New York lawyer and jurist. One of the other guests, Maria Lydig Daly, reiterated her high estimation of the Irish officer: "Corcoran seems to me to have more elements of greatness than anyone the war has as yet brought forward. He does not think of himself or of his own advancement, of what others are thinking of him[,] who can be useful, etc." During the rest of the year the Corcoran Legion helped break the siege of Suffolk (April 11–May 4) by 40,000 Confederates and took part in engagements at Edenton Road (April 15 and 24), Blackwater (May 12), Franklin (June 16 and 17), and Sangster Station (December 17). While Suffolk was under siege, Corcoran was given command of the First Division of the Seventh Army Corps, a division which included his own Irish Legion.[55]

One night in early April 1863, General Corcoran was involved in a tragic and inexplicable incident. After receiving orders to have his troops under arms by 3 a.m., the Irishman rode off to the front in the wee hours of that foggy night. A shadowy figure who appeared in the middle of the road ordered Corcoran and his aides to halt. When Corcoran courteously asked the man to stand aside, the man replied with profanities, drew his sword, and struck at Corcoran's horse. Again the Irishman asked the mysterious figure to let him pass, but in response the stranger shouted, "Not for no damned Irish son of a bitch like you or any one else." When the stranger raised his sword again and acted as if he was about to draw a pistol, Corcoran drew his own weapon and shot the man. (Corcoran later learned that the figure was Lieutenant Colonel Edgar Kimball of the Ninth New York.) In the subsequent inquiry about the incident, Corcoran was judged censurable for his action, and a court-martial was ordered, although one was never conducted.[56]

· In July 1863, Corcoran's Irish Legion was ordered to the Washington, D.C., area, where it performed garrison and picket duty for the next ten months. The 155th New York took up a position in northern Virginia in order to guard the Orange & Alexandria Railroad. During this lengthy assignment, the regiment fought off a series of Confederate cavalry raids, including attacks by Mosby's Rangers. In December about seventy men of the 155th New York successfully protected a railroad bridge from an attack by Confederate General Thomas Rosser's entire cavalry brigade of about 1,000 men.[57]

In the fall of 1864, despite the lingering effects of malnutrition caused by his imprisonment, General Corcoran returned to his legion, at that time encamped at Fairfax Court House, Virginia. In early December he invited Brigadier General Thomas Meagher to Fairfax to spend the Christmas holidays. On December 22 Corcoran accompanied Meagher as they rode to the Fairfax railroad station, where the latter officer was going to board a train to Washington, D.C., to pick up his wife and Corcoran's new seventeen-year-old bride, Elizabeth Heaney. On his return to camp astride Meagher's steed, however, Corcoran suffered some kind of accident that resulted in his being discovered on the ground in a convulsive state. Some sources state that the general was thrown by Meagher's fiery horse, while Dr. John Dwyer, the Legion's surgeon, believed that Corcoran's fall to the ground occurred only after he had dismounted. Although Corcoran's escorts got him back to camp, the thirty-six-year-old officer died within hours from what a medical director labeled "apoplexy."[58]

Funeral services for Corcoran were conducted at St. Patrick's Old Cathedral on Sunday, December 27. An account in the *New York Times* the next day reported that the cathedral doors had to be closed against the constantly increasing throng which tried to attend the requiem mass.

Among the pallbearers were Corcoran's old friend Meagher, of course, and Mathew Murphy, who had become colonel of the 69th New York National Guard Artillery at the age of twenty-three. After the funeral Corcoran's body was interred in Calvary Cemetery in Woodside, Queens, Long Island.[59]

A month later at the Cooper Institute in New York City, Meagher eulogized his fellow countryman but not before recounting the famous incident in which Corcoran had snubbed the Prince of Wales. In retelling the story, Meagher was especially sarcastic about British royalty: "Early in the Fall of 1860, there arrived in this City a young gentleman [Prince Albert Edward] of prominent family and great expectations, who had just visited a portion of his estate [in Canada] across the St. Lawrence, and was now perambulating the domains [United States] which had been lost by his great-grandfather [George III]. He was a lively and courteous young gentleman, and a startling curiosity, even among the novelties which were almost daily washed upon the shores of this great land. He was the eldest son of a Queen [Victoria], wearing the costliest diadem in the universe, and towered high in blood above the haughtiest noble of those whose ancestors had ever spurned serfs or lorded over imperial domains. He was heir to an empire belted by the zodiac, which was daily striving to monopolize the earth and invade the sky. Among an excitable people like our own [Irish], the advent of this young man produced its due effect, and found vent in extraordinary extremes. One man alone stood sternly aloof from the general impulse, and refused to participate in any honors toward the representative of that crown under which the weight of which the liberties of his country [Ireland] had been crushed. A man less fearless, less inflexible, than Michael Corcoran, would never thus have stood. ... To parade his regiment before this youth, who was one day to wear the crown which had scourged his country, would have been to cancel the oaths made for centuries by his countrymen. He would not bow to a Prince against whose land it was the darling wish of his heart one day to head his regiment. For this he was condemned, and it was urged with indignation that neither he nor his regiment could ever be relied on at a critical moment. This falsehood was answered at a later period by Corcoran, who, on the news of [Fort] Sumter, sprung from a sick bed, and was among the first with his noble men, to fly to the rescue of the land of their adoption."[60]

By the middle of May 1864, Corcoran's Legion, now commanded by Colonel Mathew Murphy of the 182nd New York, had been transferred to the Army of the Potomac. Assigned to Brigadier General John Gibbon's Second Division of the Second Corps, the Legion arrived at Spotsylvania Court House, Virginia, just in time to take part in the closing battles of that campaign. As events transpired, however, the arrival of the Legion's new troops was accompanied by a failure in communication during the action on May 18. According to Colonel Murphy, a staff officer detached the 155th and the 164th New York without informing the commander. The two remaining regiments, the 170th and the 182nd New York, forced some enemy pickets to fall back and even overran some Confederate rifle-pits. Not until then, however, did Murphy realize that he was missing two of his units. Confronted by the formidable-looking enemy position, Murphy halted his attack and went off to find his missing troops. At division headquarters he learned that they were off to the right and had been engaged for more than an hour with the 170th and the 182nd. After leading them back in the direction of the Confederate position, Murphy found Colonel James McMahon falling back with the 155th and the 164th, almost completely out of ammunition. When Murphy realized that the enemy would not mount a counterattack, he and his men dug in for a lengthy wait. When the casualties were tallied, it was found that the 164th New York had suffered the greatest losses of any regiment in battle that day: twelve killed, sixty-six wounded, and fourteen missing. (Murphy himself was wounded and did not return to command until July 14.) In his report on the engagement, General Hancock noted the Irish Legion's "good conduct," while Francis Walker, the historian of the Second Corps and no admirer of the Irish soldier, wrote that the Legion "showed itself every way worthy of the company it had come to keep."[61]

During an engagement at North Anna River, Virginia, about a week later, two of the Legion's regiments played a major role. The 170th New York encountered a severe fire barrage and suffered the loss of twenty-two killed, fifty-five wounded, and twenty-two missing. These ninety-nine casualties were the largest of any regimental losses suffered in that battle. The 182nd New York, meanwhile, posted losses of six killed, twenty-eight wounded, and six missing. For their bravery during the engagement, two Irishmen in the Legion later received the Congressional Medal of Honor. Lieutenant Colonel Michael Murphy of the 170th New York was cited for keeping his regiment on the field exposed to enemy fire for three hours, unable to return the fire because their ammunition had run out. Sergeant Major Joseph Keele of the 182nd was similarly honored for voluntarily carrying orders to the brigade commander despite the risk to his life, an act of courage which saved the defensive works that his regiment was protecting. (This may have been the Joseph Keele who had formerly served as the Second Sergeant in Company K in the 69th New York State Militia.)[62]

The Irish Legion suffered even more debilitating losses during the subsequent Union assault at Cold Harbor, Virginia, in early June 1864. As the Union line moved forward at 4:30 a.m. on June 3, the men in Corcoran's Legion noticed the marshy terrain in front of them. One of the officers who served with distinction that day was James McMahon, previously identified as lieutenant colonel of the 155th New York Volunteers. Following the death of his brother John Eugene in March 1863 from disease contracted in the service, James had been selected to succeed him as colonel of the 164th New York. At Cold Harbor Colonel McMahon led the 164th to the left, around the marshy obstacle, bearing in his hand the green Irish flag, while the 182nd moved in the opposite direction, opening up a sizeable gap in the Irishmen's line. Both Barlow's and Gibbon's divisions were halfway to the formidable Confederate works when enemy rifle fire rang out, soon followed by artillery barrages. Whole ranks of Union soldiers fell to the ground, caught in the enemy's cross fire. On Barlow's right, meanwhile, McMahon presented a gallant sight as he led the 164th with his sword uplifted and the Irish ensign clutched in his left hand. But such was the deadly enemy fire that only a few of the colonel's men followed him up the Confederate entrenchments. From there he continued to wave the green flag and urge his men to follow until he was finally cut down, his fallen body draped with the fallen banner. Although Corcoran's Legion succeeded in taking the enemy's works in its immediate front, it did so with a heavy loss of officers and men. Besides McMahon, the 164th New York lost six other officers killed, and the regiment was forced to fall back after suffering the loss of 157 men (sixteen killed, fifty-nine wounded, and eighty-two missing). In addition, the 155th New York suffered 164 casualties in about a half hour. In total, the Irish Legion sustained 900 casualties that day, more than any other brigade in either the Confederate or the Union army. Four days later, during another engagement at Cold Harbor, Irishman Patrick Doody, a corporal in Company E, 164th New York, lived up to his heritage. The citation accompanying his Congressional Medal of Honor described his heroic action: "After making a successful personal reconnaissance, he gallantly led the skirmishes in a night attack, charging the enemy, and thus enabling the pioneers to put up works."[63]

Colonel McMahon's glorious death earned for him a hallowed place in the Irish Legion's pantheon of heroes. Francis Walker, the Second Corps' historian, wrote that McMahon "had been but a brief three weeks with the Army of the Potomac; but he brought to it a lofty courage and chivalrous sense of duty which did honor even to the old corps of Sumner." Thomas Meagher eulogized the young officer in his best oratorical style: "Who . . . can forget the dashing, handsome, indefatigable soldier, with his strictly defined features, oftentimes with the enthusiasm, sometimes with the scorn and haughtiness of a true[-]blooded Celt, with a heart for hospitality, with a soul for glory, and scorn and sarcasm for what was mean, and a quick look and blow for what was treacherous — who can forget his fine bearing, erect and graceful, his rare heartiness, the decisive character of his intellect, his high pride, his humor, his physical activity, all those healthy and superior gifts which made him a soldier at the start, and qualified him even in the first hours of boyhood to be a conspicuous exponent of his martial race and kindred — who can forget all this whenever that grand picture of McMahon, planting the colors of his regiment in the face of the fire storm, and foot to foot with the desperate foe, is spoken of in the Camp and by the Survivors of the Irish Brigade of the Army of the Potomac?"[64]

McMahon was also eulogized in verse written by one of his contemporaries, an anonymous member of the Eighth New York Heavy Artillery:

*"The Brave Colonel James P. McMahon at Cold Harbor"

Would you like to have me tell you of how the Young Colonel died?
God grant my memory may not fail nor that my tongue be tied.
Twas the second weary night of that hot and bloody June,
We marched along the pickets, we camped beneath the moon.
Behind us sixty miles of death, Virginia thickets lay,
Before us was Cold Harbor, the hell to come next day.
Sitting in the tent door in the silvery dew,
We talked of old Buffalo and of the girls we knew.
Spread o'er the silent fields below, the mist lay like a pond.
We seemed to see the long dark streets, and the white lake beyond.
We charged at noon. The Colonel led green Erin's old Brigade,
While Longstreet's blazing cannon from behind their breastworks
played.
The Colonel led through fire and smoke. His sword did wave and shine.
And still the brave sound of his voice drew on our struggling line,
As o'er the surf at Wicklow I've heard the seagull cry.
His voice did rise above the storm and sounded clear and high.
Then all at once our colors sank, I saw them reel and nod
And the colonel sprang and caught them before they touched the sod.
Another leap and with a shout, the Rebs do mind it well[,]
He stood alone upon their works, waved the old Flag, and fell!
We left him at Cold Harbor. The spot was bleak and bare,
I hate to think that I'm at home and he's still lying there.
I know his sleep will not be sweet nor his gallant spirit still,
Till we lay him alone in the friendly dust of yonder slanting hill.
Where from the town he loved so well will come the daily hum,
And the lake's loud roar upon the beach when quiet nights shall come.
Well might his city rear his tomb in marble words to tell
How the bravest of her blood was shed when young McMahon fell![65]

On the following June 16–18, Corcoran's Legion was part of the Union assault on Petersburg. The 164th New York suffered fourteen men killed and mortally wounded, while the 170th sustained thirty-six similar casualties. During an attack on June 17, John Brosnan, an Irish-born sergeant in the 164th, earned the Congressional Medal of Honor for the severe wound he sustained while rescuing a comrade exposed to enemy fire. In addition, the 155th posted losses of 50 percent, enough to reduce its ranks to about seventy men when Hancock's Second Corps of the Army of the Potomac settled down for the siege of Petersburg. The battle of Reams' Station the following August proved equally disastrous for the 155th New York. The regiment was reduced in strength to a mere thirty-five men, although its ranks soon increased to between 130 and 140 with the return of soldiers who had recovered from their previous wounds. The 155th was present in the successful Union attack on Petersburg on April 2, 1865, and fought its last battle at Farmville, Virginia, five days later. On April 9 it witnessed the surrender of Robert E. Lee and his Army of Northern Virginia. During its three years of service, the regiment suffered a casualty rate of 60 percent — 189 deaths and about 280 men wounded, captured, or missing.[66]

Corcoran's Legion suffered especially heavy losses at Reams' Station. After the battle the unit numbered only about 200 men, while its loss in captured officers was severe: five from the 155th Regiment, at least five from the 164th, and six from the 170th. Other statistics were even more telling: the 155th lost forty or forty-one out of seventy-five men, the 164th had only one officer left, the 170th had one officer and about thirty men out of 150, and the 182nd lost five officers killed, wounded, or captured. Second Lieutenant Dean Wilson of the 155th New York described the disaster which befell the Irish Legion that day: "The enemy charged six times on our right, and were repulsed with slaughter. But then they brought up their batteries, I should say twenty or twenty-five pieces, and opened on us simultaneously. They were in such force they overlapped our line on the right and left, and came up in our rear. Then commenced the slaughter. From front and rear they came swarming in with their yells, and seizing the artillery, turned it immediately on our men. The lieutenant-colonel was captured while endeavoring to get the men to stand by the gun. . . . Many of our troops would not leave the pits at all, preferring capture and imprisonment to running the chances of getting out from under the destructive artillery fire that was concentrated on us from all points front and rear, right and left."[67]

During the battle of Reams' Station, the Legion lost one of its best military instructors and the Fenian Brotherhood's most effective recruiter. Captain Frank Welpley had served with the Legion from the beginning, as an officer in its original unit, the 69th New York National Guard Artillery. Though he was originally buried on the field of battle, his remains were later conveyed to Ireland and laid to rest in his native Skibbereen in County Cork. Welpley was the subject of this apparently anonymous verse:

> *"O! Eri Mo Chroidhe 'Ta M' Intinn Ort"
> ("O Erin, my heart, my mind is on thee")

To the Memory of my Beloved Comrade
Captain Welpley, Corcoran's Irish Legion.

One still Christmas night, by the Potomac river,
Our army lay cantoned in long ordered lines;
The keen frosty air made the sentinels shiver,
And icicles fringed the dark leaves of the pines.
The bells, in the distance, were cheerily ringing,
"Great tidings of joy!" to humanity bringing,
While stretched by his camp-fire, a soldier lay singing —
'O! Eri mo chroidhe 'ta m' intinn ort!'

"I've loved you, dear Eire, as the mother that bore me,
With her milk I imbibed deadly hate to your foe;
And I longed, as a man, like my fathers before me,
To strike, for your freedom, a soldier's strong blow.
But I saw, famine-stricken, your children lie dying,
And maddened, I 'rose' with my comrades, defying
Their slayers. We failed! then o'er ocean sped singing —
'O! Eri mo chroidhe 'ta m' intinn ort!'

"Since I first set my foot on this fair 'land of freedom,'
In your service I've labored by night and by day;
I have trained your true sons, hoping *sometime* to lead them
In disciplined strength on your hills, far away.
In the camp, on the march, in the hot rush of battle,
'Mid the soldier's wild cheers and the rifle's quick rattle,
When the foe fly before us like panic-stricken cattle —
'O! Eri mo chroidhe 'ta m' intinn ort!'

\*   \*   \*   \*   \*   \*   \*   \*   \*   \*   \*   \*   \*

Long he fought in the ranks of the brave "Irish Legion,"
Then fell! — his last thought on the land he loved best;
But his name shall go down Erin's history's page on,
And he sleeps in his own "Holy Isle of the West!"
On the bright wings of glory his soul fled upspringing,
To his Brothers whose thoughts are to Ireland still clinging,
'Mid angelic hosannas their voices join singing —
'O! Eri mo chroidhe 'ta m' intinn ort!'[68]

At the battle of Hatcher's Run, Virginia, on October 27, 1864, the 164th New York Infantry lost Sergeant George Tipping. This blacksmith from Buffalo had originally joined the 155th New York but was later transferred to the 164th. Just seventeen days before his death, he had written to his wife, explaining to her the practice whereby Yankee and Rebel pickets occasionally called a truce. "We make a bargain in the morning before daylight not to fire at one another all day," he wrote. "We agree to it and after breakfast we may walk any place inside our lines and chat with them all day long. They sing out the first thing in the morning to stop firing until we get breakfast. 'Say, Yank, stop firing.' 'Very well, Johnnie.' 'All day?' 'Yes, all day, Yank.' Then there is a white rag hung out on a pole with the rebs and us, and, after sundown they will sing out, 'Get into your holes, Yanks, we are going to fire,' and the firing is kept up all night until morning again."[69]

*The gave of Colonel Mathew Murphy in Calvary Cemetery in Woodside, Queens, Long Island, New York.*

When Corcoran's Irish Legion had commenced its service during the Civil War, it numbered in its ranks almost 3,500 men. Over the next two and a half years it suffered 1,943 casualties: 432 killed and mortally wounded, 1,266 wounded and recovered, and 245 dead from disease. A breakdown by each regiment reveals the following:

| Regiment | Enrolled | Killed/ Mortally Wounded | Wounded | Dead from Disease |
|---|---|---|---|---|
| 155th NY | 830 | 114 | 325 | 73 |
| 164th NY | 928 | 116 | 329 | 69 |
| 170th NY | 1,002 | 129 | 352 | 50 |
| 182nd NY | 712 | 73 | 260 | 53[70] |

Among the Legion's casualties was Colonel Mathew Murphy, first mustered into the 69th New York State Militia Regiment as a second lieutenant at the young age of twenty-two. A year later, when he and 700 other officers and men of the 69th joined Corcoran's Irish Legion, Murphy became colonel of the newly named 69th New York National Guard Artillery (later known as the 182nd New York Volunteers). He commanded the Legion from January 1863 until February 1865, when he was mortally wounded during the battle of Hatcher's Run. The young officer died of his wounds, on April 16, 1865, in a hospital at City Point, Virginia. He was buried in Calvary Cemetery in Woodside, Queens, Long Island.[71]

In July 1868, the journalist Charles Halpine, who had briefly served with the 69th New York State Militia Regiment, wrote an exceptionally long tribute for the regiment's reunion later that month. The 130-line poem was originally named "Lines for the Day" but today is better known as *"On Raising a Monument to the Irish Legion." The ode was written as preparations were under way to erect a suitable monument to the valor which the Irish soldier had displayed during the war. The tribute was Halpine's last poetic piece before his untimely death that August.

> To raise a column o'er the dead,
> To strew with flowers the graves of those
> Who, long ago, in storms of lead,
> And where the bolts of battle sped,
> Beside us faced our Southern foes;
> To honor these — th' unshriv'n, unhearsed —
> To-day we sad survivors come,
> With colors draped, and arms reversed,
> And all our souls in gloom immersed,
> With silent fife and muffled drum.
>
> In mournful guise our banners wave;

Black clouds above the "sunburst" lower;
We mourn the true, the young, the brave
Who, for this land that shelter gave,
Drew swords in peril's deadliest hour —
For Irish soldiers fighting here
As when Lord Clare was bid advance,
And Cumberland beheld with fear
The old green banners swinging clear
To shield the broken lines of France.

We mourn them; not because they died
In battle, for our destined race,
In every field of warlike pride,
From Limerick's wall to India's tide,
Have borne our flag to foremost place;
As if each sought the soldier's trade,
While some dim hopes within him glows,
Before he dies, in line arrayed,
To see the old green flag displayed
For final fight with Ireland's foes.

For such a race the soldier's death
Seems not a cruel death to die,
Around their names a laurel wreath,
A wild cheer as the parting breath
On which their spirits mount the sky;
Oh, had their hope been only won,
On Irish soil their final fight,
And had they seen, ere sinking down,
Our em'rald torn from England's crown,
Each dead face would have flashed with light.

But vain are words to check the tide
Of widowed grief and orphaned woe;
Again we see them by our side,
As, full of youth and strength and pride,
They first went forth to meet the foe!
Their kindling eyes, their steps elate,
Their grief at parting hid in mirth;
Against our foes no spark of hate,
No wish but to preserve the State
That welcomes all th' oppressed of earth.

Not a new Ireland to invoke,

To guard the flag was all they sought;
Not to make others feel the yoke
Of Poland, feel the shot and stroke
Of those who in the legion fought;
Upon our great flag's azure field
To hold unharmed each starry gem —
This cause on many a bloody field,
Thinned out by death, they would not yield —
It was the world's last hope to them.

Oh ye, the small surviving band,
Oh, Irish race wherever spread,
With wailing voice and wringing hand,
And the wild kaoine of the dear old land,
Think of her Legion's countless dead!
Struck out of life by ball or blade,
Or torn in fragments by the shell,
With briefest prayer by brother made,
And rudely in their blankets laid,
Now sleep the brave who fought so well.

Their widows — tell them not of pride,
No laurel checks the orphan's tear;
They only feel the world is wide,
And dark, and hard — nor help nor guide —
No husband's arm, no father near;
But at their nod our fields were won,
And pious pity for their loss
In streams of gen'rous aid should run
To help them say: "Thy will be done,"
As bent in grief they kiss the Cross.

Then for the soldiers and their chief
Let all combine a shaft to raise —
The double type of pride and grief,
With many a sculpture and relief
To tell their tale to after days;
And here will shine — our proudest boast
While one of Irish blood survives:
"Sacred to that unfalt'ring host
Of soldiers from a distant coast,
Who for the Union gave their lives.

"Welcomed they were with generous hand,

And to that welcome nobly true,
When war's dread tocsin filled the land,
With sinewy arm and swinging brand,
These exiles to the rescue flew.
Their fealty to the flag they gave,
And for the Union, daring death.
Foremost among the foremost brave,
They welcomed vict'ry and the grave,
In the same sigh of parting breath."

Thus be their modest history penned,
But not with this our love must cease;
Let prayers from pious hearts ascend,
And o'er their ashes let us blend
All feuds and factions into peace.
Oh, men of Ireland! here unite
Around the graves of those we love,
And from their homes of endless light
The Legion's dead will bless the sight,
And rain down anthems from above!

Here to this shrine by reverence led,
Let Love her sacred lessons teach;
Shoulder to shoulder rise the dead,
From many a trench with battle red
And thus I hear their ghostly speech:
"Oh, for the old earth, and our sake,
Renounce all feuds, engend'ring fear,
And Ireland from her trance shall wake,
Striving once more her chains to break
When all her sons are brothers here."

I see our Meagher's plume of green,
Approving nod to hear the words,
And Corcoran's wraith applauds the scene,
And bold Mat Murphy smiles, I ween —
All three with hands on ghastly swords —
Oh, for their sake, whose names of light
Flash out like beacons from dark shores —
Men of the old race! in your might,
All factions quelled, again unite —
With you the Green Flag sinks or soars![72]

On January 31, 1914, a memorial tablet in honor of Michael Corcoran was unveiled at the armory of the 69th New York Regiment at Lexington Avenue and 25th Street in New York City. The unveiling took place on the fifty-first anniversary of the Corcoran Legion's first engagement during the Civil War, a victory fought at Deserted House, Virginia. Captain John Nugent, who had shared Corcoran's captivity in the South after the first battle of Bull Run, was among the honored guests. The tablet reads:

In Memory of
Brig. Gen. Michael Corcoran, U.S.V.
Irish Patriot, Catholic Citizen, American Soldier.
Born at Carrowkeel, Sligo, Ireland,
Sept. 21, 1827.
Colonel 69th N.Y. State Militia 1859–1861
Commanding the Regiment in Volunteer
Service of U.S.
Captured at Bull Run, July 21, 1861.
In Confederate military prisons until
August 15, 1862.
Commissioned Brigadier-General, U.S. Vol's. 1862
with rank from July 21, 1861.
Organizer of Corcoran's Legion N.Y. Vol's.
Died in Service of the United States,
Dec. 22, 1863, at
Fairfax Court House, Virginia.[73]

In 1989 a new headstone was placed over Corcoran's grave in Calvary Cemetery in Woodside, Queens, Long Island, by the Sligo Men's Association. The headstone bears the motto of the 69th New York Regiment: "Gentle when stroked, fierce when provoked." The inscription is similar to that on the memorial to Corcoran at the regimental armory:

In Memory of
Brigadier General Michael Corcoran
Irish Patriot, American Soldier, Catholic Citizen
Born Carrowkeel, Sligo, Ireland
Sept. 21st, 1827
Col. 69th N.Y. State Militia, 1859-1861
Commanding the Regiment in Volunteer Service of U.S.
Organizer of Corcoran's Legion N.Y. Volunteers
Died in the Service of the U.S.
Dec. 22, 1863

His wife
Elizabeth Corcoran
Died August 1863      Aged 35 years.[74]

*The grave of Colonel Michael Corcoran in Calvary Cemetery in Woodside, Queens, Long Island. (Location: Section 4, Range 5, Plot O, Grave 13/16)*

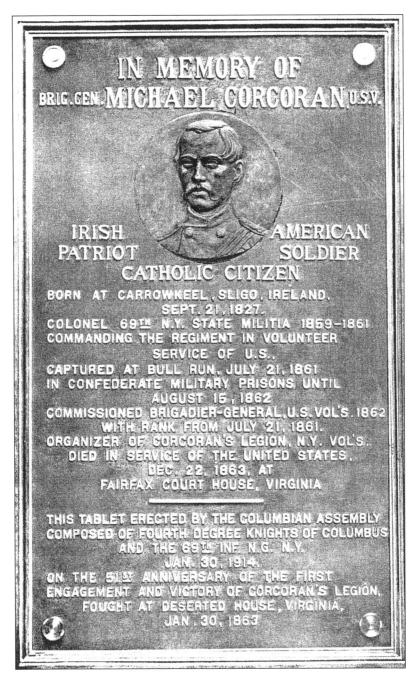

*Memorial tablet in honor of Colonel Michael Corcoran in the 69th New York Armory at Lexington Avenue and 25th Street in New York City.*

# Chapter 2

## Thomas Meagher, the 69th New York Volunteers, and the Irish Brigade

After completing three months of service to the federal government, the 69th New York State Militia Regiment returned to New York City on July 27, 1861. Of the 1,276 men and officers who had served with the 69th in Virginia, 1,034 came back with the colors. The men marched from the Battery to Union Square and from there down Fifth Avenue to the regimental armory at Essex Market. Manahan's Band led the way, playing the traditional air *"Saint Patrick's Day." Next in the line of march were four of the regiment's ten companies, followed by Lieutenant Colonel Robert Nugent (his arm in a sling from a wound suffered at Bull Run) and Father Bernard O'Reilly, the acting chaplain. The other officers — including Captain Thomas Meagher — were greeted with applause, while the wounded Captain John Breslin rode in an open barouche. The remaining regimental companies — as well as the Father Mathew Abstinence Society and the Ancient Order of Hibernians and their bands — brought up the rear.[1]

The account of this "Grand March" in the *New York Times* spared no fact — or opinion — favorable to the regiment and its Irish supporters. "[S]o conspicuous has been the service performed by the Sixty-ninth, so unquestionable its valor, so complete and heroic its willing self-devotion," gushed the reporter, "that the first word of qualified praise has not yet reached our eye." After noting that the soldiers were "browned by the fervid rays of a Southern sun, and look wirey [*sic*] and firm-limbed," the correspondent commented on the men's dusty knapsacks and their ill-fitting or unexpected clothing. "We have all heard that at the battle of Bull's Run, they stripped off their upper vestments for the comfort of 'sailing in with perfect looseness,'" wrote the journalist. "It is now apparent that after the fight some of the men got into the wrong coats, and others finding no coats at all to get into, contented themselves with a toilette in which that garment was not indispensable." At intervals along the march — so the newspaper continued — a woman would rush into the ranks and "bury herself in an immense amount of flannel and whiskers." Throwing objectivity to the wind, the correspondent gushed some more: "In that green and lovely island, where the women are all virtuous, and the men are all brave, they don't stand on ceremony, and we have Irish hearts here as true and impulsive as any that beat in Erin."[2]

Although the 69th New York State Militia Regiment was soon mustered out of federal service, on August 21 more than 500 of the men decided to offer their services to the federal government once again. Formed into a regiment now known as the 69th New York State Volunteers, they

were commanded by Lieutenant Colonel Nugent, a native of Kilkeel,
County Down, Ireland. At the same time, there was talk of organizing a
brigade of 5,000 men — all Irish recruits — under the command of General James Shields, a son of Ireland who had distinguished himself during
the Mexican War. While the possibility of an "Irish Brigade" remained
under consideration, political motivations began to play a more important role. This was especially true with regard to the conduct of Captain
Meagher. At the beginning of the war, Meagher had raised and led Company K, the "Irish Zouaves," for the 69th New York State Militia Regiment, serving under Colonel Michael Corcoran at the first battle of Bull
Run. In what was interpreted as an ungentlemanly attempt to take command of the 69th New York from Nugent, Meagher in late August offered
the services of the 69th to the War Department for three years. The War
Department accepted the offer — although Meagher later denied making
it — and it was subsequently announced that the regiment would be reorganized under "Colonel" Meagher and Lieutenant Colonel Nugent. A similar "change of plans" took place with regard to the proposed Irish Brigade. As the result of various developments, command fell not to Shields
but to "Acting Brigadier" Thomas Meagher. Though its initial regiments
were the 63rd, 69th, and 88th New York State Volunteers, the Brigade was
later augmented by the 28th Massachusetts and the 116th Pennsylvania
volunteer infantry regiments.[3]

Born in 1823 in Waterford, Ireland, Meagher was the son of a prominent merchant who for a time was a member of the British Parliament.
The younger Meagher attended the Jesuit college at Clongowes-Wood in
Ireland and Stonyhurst College in England. (At the time of his graduation
from Stonyhurst, he was known as the best rhetorician in the history of
that institution.) At the age of twenty-two he joined the Young Ireland
party in its efforts to obtain Ireland's independence from Great Britain. In
1846 he publicly broke with Daniel O'Connell's constitutionalist approach
to political change and adopted a more militant nationalist position. At a
gathering in Dublin that year he refused to forswear for Irishmen the use
of physical force in their quest for independence. In a speech which earned
him the nickname "Meagher of the Sword," he cited historical examples
of how resort to arms had gained political freedom for oppressed peoples.
"Abhor the sword — stigmatise [sic] the sword?" he asked the mayor of
Dublin. "No, my lord, for it swept the Dutch marauders out of the fine old
towns of Belgium — scourged them back to their own phlegmatic swamps
— and knocked their flag and sceptre, their laws and bayonets into the
sluggish waters of the Scheldt. . . ." Meagher even insisted that the "Lord
of Hosts . . . bestows His benediction upon those who unsheath [sic] the
sword in the hour of a nation's peril."[4]

The exalted position which Meagher occupied in the vanguard of Irish
nationalism is illustrated in the poem "The Young Patriot Leader" by

"Speranza" (the pseudonym for Lady Wilde, the mother of the famous playwright):

> O! He stands beneath the sun, that glorious *Fated One*,
>     Like a martyr or conqueror, wearing
> On his brow a mighty doom — be it glory, be it gloom,
>     The shadow of a crown it is bearing.
>
> At his Cyclopean stroke the proud heart of man awoke,
>     Like a king from his lordly down lying;
> And wheresoe'er he trod, like the footstep of a god,
>     Was a trail of light the gloom outvying.
>
> In his beauty and his youth, the Apostle of the Truth,
>     Goes he forth with the words of Salvation,
> And a noble madness falls on each spirit he enthralls,
>     As he chants his wild paeans to the nation.
>
> As a Tempest in its force, as a Torrent in its course,
>     So his words fiercely sweep all before them;
> And they smite like two-edged swords, those undaunted thunder words,
>     On all hearts, as tho' Angels did implore them.
>
> See our pale cheeks how they flush, as the noble visions rush,
>     On our soul's most dark desolation —
> And the glorious lyric words — Right, Freedom, and our Swords! —
>     Wake the strong chords of life to vibration.
>
> Ay — right noble, in good sooth, seem'd he battling for the Truth
>     When he poured the full tide of his scorn
> Down upon the Tyrant's track, like an Alpine cataract —
>     Ah! — such men wait an Aeon to be born.
>
> So he stood before us then, one of God's eternal men,
>     Flashing eye, and hero mould of stature,
> With a glory and a light circling round his brow of might,
>     That revealed his right royal kingly nature.
>
> Lo! he leadeth on our bands, Freedom's banner in his hands.
>     Let us aid him, not with words, but *doing*;
> With the marches of the brave, prayers of might that strike and save,
>     Not a slavish spirit's abject suing.
>
> Thus in glory is he seen, though his years are yet but green,

The Anointed as Head of our Nation —
For high Heaven hath decreed that a soul like his must lead,
Let us kneel then in deep adoration.

O! his mission is divine — dash down the Lotus wine —
Too long in your trancèd sleep abiding;
And by him who gave us life, we shall conquer in the strife,
So we follow but that Young Chief's guiding.[5]

In 1848 Meagher was arrested after giving a speech in which he made incendiary remarks. Several months later he was tried and condemned to death for high treason, although that sentence was soon commuted to banishment to a penal colony. (John Maguire, who was in the courtroom when Meagher was condemned to death, left a fitting tribute: ". . . I well remember . . . the proud and gallant bearing of that young and fearless tribune, who, I am convinced, would have met death calmly in the cause to which he deliberately sacrificed every hope of his youth and dream of his ambition. Had he been allowed to enter the House of Commons, when he made the attempt on the hustings of Waterford in 1847, his fate might have been quite other than it was; but the spirit of faction was too strong in those days; and so, while the British Parliament lost a brilliant orator, and Ireland an eloquent advocate and faithful representative, America gained a devoted citizen.") After about thirty months as a prisoner in Tasmania, however, Meagher escaped and arrived in New York City in May 1852. Almost from the moment of his arrival, he became the uncrowned prince of the New York Irish. After a period of time on the lecture circuit, he undertook the study of law and was admitted to the bar in 1855, thereafter combining a legal career with the editorship of the *New York Irish News*.[6]

Prior to the start of the Civil War, Meagher had often expressed his admiration for the culture and people of the southern United States. But by April 22, 1861, two weeks after the Confederate attack on Fort Sumter, he had come to the conclusion that he must fight for the Union which had given him asylum after his escape from exile in Tasmania. He also confided to a friend his hope that the involvement of Irish Americans in the war — and the military experience they would receive — would be a prelude to the day when many of those same troops would help deliver Ireland from her British oppressors. The more specific hope that the 69th New York under Meagher and Michael Corcoran would some day free Ireland finds expression in the following song. (The tale is told first by the fiancée of an enlisted soldier and then by the young man himself.)

*"The 69th Brigade"

My true love, William, to the war he is gone;
I'm in grief for his absence, I'm like a bird alone;
He's a clever, handsome fellow, besides a dashing blade.
He [en]listed with bold Meagher, in the Sixty-Ninth Brigade.

Before my true love left me, he said he'd marry me;
I long for his return, that happy day to see;
He said he'd surely marry me, of his word I'm not afraid,
He's a Patriot and soldier, in the Sixty-Ninth Brigade.

At the battle of Bull-Run, he conquer'd with each blow;
With his bayonet and his gun, he laid those Rebels low;
His Colonel there beheld him, and thus to Meagher said:
He's a credit to his Country, and the Sixty-Ninth Brigade.

One night, as I sat watching, by the light of the moon,
Who did I chance to see, but my Willie coming home?
I quickly run [sic] to meet him, for I never will degrade
My true[-]hearted soldier, in the Sixty-Ninth Brigade.

If this war was over, I'd leave you but once more:
That would be to cross the sea, to Erin's lovely shore:
To put an end, for ever, to the landlord's crow-bar brigade,
Under the gallant Leaders of the Sixty-Ninth Brigade.

They say the Queen of England went to Ireland, to try
How did her loyal subjects feel, or would their pulse beat high;
She met no grand reception, from the people, it is said;
Their hearts and souls are centered in the Sixty-Ninth Brigade.

Were she to come among you, on a visit every day,
Do not pay attention nor give heed to what she'll say;
She's trembling in her skin, she's so very much afraid
She'll shortly get a visit from the Sixty-Ninth Brigade.

When hunger, death and famine, sent one million to their grave,
She did not come among you, then, their precious lives to save;
She made up a subscription and sent you fifty pounds;
Wasn't that a blessed offering from the British royal crown?

The day is fast approaching, that all the world can see
That there must be a total end to British tyranny;
Corcoran and brave Meagher, whose deeds shall never fade,
Will free Erin's sons and daughters with the Sixty-Ninth Brigade.[7]

On August 29 an estimated 75,000 people attended a "Grand Festival" in Jones' Wood, a park on New York's East Side, to raise money for the widows and orphans of the members of the 69th who had been killed at Bull Run. So many people sought admission to the event that the ticket-takers could not keep up with the rush, and some in the crowd climbed over the fence rather than wait in line. A similar rush of human flesh surged toward the speaker's platform when Thomas Meagher, the "hero of the day," and Father Thomas Mooney took their seats. The *New York Herald* reported that "a strong and healthy" Irishwoman overpowered two policemen who attempted to stop her from ascending the platform, although she was finally removed. The *Herald* journalist commented wryly: "No doubt she entertained similar ideas of equality to her two fellow countrymen, one of whom, on a certain occasion, put the question to his companion: — 'I say, Pat, isn't one man as good as another?' to which Patrick characteristically replied, 'Of course he is, an' a grate dale bether.'"[8]

The entertainment that day included the singing of *"Corcoran to His Regiment," composed for the occasion by "an Irishman." The song's subtitle — "I Would Not Take Parole" — reminded its hearers that Colonel Michael Corcoran, captured at Bull Run, was still a prisoner in the South after refusing never again to take up arms against the Confederacy.

> Bear aloft that Flag, boys, Erin's glorious green,
> Foremost in the fight, boys, be our "Sun-burst" seen;
> Onward with that uncrown'd harp to "victory or death[,]"
> The word "Remember Limerick, and Britain's broken faith."

> Chorus
> Forward now, to aid me in my need,
> By your arms your Chief would fain be freed;
> I went into this struggle with my heart and soul,
> And though my jailors gave it me, I would not take parole.

> Raise that green Flag proudly, let it wave, on high,
> "Liberty and Union" be your battle-cry;
> FAUGH-A-BALLAGH shout from your centre to your flanks,
> And carry death and terror wild, into the foeman's ranks.

> Think how your brave fathers for your freedom fought;
> Think of those bright deeds which Irishmen have wrought;
> Meet advancing hosts, boys, let them feel your steel,
> And prove you're worthy of the land of Sarsfield and O'Neill.

> Raise that glorious Sun-burst; raise it once again,
> Let me see it shining o'er the battle plain;

With its bright rays beaming. On, my gallant band,
For God and for the Union of our dear adopted land.[9]

Later that afternoon Meagher delivered a speech designed to recruit
soldiers for the reorganized 69th New York Regiment. He first paid tribute to the members of the regiment who had fallen at Bull Run, thereby
"sealing their oath of American citizenship with their blood." He wished
eternal glory to the Irish soldiers who had gone forth without thought of
home or danger or reward to maintain in arms the authority of the government to which they had sworn allegiance and in the perpetuation of
which their interests were vitally involved. "All of them were from Ireland," he stressed, "and as the tide of life rushed out the last thought that
left their hearts was for the liberty of Ireland." To his question whether the
North's attempt to restore the Union was just, the famous orator replied
that there was no more just or sacred cause. The effort, he thundered, was
nothing less than a defense of the "most precious fruits" of the American
Revolution: "assertion of the national authority, derived, as it is, from the
free will and votes of a majority of the citizens, the conservation in its
integrity of that magnificent expanse of country over which a common
Constitution has thrown its shield, . . . the flag which no foreign hand as
yet has questioned with impunity, the enforcement of the laws of Congress, the sworn compact of the States, the inviolability of the ballot box
and the decisions that proceed from it, the sanctity of official oaths, . . . the
progress of democracy."[10]

While reminding his audience that he was a staunch Democrat,
Meagher said he cared not that President Lincoln was a Republican and
stressed that partisan politics should count as nothing when weighed
against national interests and national honor. When he asked the crowd,
"Will the Irishmen of New York stand by this cause . . . despite of all the
sacrifices it may cost . . . despite of all the bereavements and abiding gloom
it may bring . . . .? his audience roared its reply: "We will! We will!" Saying
that he asked no Irishman to do what he was not prepared to do himself,
he assured his listeners: "My heart, my arm, my life, is [sic] pledged to the
national cause, and to the last it will be my highest pride, as I conceive it
to be my holiest duty and obligation, to share its fortunes." Meagher went
on to complain that the national government had so far been too lenient
against those who had "victoriously shaken the banner of revolt and re-
pudiation in its face" and promised his support to whatever measures the
president took "to paralyze the treachery" which in New York and elsewhere had tried "to undermine and overthrow the legitimate magistracy
of the nation." Playing to the anti-British sentiments of his audience,
Meagher charged that the British government supported the "revolution"
in which the South was engaged. No Irishman, he warned, can support a
revolution which has the "patronage of an aristocracy to which for gen-

erations Ireland has ascribed her social wretchedness and political disorders." Let all Irishmen, he cried, "stand to the last by the Stars and Stripes, the illustrious insignia of the nation that, of all the world, has been the friendliest sanctuary of the Irish race."[11]

A month later, on September 23, Meagher addressed a large crowd at the Boston Music Hall. There he challenged his fellow countrymen to join the newly forming Irish Brigade and described for them the essence of the Union cause. "They who affront this Government . . . strike not at the Government, but at the people," he proclaimed, adding that the secessionists had rejected a legitimately elected government and substituted the "rule of the bayonet and the cartridge-box" for the ballot box. Through a series of rhetorical questions, he asserted that no invasion had occurred to justify the South's treason and no constitutional right of the states had been violated. Instead, he explained to his hearers, the South resented its loss of power to the Republican party after having dominated the national government for more than a half century. While admitting to his critics that he had been a "revolutionist" in his native Ireland, he proclaimed himself a conservative now that he lived in America, where "the avenues to honor, to fortune, to civic renown, and to political power . . . have been flung open to him by the genius of the Constitution." Meagher proceeded, now using a common rhetorical device: "I will not remind my countrymen," he said, that America took the Irish in when they had been driven from their homeland, that the American people had always aided the Irish in their political struggles, and that England supported the South in the current struggle. Then, recalling the American flag which he had seen at the Bunker Hill monument earlier in the day, he apotheosized the Stars and Stripes: "A national flag is the most sacred thing that a nation can possess. . . . It is the illuminated diploma of its authority; it is the imperishable epitomization of its history. . . . [I]f that flag is not worth fighting for, if the country which it typifies and over which it has a right to expand its folds, if the principles which it symbolizes . . . are not worth fighting for, . . . then I stand in the minority. But it is not so." In case gratitude and patriotism failed to motivate his listeners, Meagher appealed to honor: "[A]n Irishman never fights so well as when he has an Irishman for his comrade. . . . An Irishman going into the field in such a cause as this . . . has this as his richest reward in anticipation — that his conduct, if it be exemplary and courageous, will reflect honor upon that land which he will see no more." Henceforth, Meagher proclaimed, the Irish soldier will "take his stand proudly by the side of the native-born, and will not fear to look him straight and sternly in the face, and tell him that he has been equal to him in his allegiance to the Constitution."[12]

Despite his growing reputation as the spokesman for the pro-Union members of the New York Irish community, Meagher had begun to alienate some prominent people by his remarks. Maria Lydig Daly, whose husband, Judge Charles Daly, was an enthusiastic supporter of the fledgling 69th New York State Volunteers, took issue with Meagher when he criticized the men of Corcoran's former regiment who did not join the new volunteer unit. In a diary entry for October 14, Mrs. Daly wrote, "Had Corcoran been here to lead them, doubtless they would have gone, but in Meagher they do not place such reliance." She continued in a more biting vein: "A countryman said of him [Meagher] a few days ago that God Almighty had just made him to step off a scaffold [platform] with a big speech in his mouth. He has a very domineering, arrogant disposition. He is very jealous too. . . ." Almost three weeks later Mrs. Daly confided to her diary: "Meagher is not very officer-like. He is tempted to try a brigadiership, and his wife will urge him on." In an entry of November 10, the judge's wife returned to her theme: "Meagher is evidently double-faced. On Tuesday last, he said nothing would induce him to be a brigadier; on Saturday last, he begged Mr. [John] Savage to push the matter with some influential men in Washington." (Savage was a member of the executive committee of a civilian organization formed in New York to help create the Irish Brigade.)[13]

At the end of October, Meagher, soon to be named brigadier general, ordered his recruits to report to Fort Schuyler on Long Island Sound. Although the overwhelming number of men in the Brigade were from the laboring classes, some were lawyers, teachers, merchants, businessmen, and public officials. Some had even fought for the pope in Italy or served with the British in India and the Crimea. Because the men in the camp were often visited by their families and friends, Meagher was soon complaining of "difficulty in reducing the recruits to order and docility," a frustration highlighted by the following episode. When a newly arrived lieutenant noticed one of his men lazing on the lawn at Fort Schuyler and smoking a pipe, he asked him how he was getting along. The private, without standing to attention, puffed out a cloud of smoke and replied, "First rate, thank you. . . . an' it's sorry I am that I didn't 'list [enlist] years ago." Despite this uncertain beginning, Meagher in the months and years to come invariably held up to emulation the noble character of the men who served with him in the Irish Brigade. Two years after the war, for example, he described the sense of duty which had motivated them as both chivalrous and religious, adding that "many of my gallant fellows left comfortable homes, and relinquished good wages, and resigned profitable and most promising situations, to face the poor pittance, the coarse rations, the privations, rigours, and savage dangers of a soldier's life in the field."[14]

By mid November 1861, three regiments of the Brigade — the 63rd, the 69th, and the 88th New York Volunteers — were ready to join the Union army in Virginia. Before departing for the front, however, the last two units were presented with their regimental colors at a ceremony in front of Archbishop John Hughes's residence on November 18. Because the arch-bishop, a native of County Tyrone, Ireland, was in Europe on a mission for President Lincoln, the cleric's vicar general presided at the ceremony. But it was Judge Daly who actually presented the 69th New York with its regimental flag. In his remarks that day the jurist compared the secession-ist doctrine which had disrupted the American Union with the centrifu-gal forces which had undermined the unity that *Brian Boru had brought to Ireland. Drawing on the memory of such Irish patriots as *Wolfe Tone and *Edward Fitzgerald and of the *three Irish-born signers of the Decla-ration of Independence, Daly urged all Irishmen to preserve the republi-can form of government for which these men had either died or pledged their sacred honor. The American experiment, he said, had rewarded the Irishman's "native energy" and had given his race a degree of political influence not found in his native land. Daly then urged the regiment to live up to the reputation which the Irish recruit had so valiantly earned: "The Irish soldier has been distinguished by military critics for his recog-nition of the necessity of implicit military obedience, for the cheerfulness with which he endures the privations and hardships incident to a military life, and for his daring impetuosity in battle." Finally, the judge alluded to an earlier Irish Brigade — one that had so valiantly served eighteenth-century France on the battlefields of Europe, most notably at Fontenoy in 1745. Turning to Colonel Robert Nugent, the regiment's commander, Daly reminded him that Irish horsemen under an *earlier Colonel Nugent had defeated Imperial infantry at the battle of Speier.[15]

The 88th New York, meanwhile, received its regimental flags from Meagher's wife, Elizabeth. On her behalf Malcolm Campbell stressed the political ideals which motivated the Irish in the Union army. They had gone into battle, he said, "willingly and freely, sacrificing all personal and minor considerations, rising not in passion or with vindictiveness, but with calm dignity, to enforce their own sovereignty, as integral parts of a popular government, to assert and prove the superiority in power of the ballot over the bayonet, to maintain the great principle of the capacity of man for self-government." He then charged the men of the new Irish Bri-gade with a sacred trust: "Guard [these standards] well — bear them firmly through the battle — make the flaunting flag of sedition trail in the dust before these insignia of the majesty of the people, and return them, in tattered shreds if you will, dyed in blood, and begrimed with the dust and smoke of battle, but free from the slightest stain or speck of dishonor. Do this, and there is still hope that the wish that lingers on the lips of your dying patriots may yet be gloriously realized, 'That in the days to come *the Green shall flutter o'er the Red.'"[16]

Earlier that November a delegation of Irish-Americans headed by Gen-eral Meagher himself arrived at David's Island in the East River to present the 63rd New York with an American flag and the traditional green banner of Ireland. In making the presentation, William Robinson denounced the South's treason against the Stars and Stripes: "that flag, which Irishmen at home had idolized — the glories of which had been sung over their cradles, and whose stars had lighted their pathway across the dark and stormy ocean — beneath whose folds they had found blessings innumerable, denied them at home." In addition, he said, the war record of the Irish soldier had disproved the claim that Catholics and naturalized citizens were unworthy of American citizenship. Colonel Richard Enright accepted the banners, while the regiment's chaplain, Father James Dillon, asked the men whether they were willing and ready to defend "these emblems of freedom" with their lives. "We are! We are!" replied almost 800 voices. The chaplain then reminded his eager charges of their solemn duties: "Then go forth to battle, my friends and comrades, and never let it be said that the Sixty-third regiment — which is to hold the second place of honor in the Irish Brigade — permitted their flag to fall into the hands of the enemies of the Union and liberty. Let me impress on you the fact that to be faithful, brave soldiers, you must be practical Christians. There is no braver soldier in this world, in any country, under any form of government, than a consistent Catholic. The fathers of most of you have fought on every battlefield, from *Fontenoy to Chapultepec[,] and their bayonets were ever in the van. Let it be said of you, ere this causeless rebellion is suppressed, that the soldiers of the Irish Brigade have emulated the heroism of their forefathers. Ours is a country and cause worth fighting for — dying for!"[17]

Each regimental flag was deep green in color and bore in the center an embroidered golden Irish harp, with a sunburst above it and a wreath of shamrocks beneath. Above and below these symbols were two crimson scrolls: the higher one bearing the regimental designation (e.g., "1st Regt. Irish Brigade" for the 69th New York Regiment), and the lower one bearing, in Irish letters and in the Irish language, the motto *Riam Nar Druid O Sbairn Lann* ("Who Never Retreated from the Clash of Spears").[18]

The iconography of these regimental flags was derived from a variety of sources. The harp's association with Ireland has its roots in Celtic mythology. The god Dagda ("Good God") owned a living harp, which, as he played it, was able to summon the seasons in their proper order. (Dagda's son Angus had a golden harp.) From early Druid days Celtic harpers were closely associated with Druidic priests and were regarded as next to the king in importance. But it was Ireland's English conquerors who promoted the harp as a national symbol of sorts. Henry VIII introduced it into his Irish armorial bearings, and Elizabeth I placed it on her Great Seal of Ireland, while her successor, James I, placed the harp in the Royal Arms. In 1641–1642, Irish Catholic rebels fought under a banner emblazoned with a harp on a green background, and a century and a half later the United Irishmen used the harp as a symbol of Irish nationalism. The shamrocks depicted on the regimental colors were symbolic of Ireland's acceptance of Christianity and were derived from St. Patrick's alleged use of the shamrock to explain the Trinity. The sunburst, meanwhile, was a favorite symbol of the Fenians, a revolutionary group which sought the creation of an Irish republic. The motto on each flag's lower scroll was taken from a tale about Oisin, a mythological figure who rejected St. Patrick's attempt to convert him and instead treated the saint to tales about *Fionn MacCumbal and his companions. When the saint insisted that they would all be condemned to hell because of their unbelief, Oisin replied:

"Were Fionn and Mac an Loin [Fionn's spear] with me, —
(Two who never retreated from the clash of spears;)
Despite thy clerics, bells and thee —
We'd hold — where Satan domineers."[19]

As originally planned, the Irish Brigade was to have contained six regiments: three from New York (63rd, 69th, and 88th), one from Philadelphia (115th Pennsylvania), another from Boston (28th Massachusetts), and a combined infantry and cavalry regiment raised from New York and Philadelphia. Although the three New York units belonged to the Brigade from the beginning, the 115th Pennsylvania Volunteer Regiment was placed in the Third Corps and never became part of the Brigade. The Massachusetts regiment, meanwhile, was sent to North Carolina and became part of the Brigade only in November 1862, just before the battle of Fredericksburg. The sixth regiment was never completely organized. As a result, when the Brigade sailed for Virginia in November and December 1861, it was composed of only the three New York regiments. The 69th — with 950 men — was under the command of Colonel Robert Nugent, while Colonel Richard Enright and Colonel Patrick Kelly led, respectively, the 63rd (with 750 men) and the 88th (with 800). All three units were commanded by Thomas Meagher, who was finally confirmed as brigadier general in February 1862.[20]

By the time the three New York regiments left Fort Schuyler, two batteries of artillery seem to have been raised with the intention that they would eventually become part of the Irish Brigade. These artillery sections, known at the time as the Brigade's Fifth Regiment, were commanded by Captain William Hogan and Captain James McMahon. After a few months of training on Capitol Hill, in April the regiment was sent to join the Irish Brigade, which, at the time, was encamped outside Yorktown, Virginia. By then the artillery sections boasted 154 men, 115 horses, and six ten-pounder Parrott guns. This fifth regiment's association with the Brigade was short-lived, however, because General George McClellan ordered it divided into three sections and assigned to other batteries in his division.[21]

Each of the three original regiments in the Brigade had its own Catholic chaplain. Father William Corby and Father James Dillon of Notre Dame

College served, respectively, with the 88th and the 63rd New York regiments, while Father Thomas Ouellet, a Jesuit from Fordham College, ministered to the 69th. Corby, the most famous of the three, had been born in 1833 in Detroit, where his father, a native of Ireland, had settled. When he was twenty years old, the future priest entered Notre Dame College and within a year had joined the Congregation of the Holy Cross, the teaching religious order which administered the university. After his ordination, he combined pastoral work with his duties as a professor and the director of the Manual Labor School at Notre Dame. As chaplain of the 88th New York, he participated in all the campaigns of the Army of the Potomac. After the war Corby returned to Notre Dame, assuming administrative duties, including those of president, and then serving as provincial general of the Holy Cross Congregation in the United States.[22]

That the moral well-being of their soldierly charges was foremost in these chaplains' minds is documented in the pages of Father Corby's *Memoirs of Chaplain Life*, published a generation after the war. Corby alluded to the goal of his wartime ministry by describing the relationship between military valor and the practice of religion. "Men who are demoralized [i.e., morally corrupted] and men whose consciences trouble them make poor soldiers," he wrote. "Moral men — men who are free from the lower and more degrading passions — make brave, faithful, and trustworthy soldiers. . . . [T]he soldier is all the better as a soldier when assisted by religion. When he is gently induced to practice his duty to God and to keep alive in his heart his love of virtue, he is not made a coward by his guilty conscience; on the contrary, he is willing, if necessary, to lay down his life for justice or for his country, and to leave to posterity an example worthy of emulation."[23]

Father Dillon also acknowledged the importance of sound morality to civic virtue and military prowess. In mid November 1861, in a sermon to the approximately 700 men of the 63rd New York encamped on David's Island in New York's East River, he announced the formation of a temperance society within the regiment. Labeling intemperance as the "father of all crimes," the priest challenged the men: "Show me an Irish Catholic who is not addicted to the vice of drunkenness, and I will find a good citizen of the Republic. Give me an abstainer from the cup that inebriates, and I will show you an obedient, brave soldier willing to die for the flag. . . . Go, then, to the front as temperate men. If you do, you will be equal to all emergencies." Father Corby noted that several secretaries were needed to record the names of the 700 men who immediately took the pledge, the effects of which were soon apparent: "Daily and Sunday attendance at Mass was sensibly augmented, and there was a decided diminution in camp carousals."[24]

When the 63rd New York prepared to sail from the Battery in Manhattan on November 28, there occurred an incident which stood in sharp contrast to Father Dillon's temperance message. As reported in the *New York Times*, the first three companies filed through the gate onto the pier where a waiting boat was docked. The men conducted themselves "in good military style" until a guard turned back several women trying to follow the soldiers onto the pier. This exclusion caused "considerable excitement" among the troops, many of whom broke ranks and proceeded to the local saloons. "Soldiers, who a short time before were orderly and obedient, were now either raving with passion, or so stupidly intoxicated as to be unable to walk," reported the *Times*. In the commotion that followed attempts by friends and family members to enter or exit the gates, bayonets, knives, and other weapons were drawn and several people were seriously wounded. Two soldiers fell into the water, and one of them reportedly drowned. Only after an hour were Colonel Enright and his officers and the police able to restore order. The following day a steamer returned from New Jersey with the bodies of two privates from the 63rd — John Gautley of Company C and Dennis Reagan of Company B — both of whom had died soon after leaving New York. The coroner ruled that the two men had died "from intemperance."[25]

When each of the three initial regiments of the Irish Brigade arrived in Virginia, they bivouacked at Camp California, a site near Alexandria so named because their division commander, Major General Edwin Sumner, had recently returned from the Pacific coast. That winter Father Ouellet, the French-Canadian chaplain of the 69th New York, was a familiar figure in camp. He not only celebrated Sunday mass but also comforted the sick soldiers in their tents, heard confessions in the evenings, and socialized with the men around their camp fires. According to *Captain David Conyngham, the Irish Brigade's historian, Father Ouellet used "the force of his eloquence and logic" to almost eradicate gambling, profanity, and intemperance from the regiment's camp. In addition, when the men of the 69th received their first military pay, the chaplain helped the men send the money to their families back home. He was especially vigilant that the men did not squander their wages at the gambling tables or in the sutlers' canteens. Father Ouellet accompanied the 69th in all its battles from Yorktown to Antietam, bravely administering the last rites in the thick of the fighting and spending days and nights among the wounded, often washing their scars with his own hands. Sometime during the winter of 1862–1863, he left the 69th New York and served in North Carolina under the command of General John Gray Foster.[26]

Understandably, the thoughts of the men in the Irish Brigade turned homeward on their first Christmas Eve in camp. "[T]he soldier's heart fled back to his home, to his loved wife, to the kisses of his darling child, to the fond Christmas greeting of his parents, brothers, and sisters, until longing eyes were dimmed with the dews of the heart," wrote Conyngham. To dispel this homesickness, the men spent the evening telling stories, singing traditional Irish airs, and dancing jigs and reels around their camp-fires. Thoughts turned serious, though, when the tinkling of a bell summoned the men to midnight mass celebrated by Father Dillon and Father Ouellet. Quartermaster Patrick Haverty and Captain Michael O'Sullivan answered the Latin responses, "while the attentive audience crowded the small [tent] chapel, and were kneeling outside on the damp ground under the cold night-air." Even more men attended the Christmas morning mass, after which the soldiers and their officers tried to pass the holiday in camp as pleasantly as possible, visiting one another's tents, toasting family at home, and enjoying their pipe tobacco.[27]

Sometime that winter an ugly incident took place one Sunday morning between Father Ouellet and an officer generally believed to have been Captain Felix Duffy of the 69th New York. As a military chaplain, it must be pointed out, Father Ouellet received the same pay and allowances as a captain of mounted troops. Before mass that morning the priest was heard reproving Captain Duffy for using language toward some members of his company that the chaplain found objectionable. The indignant officer replied, "Do you know, sir, I am a captain of this regiment, and you are only a captain of cavalry on detached service?" Ouellet, realizing that further argument would be useless, broke off and proceeded to church. During the sermon, though, he took the offending officer to task in a most public way: "I have been told to-day, by an officer of my regiment, when reproving him for profanity in the presence of his men, who are to share with him on the battlefield the dangers of a soldier's life, that I was only a captain of cavalry, and had no business to interfere in the discharge of his duties. I never intended to interfere in the discipline of the regiment, but I want to tell that captain, as well as all here assembled to worship God, that I did not enter the army as a captain of cavalry, but as a soldier of the Saviour to preach the doctrine of our holy Church, and I shall, on all occasions, as one of the spiritual directors of this command, reprove vice, and preach to you, undefiled, the religion of your fathers."[28]

Following his appointment as commander of the Irish Brigade in February 1862, Brigadier General Thomas Meagher rode out from Washington, D.C., to Camp California to meet his men. In response to their boisterous toasts, he expressed his confidence in "their readiness to obey, their aptitude to learn, and their zeal in the execution of the more perilous duties of the service." He then assured them that, as long as he was their chief, "the humblest soldier shall have in me a protector . . . and a friend in whom he can trust . . . ." Then, as was his wont, he contrasted the political subjugation of Ireland with the "wit, poetry, song, creative faculty or power of golden speech" of her people. He reminded his hearers — many of them Fenians — that the discipline and self-abnegation which they acquired in this war would some day bear fruit for Ireland. He ended his speech with the hope that, should he be killed in the present war, his gravestone be inscribed with the following epitaph: "Fighting for the honor and integrity of the Irish exile's happiest, proudest, and most prosperous home, Thomas Francis Meagher, an Irish exile, died at the head of the Irish Brigade."[29]

One of the most colorful and fun-loving men in the Brigade was John Gosson, formerly captain of Company C in the 69th New York State Militia. "Captain Jack" was a native of County Galway, Ireland, and had entered the military service of Austria through the influence of the Irish patriot Daniel O'Connell. Gosson served as a lieutenant under his friend General Count Nugent in Styria, a duchy in southeastern Austria. (Nugent was one of five descendants of an Irish Catholic family from County Dublin who served in the Austrian military.) Gosson was subsequently commissioned in the Seventh Hussars of Austria, a Hungarian regiment commanded by Prince Frederick Liechtenstein. After returning to Ireland, Gosson was welcomed as the very model of the handsome soldier and quite naturally became the favorite of the ladies. At the outbreak of the American war, he threw in his lot with Meagher and served as his aide-de-camp. In mid March 1862, when Major General Sumner became one of the four corps commanders in the newly reorganized Army of the Potomac, the Brigade was placed under the command of General Israel Richardson. To create among the men of the Brigade a favorable impression of their new commanding officer, Gosson spread the false rumor that Richardson had sent each regiment of the Brigade a complimentary barrel of whiskey. Gosson's practical joke had its desired effect. When Richardson arrived in camp, the men cheered him warmly. About Gosson's service during the Civil War, an officer of the U.S. Regular Army said that in his manners, his dress, his speech, his history, this "gallant and dashing soldier" had no peer.[30]

Another officer whose wit was legendary, and whom General Meagher regarded as the model of the dashing, cultivated gentleman, was Captain Maxwell O'Sullivan of the 88th New York. O'Sullivan had been educated for the law and had practiced it in his native Ireland. Blessed with a rich, mellow voice, he became a member of various musical societies in Dublin and Cork before emigrating in 1860. After settling in New York City, he joined the choir of St. Bridget Church and became the director of the music school connected with it. During the first months of the Civil War, he served with the 69th New York Militia Regiment and then formed a company in the newly raised Irish Brigade. He met an untimely end when he died of injuries sustained from a tent fire in Camp California on April 2, 1862.[31]

The Union strategy still revolved around the belief that putting pressure on the Confederate capital at Richmond was the best guarantee of protecting Washington. To this end, the Army of the Potomac — and the Irish Brigade — sailed from Alexandria at the end of March 1862 for the peninsula between the York and the James rivers. As General George McClellan pushed his troops up the peninsula toward Richmond, they met resistance from Confederate soldiers under Major General John Magruder, entrenched at Yorktown. McClellan laid plans for a lengthy siege, and the men of the Brigade celebrated May Day by decorating their circus-tent chapel with wild flowers. But three days later, after Magruder learned that 40,000 Union troops under General Irwin McDowell were on their way, the Confederate officer decided to abandon his position. By the end of May, McClellan had established his lines at the Chickahominy River, between seven and twelve miles from Richmond.[32]

To strike at McClellan's army before McDowell could bring in reinforcements, the Confederate general Joseph Johnston attacked. The resulting battle of Fair Oaks (or Seven Pines) on May 31 began while the Irish Brigade was finishing up its "Chickahominy Steeplechase." The day had featured a football game and horse racing, the latter competition open only to the officers of the Brigade. Some of the steeds bore the allusive names "Mourne Boy," "Tipperary Joe," and "Faugh-A-Ballagh" (Irish for "Clear the Way"). For riding the winner — "Katie Darling" — Major James Cavanagh received a tiger skin, compliments of General Meagher himself, the trophy of a Central American hunt. The drummer boys were just about to start their mule race when the Brigade heard artillery fire off in the distance. This sudden development put an end to the festivities and prompted the cancellation of "The Limerick Boy," the "screaming farce" planned for the evening's entertainment.[33]

Preliminary to their going into battle to reinforce the Third and the Fourth Corps, General Sumner told the Irish Brigade that if they failed him the contest was lost. "I know the Irish Brigade will not retreat," he said confidently. "I stake my position on you." A sergeant replied, "General, we have never run yet, and we are not going to do it now." (What may be a variant of this story or an entirely different one says that Sumner pointed to his epaulets and said: "Boys, I stake my position on you. If you run away to-day, I will tear these off and run with you.") When the 69th and the 88th New York finally entered the fray, they charged with their distinctive battle cry — half-English, half-Gaelic — while the 63rd New York guarded a bridge and retrieved some field guns mired in a swamp. Despite the Union victory, the day was marred by the death of Michael Herbert of the 69th, the Brigade's first fatality. (Earlier in his career Herbert had fought with the British in India and with the Papal Brigade in Italy.) The Irish Brigade suffered thirty-eight additional casualties.[34]

Dr. Thomas Ellis, a surgeon in the Union army, left a telling description of the Brigade's *joie de combat* at Fair Oaks. "Other men go into fights finely, sternly, or indifferently," he wrote, "but the only man that really loves it, after all, is the green, immortal Irishman. So there the brave lads from the old sod, with the chosen Meagher at their head, laughed and fought and joked as if it were the finest fun in the world. We saw one sitting on the edge of a ditch, wounded, with his feet in the water, and both the sun and the water, too, very hot. As we rode by, he called out to know if we had ever seen 'a boiled Irishman.'"[35]

Shortly after the Union victory at Fair Oaks, Peter Rafferty, a sixteen-year-old private in the 69th New York, searched the battlefield for "souvenirs." As he and one of his comrades passed the dead body of a Confederate, they noticed that the Rebel wore a fine pair of leather boots. Intending to come back for the attractive footwear, the two scavengers moved on and soon came upon a field of dead and wounded Rebels as well as a barrel of whiskey. After filling five canteens with the "water of life" and relieving the dead of their pipes and money, the pilferers began to head back to camp. En route, though, they met Father Ouellet, their chaplain, who asked them for some of the "water" in their canteens. The two soldiers obliged, but they were well on their way before the priest realized what the canteens contained. When Rafferty and his companion returned to the Rebel whose footwear they coveted, they discovered that someone else had stolen the dead man's boots.[36]

The day after the battle, George Townsend, a correspondent for the *New York Herald,* paid a visit to General Meagher's headquarters. "Every adjunct of the place was strictly Hibernian," he later reported. "The emerald green standard entwined with the red, white, and blue; the gilt eagles on the flag-poles held the Shamrock sprig in their beaks; the soldiers lounging on guard, had '69' or '88'[,] the numbers of their regiments, stamped on a green hat-band; the brogue of every county from Down to Wexford fell upon the ear." Perhaps because of other things he saw, though, Townsend betrayed a common misgiving about the Irish: They appeared to be "good for a fight, a card-party, or a hurdle-jumping, — but entirely too Quixotic for the sober requirements of Yankee warfare. . . . [O]rdinarily, they were regarded, as a party of mad fellows, more ornamental than useful, and entirely too clannish and facetious to be entrusted with power." Yet, even in this early period of the Irish Brigade's career, Townsend was quick to admit that when "anything absurd, forlorn, or desperate was to be attempted," the Irishmen were called upon.[37]

About Meagher himself Townsend was equally descriptive but less ambivalent. "[H]e welcomed me in the richest and most musical of brogues," the journalist reported. "Large, corpulent, and powerful of body; plump and ruddy — or as some would say, bloated — of face; with resolute mouth and heavy animal jaws; expressive nose, and piercing blue eyes; brown hair, moustache, and eyebrows; a fair forehead, and short sinewy neck, a man of apparently thirty years of age, stood in the doorway, smoking a cigar, and trotting his sword fretfully in the scabbard. . . . He was fitfully impulsive, as all his movements attested, and liable to fluctuations of peevishness, melancholy, and enthusiasm. . . . He was, to my mind, a realization of the *Knight of Gwynne, or any of the rash, impolitic, poetic personages in *Lever and Griffin. . . . His address was infatuating: but there was a certain airiness, indicative of vanity . . . . He loved applause, and to obtain it had frittered away his fine abilities, upon petty, splendid, momentary triumphs. He was generous to folly, and, I have no doubt, maintained his whole staff."[38]

Twenty years later Frank Moore included among his anecdotes from the war a lengthy narrative about an incident at Fair Oaks. Among Meagher's men that day, it seems, was a soldier named O'Neill, "dark complexioned, robust, and undoubtedly full of pluck." The story continues: "On that terrible Sabbath morning a portion of the Irish brigade swept over the railroad and into an adjacent swamp, full of dead horrors . . . . A rebel Lieutenant, at the head of those who remained in his company, dashed madly on the Irish line of steel, which stood firm as the *rock of Cashel; and the impotent, insurrectionary wave was repelled with a reactionary shock that scattered it like spray. Forty rebels lay dead and wounded; and foremost among them all the young Lieutenant, a bullet having shattered his left knee. Of course he fell into our hands a prisoner, and with his companions was thereafter soon carried to the rear. This young man — long hair, dark eyes, straight and soldierly — was admired for his bearing, which was that of a proud foe, foiled, but not vanquished. There was a halt near the station, where the O'Neill alluded to above then was, as temporary guard over some other prisoners. As he gazed at the wounded rebel officer, a visible change overspread his features. He asked one of his superiors if he might speak to the Lieutenant. His joy knew no bounds when he learned that this was Phil O'Neill, C.S.A., a younger brother, of whom the family had had no tidings for fifteen years. He had lived as a clerk in Savannah, had enlisted as a private, for good conduct had been promoted, and was at length a prisoner. The young Confederate, when fully aware of the interesting discovery, again wept tears of joy and the scene was one never to be forgotten. The romantic circumstance was made known to General Meagher, to whom the Lieutenant was introduced, and for whom the General did everything in his power. Though the captured officer would not fight on our side, he would not be exchanged, and went North, where, in a brief period, he took the oath of allegiance. His brother was killed while butting under *Burnside against the stone wall at *Fredericksburg . . . ."[39]

As camp life returned to normal after Fair Oaks, the Spanish general Juan Prim visited the Army of the Potomac and happened to notice a group of men whose "stalwart appearance and martial bearing" attracted his attention. When informed that they were members of the Irish Brigade, the foreign officer alluded to the role which earlier sons of Erin had played in the military history of his country. "Spain had reason to appreciate Irish valor," he acknowledged. "Spain and Ireland were old friends from ancient times, and their soldiers had often stood side by side together on many a hard-fought field." As Prim and his escorts galloped off, the Irishmen gave him a rousing cheer, an adieu that prompted the Spaniard to quip, "I don't wonder the Irish fight so well; their cheers are as good as the bullets of other men." (Another version claims a bit different wording: "Soldiers who can cheer like that must fight well. Such cheers are better than cold lead.")[40]

About two weeks later the Brigade was reinforced by the arrival of the 29th Massachusetts, a thoroughly Yankee regiment commanded by Colonel Ebenezer Pierce. (Among its members were descendants of the early settlers of the Plymouth and Massachusetts Bay colonies.) Private William Osborne, who later wrote a history of the 29th Massachusetts, recorded seeing Meagher at this first meeting "sitting on his horse, wet to the skin, asking and receiving a hot dipper of coffee from a man of the Irish Brigade." In light of the traditional political and cultural rivalry and frequent hostility between Celt and Yankee in New England, this assignment seemed bound to result in friction. But, according to Osborne, the new recruits were "cordially welcomed" to the Brigade by the latter's officers and men.[41]

On June 26, while pushing on to Richmond, General McClellan's troops came under Confederate attack in the first of a series of engagements known as the Seven Days battle. Under a barrage of Confederate fire, the Union right withdrew to Gaines' Mill, where the Irish Brigade reinforced the collapsing Union line and covered its retreat. The first regiment thrown into the fight to check the advance of "Stonewall" Jackson's 20,000 men was the Ninth Massachusetts, an Irish unit under the command of Colonel Thomas Cass. When Jackson saw the Ninth advance under its green banner, he mistook that regiment for the Irish Brigade and ordered his reserves to sweep away "that damned Brigade." The Ninth Massachusetts took the brunt of Jackson's attack and was forced to fall back, though the Bay State Irishmen continued to put up a fight. Just then the Irish Brigade rushed onto the scene, a development that caused Cass to take heart and to reenter the fray with his handful of men. When General Meagher saw Cass in his bloodied shirt, he called out, "Colonel Cass, is this you?" "Hallo, General Meagher, is this the Irish Brigade?" replied the colonel. "Thank God, we are saved." Despite the favorable outcome, Meagher took steps to protect the 88th's regimental flags from capture. Unwilling to see them displayed in Richmond by the enemy, he gave Captain Patrick Clooney a box of matches with orders to distribute them among the men of the color company. Rather than allow the Irish banners to be seized, the color-bearers were to burn them.[42]

After concluding that McDowell's reinforcements were not coming, McClellan decided to move his base to a point across the peninsula on the James River. But at every turn rebel troops challenged the Union commander, hoping to cut him off before he reached the James. On June 29, at Savage Station, the Irish Brigade went into battle "with a roar that might have drowned the musketry," drove off a group of Virginia artillerymen and their supporting infantry, hauled away and spiked two guns, and chopped the carriages to pieces. For leading a successful attack on a Confederate battery of six guns that day, *Major James Quinlan of the 88th New York later received the Congressional Medal of Honor. Several other regiments had attempted to silence the battery but to no avail. Before General Sumner ordered the attack, he said to Quinlan, "I know your regiment well, can you silence that battery?" After answering, "I will try, sir," the Irishman led the command forward. Although many of the 88th fell during the bayonet charge, many others reached the guns, where bitter hand-to-hand fighting resulted in a victory. About Quinlan's gallantry the official record reads: "He led his regiment on the enemy's battery, silenced the guns and held the position against overwhelming numbers, and covered the retreat of the 2nd Army Corps."[43]

The next day the Brigade was deployed at White Oak Swamp, where it supported some batteries firing into the enemy position and where Meagher was seen repeatedly riding a horse up and down the firing line. When some officers tried to get him to take cover, he cried out to them, "If I am killed, I would rather be killed riding this horse than lying down." Just before the 63rd New York was called into action, the regiment's chaplain, Father James Dillon, urged the men to prepare themselves to meet their Creator. "Let every soldier," exhorted the priest, "officer and private, Catholic and Non-Catholic, fall on his knees and repeat with me a sincere act of contrition for their past sins, after which I will impart absolution in the name of Christ." Major John Dwyer described the scene: "The regiment of bronzed soldiers were promptly on their knees, and then to the music of bursting shells, the swish of round shot, and the buzz of rifle balls, the solemn act of devotion was performed."[44]

In his description of the battle at White Oak Swamp, Lieutenant James Turner of the 88th New York described the Irish Brigade's typical use as a reserve unit. "We are the reserve — our corps is the reserve of the army; and it is only when the black need comes that we press forward to the work. The dead, the wounded, the beaten, the broken and disheartened line our path — but our cheers reanimate — our *élan* gives them hope. I pledge you my word that when the Irish Brigade approaches the turning point of the battles, the hearts of that portion of the army that see them are moved within them, the most graceful and glad cheers greet us all the way, the wounded take heart, and the beaten and broken, reassured, join in our sturdy ranks and go along with renewed courage to the battle front. 'That is the Irish Brigade' — 'that is General Meagher,' uttered in tones of hope, are the words you hear as you march along." General McClellan himself was especially appreciative of the Brigade, on one occasion saying to Meagher, "I wish I had twenty thousand men like yours." Twenty-four years later General William Franklin recalled the Irish Brigade's performance at White Oak Swamp: "It was subjected to a very severe artillery fire during nearly the whole day, under which it never flinched. . . . I always thought its behavior that day was in the highest degree suggestive of Irish pluck and endurance."[45]

At Malvern Hill, at the end of the Seven Days campaign, the Confederates failed to capture that elevated plateau from the Union army. During the battle the Irish Brigade pushed back the rebel assault. Again Meagher was conspicuously in the front lines, brandishing his sword and commanding his men to charge with bayonets. It was during this battle on July 1 that a Confederate aide-de-camp alluded to one of the Brigade's distinctive ensigns when he informed his superior officer, "Here comes that damned green flag again!" When the 88th New York Regiment clashed with the famous "Louisiana Tigers," both sides were so taken by surprise that the former used their muskets as clubs while the latter fought with pistols and bowie knives. At the height of the melee a gigantic member of the 88th spied a mounted officer cheering on the Tigers. When the Union soldier strode up to the mounted Confederate, he grabbed him with his enormous hand, exclaiming "Come out o' that, you spalpeen [rascal]!" and dragging him from his steed. During the battle Father Ouellet sought out the wounded, asking whether they were Catholic and wanted absolution. One badly wounded man replied that he was not a Catholic but that he would like "to die in the faith of any man who has the courage to come and see me in such a place as this."[46]

The 69th New York was ordered into the fighting at Malvern Hill about 6 p.m. that day. In doing considerable damage to the enemy, the regiment suffered a large number of wounded and was forced to fall back when it ran out of ammunition. At 8:30 that night the 69th was again ordered into action. Private Peter Rafferty, now turned seventeen and wounded in the earlier clash, was directed to stay in the rear. When he protested to Thomas Leddy, his company captain, the superior officer relented and allowed Rafferty to limp off into battle with his comrades. During the engagement Rafferty was again wounded. Two balls struck his mouth and part of his jaw, smashing the bones and tearing away part of his tongue, while a third went through his foot. His regiment, however, helped rout and beat the 10th Louisiana with bayonets and musket butts. Three of Rafferty's wounds broke bones, and he was left on the field. Two days after the battle he was picked up by the enemy and sent to Libby Prison in Richmond, Virginia. There he received little or no medical attention for several weeks, until some Sisters of Charity tended to his wounds. The young soldier was finally exchanged after two months of imprisonment. In 1897 he was awarded the Congressional Medal of Honor. The citation with the award read: "Having been wounded and directed to the rear, [he] declined to go, but continued in action, receiving several additional wounds, which resulted in his capture by the enemy and his total disability for military service." The day after the battle, when General Sumner noticed a pile of broken muskets in camp, he exploded in anger, mistakenly thinking that they had been damaged by stragglers. The general's anger abated when he learned that the weapons had been damaged because "the byes [boys] wint for the Rebs in the way they wor used to."[47]

One of the other casualties which the 69th New York Regiment suffered at Malvern Hill was Lieutenant John Donovan of Company D. While he charged with his men, a bullet struck his right eye and exited the ear just under the brain. The officer survived, however, and showed unusual wit when General Hill remarked that Donovan — given his injuries — would no longer need his side arms in the future. "I think differently, general," Donovan replied indignantly. "I think I have one good eye left yet, and will risk that in the cause of the Union. Should I ever lose that, I'll go it blind." On another part of the battlefield, Sergeant Driscoll shot a Confederate officer whose men fired so accurately that they prevented a company of the Irish Brigade from advancing. Ordered to see whether the Rebel officer was dead, Driscoll turned over the stricken man — only to discover his son, who had moved to the South before the war. The elder man's grief was cut short, though, when he himself was cut down during the next charge. Private William Osborne of the 29th Massachusetts, the Brigade's only non-Irish unit, received the Congressional Medal of Honor for his actions that day: "Although wounded and carried to the rear, he secured a rifle and voluntarily returned to the front, where, failing to find his own regiment, he joined another and fought with it until again severely wounded and taken prisoner."[48]

According to Osborne, General Meagher complimented the 29th Massachusetts for its showing during the battle. Besides saying that its men had proved themselves equal to any others in the Brigade, the general added that the 29th had no superiors in the army. (While Meagher was speaking, though, some of the soldiers in the 29th stole nearly all the whiskey in the Irish officer's tent.) When the regiment's commander, Colonel Ebenezer Pierce, heard about Meagher's remarks, he expressed his appreciation and returned the compliment. In a letter to Governor John Andrew of Massachusetts, Pierce wrote that the 29th "has added to its reputation by the mere fact of its being connected with the Irish Brigade; and it has been our endeavor that the brigade should not by our acts lose any of their already acquired reputation. . . . The general said to the whole regiment, 'The Twenty-Ninth Massachusetts has been tried, and, I am proud to be able to say, has proved itself an honor to the Irish Brigade and to the country.' This is nearly his precise language, and it was the proudest moment the regiment had seen."[49]

By the beginning of July, McClellan's army had completed its strategic retreat from the York River to Harrison's Landing on the James. On July 8 President Lincoln visited the army and conferred with McClellan and his corps commanders. While the president was still in camp, First Lieutenant James Birmingham of the 88th New York happened to take a swim in the James River. After emerging from the water in his underwear, he headed over to the camp of the 69th New York Regiment to visit his brother. En route, Birmingham noticed that the president and General McClellan and General Sumner were talking with Colonel Robert Nugent. After finding cover, the under-dressed officer eavesdropped on the conversation but without taking his eyes off the scene. One can only imagine his surprise when he saw Lincoln lift a corner of the 69th's regimental flag and kiss it, exclaiming "God bless the Irish Flag."[50]

At their new headquarters the men of the Irish Brigade recuperated and entertained one another with their often exaggerated stories. In his classic account of the Brigade's exploits during the Civil War, Captain David Conyngham included an episode recounted by Major James Cavanagh of the 69th New York at their new encampment:

"After Malvern Hill, when we were falling back, I [Cavanagh] came across a young officer. He was lying up against a tree, with the pallor of death on his brow. I at once saw that he was a Confederate officer. Something in his appearance struck me. So I alit, gave him a drink from my flask. It revived him a little, and he muttered —

'I think I know you; aren't you James Cavanagh?'

'I am, and your face is familiar to me.'

'Don't you remember Arthur Scanlon, that went South some years ago?'

'Scanlon, Scanlon, my dear friend, is this you? Oh, in God's name, what brought you here?'

'You know, Cavanagh, I went to live with an uncle in Charleston, some eight years ago. He was a bitter rebel; so was every one I associated with, and it is no wonder that I became one. I joined the ranks; was commissioned for my bravery; was in that desperate charge in the morning. But, Cavanagh, when I saw the dear old green flag, my heart failed me. I was almost glad to have us driven back. I knew it was the Irish Brigade did it; but as we retreated ye followed with a vengeance, and I was shot through the breast, and here I am.'

'Alas! alas! dear old friend! it is too bad that we Irishmen should be killing one another, and we so much wanted at home. But can I do any thing for you? Let me bandage your wounds.'

'No, Cavanagh, it's no use. I have but a few minutes to live, and if you remain long here, you'll fall into the hands of our men.'

'No, my dear fellow, I'll not leave you!'

He took my hand and squeezed it, and I thought a tear stole down his pale cheeks."[51]

The strong emotional attachment which the Irish soldier felt for that "dear old green flag" is evident in the following song by an anonymous New York Irishman. The many allusions in the second and third stanzas are to battlefields — both in Ireland and abroad — on which the green banner was proudly unfurled.

*"The Green Old Flag"

Over Erin's isle on high
Waves a Green Old Flag —
Erin's son, to do or die,
Guard that Green Old Flag —
It has waved, for myriad years,
O'er sages, saints and seers,
Over bloodshed, gloom and tears
Waved that Green Old Flag.

O'er warriors true and brave
Waved that Green Old Flag —
Over many a gory grave
Waved that Green Old Flag —
O'er Clontarf's tide in joy —
O'er Benburb and Dunboy —
On the fields of Fontenoy
Waved that Green Old Flag!

In climes beyond the sea
Waved that Green Old Flag —
With France's *fleur-de-lis*
Waved that Green Old Flag —
With Columbia's Stripes and Stars,
In Freedom's righteous wars,
O'er that bold Brigade of Meagher's
Waves that Green Old Flag.

Without stain on glittering fold
Waves that Green Old Flag;
With its harp of burnished gold
Waves that Green Old Flag —
O'er a nation's proud array —
O'er England's might at bay —
O'er united hearts today
Waves that Green Old Flag.[52]

In an article for the *New York Tablet*, General Denis Burke recounted an episode which occurred on the Brigade's first Sunday encamped at Harrison's Landing. As the time for morning mass approached, Father Ouellet, chaplain of the 69th New York, noticed that some of the men were still in their tents, their breakfast and coffee cups outside betraying a concern for their stomachs rather than for their souls. With excessive but good-intentioned zeal, the chaplain stormed through the tent-lined streets, kicking over the men's coffee cups, spilling the prized liquid, and prompting angry howls from the hungry soldiers. During the mass the righteous priest scolded the Brigade's backsliders, in the process popularizing two words that later became common in military parlance. "I know [who you are] regardless of your regimental designation," he said, probably thunderously. "I can tell the good and bad of you. The good came here this morning to thank God for their deliverance from death, and the rest who remained to satisfy their appetites were fellows that were *coffee-coolers* and *skedaddlers* during our retreat." Burke concluded his tale approvingly: "Ever afterward, there was little necessity for the chaplain to call the attention of the men when circumstances permitted the celebration of the Mass. They all attended, especially if Father Ouellet was in camp."[53]

To move against the Confederate capital again, the Union army needed reinforcements. This was especially true of the Irish Brigade, which had lost 700 men during the Seven Days campaign. The three New York regiments now numbered in their ranks only 1,245 men, down from their original 2,500. (The 69th had 295; the 88th, 400; and the 63rd, 550.) So once again General Meagher returned to New York to recruit for the sorely depleted Brigade, but unlike his earlier missions this one was woefully unsuccessful. In fact, during a huge rally at an armory in New York City on July 25, he was greeted by hecklers who claimed that the Democratic Irish had already done their part and that Meagher should seek recruits among the abolitionist wing of the Republican party. To counter such hostility, Meagher used his legendary eloquence, explaining that the Brigade had indeed done more fighting than most of the other units and had suffered such staggering losses because of its fidelity, courage, and "utter disregard of life in the discharge of their duties." He urged his listeners "to throw themselves forward, and pledging themselves in life and death to it, to stand to the last by that noble little brigade which has been true to its military oath, true to the Republic, against the enemies of which it strikes . . . ." Reminding his hearers that America had been to the Irish "a shelter, a home, a tower of impregnable security," Meagher conjured up the heroic figures from the homeland. To the names of O'Neill and Emmet, he added those of Richard Montgomery, Andrew Jackson, James Shields, and Michael Corcoran— men of Irish birth or ancestry who had distinguished themselves in the past by fighting for their adopted land. In the end, though, only 250 recruits — rather than the 1,000 Meagher had hoped for

— joined the Brigade in the next two months. In contrast, Michael Corcoran, released from Confederate prison that August, was much more successful in recruiting for his newly formed "Corcoran's Legion." About 700 men from the former captive's Old 69th New York State Militia enlisted immediately, while another 1,800 men signed up within only three weeks.[54]

Despite the earlier expectation that the Army of the Potomac would renew its campaign to take Richmond, that force was ordered to withdraw from the Peninsula. Now that the Confederate capital was no longer threatened by an imminent Union attack, General Robert E. Lee moved north to reinforce "Stonewall" Jackson and attack Major General John Pope, to whose newly formed Army of Virginia McClellan's troops had recently been assigned. On August 29 and 30, Pope suffered a disastrous defeat at the second battle of Bull Run. The Irish Brigade played no part in this clash except for a brief encounter with Confederate cavalry while the Brigade covered the Union retreat. At the beginning of September, the Army of the Potomac, once again under McClellan's command, pursued Lee into western Virginia, hoping to stop a threatened Confederate advance to Harrisburg, Pennsylvania. Although Lee's immediate objective was to destroy the railroad bridge across the Susquehanna River, and thus cut off east-west communications, such an advance would also directly threaten Philadelphia, Baltimore, and Washington.[55]

Before McClellan caught up with Lee, however, there occurred an episode involving the Irish Brigade's irrepressible Captain Jack Gosson. After rousing himself from the top of a haystack where he had slept one night, Gosson slid to the ground but not before landing on someone below. Captain Conyngham described the scene:

"'Oh, dear! — my ribs are broken, you scoundrel; who the devil are you?' exclaimed the injured party, trying to extricate himself from the hay.

"'And who the h—l are you? Get up out of that,' and Jack gave him an application of his boot to accelerate his movements.

"He did get up in a rage, using very strong language, and faced Captain Jack. The latter fell back a pace or two, and exclaimed: 'Bless my soul, General Richardson, who the h—l could think I was kicking you; I assure you I am sorry for it, general, an' I have a small drop, it's good, here in my flask, and the morning air is a little bitter.'

"'Captain Jack, my dear fellow! Oh, dear, my ribs pain me; but I know you couldn't help it, or you didn't know who was in it. That's good, Captain Jack — I feel better; I'll have another pull.'"[56]

As McClellan's army advanced into Maryland, his troops were seized by what Francis Walker, the historian of the Second Army Corps of the Army of the Potomac, called a mania for killing sheep. In vain did the officers forbid the practice, in vain did they storm and threaten, and in vain did they court-martial the "ovicides." Although the Irish Brigade was most often blamed for this proscribed practice, Walker seems to have accepted General Meagher's claim that a large number of the sheepskins found in his camps had been placed there by the men of the Fifth New Hampshire after they had eaten the carcasses. Nevertheless, General Hancock decided to make an example of some soldiers from the Irish Brigade who had fallen out of ranks and taken to the woods, presumably intent on finding some sheep. When General Hancock, on horseback, intruded on the soldiers as they gathered around their "unfortunate victim," he confronted the leader of the group with drawn sword and flashing eyes. "Arrah, dear general, don't be the death of me," pleaded the presumed malefactor. " I didn't do it, indade I didn't." "You infernal liar," shouted Hancock, "what do you mean by telling me that? I saw you, you scoundrel! I'll teach you to disobey orders. I'll teach you to kill sheep!" Walker recorded the episode's unexpected ending: "And, with this, crushing out the last hope of poor Paddy, he [Hancock] flourished his sword as if about to begin execution; when, in the most opportune moment, up jumped the innocent subject of the controversy, and giving vent to its feelings in a quavering ba-a! ran off, while, amid the shouts of the staff, the general put up his sabre and rode away."[57]

When Lee and McClellan finally came face to face along Antietam Creek near Sharpsburg, Maryland, little did they know that the next day's battle would be the most savage and costly of the war. Although Union forces would stop the Confederate advance into the North that September 17, it would be at a cost to both sides of 23,000 dead and wounded. After two unsuccessful Union attacks at Antietam, the Irish Brigade was called into action with the rest of Sumner's corps. With General Meagher commanding, the three New York regiments and the 29th Massachusetts advanced to a split rail fence that partially barred their further advance. Along the way Father William Corby, one of the regimental chaplains, rode back and forth across the front line, shouting the words of conditional absolution. In his memoir of life with the Irish Brigade, Corby described the horrors of that advance: "I shall never forget how wicked the whiz of the enemy's bullets seemed as we advanced into that battle. As soon as my men began to fall, I dismounted and began to hear their confessions on the spot. It was then I felt the danger even more than when dashing into battle. Every instant bullets whizzed past my head, any one of which, if it had struck me, would have been sufficient to leave me dead on the spot, with many of my brave soldiers, as the bullets came from the Confederates at very close range."[58]

After reaching the fence and dismantling it under intense fire, the men of the Brigade saw that the Confederate barrage came from a sunken road about 150 yards past the fence and behind a small knoll. Alarmed at the number of casualties which his men had already suffered, Meagher finally gave the command: "Irish Brigade! Raise the colors and follow me!" Soon later Meagher yelled his strategy to Lieutenant Colonel James Kelly, alluding to a battle which another Irish Brigade had helped win for France: "It will be Fontenoy again, Colonel, Fontenoy! We shall march to the top, give them two volleys, and then go in with the bayonet." As the Irishmen pushed on to the top of the hill, they again faced withering Confederate fire.[59]

When every one of the Brigade's color-bearers was downed, Captain Patrick Clooney of the 88th New York ordered his men to recover the regimental flags. One of the casualties, the color-bearer of the 69th New York, dropped his green flag, and in minutes seven more flag-bearers fell. While the Irish green lay in the dust, Meagher again shouted out from his white steed, "Boys, raise the colors, and follow me!" Instantly Captain James McGee of the 69th retrieved the fallen ensign. Although a Confederate bullet snapped the standard in two and another ripped through McGee's cap, the native of County Antrim charged ahead, waving the banner as the men cheered. One of McClellan's aides, seeing the colors fall so often, cried out, "The day is lost, general — the Irish fly!" McClellan replied, "No, no! their flags are up — they are charging!"[60]

Frederick Hitchcock, the adjutant of the 132nd Pennsylvania Regiment, later described the charge. "General Meagher," he wrote, "rode a beautiful white horse, but made a show of himself by tumbling off just as he reached our line. The boys said he was drunk, and he certainly looked and acted like a drunken man. He regained his feet and floundered about, swearing like a crazy man. The brigade, however, made a magnificent charge and swept everything before it." Elsewhere on the field, sixteen-year-old John Hartigan of the 63rd New York marched in advance of the regiment, boldly waving the colors in the very face of the enemy. The whole Brigade gave a cheer that echoed along the lines for a mile, and then the men advanced up the rising ground and drove the enemy from its position. According to one eyewitness, "The rebels seemed to have a special spite against the [63rd Regiment's] green flag, and five color-bearers were shot down successively in a short time. . . . 'Big Gleason,' Captain of the Sixty-third, six feet seven, sprang forward and snatched it up. In a few minutes a bullet struck the staff, shattering it to pieces; Gleason tore the flag from the broken staff, wrapped it around his body . . . and went through the rest of that fight untouched." In all, sixteen men fell bearing the colors of the 63rd New York that day.[61]

The Brigade pushed ahead, though, smashing the 16th Mississippi and forcing the Rebels to take cover in the sunken lane. After advancing to within thirty paces of the enemy, the Brigade formed in front of the sunken lane and fired ferociously into the Confederate ranks. General George Anderson's North Carolina Brigade replied in kind. Meagher, in desperation, called out to Colonel Francis Barlow, the commander of a regiment held in reserve — "For God's sake, Barlow, come up and help!" But Barlow replied that he could not move without orders. Soon later

Meagher's mount was shot from under him, and the general was carried from the field unconscious. One of his aides, Captain Gosson, lost one horse and found another but ended the day covered with blood from a wound to the neck of his second mount. Major James Cavanagh continued to encourage the few remaining men of the 69th New York to keep up their fire. From the sunken road came a Confederate taunt to the 69th — "Bring them colors in here!" The men of the 69th responded with a challenge of their own — "Come and get them, you damned rebels!" As if to make the enemy's task easier, two 69th color-bearers ran toward the Confederate lines and boldly waved their banners in the rebels' faces.[62]

Rapidly loosing men and ammunition, the Irish Brigade was finally relieved by troops under General John Caldwell and Colonel Barlow. During the transition, though, the 29th Massachusetts, the Irish Brigade's all-Yankee regiment, joined in a renewed attack. When their Irish comrades-in-arms saw the 29th advance, they cheered themselves hoarse and then rushed into the fray. After the Irish Brigade had finally withdrawn, Major General Richardson, the division commander, said to Captain Patrick Kelly, "Bravo, Eighty-Eighth, I shall never forget you!" Overwhelmed by troops under Caldwell and Barlow, the Confederates broke ranks and ran from the sunken road.[63]

The most heartbreaking loss to the Brigade that day was the death of Captain Patrick Clooney of the 88th New York. Though his knee had already been struck by a bullet, he grabbed the regiment's green flag and urged his men forward. But he was hit again — this time in the head and the chest — and fell to the ground and died. Conyngham left an eloquent tribute to the heroism of this native of Waterford, Ireland: "On the battlefield of Antietam his commanding form could be seen remarkably conspicuous among his comrades. High above the din of battle, his rich, manly voice could be heard encouraging his men and inspiring them to action. To see him unflinchingly and fearlessly stand, like one of the heroes of Grecian lore, sword in hand, his green plume waving in the wind, whilst the leaden hail flew thick and fast around him, you would perceive a sublimity of person, appearance, and of action no pen can portray nor words express." He was buried where he fell, his grave marked by a wooden cross engraved with the words, "He like a soldier fell." Clooney's fellow soldiers later raised money to rebury their captain in Calvary Cemetery in Woodside, Queens, Long Island. Several months after the battle, a memorial to the fallen Celt was erected in the yard of Ballybricken Church in Waterford, Ireland. The four-sided stone was inscribed in part: "To the memory of Captain Patrick J. Clooney of the Pope's Irish Brigade and subsequently of Meagher's Irish American Brigade who fell gallantly leading his company at the Battle of Antietam, September 17, 1862, aged 21 years. Requiescat in pace."[64]

During this bloodiest of Civil War battles, the Irish Brigade played a conspicuous part in the Union victory by pushing the enemy back to its second line. Various sources place the total number of casualties suffered by the four regiments of the Brigade at between 525 and 540 men, of whom 113 were fatalities. The three New York units lost 498 men, about 52 percent. (The 88th New York sustained a casualty rate of 34 percent, and the 63rd New York one of 59 percent. The 69th alone suffered 194 casualties, or 61 percent.) The fourth regiment, the 29th Massachusetts, had only twenty-eight casualties. Sadly, seventy-five of the casualties that day were recruits who had joined the Brigade only the day before. Because of the carnage which took place along the sunken road at Antietam, the site has ever since been known as the "Bloody Lane."[65]

Tributes to the fallen heroes of the Brigade came in from friend and foe alike. General McClellan acknowledged the role of the men who had always supported him: "The Irish Brigade sustained their well-earned reputation, suffering terribly in officers and men, and strewing the ground with their enemies, as they drove them back." Even an officer of the Second Mississippi Battalion saluted the Irishmen: "I wish here to bear witness to the gallantry of the men of Meagher's Brigade and the superb courage of their commanding officers on that bloody day. They stood in line on their ridge, in plain view, with three flags as colors — One the Stars and Stripes, one a Pennsylvania [actually, Massachusetts] State flag and one the green flag with the Harp of Erin. Our men kept those flags falling fast, while just as fast they raised [them] again. Several times the deadly fire of our rifles broke the ranks of those men and they fell behind the ridge, but quickly re-formed each time and appeared with shorter lines but still defiant."[66]

In addition to Clooney, the Brigade lost nine other officers at Antietam, most notably Captains Felix Duffy (69th), John Cavanagh (63rd), and John Joyce (88th) — all sons of Erin. In a letter to the New York *Irish American*, Lieutenant James Turner, who was wounded during the battle, described the effect of these and other losses on General Meagher: "Often and often has he been heard to say that Joyce and Clooney and O'Donohue [killed at Malvern Hill] and the others were his children. They had been with him from the beginning. They had served with him in his old Company [K] in the 69th Regt. They were high-souled, high-toned young Irish patriots, who had imbibed from his lips their passionate love of Ireland, and the hope in which they died, that some day or another they would have an opportunity to draw their swords under him, and display their soldierly skill to some purpose, in the ranks of men fighting for the Fatherland." Elsewhere in the pages of the *Irish American*, Turner eulogized all the men of the Brigade, whose lives, he said, would form "one of the brightest biographies of heroism": "So much individual pluck, courage, dash, enthusiasm and valor, has rarely in any age been marshalled together for the fight. After all it is some consolation to know, even although the Brigade is melting by degrees away, that there was in our times so much that was proud, noble and invincible among our people on this continent. It will be a glorious heritage to leave to your posterity the record of your valor, and one of the proudest assertions that can be made by any Irishman of our day, will be that he, too, was a member of the Irish Brigade that fought for the American Republic."[67]

As had been the case after the battle of Bull Run, reports about Meagher's role at Antietam were often contradictory. In his official report Meagher paid tribute to his men's bravery and explained that he was injured when thrown from his horse while leading his men and thus had to be carried from the field. The *New York Herald* painted the general as a larger-than-life hero, wounded while leading his men — almost quite literally — into the breach. Whitelaw Reid, a correspondent for the *Cincinnati Gazette*, however, presented an extremely different picture about Meagher: "The General . . . was not in the charge at all! — did not lead or follow it! He was too drunk to keep the saddle, fell from his horse . . . several times, was once assisted to remount by Gen. Kimball of Indiana, almost immediately fell off again, was too stupidly drunk to answer the simplest question Gen. Kimball put to him about the disposition of his brigade, and was finally taken up on a stretcher, covered with a cloth, and carried off the field — the bearers circulating the story as they went that Gen. Meagher was dangerously wounded." Colonel Davis Hunter Strother of the headquarters staff confirmed Reid's story, recording in his journal the day after the battle that Meagher had fallen from his horse drunk.[68]

In sharp contrast to the images of carnage which filled the collective memory of the Irish Brigade after Antietam stands another story about Captain Jack Gosson. A week after the battle the dashing officer on General Meagher's staff was attending a concert in a theater in the nation's capital. As was his wont for all grand events, Gosson wore a gold-laced cap and jacket, a broad gold-embroidered cross-belt clasped with a lion's head, an enameled leather cartridge box, and a leather satchel suspended from his sword belt. Such a display naturally attracted attention to his box, and such was the reaction from the evening's principal actress. During her superb rendition of a patriotic song — to which she added a compliment to the soldiers in the audience — she shot a "bewitching glance" at the glittering Gosson. A likely eyewitness left a lengthy description of the startling drama which ensued from the edge of Captain Jack's box:

"[T]he conspicuously handsome cavalier so favored by the beautiful minstrel, rose to his full height, and with his hand on his heart, bowed his thanks to the charmer. While on his feet our hero noticed in the box beneath him a portly bald-headed old gentleman dangling tremulously in his fat hand a beautiful bouquet of the rarest flowers. Stimulated by innate gallantry, combined with the irrepressible spirit of deviltry so characteristic of his daring impulsive nature, Jack drew his sword, and with its point gently lifted the bouquet and tipped it to the lady's feet, amid uproarious cheers and laughter.

"The astonished old gentleman turned up his purple-hued face to his despoiler, and, in a voice half-choked with rage, gasped out: —

"'Who are you, sir! How dare you?' —

"'Shut up! you cantankerous old codger,' shouted Jack, 'or I'll jump down your throat — boots, spurs and all, by — !'

"The interlocutor suddenly collapsed. A storm of commingled cheers and laughter reverberated through the house with, here and there, a cry of 'shame!' from some stickler for the 'proprieties.' Our hero stood gazing placidly on the sea of excited faces until the uproar had ceased, and then, in cool and measured tones, said: —

"'Gentlemen, I am a soldier of the 'Irish Brigade!' I am Captain Jack Gosson, of General Meagher's staff. If, in response to a lady's appeal, I have given offense to any gentleman here, I will be found at Willard's Hotel to-morrow ready to give him adequate satisfaction.'

"There was no dissenting interruption to the cheering this time; neither was [sic] there any seekers for 'satisfaction' calling at Willard's next day."[69]

---

Just over a hundred and thirty-five years later, on October 25, 1997, the role which the Irish Brigade played on the battlefield at Antietam was commemorated with the dedication of a memorial along the infamous "Bloody Lane." During the commemorative event, Archbishop Edwin O'Brien quoted the words which Father Corby uttered at a ceremony twenty-five years after the battle of Antietam. "Oh, you of the younger generation," the Civil War chaplain had prayed, "think what it cost your forefathers to save our glorious inheritance of union and liberty! If you let it slip from your hands you will deserve to be branded as ungrateful cowards and undutiful sons. But no! You will not fail to cherish the prize — it is too sacred a trust — too dearly purchased."[70]

The ten-foot-high memorial includes two bronze sculptures embedded in Irish granite. The bronze on the front depicts the Irish Brigade — and its famous flag — on the battlefield, while a bas-relief of Brigadier General Meagher adorns the back.

The inscription on one of the side panels summarizes the history of the Brigade: "Formed in November 1861, the brigade was largely recruited in New York, Massachusetts and Pennsylvania. Its initial regiments were the 69th, 88th and 63rd New York State Volunteers. Other units identified as part of the brigade included the 29th Massachusetts, 116th Pennsylvania and 28th Massachusetts volunteer infantry regiments. The brigade fought in all of the major campaigns of the Army of the Potomac. It lost over 4,000 men during the war. This total is larger than the number of

The Irish Brigade Memorial
on the Antietam battlefield
includes two bronze sculptures embedded in Irish
granite. The bronze on the
front depicts the Irish Brigade — and its famous flag
— on the battlefield, while a
bas-relief of Brigadier General Thomas Meagher
adorns the back.

soldiers who served in the brigade at any single time. Eleven brigade members were awarded the Congressional Medal of Honor. Of the five officers who commanded the brigade, three were killed or mortally wounded: Colonel Richard Byrnes (Cold Harbor), Colonel Patrick Kelly (Petersburg), and Brigadier General Thomas Smyth (Farmville). The brigade was mustered out in June 1865."

The other side panel recounts the Brigade's exploits at Antietam: "On 17 September 1862, the brigade crossed Antietam Creek (9:30 a.m.) at Pry's Ford. As it formed at the edge of a cornfield, Father William Corby, chaplain, rode along the line giving absolution to the soldiers. The 69th New York occupied the right, then the 29th Massachusetts, the 63rd and 88th New York. Crossing the cornfield, the command encountered a rail fence which was torn down under severe fire. An opposing Confederate column advanced within 300 paces of the brigade. After several volleys, the Irish Brigade charged with fixed bayonets at 30 paces. It poured 'buck and ball' into General George Anderson's brigade (Second, Fourth, 14th, and 30th North Carolina infantry regiments), which fell back to 'Bloody Lane.' After fierce combat, its ammunition exhausted, the Irish Brigade was relieved."

Inscribed on the back of the monument, below the bas-relief bust of Thomas Francis Meagher, are the following words: "The Irish Brigade commander was born in Waterford City, Ireland on 23 August 1823. A well-educated orator, he joined the Young Ireland movement to liberate his native land. This led to his exile to a British penal colony in Tasmania, Australia in 1849. He escaped to the United States in 1852 and became an American citizen. When the Civil War broke out, he raised Company K, "Irish Zouaves," for the 69th New York State Militia Regiment, which fought at First Bull Run under Colonel Michael Corcoran. Subsequently, Meagher raised the Irish Brigade and commanded it from 3 February 1862 to 14 May 1863. He later commanded a military district in Tennessee. After the war, Meagher became secretary and acting governor of the Montana Territory. He drowned in the Missouri River near Fort Benton on 1 July 1867. His body was never recovered."[71]

When, after Antietam, General Robert E. Lee saw that his invasion of Maryland in September 1862 had failed, he recrossed the Potomac River and the Confederates withdrew from Harpers Ferry. Within days General Sumner's corps — including the Irish Brigade — was encamped at Bolivar Heights, above the town of Harpers Ferry. There they rested and turned to their music-making and story-telling. Among the visitors to the camp were President Lincoln and General Meagher's wife, Elizabeth. Father Corby described the latter guest as "a lady of marked character and possessed of more than an ordinary degree of refinement and excellent social virtues. She was a devout convert to the Catholic Church, and was highly respected by the army officers, many of whom had known her and her family in New York long before the war." On Sundays the three Catholic regiments in the Brigade were marched to the parish church above town.[72]

While the Brigade was still at Harpers Ferry, its ranks were briefly increased in size with the addition of the 116th Pennsylvania. Though the men of this regiment were mostly American born, it contained a large number of Irish natives. Its colonel, Dennis Heenan, haled from Tipperary, while its lieutenant colonel, St. Clair Mulholland, was a native of County Antrim. Mulholland had arrived in America in 1839 at the age of seven, first settling with his parents in New Jersey and then moving with them to Philadelphia. He attended parish schools in the City of Brotherly Love and later worked as a printer's assistant and a window-shade painter. Before the war he served with the Pennsylvania militia and earned a reputation as an expert drill instructor. In 1862 he recruited two companies for what later became the 116th Pennsylvania. (The regiment's first camp was named after Temple Emmet, an aide to General Meagher and the grand-nephew of the famous Irish patriot Robert Emmet.) Mulholland's reputation as a disciplinarian can be seen in an episode in which a teamster refused to move his wagon from the path of the Irishman's regiment. Mulholland threatened to kill each of the teamster's mules — and then the teamster himself — if the latter failed to comply with the officer's command. When Mulholland shot the first mule, the teamster quickly obliged.[73]

In his famous history of the 116th Pennsylvania, Mulholland described his impression of the Brigade's commander at their meeting at Harpers Ferry. "Meagher was a handsome man, stately and courteous," he noted, "with a wonderful flow of language and poetic ideas. When the canteen had been passed around[,] the conversation became animated, Meagher displaying a most gracious manner that was captivating and charming to a remarkable degree, forming a strange contrast to his mood at times when he tried to be stern and when his manner was not affable." Mulholland went on to describe the Irish Brigade as "renowned for hard fighting and famous fun," adding that the "very name of this brigade was redolent of dash and gallantry, of precision and evolution and promptness of action." Just before leading the Brigade into nearby Charleston that October, Meagher urged his men to be steady and to do their duty. Private William McCarter of the 116th Pennsylvania believed that Meagher intended this bit of encouragement particularly for his regiment, "all its members being raw, green and untried men." Meagher later reported that the 116th had acted "Nobly, worthy of being a part of the Irish Brigade."[74]

In his memoir of life in that famous unit, Private McCarter left a lengthy sketch of Meagher based in part on his own experiences with the general during this encampment at Harpers Ferry. The young soldier wrote that Meagher stood five feet eight or ten inches in height, had a dark brown moustache, and spoke fluently not only in English but also in Greek, Hebrew, French, German, Welsh, and Irish. According to McCarter, Meagher had no equal in the army for gentlemanly manners, military skill, and courage on the battlefield. In addition, said the young soldier, the general always presented a clean, soldierly appearance and, except when in battle, almost always wore the full dress of his rank. About Meagher's devotion to his charges, McCarter was equally laudatory:

"In kindness and thoughtfulness for his men, he was the shining light and bright star of the whole Union Army. Meagher made unceasing efforts to have his soldiers all well provided for and made comfortable. He often brought some poor, sick or perhaps dying soldier into his own private tent in cold weather. Wrapping him up there in blankets, Meagher administered with his own hands such medicine as was prescribed by the brigade head doctor. In the surgeon's absence, the general prescribed for and administered himself such remedies as he thought were needed. As a physician, Meagher had considerable judgment.

". . . . [H]is many acts of kindness, bravery and heroism will long be remembered and cherished with pleasure and pride by many an American and by thousands of his own native countrymen of the Emerald Isle."[75]

Meagher's critics, however, were far less flattering, charging that the general often imbibed "the whiskey" to excess. Apropos of this accusation, two men who had many opportunities to witness the Irishman left interesting characterizations. Father Corby, chaplain of the 88th New York, insisted that Meagher was not a drunkard. Although the priest admitted that Meagher's "convivial spirit would lead him too far," especially during the lulls between fighting, he attributed Meagher's drinking to his love of sport and joviality and insisted that these occasions were "few and far between." Private McCarter, who had come to the general's attention because of his exemplary penmanship and ability to write clear military communications, recorded a dramatic scene about his superior officer. One night in November 1862, McCarter, a native of Derry, Ireland, noticed that Meagher was "very drunk" and kept himself from falling to the ground only by holding on to one of the poles in front of his tent. McCarter was especially concerned about Meagher's safety because only a few yards from the general burned an immense campfire, into which he would tumble if he lost his grasp. As the private feared would happen, Meagher let go of the pole and began to fall headlong toward the fire. Instantly, though, McCarter stopped the general's momentum by pushing the unconscious officer to the ground with his bayonet. In the commotion McCarter's musket accidentally fell into the fire and was damaged. The following day, after reporting to the general's tent to copy some papers, McCarter was presented with a beautiful new musket and bayonet. Although Meagher never directly alluded to his brush with disaster, his subsequent acts of kindness to McCarter confirmed the young private's belief that the general was truly grateful to him. McCarter ended his account of this episode by writing that "To his honor and credit, I never saw General Meagher intoxicated again."[76]

At the beginning of November 1862, the War Department recalled General McClellan and replaced him as commander of the Army of the Potomac with General Ambrose Burnside. McClellan had always been a favorite of the Irish Brigade, and they could not understand his removal, especially after his bold invasion of Virginia less than two weeks before. That McClellan had been the victim of political rivalry seemed clear to many soldiers, as Lieutenant Thomas Galway of the Eighth Ohio Regiment wrote: ". . . The President [Lincoln] is in the hands of two men who are bitterly opposed to McClellan. One, a popinjay soldier [Halleck] who has never shown any anxiety to smell powder, the other a lawyer [Stanton] of extraordinary ability, but who has some other ends to compass which are to him of more importance than any *present* success of our army. The one a fool and the other a knave will together thwart us, as they have done before." When some of Meagher's officers threatened to resign in protest over McClellan's removal, the Irish general reminded them that loyalty to the Union should take precedence over their loyalty to an individual.[77]

In the middle of the month, the Army of the Potomac, now under General Burnside, moved to Falmouth, Virginia, on the north side of the Rappahannock River opposite Fredericksburg. En route, the Irish Brigade decided to impress its new division commander, Winfield Scott Hancock, with a daring raid against a Confederate battery along the river. After crossing to the opposite bank, the Brigade surprised and routed the artillerymen, kicked over their tents, and returned with two cannon. "I have never seen anything so splendid," Hancock said to Meagher. Although General Sumner was eager to attack Fredericksburg immediately, Burnside overruled him, a decision which allowed the Confederates to fortify their position and which lulled the men of the Irish Brigade into thinking they would be spending the winter at Falmouth.[78]

During this time some of the men broke the monotony of camp life by attending the monthly meeting of the Potomac Circle of the Fenian Brotherhood. Dedicated to the forceful overthrow of British rule in Ireland, the Fenians at Falmouth were part of a larger American group which by 1863 numbered 15,000 in the northern states alone. The Fenians within the Irish Brigade were led by Dr. Lawrence Reynolds, surgeon of the 63rd New York Regiment, and met in the Brigade's hospital tent. Thomas Galwey, an officer in the Hibernian Guard Company of the Eighth Ohio Volunteer Infantry, recorded his attendance at one of these meetings in his memoir of the war. He noted that Reynolds was in the habit of brewing and serving a "milk-punch," a concoction of whiskey, hot water, condensed milk, and nutmeg. About the most important ingredient, Galwey concluded: "Whiskey is a great thing in the army. At times we have 'lashins' ["lash-

ings," an abundance] of it, as they say in the Irish Brigade, and then it is
sometimes very hard to find."[79]

Like Meagher, Reynolds was a native of Waterford, Ireland, and as a
young man he had assisted his brothers in the publication of a newspaper.
After moving to England, he studied for a career in medicine and subsequently set up practice in Liverpool. There he became the acknowledged
leader of his countrymen until his revolutionary politics caused him to
emigrate in 1848. After settling in New York, he resumed his medical practice, which by the time of the Civil War had become quite lucrative. When
the Irish Brigade was being raised, he joined the 63rd New York and served
in every battle in which the Brigade fought. For his service in the field he
was promoted to the rank of lieutenant colonel. Michael Cavanagh,
Meagher's biographer, described "Old Larry" in superlative terms: "Skillful and experienced in his profession, a highly-educated Irish gentleman,
a versatile writer, orator and poet, and an earnest, active worker in the
cause of Irish nationality for over half a century, he well merited the respect of his fellow officers, and the enthusiastic affection which was accorded him by his compatriots of the rank and file. . . . He was the very
personification of cheerfulness and good nature — his beaming counte-
nance — like the sun — suffused warmth wherever it shone. . . . The victims of his playful humor enjoyed his jokes most keenly, for, in general,
they were among his most intimate friends."[80]

The secretary of the Fenian group in the Brigade was Captain James
McKay Rorty, a native of County Donegal, Ireland, who had arrived in
New York in 1857. When the Civil War broke out four years later, Rorty,
already a member of the Fenian Brotherhood, enlisted for ninety days in
the 69th New York State Militia. During the battle of Bull Run in July 1861,
he was one of about a hundred men who, along with Colonel Michael
Corcoran, were captured by Confederate forces. On September 18, however, Rorty and two other members of the 69th escaped from imprisonment in Richmond, Virginia. After eventually reaching New York, Rorty
was mustered out of the 69th New York State Militia but soon accepted a
position as second lieutenant in the Second Battalion of the New York
Light Artillery, the little-known fifth regiment of the Irish Brigade.[81]

To mark Rorty's promotion, Captain Patrick Phelan, a fellow Fenian,
presented the new lieutenant with a saber, a sash, and a belt. The grateful
young officer replied with his typical idealism: "My political faith as an
Irishman has only one article — a firm belief in the future resurrection of
Ireland. And whether death meets me, as I hope it will, on an Irish battlefield, or whether it overtakes me battling for freedom on the hot plains of
the South, it will ever find me as firm in that faith as it finds the dying
Christian in the faith of his own resurrection." Only two weeks earlier
Rorty had written his parents explaining why he had broken his promise
not to re-enlist. To his claim that he had no talent for or inclination to a

commercial career, he added his belief that his earlier service in the 69th New York had been the "realization of many a cherished dream." He continued with details of his moral and physical transformation: "I joined the 69th a shy, morose, and gloomy being, weak in body and with fluctuating health . . . . After enduring extraordinary fatigue and hardships[,] I returned, in less than six months[,] with every trace of asthma or consumption gone . . . my sinews braced and invigorated as if they were turned into iron ones, my nervousness gone, . . . and in its place a cool, steady self possession that thank God will keep me out of panics at any rate, and in short time such an entire improvement in my size, weight and appearance, that it takes an intimate friend to recognize me." Rorty would die on the field of Gettysburg, killed while he and his battery crew manned their guns during Pickett's Charge.[82]

During the second half of November 1862, General Meagher varied the routine of camp life at Falmouth by honoring the 29th Massachusetts, the only non-Irish regiment in the Brigade. For its impressive showing at Antietam, Meagher called the Yankees "honorary Irishmen" and made plans to present their lieutenant colonel, Joseph Barnes, with a green flag like the banners flown by the three New York regiments. When Barnes learned that his regiment was expected to fight under the Irish banner, however, he balked at the prospect. The embarrassing situation was overcome when the 29th Massachusetts left the Brigade and was replaced by the 28th Massachusetts under Colonel Richard Byrnes. (Some time later the green banner was given to the Ninth Massachusetts, a predominantly Irish regiment, but only after the "2" in "29" had been removed.)[83]

Born in County Cavan, Ireland, in 1832, Richard Byrnes had come to the United States at the age of twelve and joined the U.S. army five years later, in 1849. During the next decade he fought with the Second U.S. Cavalry against Indians in Florida and Oregon and rose to the rank of sergeant major of the First Cavalry. He was severely wounded in a battle with Apache Indians near Taos, New Mexico, in 1854. With the onset of the Civil War, Byrnes served with the U.S. cavalry at Bull Run in July 1861. Although later that month he was sworn in as a second lieutenant in the 17th U.S. Infantry, his first love continued to be with the cavalry. For this reason he secured a transfer to the Fifth Cavalry the following September and found himself subordinate to Second Lieutenant George A. Custer.[84]

About a year later Byrnes was being considered for command of the 28th Massachusetts after that regiment found itself with serious organizational problems. Not only had the 28th's original colonel been forced to resign after several drinking incidents, but its lieutenant colonel had also stepped down and its major was recovering from wounds sustained at the second battle of Bull Run. When Byrnes was finally appointed, his regimental officers resented the fact that one of them had not been selected for the position. Faced with threats of resignation, the new colonel set out to instill discipline into the unit and to restore its fallen numbers. The famous letter-writer Peter Welsh of Company K wrote his wife that he expected Byrnes to bring better order and discipline to the regiment. When the 28th Massachusetts was transferred to Meagher's Irish Brigade at the end of November 1862, Byrnes saw the new arrangement as an opportunity to remake his regiment in the image of the Brigade, a unit already known for its gallantry.[85]

Around the time of this transfer, Meagher appointed Private William McCarter of the 116th Pennsylvania his private secretary. The young man's first assignment was to copy into Meagher's scrapbook — a gift from his friends in Ireland — a poem of almost forty verses composed by the general himself and entitled "Midnight on the Potomac." The private was so overcome with emotion by the appointment that he burst into tears, recalling at the same time the incident in which he had saved the general from falling into the campfire. A week later, but before Meagher had seen McCarter's completed assignment, the general informed the young soldier that he had placed his name on the list of men to be promoted to "adjutant," one of the army's official secretaries or clerks. The following day McCarter presented his commanding officer with his scrapbook, newly inscribed with the general's poem. So impressed was Meagher by the scrivener's work that he publicly praised McCarter to his fellow officers, adding that he was especially proud that the man who had executed it was a member of his command. To show his gratitude for transcribing the poem, Meagher gave McCarter what the private at first thought was a $5 bill. Not until the young secretary made a purchase from the brigade sutler did he realize that the greenback was actually worth $50. Though McCarter remonstrated with his patron that the gift was entirely too much, the Irish officer insisted that the young man keep the gift. When McCarter said he intended to send the money to his wife and family in Philadelphia, the general confessed that he thought more of his scribe than ever and then forced another $10 into the private's hands. McCarter ended this lengthy account of his relationship with Meagher with additional praise for his superior officer: "Do I say too much in terming General Thomas Francis Meagher, a soldier and a gentleman, my benefactor and my friend? Certainly not. He possessed traits of character rarely combined in any one man at the present day. As a soldier, he was second to none in the American army. Meagher was cool, collected and brave in the most trying and dangerous military duties. As a gentleman, he was not excelled by any. The general was polite, obliging and kind to all, especially to the common private soldier in the ranks."[86]

Earlier that November Meagher had sent a delegation of officers under Lieutenant Colonel James Kelly to New York to turn over the Brigade's tattered regimental flags to Daniel Devlin, the chairman of the executive committee of the Irish Brigade. In a ceremony marking the return of the battle-scarred standards, Devlin spoke of them with the ornate rhetoric that befitted such a solemn occasion: "Oh, could these tattered flags but tell us how often, when the storm of battle raged to its very height — when comrades had fallen in frightful heaps on every side, and other flags had been stricken down or had disappeared in the grasp of a hostile hand, and hope seemed fast receding on the swelling tide of blood, they were still borne aloft, as it were with newborn strength, were seen far and wide to beckon on and on to the point of deadliest encounter; and could they tell us how, as the tumult of the onset ceased and the smoke of the battle swept from the plain, they still were seen aloft waving in triumph, amid the shouts of victory, then would not every Irish and every patriotic heart swell with honest pride . . . .?" Henry Spaulding then presented the new regimental flags in an especially appreciative tone: "Allow us, American-born citizens, to present them in grateful commemoration of the gallant deeds of your Brigade in the army of the Potomac, on the battle-fields of Virginia and Maryland, in the war to maintain the national domain and the honor and integrity of the American Union. . . . [M]ay the 'sunburst' on the flag of Erin prove prophetic of that peace which shall soon break gloriously through the storm of war which now desolates our beloved country. Then shall old Erin's harp be tuned afresh to the proud song of 'The Land of the Free and the Home of the Brave.' Then shall we represent 'one country, one constitution, one destiny.'" Meanwhile, to mark the arrival of the new flags at the Brigade's camp in Falmouth, Meagher planned a banquet for the returning officers and the civilian delegation which would accompany them. The soldiers in the Brigade erected a large log structure — the Green House — in which the dinner and an appropriate ceremony were scheduled to be held on December 13.[87]

A few days before that date, General Burnside decided to launch a frontal assault on the Confederate position on Marye's Heights behind Fredericksburg. Although the Union field generals vehemently opposed the plan, orders were given to prepare for an attack. In a show of force intended to clear the way for the construction of pontoons across the Rappahannock, the federal battery of 150 cannon rained destruction on Fredericksburg for eighteen hours. St. Clair Mulholland, the lieutenant colonel of the 116th Pennsylvania Regiment, described the terrifying sight: "Tons of iron were hurled into the town; shells, solid shot, shrapnel and canister raked and swept the streets. We could not see yet; we could hear the walls crumbling and the timbers crashing; then a pillar of smoke rose above the fog; another, and another, increasing in density and volume, rose skyward and canopied the doomed city like a pall. Flames leaped high out of the mist — the city was on fire."[88]

During the night of December 11 and in the early hours of the next morning, some of the troops took advantage of Fredericksburg's misfortune and plundered the city. Though lamenting what he called "some downright, wicked mischief," the eyewitness Francis Walker asserted that there was nothing contrary to the laws of war in the depredations. Fredericksburg had refused a formal demand to surrender, he noted, and the town had been the object of a fierce contest between rival forces. Under the circumstances, he concluded, the conquerors had the "right to sack and pillage." In further extenuation he added that most of the mischief was committed by a small number of soldiers and that it was done out of "a spirit of fun, rather than of hatred." Walker especially recalled seeing four members of the Irish Brigade with their "spoils of war": two soldiers sported bonnets, a third carried off a ten-gallon coffee pot, and the last staggered under the weight of a huge feather bed.[89]

On the morning of December 12, Meagher led the Irish Brigade across a pontoon bridge into Fredericksburg, and the whole Second Corps followed. To the overly eager undertakers who distributed their business cards to the men as they entered the town, one Irishman replied sarcastically, "Well, only that we were in a bit of a hurry we'd be after givin' yez the natest [neatest] koind av a jig in the air." Because the three New York regiments had sent their battle-tattered flags to New York for replacement, Meagher the next day told his men to identify themselves by putting green sprigs of boxwood into their hats. When Colonel Robert Nugent of the 69th New York placed a sprig of boxwood in the hat of Father Thomas Ouellet, the regiment's French-Canadian chaplain, the officer said he would make an Irishman of the priest that day. Lieutenant Colonel Mulholland wrote that wreaths of boxwood were "hung upon the tattered [U.S.] flags, and the national color of the Emerald Isle blended in fair harmony with the red, white, and blue of the Republic." Luckily, the 28th Massachusetts still had its regimental banner — decorated with the familiar harp, sunburst, shamrocks, and Gaelic motto *Faugh A Ballagh* ("Clear the Way"). Before proceeding, Meagher reminded his soldiers of their duty to support the Union cause and to uphold their reputation as fighters.[90]

To the men of the 88th New York, Meagher directed special words of solicitude. Private William McCleland recorded the scene and the general's speech in a letter to the *Irish American*. "In a few moments you will engage the enemy in a most terrible battle, which will probably decide the fate of this glorious, great and grand country — the home of your adoption," the private quoted Meagher as saying. "The General hesitated a moment, and then with eyes full to overflowing, through which he could hardly speak, he said: 'Soldiers — This is my wife's own regiment, 'her own dear 88th,' she calls it, and I know, and have confidence, that with [that] dear woman's smile upon you, and for woman's sake, this day you will strike a deadly blow to those wicked traitors who are now but a few hundred yards from you, and bring back to this distracted country its former prestige and glory. This may be my last speech to you, but I will be with you when the battle is the fiercest; and, if I fall, I can say I did my duty, and fell fighting in the most glorious of causes.' The Regiment then gave three cheers, such as the 88th alone can give."[91]

The Irish Brigade finally advanced, crossing a millstream by means of a narrow bridge, all the while under intense Confederate fire. Two companies of the 69th New York were ordered to protect a knoll to the right of the main action, a command that spared their sixty-nine men from the slaughter that soon followed. As the rest of the Irish Brigade stopped to form a battle line, they could see Marye's Heights rising 150 yards ahead and crowned by a stone wall bristling with Confederate rifles. (Ironically, the Confederates on Marye's Heights were mostly Irish — from Thomas Cobb's Georgia Infantry and Joseph Kershaw's South Carolina Infantry.) The Brigade watched as General William French's division, sent ahead first, was repulsed and scattered. When it was the Irishmen's turn, they rushed past the first fence, but an ulcerated knee joint prevented Meagher from leading his men on foot. According to Lieutenant Colonel Mulholland, when the Georgians recognized the green sprigs in the enemy's caps and the green flag of the 28th Massachusetts, the Confederates cried out, "Oh, God, what a pity! Here comes Meagher's fellows!" Captain Thomas Galwey of the Eighth Ohio observed that each of the charging Irishmen had a sprig of green in his cap and "a half-laughing, half-murderous look in his eye." But at the second fence the men of the Brigade were cut down by rifle fire from behind the wall.[92]

About thirty yards from the stone wall, the Irish Brigade halted and began to fire a barrage into the Confederate line. William Tyrrell, the color sergeant for the 116th Pennsylvania, was struck six times, while another dozen bullets ripped through the Stars and Stripes. Though Tyrrell finally fell to the ground, he miraculously survived. Lieutenant Francis Quinlan saved the flag by clasping it tightly to his breast and rolling with it to safety. Private William McCleland later reported that none of the men in the 88th New York Infantry fell until they were within thirty or forty yards of the rifle pits, where they met a blistering hail of bullets from three lines of enemy. "Our men were mowed down like grass before the scythe of the reaper . . . ," McCleland added. "The men lay piled up in all directions."[93]

Meanwhile, William McCarter, Meagher's adjutant, suffered minor wounds to the left shoulder and the left ankle before being seriously hit in the right arm as he rammed a cartridge into his musket. "A stream of blood now came rushing down the inside and outside sleave of my uniform, then down the side of my pants into my right foot shoe until it overflowed," he wrote twenty years later. "Next, a dizziness in the head and partial loss of sight came over me, accompanied by violent pain in the wounded part." As he lay on the ground within fifty feet of the Confederate wall, he was an easy mark. One ball hit his left wrist, and another thirty-three bullets would have struck him but for the blankets that protected his head and body. Irishman Timothy Donoghue, a private in the

69th New York, was struck while carrying a wounded officer off the field between the lines, an act of heroism for which he was awarded the Congressional Medal of Honor thirty-two years later.[94]

According to Captain Conyngham, the men of the Irish Brigade had not a single piece of artillery to support them. "[A]nd yet," he said, "they stood against shot and shell, grape and canister, minie and conical balls, to fight a formidable enemy, artillery and infantry, posted behind stone walls and fortifications." Another officer wrote that the Brigade charged the enemy, "who were well protected behind a stone wall, and received a murderous fire from both musketry and artillery, and, what was worse than all, they were caught between two fires. The musketry fire began at half-past nine o'clock, and continued without an instant's cessation until a quarter to seven in the evening — the longest and at the same time the heaviest fire of musketry on record." Nevertheless, some of the men persevered until they were within twenty-five feet of the enemy, only to be killed or wounded. Conyngham's description of the battlefield that night still chills the blood: "Thousands lay along that hill-side, and in the valleys, whose oozing wounds were frozen, and whose old limbs were stiffened, for they had no blankets; they had flung them away going into the fight. Masses of dead and dying were huddled together; some convulsed in the last throes of death; others gasping for water — delirious, writhing in agony, and stiffened with the cold frost. The living tried to shelter themselves behind the bodies of the dead."[95]

Tributes to the Brigade's valor came from participants on both sides of the conflict. After the war Colonel William Brooke, who commanded the 53rd Pennsylvania Regiment at Fredericksburg, said that the dead found nearest the wall belonged to the 69th New York, the Fifth New Hampshire, and the 53rd Pennsylvania. Colonel Mulholland made a more precise claim — that the two bodies "nearest the enemy" were those of Major William Horgan and Adjutant John Young, both of the 88th New York. Confederate General J. E. B. Stewart's chief of staff, meanwhile, summed up the carnage by saying that the greater part of the 1,200 bodies found on the plain between Marye's Heights and Fredericksburg belonged to "Meagher's brave Irish Brigade, which was nearly annihilated during the several attacks." Another Confederate wrote admiringly: "In the foremost line we distinguished the green flag with the golden harp of old Ireland, and we knew it to be Meagher's Irish Brigade. On they came in beautiful array, but our fire was murderous, and no troops on earth could stand before the *feu d'enfer* [fire of Hell] we were giving them, but the gallant enemy pushed on and fought, and left their dead within five and twenty paces of the sunken road." The enormity of the loss was expressed by General Hancock's adjutant general: "I looked with my field-glass, and I looked for a long time before I was certain of what I saw. I at first thought that the men of the Brigade had lain down to allow the showers of shot and shell to pass over them, for they lay in regular lines. I looked for some movement, some stir — a hand or a foot in motion; but no — they were dead — *dead every man of them* — cut down like grass."[96]

Statistics on the total number of casualties which the Irish Brigade sustained at Fredericksburg vary. Colonel Robert Nugent asserted that the Brigade had suffered 545 casualties, 43 percent of the 1,257 men who went directly into the battle. (Francis Walker, the historian of the Army of the Potomac's Second Corps, records the same number of casualties but a larger number of men — 1,315 — taken into battle.) According to Nugent, the three New York regiments lost about 50 percent of the number engaged in the fight. The 69th New York listed among the killed and wounded 112 of the 173 enlisted men — and each of the sixteen officers — in the assault (68 percent). The 88th New York suffered 127 casualties (52 percent); the 63rd New York, forty-five (28 percent); the 28th Massachusetts, 156 (37 percent); and the 116th Pennsylvania, eighty-nine (36 percent). According to the Official Records, the Irish Brigade lost forty-six killed, 416 wounded, and seventy-four missing. The casualties for each of the five regiments were as follows: 128 in the 69th New York, 127 in the 88th New York, forty-four in the 63rd New York, 158 in the 28th Massachusetts, and eighty-eight in the 116th Pennsylvania.[97]

Even before the official tally could be made, the degree to which the

*Located along the Rappahannock River in Fredericksburg, Virginia, this memorial to the Irish Brigade notes that the 69th New York lost 128 men killed, wounded, or missing during the Brigade's assaults on Marye's Heights on December 13, 1862.*

Irish Brigade had been decimated became evident. At inspection the following day, one company presented only seven men, while another mustered a solitary soldier. When General Hancock noticed three privates from
the Brigade parading by themselves, he cursed them and asked why they
did not close up with their company. After returning a salute, one of the
privates replied, "General, we are a company." Since the siege at Yorktown
the previous April and May, the Irish Brigade had lost — killed and
wounded — ninety-six officers and 1,521 enlisted men.[98]

The roster of wounded officers was particularly devastating. Among
those casualties were Captain Thomas Leddy (severely wounded in the
left arm), Lieutenant Patrick Callaghan (wounded in four different places),
Second Lieutenant David Burke (severely wounded in the left shoulder),
Captain O'Donovan (struck in the left breast by a spent shell), Major James
Cavanagh (shot in the hip), and Lieutenant James Birmingham (both thighs
broken). In addition, three of the Brigade's five regimental commanders
were wounded: Major Joseph O'Neill of the 63rd New York, Colonel Robert Nugent of the 69th New York, and Colonel Dennis Heenan of the 116th
Pennsylvania. Describing the mood after Fredericksburg, one officer wrote
that the remnant of the Brigade "were the most dejected set of Irishmen
you ever saw or heard of."[99]

Although the 28th Massachusetts suffered a casualty rate of 37.5 percent in its first battle under Colonel Richard Byrnes, the Irish officer received high praise from his superiors. General Meagher expressed his pleasure with his new regimental commander: "[He] eminently distinguished
himself by the perfect fearlessness of his conduct, his gallant bearing, and
his devotion to the orders he had received — leading his men up within
pistol-range of the enemy's first line of advance, and there holding his
ground until the rest of the Brigade being hopelessly reduced, and his
own command left without support whilst it was considerably weakened,
he brought the 28th with honor from the field." Though using fewer words,
General Hancock concurred with Meagher's assessment: "The conduct of
Col. Byrnes at Fredericksburg was excellent: the loss of officers and men
in his Regt. was quite great. I think him entitled to a Brevet for that action.
Col. Byrnes has a fine, disciplined regiment." No promotion was forthcoming, however.[100]

Serious efforts to retrieve the Union dead and wounded could not be
made until the night after the battle. To rescue John Sheridan, a wounded
sergeant of the 88th New York, four of his comrades crawled out onto the
battlefield on their stomachs, thus avoiding sporadic Confederate gunfire. Because Sheridan had a fractured leg, a rescue at first seemed impossible until Sergeant Slattery devised a plan. "Begob [By God], boys,"
Slattery said, "did yez ever see rats trying to get away with a goose egg?
One rat lies down, the others roll the egg on top av him, he holds it in
place wid his four paws, and then they pull him off by the tail. Now I will

lie down on my back, you lift Sheridan on top av me and I will do my best to kape his leg even." Mulholland described the outcome: "The men would push themselves on [forward] a couple of feet, then pull Slattery, with his precious load, up to them, and so on, until before daylight, they all reached the city and had Sheridan attended to, and his leg amputated; too late, however, to save the poor fellow's life. He died from exhaustion. The clothes were literally ground off Sergeant Slattery's back . . . ."[101]

While recuperating from injuries suffered at Fredericksburg, Captain John Donovan of the 69th New York mused about the future of the Irish Brigade. "I can say that as an 'Irish Brigade' it has 'fought its last battle,'" he informed the *Irish American*, "and could the spirits of its honored and immortal dead, whose rude graves spot the soil of Virginia and Maryland, but have the privilege or power to look down upon the future of this Republic, they can now tell whether or not the cause for which they offered up their lives is to perish; and if it is to perish, better on the battlefield, than to have survived as cripples to experience the agonies of the awful wreck. If it is not to perish, but on the contrary to triumph, their noble souls could not have [given] up their lives for a more glorious or greater earthly heritage; and their surviving comrades, although deprived of sight and limb, will have ample reason to shed tears of joy and gratitude for having lent their aid and spilled their blood in defense of so great a cause, and in contemplation of so grand and noble an object."[102]

The heroism which the Brigade showed at Marye's Heights earned it universal admiration and praise. Thomas Galwey of the Eighth Ohio recorded the carnage in his diary: "[The Irish Brigade] pass just to our left, poor fellows, poor, glorious fellows, shaking goodbye to us with their hats! They reach a point within a stone's throw of the stone wall. No farther. They try to go beyond, but are slaughtered. Nothing could advance further and live. They lie down doggedly, determined to hold the ground they have already taken. There, away out in the fields to the front and left of us, we see them for an hour or so, lying in line close to that terrible stone wall." Another eyewitness, the Confederate general George Pickett, described his men's feelings as they watched "those sons of Erin" rush fearlessly to their death: "[W]e forgot they were fighting us, and cheer after cheer at their fearlessness went up all along our lines." Francis Lawley, a correspondent for the London *Times*, was especially effusive: "Never at *Fontenoy, Albuera, or at Waterloo, was more undoubted courage displayed by the sons of Erin, than during those six frantic dashes which they directed against the almost impregnable position of their foe . . . . The bodies which lie in dense masses within forty yards of the muzzles of Colonel Walton's guns are the best evidence of what manner of men they were who pressed on to death with the dauntlessness of a race which has gained glory on a thousand battle-fields, and never more richly deserved it than at the foot of Marye's Heights on the 13th December, 1862." Even

Robert E. Lee remarked: "Never were men so brave. They ennobled their race by their splendid gallantry on that desperate occasion. Though totally routed, they reaped harvests of glory. Their brilliant, though hopeless assaults on our lines, excited the hearty applause of our officers and soldiers."[103]

Despite the plaudits which the Brigade received for its heroic showing at Fredericksburg, its commander came under fire for what one of his critics called another example of cowardice. In his official report of Fredericksburg, Meagher noted that a painful ulcer in the knee-joint — "which I had concealed and borne up against for days" — had caused him to leave the field of battle early that day. He added, however, that he had returned on horseback, only to be greeted by fleeing members of the 63rd and 69th regiments. He argued that his subsequent decision to transfer his men to the north bank of the Rappahannock had been actuated by a desire to safeguard the many wounded men under his command. In effecting this transfer, he claimed, he had acted on the belief that he possessed "a conditional authorization" from General Hancock, an assumption which he later realized was unwarranted. The newspaper reporter Henry Villard, however, saw Meagher's retreat — without orders — in a different light: "nothing but a piece of arrant cowardice, for which, however, he never received punishment on account of his popularity among the Irish."[104]

Whatever may have been General Meagher's role in the battle of Fredericksburg, the Brigade's charges at Marye's Heights became celebrated in the annals of military history. Few people so adequately expressed the psychological results of the Brigade's bloody sacrifice that day as Lieutenant Colonel Mulholland of the 116th Pennsylvania: "Save one regimental flag, no trophies of the fight remained. Yet the field was redolent with acts of noble daring. The troops that marched on Marye's Heights more than equalled, in the grandeur of their bravery, the *gallant six hundred immortalized by the poet laureate, while by their sacrifice, though they did not gain a victory, they raised a monument more enduring than marble or brass to the valor and heroism of our times and our people; and in other ages, when the memories of the contest will have been mellowed by the lapse of centuries, in the bloodshed will be seen a holocaust at the altar of freedom in the smoke of the battle, sweet incense at the shrine of human liberty. The Union troops failed — so did *Leonidas of Sparta, yet what son of Hellas [Greece] but shares even to this day in the glory of old Thermopylae, and what American, even to the most remote period of the future, but will share in the glories that cluster around the plain of Fredericksburg? Those fields, resplendent with the great deeds of our people, where the verdure and every blooming flower is nurtured and enriched by martyr blood, will ever be hallowed places in the land, around which will crystallize the warm, full gratitude of a nation saved."[105]

In his poem *"At Fredericksburg — Dec. 13, 1862," John Boyle O'Reilly, the famous Irish exile and the editor of the Boston *Pilot*, described not only the Irish Brigade's six heroic charges at Marye's Heights but also the transformation which the nation had undergone at the start of the war.

> God send us peace, and keep red strife away;
> But should it come, God send us men and steel!
> The land is dead that dare not face the day
> When foreign danger threats the common weal.
>
> Defenders strong are they that homes defend:
> From ready arms the spoiler keeps afar.
> Well blest the country that has sons to lend
> From trades of peace to learn the trade of war.
>
> Thrice blest the nation that has every son
> A soldier, ready for the warning sound;
> Who marches homeward when the fight is done,
> To swing the hammer and to till the ground.
>
> Call back that morning, with its lurid light,
> When through our land the awful war-bell tolled;
> When lips were mute, and women's faces white
> As the pale cloud that out from Sumter rolled.
>
> Call back that morn: an instant all were dumb,
> As if the shot had struck the Nation's life;
> Then cleared the smoke, and rolled the calling drum,
> And men streamed in to meet the coming strife.
>
> They closed the ledger and they stilled the loom,
> The plough left rusting in the prairie farm;
> They saw but "Union" in the gathering gloom;
> The tearless women helped the men to arm;
>
> Brigades from towns — each village sent its band;
> German and Irish — every race and faith;
> There was no question then of native land,
> But — love the Flag and follow it to death.
>
> No need to tell their tale: through every age
> The splendid story shall be sung and said;
> But let me draw one picture from the page —
> For words of song embalm the hero dead.

The smooth hill is bare, and the cannons are planted,
Like Gorgon fates shading its terrible brow;
The word has been passed that the stormers are wanted,
And Burnside's battalions are mustering now.
The armies stand by to behold the dread meeting;
The work must be done by a desperate few;
The black-mouthèd guns on the height give them greeting —
From gun-mouth to plain every grass blade in view.
Strong earthworks are there, and the rifles behind them
Are Georgia militia — an Irish brigade —
Their caps have green badges, as if to remind them
Of all the brave record their country has made.

The stormers go forward — the Federals cheer them;
They breast the smooth hillside — the black mouths are dumb;
The riflemen lie in the works till they near them,
And cover the stormers as upward they come.
Was ever a death-march so grand and so solemn?
At last, the dark summit with flame is enlined;
The great guns belch doom on the sacrificed column,
That reels from the height, leaving hundreds behind.
The armies are hushed — there is no cause for cheering;
The fall of brave men to brave men is a pain.
Again come the stormers! and as they are nearing
The flame-sheeted rifle-lines, reel back again.
And so till full noon come the Federal masses —
Flung back from the height, as the cliff flings a wave;
Brigade on brigade to the death-struggle passes,
No waving rank till it steps on the grave.

Then comes a brief lull, and the smoke-pall is lifted,
The green of the hillside no longer is seen;
The dead soldiers lie as the sea-weed is drifted,
The earthworks still held by the badges of green.
Have they quailed? is the word. No: again they are forming —
Again comes a column to death and defeat!
What is it in these who shall now do the storming
That makes every Georgian spring to his feet?

"O God! what a pity!" they cry in their cover,
As rifles are readied and bayonets made tight;
"'Tis Meagher and his fellows! their caps have green clover;
'Tis Greek to Greek now for the rest of the fight!"
Twelve hundred the column, their rent flag before them,

With Meagher at their head, they dashed at the hill!
Their foemen are proud of the country that bore them;
But, Irish in love, they are enemies still.
Out rings the fierce word, "Let them have it!" [—] the rifles
Are emptied point-blank in the hearts of the foe;
It is green against green, but a principle stifles
The Irishman's love in the Georgian's blow.
The column has reeled, but it is not defeated;
In front of the guns they re-form and attack;
Six times they have done it, and six times retreated;
Twelve hundred they came, and two hundred go back.
Two hundred go back with the chivalrous story;
The wild day is closed in the night's solemn shroud;
A thousand lie dead, but their death was a glory
That calls not for tears — the Green Badges are proud!

Bright honor be theirs who for honor were fearless,
Who charged for their flag to the grim cannon's mouth;
And honor to them who were true, though not tearless, —
Who bravely that day kept the cause of the South.
The quarrel is done — God avert such another;
The lesson it brought we should evermore heed;
Who loveth the Flag is a man and a brother,
No matter what birth or what race or what creed.[106]

Despite the Irish Brigade's tremendous losses at Marye's Heights, Meagher went ahead with the banquet he had planned to mark the arrival of the civilian committee bearing the Brigade's new regimental flags. Because the banqueting hall which the men had built at Falmouth, across the river, was now inaccessible, the honors were conducted in the theater in Fredericksburg. Surrounded by twenty-two generals, the surviving officers of the Brigade, and his civilian guests, Meagher expressed his pride in his men and thanked his guests for the new banners. However, because the Brigade's numbers had been so sharply reduced, he asked the committee to keep the flags until new recruits could bring the Irish unit back to full strength. Meagher also used the opportunity to take a swipe at the political partisanship which he believed was partly responsible for the slaughter which had occurred only two days before. While making a toast to Brigadier General Alfred Sully, an Irish-American officer sitting next to him, Meagher proclaimed: "I want you to understand, gentlemen, that *he* is not one of your 'Political Generals,' but a brave and accomplished soldier — *who attracted his 'star' from the firmament of glory — by the electricity of his sword!*" All the while could be heard outside the screaming sound of shells from Confederate batteries trying to bring the theater into range.

Even when the firing tore part of the roof away and shattered windows, the "death feast" continued. Only after a waiter walked up to Meagher bearing a cannonball that had worked its destruction on a nearby build-ing did the assembled guests admit that discretion is the better part of valor. Even then some of the gentlemen camouflaged their quest for safety with the remark that, "it being Sunday [morning], they thought it well to close the feast a little early that they might attend divine service." As the men and their guests left the theater, General Hancock commented that only the Irish could follow such a fight with such a feast.[107]

The new flags which were presented to the Brigade's three New York regiments were a rich green in color and, like the original banners, mea-sured six and a half feet on the fly and six feet on the pike. Each flag bore the traditional insignia: a harp, a sunburst, a wreath of shamrocks, and two scrolls bearing the name of the respective regiment and the inscrip-tion "Irish Brigade." The banner of the 69th New York regiment, for ex-ample, was inscribed in the lower left-hand quarter with the legend: "Pre-sented by the Citizens of New York to the 69th N.Y.V. (1st Regiment Irish Brigade) Brigadier Gen. Thomas F. Meagher Commanding. In grateful ap-preciation of their gallant and brilliant conduct on the Battlefields of Vir-ginia and Maryland in the War to maintain the National Domain and the American Union. Nov. 1862." The right-hand side of the flag bore the names of nine battles: Yorktown, Fair Oaks, Gaines' Hill [Mill], Allen's Farm, Savage's Station, White Oak Bridge [Swamp], Glendale, Malvern Hills [Hill], and Antietam. The names of four other battles were added later: Fredericksburg, Chancellorsville, Gettysburg, and Bristoe Station. In 1963 the flag of the 69th New York was presented to the Republic of Ireland by President John Kennedy and today is enshrined in Leinster House, the site of the Irish parliament. The 63rd New York Regiment's banner is lo-cated in the library of the University of Notre Dame in South Bend, Indi-ana, while the flag of the 88th is in the armory of the 69th New York Regi-ment in New York City.[108]

During the week after the presentation of the new regimental flags, Michael Sullivan, a member of the Georgia regiment that had poured fire into the Irish Brigade as it charged up Marye's Heights, crossed into the Union camp at Falmouth. To the surprised Meagher and his men, Sullivan told how, during the battle, he had seen one of the Brigade's color-bearers shot down. Later that night, Sullivan said, he had crawled out onto the field and retrieved the green flag from under the color-bearer's body. His tale told, Sullivan unwound from his waist a green flag with the familiar harp and sunburst — the colors of the 28th Massachusetts.[109]

The following Christmas was a sad one for the families whose men had fallen at Marye's Heights. "It will be a sad, sad Christmas by many an Irish hearthstone in New York, Pennsylvania, and Massachusetts," wrote one officer. Nevertheless, the survivors in the Brigade celebrated the holiday as best they could. Lieutenant Colonel Mulholland of the 116th Pennsylvania wrote that "many boxes of good things from home were received, and shared by the recipients with comrades less fortunate. Some of the boys were a little homesick, to be sure, but enough were sufficiently light of heart to drive dull care away. A large Christmas tree was erected in the centre of the camp, and peals of laughter and much merriment greeted the unique decorations, tin cups, hardtack, pieces of pork and other odd articles being hung on the branches. At night the camp fire roared and blazed, the stars shone above the tall pines, the canteen was passed around, and care banished for the hour."[110]

A few days before Christmas, General Meagher had traveled to New York City. Besides hoping to recuperate from his ulcerated knee, he had made the trip to accompany the body of Major William Horgan of the 88th New York, one of the fatalities at Fredericksburg. While still in the Empire City, Meagher attended a requiem mass for the Brigade's dead on January 16, 1863. The mass, held at St. Patrick's Old Cathedral, was sung by Father Thomas Ouellet, the chaplain of the 69th New York Volunteers, while Father O'Reilly, the chaplain of the 69th New York National Guard, preached the sermon. The latter priest praised the fallen heroes for their Christian obedience to their commanders and for their religious observance. "They have done their duty as men, as citizens, and as Christians, and their families, their country and the Church have a right to be proud of them," he was quoted as saying by the *New York Times*. In a speech after the services, Meagher showed that he had moderated his earlier animus against the Southern cause and even toasted the "heroism of both armies." Colonel Robert Nugent of the 69th New York then proposed a toast to Meagher — "the General who does not say, 'There are your orders — go,' but who says, 'Come, boys, come,' and who has been with his brigade on every battlefield."[111]

As a fitting accompaniment to the memorial mass, the journalist John Savage wrote *"Requiem for the Dead of the Irish Brigade" in honor of those who had died while serving with the famous unit:

> Come, let the solemn, soothing Mass be said,
> For the soldier souls of the patriot dead.
> Let the organ swell, and the incense burn,
> For the hero men who will ne'er return.
>
> Men who had pledged to this land their troth,
> And died to defend her, ere break their oath.
>
> But if high the praise, be as deep the wail
> O'er the exiled sons of the warlike Gael.

From their acts true men may examples reap;
And women bless them, and[,] glorying, weep.

Proud beats the heart while it sorrowing melts
O'er the death-worn fame of these truthful Celts.

For the scattered graves over which we pray
Will shine like stars on their race alway.

Oh, what doth ennoble the Christian man,
If not dying for truth in freedom's van!

What takes from Death all its terrors and gloom?
Conscience to feel Justice blesses the tomb!

And oh! what doth build up a nation's weal
But courage to fight for the truths we feel!

And thus did these braves, on whose graves we wait,
Do all that make nations and races great.

*Oremus.*
Ye living, your hearts combine
In praise and prayer, to the heavenly shrine:
Ye widowed and stricken,
Your trustfulness quicken
With faith in the Almighty Giver;
And may blessed repose
Be the guerdon of those
Who fell at Antietam and James's river,
By the Rappahannock and Chickahominy;
*Requiem aeternam dona eis domine!*
May their souls on the Judgment-day arise;
*Et lux perpetua luceat eis.*[112]

Before leaving New York to rejoin the Brigade in Virginia, General Meagher met with various civilian patrons of the Brigade to acknowledge their gift of new regimental flags the previous December. In doing so, he reminded his listeners that the officers of the Brigade had declined the gift because the unit was not numerically strong enough to protect the new banners and to carry them with the honor they deserved. In response, Henry Spaulding, on behalf of the donors, praised the Brigade for its noble efforts: "If the words inscribed on the banners had been prepared in letters of gold, and if the staff had been studded with diamonds and rubies, the gift would not meet the merits of the noble Irish Brigade, which had fought so gallantly for the land of their adoption. Nothing that American citizens could offer would be too much for the adopted citizens who perilled life and everything for the preservation of the republic." In a more formal acknowledgement written to Spaulding early in February, Meagher assured him that "whilst this Republic, as Washington inaugurated it and Andrew Jackson confirmed it, demands for its salvation a strong arm and a devoted heart, even unto death — neither the one nor the other shall fail to find a Champion whilst there lives a soldier of the Irish Brigade."[113]

It was during this same visit to New York that Meagher received from his officers an elegant medal inscribed in his honor and decorated with an Irish harp and the American and Irish flags. With his customary rhetorical flourish, the general described the gold gift as his most precious treasure and promised to bequeath it to his son "as the greatest legacy he could receive — with the hope that, taught and inspired by its memories, its inscriptions and its emblems, he may endeavor to serve Ireland as I have tried to serve America." He then assured his officers that no advancement in rank could confer on him a greater dignity than that he had enjoyed as general of the Irish Brigade in America.[114]

Meanwhile, back at camp near Fredericksburg sometime that winter, Captain Jack Gosson decided to break the monotony with a show of his legendary horsemanship. Though the ground was covered with ice, the Irishman dashed off on his mount. When almost immediately the horse slipped, Gosson was thrown to the ground, where he lay senseless, his collarbone broken. By the time Father Corby arrived on the scene, however, the humbled horseman had regained consciousness and was lamenting not his scrape with death but the fact that he had fallen on level ground. The chaplain provided some insight into the character of the "disgraced" Captain Jack: "If it had been going over a stone wall or down a precipice fifty or a hundred feet, there would have been some glory in it; but to be broken up, and perhaps killed, on level ground was ignominy he could not endure. How would such an unworthy action sound in history? What would his New York and European friends say? He thought they would drop his name from the roll of chivalric knighthood forever!"[115]

Since the debacle at Fredericksburg, General Meagher had worked to have the three original regiments of the Brigade recalled to New York so his men could rest and replenish their numbers. (The three units together numbered only 531 enlisted men.) Having received no reply from the military authorities, he wrote to the secretary of war on February 19, 1863. In the general's extremely lengthy letter, he recounted the Brigade's heroic deeds and argued that no brigade in the United States army "has more assiduously, unremittingly, bravely, nobly done its duty." He pointed out that other regiments similarly decimated had already been ordered home and that silence on his part would jeopardize the Irish Brigade's reputation. The relief of his three regiments from duty in the field, he concluded, "will result in an important accession to their ranks, and so enable the Irish Brigade to render, in support of the Constitution and the legitimate Chief Magistracy of the United States, services not less faithful and chivalrous than those they have already permanently imprinted with their blood upon the national records of this war."[116]

Despite the precarious situation of the Brigade, Meagher and his men planned to celebrate St. Patrick's Day with their usual enthusiasm and camaraderie. On the appointed day, March 17, Father Corby celebrated a "military Mass" in a rustic chapel specially constructed for the service, during which Meagher himself directed the military band. After the liturgy Father Joseph O'Hagan, the chaplain of the Excelsior Brigade (the 70th through the 74th New York Volunteers), preached a sermon. By about 11 a.m. an estimated 10,000 soldiers, officers, and invited guests had gathered to watch the traditional steeple chase over a course a mile and three-quarters in length. Among the guests was Thomas Galwey of the Eighth Ohio Infantry, who noted that St. Patrick's Day ranked with the Fourth of July in importance in the Army of the Potomac "among all but a few of the bluest of Yankees." Two of the most conspicuous figures on the field were Meagher himself — dressed in white hat, blue swallow-tail coat, and buckskin knee breeches — and Captain Jack Gosson, the winner of the first race. Later that day, under a shady bower, the most important guests dined on fare provided by the quartermaster: thirty-five hams, a side of a roasted ox, numerous poultry, eight baskets of champagne, ten gallons of rum, and twenty-two of whiskey. The afternoon was devoted to the customary contests: foot racing, casting weights, catching a soaped pig, and Irish dancing. At an appropriate time between events, Major General Joseph Hooker, the new army commander, proposed three cheers for "General Meagher and his Irish Brigade, God bless them." The evening's diversions included a "poetical address" composed and read by Dr. Lawrence Reynolds, a member of the 63rd New York Regiment and the poet laureate of the Brigade.[117]

*"Poetical Address Before the Irish Brigade"

Whether he's fated in far lands to roam,
Or pines beneath a stranger's sway at home,
There is, in every year, one sacred day,
When Ireland's son feels full of hope and gay,
Sees sorrow's sad shade from life's scenes depart,
And faded joys flash fresh upon his heart;
While fancy tells the blissful time will come
When fame and freedom yet shall bless his home.
Why should we not, on this our hallowed day,

On freedom's soil, feel full of hope and gay?
When every hill around, and every vale
Tells to all time a spirit-thrilling tale,
That here the conflict for the rights of man,
Man's natural rights and dignity began.
That hence were chased by freemen of all lands
The monarch's minions and his hireling bands.
That in this happy country, none shall bleed
For difference of thought, or race or creed;
But all shall dwell in holy unity,
The sons of order, love and liberty.

What has Columbia by just laws become?
Her children's Eden and the exile's home.
'Tis only on her shore, since time began,
Man walked in pride, and felt himself a man;
Looked up to God, and down on such vile things
As flattering courtiers and inflated kings;
Gave proud defiance to each threat'ning foe,
And cordial welcome to each child of woe.

Oh! shall we ever, ever be again
The peaceful, happy people we were then?
Each by the other's skill and friendship blest,
The enterprising East, the fertile West,
The South by love cemented to the North —
The modern envied Eden of the earth.

Alas! as in the world's young sinless hours,
The wily serpent lurked in Eden's bowers,
And blasted all the peace and rapture there;
So breathed the serpent words of misery here,
Burst every bond of holy brotherhood,
And bathed the country in fraternal blood.
The crafty politician's guilesome tongue
Poured cheating words the mislead crowd among,
And brought that plague, than famine direr far,
That heaviest curse of mankind, civil war.

The storm came on, the crouching coward bowed
His craven head beneath the murky cloud:
In his concealment trembled in his soul,
To see the flash and hear the thunder roll.
At once you gallant Irish, you came forth,

And proved your manhood, loyalty and worth;
And, unseduced, unwavering, undismayed,
You raised for battle your renowned Brigade,
And proved how pure the loyalty you vowed,
By deeds of daring, and by floods of blood.

Your chief you chose to lead you to the war,
Your native chieftain, the intrepid Meagher,
Who dared already in his early youth,
The patriot's doom for freedom and for truth;
And never since from foeman's fire he shrank —
Our first in danger, as our first in rank.

You fought, how gloriously you fought, how well,
The page of wondering history shall tell.
On Yorktown's walls, the rebel flag was seen
To droop its folds beneath the Irish green.
From Williamsburg, the traitor legion fled
From the fierce charge by Irish valor led;
And Fair Oaks saw the victors of a day
Before your green flag fade like mists away.
Already Richmond lay before your view,
And owned her destined conquerors in you.
But politicians, to the nation's grief,
Marred the wise projects of your youthful chief.
Why was withheld the stipulated aid?
Why was McDowell's promised corps delayed?
While Southern thousands rushed to Richmond's aid
And closed the gaps that Irish valor made.

From that came on that trial most severe,
Which gallant heroes are compelled to bear;
To leave a conquest all but won, and fly
Before an oft-defeated enemy.
In countless thousands, on the rebels came,
With cries of vengeance and with hearts of flame —
They came to hurl destruction on our rear,
But you, Green Erin's bold Brigade[,] were there,
And glorying in the post given you by Mac,
The thundering tide of traitors you tossed back.

Bright on the warrior's memory flashes still,
Your bright advance at eve on Gaines's [sic] Mill.
From early dawn you heard the cannon's roar,

And every hour it deepened more and more —
Nearer and nearer comes the battle's sound —
Your General moves your ready ranks around,
That chafe at every moment of delay:
"Advance!" You cheer, and cheering, bound away.
The battle raged from morning until eve;
The field, the Union forces slowly leave.
On came the rebels, in a countless host,
They cleave the loyal ranks, and all is lost;
Horse, foot, artillery, one jumbled mass;
Over that narrow bridge: how shall they pass?
They gnash their teeth, and scowl in fierce despair.
The stream before — the foemen in their rear.
Who, who are they, who through the flying crowd
Pass, with firm tread and bearing sternly proud?
Who, who are they, whose green flags gaily fly?
They near the hill: they face the enemy;
With hurried pace they mount — from on the hill,
They wave their flags of green, and all is still.
The foe retires; pursuit and panic cease,
And all is silence, sweet repose and peace;
Save where brave Porter's rescued corps rend Heaven
With grateful shouts for Ireland's warriors given.

Still in the rear the loyal lines we close;
And slow retiring, keep at bay our foes.
At Savage Station next the Irish band,
Calm and resolved, before their vanguards stand.
They come; they cheer and rush, our ranks to pierce;
Our cannon greets them with a welcome fierce;
Our bullets whistle thick around their ears;
Our changing lines advance with heavy cheers.
High in our front ranks streams the banner green;
Our foes look on it, and desert the scene.
With each repulse, inflamed to greater wrath,
Like famished wolves they follow on our path.
O'er White Oak Swamp, we break the narrow bridge,
And wait their onset, on the rising ridge.
Along the line a dreadful fight soon rose:
Here our troops conquered, there prevailed the foes.
A weak point in our line their leader found,
And moved, to flank us, and our troops surround.
The veteran Sumner still kept fighting on,
But saw his forces yield, hope almost gone.

When on his eye a gladsome vision broke,
Our coming green flag, and the hero spoke:
"Irish brigade, while through the day I fought,
Your gallant band with anxious eye I sought,
But now I care not, since you are with me,
For all the hosts of Jackson and of Lee."
The veteran spoke, we cheered, the charge he led,
Our bayonets glittered, and the foeman fled,
And unattacked along our road we go,
And stand at Malvern Hill, to meet the foe.

When the sun rose on mountain, vale, and rill,
What scene so lovely as sweet Malvern Hill?
The noble mansion topp'd the gradual slope,
And gave the view variety and scope.
The fertile plain diversified and broke
By graceful fir-tree, and by lordly oak;
The plump sheep fed, and sheaves of heavy grain,
Were frequent piled throughout the broad domain,
While in the rear, the James's [*sic*] River flowed,
Whose winding tide with gorgeous grandeur glowed.

The noon stole on, the beauties of that hour
Ask Titian's coloring and Caracchi's [*sic*] power;
The painter and the poet here might gaze,
Paint scenes sublime and pen immortal lays.
What pity that war's tumults harsh and rude,
Should e'er on this sweet solitude intrude,
That the wild havoc, and sad waste of war,
Should nature's bounties and her beauties mar.

The cannon now resounds, the hurrying drum
Loud beats to arms and tells the foemen come,
Quick forms in line and marches our Brigade,
As gay as if they formed for their parade,
Upon their bayonets bright the sunbeams dance,
The skirmishers come out, spread wide, advance.
The leaders on each side exhaust their skill,
But hours wear on and they but skirmished still.
At length Magruder heads his tiger band,
And boldly seeks to meet us, hand to hand;
Like beasts of prey o'er th' intervening space,
His frantic followers loudly yelling, race.
Quick from our rear impetuous courtiers bound,

Their rapid gallop shakes the echoing ground;
Rushing along, "give way, give way," they cry,
Comes on their heels, the horse Artillery.

They sweep by, while a cloud of dust conceals
The panting horses and the whirling wheels;
Down the steep hill with headlong haste they go,
Wheel round their guns and point them at the foe.
Magruder comes, the word to fire is given,
And gaping earth and quivering man are riven;
A new host rushes o'er the gory plain —
Again the cannon roars, that host is slain.
Once more the desperate charge Magruder led,
Once more the cannon roared, and all lay dead.

The crimson sun was sinking from the sky,
Tinging the light clouds with a saffron dye;
The battle's smoke and the advancing night,
Concealed that sun — those clouds so fair and bright.

'Tis darkness, yet not silence, on the throbbing ear
Peals the war's tumult and the Irish cheer;
Now lurid lightnings through the darkness shine
As the last volley flies from all our line.
Our rifles rattle and our cannons roar,
But to our challenge foes reply no more.

That night we marched, and on the coming morn
In safety camped, held our foiled foes in scorn;
On the damp ground our wearied limbs we toss;
Our comrades welcome, or lament their loss.
From very peril saved, and every ill,
By our own courage, and McClellan's skill.
We leave Virginia's desolated soil,
A desert, where no thrifty peasant's [sic] toil,
Whence the green grass and golden grain have fled —
A country now, the country of the dead.
To fairer scenes we're called away by war.
That loyal State may warfare never mar —
Sweet Maryland, thou brave and peaceful State
'Mid tumult calm, 'mid turbulence sedate.
Were all they sister States true, firm like thee,
This nation from war's ravages were free.
When our lov'd country's madness shall be past

And peace and late repentance come at last,
All shall before thy useful virtues bow,
And own the noblest of her States are thou.
We marched, the land one blooming garden seemed,
With cattle and with grain, the rich land teemed.
A bluer sky, a milder atmosphere,
A halo shed by peace, was beaming there;
The gentlemen we met there frank and warm,
Saw woman's lovely face, and graceful form.

At home, in peace, too little do we prize,
The love-light beaming in fond woman's eyes,
The kind attentions and the gentle tone,
That tell the heart that beats for us alone.
But when in toil and danger far we roam,
From all the comforts and the love of home,
How cold we look upon the sunny sky,
The tree with branches broad, or towering high,
The fairy glen, the river fleet and bright,
And all that nature forms to glad the sight;
Oh! then we own this world a joyless place
Without dear woman's form and angel face.

The promises by the arch plotters made
To their deluded followers, quickly fade;
Where splendor and profusion reigned, that home
Has a sad scene of poverty become.
There's nothing now in all the beggared South,
To clothe the naked back, or feed the mouth,
And Lee and Jackson the sad desert leave,
Rich Maryland to plunder and deceive.
In gangs their hungry followers throng the road,
The baggage that they bear is no great load;
To all they meet, they're most polite and kind,
And scatter proclamations on the wind;
Yet take the people's goods and food away,
And in return give promises to pay;
But no recruits her sturdy patriots give,
And the foiled traitors are compelled to leave.
They leave in haste, they have no time to spare;
They hear McClellan close upon their rear;
They leave a guard his progress to delay,
While the main body flies in fear away.
South Mountain's pass the onward road commands,

And there their strong rear guard for battle stands,
Not long it stands — bold Burnside's rapid horse,
Leads to the charge, th' avenging Union force;
His soldiers following, mount the hill and shout,
Rush to the assault, and the scared rebels rout.

When next morn's sun upon the bright earth burst
We followed fast, our bold Brigade the first —
Ever the first to meet the foe in fight,
Ever the last to guard the rear in flight.
The gladdening peasants crowding to the road,
The path the foemen took, unquestioned showed;
A curious spectacle was witnessed then,
Six thousand following sixty thousand men.
O'ertaken, all their force they mass, and stand;
Without a fight they cannot leave this land:
And a position strong their leader chose,
McClellan's further progress to oppose.

Through rich deep soil the clear Antietam glides,
And tall hills grandly rise on both its sides;
That on the east, like a huge sentinel,
Looks down upon the plain, and western hill.
There, in a wide gap, cut through the tall wood,
Our chief McClellan, through that conflict stood;
Guiding with counsels, ever wise and right,
The varying fortunes of that desperate fight;
While on the west side, Jackson, Hill and Lee
Drew out the flower of Southern chivalry.

The gallant Hooker on our right, the first
Upon the foeman's flank, with fury burst;
Close by his side a lofty hill arose,
Defended by a triple line of foes.
And from that hill those foes to force, was made
The arduous duty of our brave Brigade.
You Irish lads, e'er full of mirth and fun,
How gay your hearts when rose that morning's sun;
With laughter loud you waded through the rill,
With manly bearing, breasted the steep hill;
Beyond that hill a well-protected road,
To aid our foes, a rifle-pit bestowed;
Above its banks they scarcely raise their head,
On our advance they rained a shower of lead;

Down falls the Green Flag, on the crimson plain,
Crowds rush to seize it, and it floats again;
The standard-bearer falls, a third, a score,
Still the unwavering line, it flutters o'er;
An anxious group around McClellan stand,
The spy-glass turned on us from every hand:
An Aide-de-camp cries out in agony —
"The day is lost to us, the Irish fly";
McClellan gazing on the battle scene,
Sees raised again, the glorious flag of green;
Sees, while his eyes with victory's radiance shine,
The volley flying from our closed-up line,
The foe retiring, and exclaims "Hurra[h],
The Irish win the hill, and win the day."
All looked; the Irish on the hill-top stood,
The foe were hid amid the neighboring wood;
What now can Lee, what now can Jackson do?
How 'scape the conquering foeman that pursue,
How back to their homes, can they ever get?
McClellan holds their whole host in a net.

High o'er the river, Harper's [sic] Ferry stands
And from its heights the neighboring roads commands;
A force placed there, the foeman to oppose,
Basely resign that fortress to our foes.
Then Jackson rushed through with his aid to Lee,
And now through it their beaten armies flee:
Oh! had some heroic chief held Bolivar,
The foe were seized, and ended this sad war.

Along the country with proud hopes we go,
With conquest flushed, and careless of the foe,
Already we see Richmond's battered wall
At last before McClellan's genius fall.
When, lo! a letter to our camp is brought,
A letter with terrific misery fraught;
And 'mid his conquests from us is removed —
The chief we trusted in, the man we loved.

Who can forget, while memory holds her power,
The bitter sorrows of that parting hour?
While the old cannon poured his last salute,
Each heart beat wildly, tho' the tongue was mute.
Tremble the standard-bearers, strong and brave,

While the green flags he loved, they sadly waved,
And many an eye that fired at threat'ning death,
Now droops the load of manly tears beneath,
And gratified, yet weighed down by our grief,
A woman's weakness, conquers our brave chief.

Yet we performed the loyal patriot's part,
And marched along with sad foreboding heart.
At Falmouth with the foe's outposts we fight, —
They fly and burn the bridge they crossed in flight;
Sumner at once would o'er the river dash,
But young men think the veteran too rash —
"We'll wait a day, — and cross with the pontoon,
They're ordered 'long, and must be with us soon."
We wait another and another day,
And still the pontoons linger on the way.
Ah! now at last, indeed the tale is true,
The lazy pontoons slowly creep to view,
Yet wait — to cross so early is not fit,
They have not finished quite their rifle-pit.
Wait some days longer till the Richmond train,
Shall bring down corps of chosen men again.
Wait, wait! that stone-wall upon Mary's Hill [sic]
Is not quite finished, Lee is at it still.
Those triple rows they're forming for defense,
Will not be ready for some few days hence.
Now all that Lee and Jackson planned is done,
Now throw the bridge across, and boys charge on.

We crossed the bridge, at our success amazed,
On Fred'ricksburgh [sic] our gallant soldiers seized,
Formed where the railroad thro' the city run,
In streets commanded by the foemen's guns.
Thence thro' the water, up the hill we go,
To fire through stone-walls, at our laughing foe.
Our cannons fire behind us, with great skill,
But fire[,] like water, won't run up the hill,
And Lee and Jackson think it a good joke,
To hear our cannon and to see our smoke.
What crowds of wounded combatants we meet
Hurrying along thro' every dangerous street;
And, oh, what numbers, miserably slain,
Die, unavenged, upon the battle plain;
Yet even there, the Irish won renown,

And with new glory left the riddled town.
The nearest slain, close by the stone-wall gap,
Wore the green box-wood in their Irish cap.

We miss full many of the light of heart,
Who in our perils and our sports took part;
They died, for every man is born to die:
For them we shed no tear, we heave no sigh,
But tell with admiration and with pride,
How well they fought, how gallantly they died.
Is there who wearies Heaven with coward prayer,
His life to age's helplessness to spare?
Who begs this boon, on his sick bed to lie,
And of diseases inch by inch to die?
More glorious was our lost companions' lot,
To fall where raged the battle loud and hot,
And bound from their post on that crimson sod,
Where freedom triumphed, to the breast of God.
Their last gaze fixed upon their flag of green,
Which waved in glory — o'er the battle scene.
And the last sound that feel upon their ears
Their comrades' volley and their comrades' cheers.
Like them we swear to fill a hero's grave,
Like them to perish, or the Union save.

No hatred, no desire of gold accursed,
Called us to mingle in this strife at first,
But human wisdom, human love ne'er planned,
Laws like our laws, a Government so grand;
We shared its glory, and its peril share,
And here before that God, who hears, we swear,
The stars may fall from yon blue vault of Heaven,
But not one Star shall from that flag be riven;
Which o'er his troops, when human rights were won,
Was waved by mankind's hero — Washington.
The earth may melt, the sun the ocean drain,
Those laws shall stand, that Government remain.

Welcome, brave comrades, to our sports to-night,
You whom we met, in many a desperate fight,
Your birth, your valor, and your flag the same,
You're our Brigade in everything but name.
Welcome, you Irish Ninth, come from that shore,
Against whose granite ocean's billows roar;

And ne'er tossed back those billows, that proud rock
As you e'er backward hurled the foeman's shock.
At Gaines' Mill, with what true aim you fired,
What numbers fell, as slowly you retired.
With stubborn strength, you fought thro' all the day,
And kept the numerous foe, in fear away.
And when at eve, our banners topped the hill,
The foeman thought the Ninth opposed them still:
They fled, the green flag which they gazed upon,
And we gained glory, that your prowess won.
At Malvern Hill we saw your heroes pass
From fight, with your lost Colonel — gallant Cass.
Glory and peace to him, who left behind
No bolder spirit, and no nobler mind,
And welcome here, brave Thirty-Seventh, no band
E'er gave more honor to green Erin's land.
Brave Kearney's [sic] pet, the favorites of him
Whose glory makes great heroes' glory dim.
At Williamsburg, how bold you charged the foe;
At Fair Oaks, hosts of foemen you laid low.
Fierce, fierce the fray, and bloody is the work
When charge the Irish Rifles of New York.
Welcome, brave Sixty-Ninth, you gallant band,
That give to fame, fair Pennsylvania's land,
We thank you for your presence here to-night,
We thanked you for your aid in many a fight.
Although you're robbed of glory's envied wreath,
At Savage Station our famed Eighty-Eighth,
They rushed to charge the foe, and end the fight;
They came too late, you put the foe to flight.
But when did brave men ever charge in vain,
When led by such a hero as O'Kane.

Welcome, brave Second, to a merrier scene,
That when at Glendale, waved your flag of green,
When flying foemen hurried from your cheer,
Your voice is much more pleasant to us here.
And welcome Houston [sic], to our sports to-night —
The gay, the gallant, generous and polite.
And last, not least, our bosom friends we see,
Our brave, kind-hearted friends of Tammany.
And welcome Hooker, with a soldier's cheer,
We greet our noblest soldier's presence here;
McClellan's right hand, Valor's favorite son,

The honors that you wear you nobly won.
Full many a gem left California's mine,
But none so precious as that heart of thine:
A heart no danger or no foe can bend,
That none can ever conquer but a friend.
Since by your sway our Army has been blest,
You proved the generous feelings of your breast;
A father's care for every man you showed,
Cared for his comfort, clothing, tent and food;
Shed o'er our gloomy souls a lambent light
And fired our bosoms for the coming fight.
There's not one man, our famed green flag beneath,
But follows thee, to victory or death.
Yet Richmond shall behold her 'leaguered wall
Before the might of Hooker's soldierly fall;
He shall command, the woes of war to cease,
And by his valor give our Country peace:
A hapless fate shall fall upon the foe,
That hears our battle-cry, Hurrah for Joe![118]

After Dr. Reynolds finished his extremely lengthy recitation, Captain John Blake of the 88th New York Infantry sang a song described as the work of "a poetical rival of the doctor's":

*"Song of the Irish Brigade"

We've never swerved from our old green flag,
Upborne o'er many a bloody plain;
'Tis now a torn and tattered rag,
But we will bear it proudly oft again.
We'll raise it high, this dear old flag,
From Liffy's [sic] banks to Shannon's stream,
'Till victory o'er the pirate rag
Upon our sacred cause shall beam.

Chorus:
Hurrah! Hurrah! for our dear old flag,
Hurrah for our gallant leader, too;
Though 'tis a torn and tattered rag,
We would not change it for the new.

We've borne it with the Stripes and Stars,
From Fair Oaks to Frederick's bloody plain;
And see, my boys, our wounds and scars

Can tell how well we did the same.
But sure, our chieftain, of his race,
Was ever foremost 'mid the brave,
Where death met heroes face to face,
And gathered harvests for the grave.

Chorus

We miss full many a comrade's smile,
The grasp of many a friendly hand,
We mourn their loss, and grieve the while
They had not died for fatherland.
But o'er their fresh and gory graves —
We swear it now, and evermore —
To free green Erin, land of slaves,
And banish tyrants from her shore.

Chorus

Now we're pledged to free this land,
So long the exile's resting-place;
To crush for aye a traitorous band,
And wipe out treason's deep disgrace.
Then let us pledge Columbia's cause,
God prosper poor old Ireland, too!
We'll trample on all tyrant laws:
Hurrah for the old land and the new![119]

Although John Savage, the New York journalist, was unable to accept
Meagher's invitation to the St. Patrick's Day celebration, he replied to the
general in a tone both nostalgic and sentimental. The writer first alluded
to Meagher's and his own participation in the unsuccessful uprising in
Ireland in 1848. Then Savage wrote that the invitation had reminded him
"that at a time of great civil war, when the best government devised by
man was waylaid by the most stupendous treason — when the fate not
only of that government, but the hopes and blessings its example kindled
and its success sustained, was at stake, the Irish rushed in thousands to
the standard of Democratic government and civilization." The journalist
ended his reminiscing with a wish: "Long live the Republic, one and indi-
visible. May the Irish citizens as well deserve its honors in peace, as the
Irish Brigade has won them in the war for its defence."[120]
        Although the disastrous fate which the Irish Brigade had suffered at
Fredericksburg was no longer foremost in the men's thoughts, the memory
was still fresh in the mind of Kate M. Boylan of Jersey City, New Jersey. In

a poem dated March 17, 1863, she eulogized the Irish soldiers who had fallen on the field of battle three months before. (The poem was printed in the *Irish-American* in New York City on May 2, 1863.)

*"The Irish Dead on Fredericksburg Heights"

Softly let thy footprints fall,
Upon this holy ground,
In reverence deep,
For those who sleep,
Beneath each lowly mound.

Here hath many a noble son,
Of trodden mother land,
Whose joy thro' life,
Was hope of strife[,]
For their love of native land.

They came from Carlow's fertile plains,
And Wexford's woody vales,
From Innisbowen,
And green Tyrone,
And Wicklow's hill and dales.

They came to seek amid the free,
Homes to reward their toil,
In which to see
That Liberty
Unknown on Erin's soil.

And well they loved the chosen land;
When menaced was her might,
Each grateful heart
A willing part
Took in her cause to fight.

And here they lie in unblessed earth,
No kindred eye to weep;
Far, far away,
From the abbey's [*sic*] grey[,]
Where their sires and grandsires sleep.

Oh! many a matron, many a maid,
Mourn in their native isle,

> For the dear ones here,
> Who no more shall cheer
> Their hearts by their gladsome smile.
>
> In many an ancient chapel there,
> Nestled on the green hill side,
> Will the good priest pray,
> On the Sabbath day,
> For his boys who in battle died.
>
> Let us offer[,] too, our orisons,
> For each of the martyr band,
> Who nobly gave
> Their lives to save
> The might of their adopted land.[121]

At the end of April 1863, General Joseph Hooker was so confident of his numerical strength — 104,000 to Lee's 60,000 — that he ordered an ambitious offensive. Within days he brought his troops south across the Rappahannock and threatened Lee's rear. But, like McClellan before him, Hooker lost his nerve and failed to press his advantage. This failure of resolve allowed "Stonewall" Jackson to strike first at the Union's right flank and then at its center, hoping thereby to seize control of the area around Chancellorsville. On May 3, as thirty Rebel cannon pounded the Union line, they met only token response from a battery of six guns belonging to the Fifth Maine Regiment. In the inevitable Union retreat which followed, the 116th Pennsylvania saved the guns of the Maine battery by dragging them off the battlefield, while the rest of the Irish Brigade provided its customary support to yet another withdrawal. The Rebel losses amounted to 12,000; the Union's, 16,000. The Brigade, which had numbered 520 men at the beginning of the engagement, suffered 102 casualties. Father Corby summed up the failed campaign with a tinge of irony: "We accomplished little — sent a few souls to heaven, exceedingly rejoiced, it may be, to be out of this wicked world — and our only consolation was that, as far as human weakness goes, we had all tried to do our duty to our fellow-man in his time of need, either of body or soul."[122]

During the renewed battle of May 4–5 occurred two incidents which won for *Major St. Clair Mulholland, the commander of the 116th Pennsylvania, the Congressional Medal of Honor. The Confederates had set fire to the woods in front of the Second Corps line, hoping that the wind would spread the flames to the Union position. General Hancock had repeatedly ordered his men to extinguish the flames, but every effort failed, the aim of the enemy's sharpshooters proving deadly. By the afternoon, when the flames had come within fifty feet of the Union abatis, Hancock asked Mulholland to take command of the picket line and from there try to extinguish the fire. Hancock's brother, Major John Hancock, later wrote that "Mulholland formed squads of men, and, by showing great personal bravery in leading them into the flames, succeeded in beating out the fire and saving our line." Later, when General Hancock decided that it would be necessary to sacrifice some officers and men in order to safely withdraw his army from the field, Mulholland either volunteered for the assignment or was ordered to accept it. According to one source, Hancock *ordered* the Irish officer to remain in command of the picket line and to keep up a continuous fire during the night until the army had recrossed the river. Hancock's brother, however, emphasized the voluntary nature of the assignment in his description of the outcome: "Major Mulholland volunteered to do so with the distinct understanding that he should remain and be captured by the enemy; and, after accepting the trust, a promise was made him in my presence, that the Government should tender him suitable recognition for the sacrifice. He held the enemy in check on the picket line until seven o'clock on the morning of the 5th, when, all the Army being safely over the Rappahannock, he was notified that he might abandon the line. He then succeeded in saving nearly all the pickets and getting them over the river. Major Mulholland was not captured by the enemy, but it was not his fault that he escaped. He remained on the picket line in good faith, until the whole army had re-crossed the river, and with the understanding that he would be left in the hands of the enemy."[123]

Having received no reply to his requests to recruit more men for the Irish Brigade, Meagher finally resigned as brigadier general in a letter to divisional headquarters. In that missive he repeated his intention not to endanger the lives of his men, now reduced in number to about 500. (The three New York regiments originally had about 2,500.) In a moving speech on May 19, he bade adieu to the Brigade, but not without first expressing the "gratitude and pride with which I revert to the first days of the Irish Brigade, when it struggled in its infancy and was sustained alone by its native strength and instinct." He then described the source of his men's intense loyalty to him: his habit of "Sharing with the humblest soldier freely and heartily all the hardships and dangers of the battle-field — never having ordered an advance that I did not take the lead myself." He ended his remarks with the promise "that, as long as there remains one officer or soldier of the Irish Brigade, so long shall there be found for him, for his family and little ones, if any there be, a devoted friend in Thomas Francis Meagher." The general then walked along the lines, shaking each soldier by the hand, before turning over command of the Brigade to Colonel Patrick Kelly of the 88th New York. Later that month the officers of the three New York regiments expressed their sorrow at the loss of their commander in a printed farewell address. The noncommissioned officers of the 88th New York pledged their loyalty to Meagher, saying that they would "always rally at your call around that flag for which you have sacrificed so much, and braved so many dangers." The officers of the 116th Pennsylvania, meanwhile, grieved over the loss of a leader whom they would have followed to death, if necessary — "a leader whose name was sufficient to strike terror into the hearts of his foes, and excite admiration in the hearts of his copatriots [*sic*] in arms." The memorial went on to say that Meagher possessed the qualities of a true soldier — "when on duty a strict disciplinarian, and when off duty an affable, agreeable, and kind companion."[124]

Colonel Patrick Kelly, the Brigade's new commander, was a native of Ireland, having been born in Castlehackett, County Galway, in 1821. He came to America at the age of twenty-nine and settled in New York, where his wife died in 1858. When civil war engulfed the nation, Kelly joined the 69th New York State Militia, quickly becoming lieutenant of Company E. By the end of 1861, he had been named lieutenant colonel of the 88th New York and by the following October its colonel. Captain William O'Grady of the 88th — a former officer in the Royal Marines Light Infantry Battalion — left an interesting description of his commanding officer: "He was not a large man to look at, but his looks were deceiving. He had the physique of a Hercules, broad and deep-chested. He was handsome, with a noble forehead, brilliant black eyes, fine nose, the blackest hair and beard and a dark complexion — which is not uncommon among the people of Galway and Limerick, who in old days, were socially and politically in close alliance with Spain."[125]

The succession of Union defeats and a growing antiwar sentiment in the East prompted General Robert E. Lee to plan another offensive into the North, this time through Pennsylvania. Toward the end of June the Confederate commander moved his entire army into Maryland and by June 28 had arrived in York and Carlisle in southern Pennsylvania. In the meantime, General Hooker had left the Rappahannock and moved the Army of the Potomac north as far as Frederick, Maryland. En route, the Irish Brigade halted briefly during a downpour on the battlefield at Bull Run. There the men noticed that the steady rain had washed away the soil to expose the remains of the soldiers killed and buried there almost two years before. Following a disagreement with his superiors in Washington, Hooker was replaced by General George Gordon Meade. The new commander was a descendant of an old Irish family in Philadelphia and had been wounded in the Peninsular Campaign. He had led a division at Antietam and Fredericksburg and had commanded a corps at Chancellorsville. The men in the Irish Brigade no doubt welcomed Meade's appointment, but they were also cheered by what turned out to be a false rumor that McClellan — their special favorite — had been restored to command.[126]

By July 1 the Union's Second Corps, including the Irish Brigade, had arrived at Taneytown, Maryland, not far from the Pennsylvania border.

The Brigade now numbered 530 men: the three New York regiments totaled 240, the 28th Massachusetts counted 224 men available, and the 116th
Pennsylvania had only sixty-six. Near Taneytown the officers of the Second Corps learned that the Confederates had driven the First Corps and
the Eleventh Corps back through the town of Gettysburg. In response,
Hancock took up a strong defensive position on Cemetery Hill near that
southern Pennsylvania town.[127]

At dawn on July 2, the Irish Brigade, along with the rest of the Second
Corps, filed off toward Gettysburg and halted near the Union defensive
line at Cemetery Hill and Cemetery Ridge. The corps was soon moved
into position on Cemetery Ridge between Major General Sickles' Third
Corps and components of the ill-fated First and Eleventh Corps. The Confederates, meanwhile, had established themselves on a ridge about a mile
to the southwest, beyond which lay a wheatfield and a peach orchard.
About midday Sickles led his 10,000 men from Cemetery Ridge and the
Round Tops toward the Peach Orchard. The resulting gap left the Second
Corps' left flank — and the Irish Brigade — vulnerable, a situation which
worsened when Sickles' men retreated under attack from Lieutenant General James Longstreet's Confederate corps of almost 15,000. To cover the
Third Corps' unprotected flanks, Meade sent out Sykes's Fifth Corps and
ordered Caldwell's First Division, which included the Irish Brigade, to
prepare to support Sykes.[128]

The Brigade was ready to move at about 4:30 p.m. Shortly thereafter
Colonel Kelly asked Father William Corby to give the men general absolution. In a letter which the priest wrote in 1879, he recorded his recollec-
tion of his words to the assembled troops that day: "My dear Christian
friends! In consideration of the want of time for each one to confess his
sins in due order as required for the reception of the sacrament of pen-
ance, I will give you general absolution. But my dear friends[,] while we
stand here in the presence of eternity — so to speak — with a well[-]armed
force in front and with missiles of death in the form of shells bursting over
our heads, we must humble ourselves before the Great Creator of all men
and acknowledge our unworthiness and conceive a heartfelt sorrow for
the sins by which we ungratefully offended the Divine Author of all good
things . . . ."[129]

Twenty-six years later St. Clair Mulholland, the Irish-born commander
of the 116th Pennsylvania Regiment, recalled the scene. His account is
rich in imagery: "Father Corby stood upon a large rock in front of the
brigade. Addressing the men, he explained what he was about to do, saying that each one could receive the benefit of the absolution by making a
sincere act of contrition and firmly resolving to embrace the first opportunity of confessing their sins, urging them to do their duty well, and reminding them of the high and sacred nature of their trust as soldiers and
the noble object for which they fought, ending by saying that the Catholic

church refuses Christian burial to the soldier who turns his back upon the foe or deserts his flag. The brigade was standing at 'order arms', and as he closed his address, every man fell on his knees with head bowed down. Then, stretching his right hand toward the brigade, Father Corby pronounced the words of the general absolution, *Dominus noster Jesus Christus vos absolvat, et ego, auctoritate ipsius, vos absolvo ab omni vinculo excommunicationis et interdicti in quantum possum et vos indigetis; deinde, ego vos absolvo a peccatis vestris in nomine Patris, et Filii, et Spiritus Sancti. Amen!* [May our Lord Jesus Christ absolve you, and I, by his authority, absolve you from every bond of excommunication and interdict as far as I am able and you have need; moreover, I absolve you of your sins in the name of the Father and of the Son and of the Holy Spirit. Amen.] The scene was more than impressive, it was awe-inspiring. Nearby stood Hancock, surrounded by a brilliant array of officers, who had gathered to witness this very unusual occurrence, and while there was profound silence in the ranks of the Second Corps, yet over to the left, out by the peach orchard and Little Round Top, where *Weed, Vincent and Hazlett were dying, the roar of the battle rose and swelled and re-echoed through the woods, making music more sublime than ever sounded through cathedral aisles. The act seemed to be in harmony with all the surroundings. I do not think there was a man in the brigade who did not offer up a heartfelt prayer. For some it was their last; they knelt there in their grave clothes — in less than half an hour many of them were numbered with the dead of July 2d. Who can doubt that their prayers were good? What was wanting in the eloquence of the priest to move them to repentance was supplied in the incidents of the fight. That heart would be incorrigible, indeed, that the scream of a *Whitworth bolt, added to Father Corby's touching appeal, would not move to contrition."[130]

Two additional accounts illustrate the significance which both the chaplain and the typical soldier accorded the unusual scene. In his *Memoirs of Chaplain Life*, Father Corby shed light on his intentions during that historic moment: "In performing this ceremony I faced an army. My eye covered thousands of officers and men. I noticed that *all*, Catholic and non-Catholic, officers and private soldiers showed a profound respect, wishing at this fatal crisis to receive every benefit of divine grace that could be imparted through the instrumentality of the Church ministry. Even Maj. Gen. Hancock removed his hat, and, as far as compatible with the situation, bowed in reverential devotion. That general absolution was intended for all — *in quantum possum* [as far as I am able] — not only for our brigade, but for all, North or South, who were susceptible of it and who were about to appear before their Judge. Let us hope that many thousands of souls purified by hardships, fasting, prayer, and blood, met a favorable sentence on the ever memorable battlefield of Gettysburg." Private Robert Laird Stewart of the 140th Pennsylvania witnessed Father Corby's absolution and recalled the sight many years later as a Presbyterian minister: "At a given signal every man of the command fell on his knees and with head bowed low received from him the sacrament of extreme unction [sic]. Instinctively every man of our Regiment took off his cap and no doubt many a prayer from men of Protestant faith, who could conscientiously not bow the knee in a service of that nature, went up to God in that impressive and awe-inspiring moment. . . ."[131]

Following this rarely seen religious rite, the Irish Brigade advanced down Cemetery Ridge, ordered to support Sykes's hard-pressed Fifth Corps, itself sent in earlier to help cover the Third Corps' exposed flank. When Confederate batteries near the Peach Orchard opened fire, though, the Brigade moved to the left and reached the valley in front of Little Round Top. When the Irish were about twenty yards from Stony Hill, a belt of woods at the edge of the Wheatfield, they came under heavy fire from the 800 men in General Joseph Kershaw's Third and Seventh South Carolina infantry regiments. But since the Carolinians were shooting down a slope, they overshot their mark, thereby allowing the Brigade to reply with a devastating volley. After climbing the hill, the Irishmen found the crest covered with enemy dead. The fighting continued into the woods, where the Brigade killed four color-bearers from the Third South Carolina. Although some of the Confederates surrendered, fresh Rebel troops rushed out of the Peach Orchard and soon flanked the Irish Brigade. In addition, the remains of Kershaw's South Carolina Brigade and Semme's Brigade threatened the Irishmen's other flank.[132]

The Irish Brigade's only chance of escape was through the Wheatfield. Their line of flight, however, was flanked by Confederates, whose ranks were so close together that the rebels were firing into one another. Seven or eight men from the 116th Pennsylvania were probably killed in the flight through the Wheatfield. The 116th's most conspicuous casualty was Martin Gallagher — nicknamed "Jersey" by his comrades — who fell to the ground with a broken leg. Although he was subsequently struck six or eight more times as he lay in the field, he eventually recovered from all his wounds. When Captain Richard Moroney, the commander of the 69th New York, was wounded, Lieutenant James Smith of County Monaghan, Ireland, assumed command of the regiment. Colonel Richard Byrnes, meanwhile, re-formed the 28th Massachusetts and joined the other remnants of the Brigade. The cost to the Brigade was high: 202 killed, wounded, and missing — almost 40 percent of its strength. The 28th Massachusetts suffered the most, losing almost half of its men. Despite these losses the Brigade had cleared the Wheatfield, at least blunted the Carolinians' assault, and gained valuable time for Hancock to reinforce the Union left. Later that afternoon Hancock ordered the Brigade and the rest of Caldwell's division back to Cemetery Ridge, not far from their original position.[133]

At 1 p.m. the following day, July 3, the Brigade watched from its vantage point as the Southern artillery on Seminary Ridge opened fire on the Union troops along Cemetery Ridge. For two hours 147 field guns blasted the Union center, preparatory to an infantry attack by General George Pickett. Among the Union artillery units which replied in kind was Battery B, First New York Light Artillery, a unit made up of 114 men and four Parrott guns and commanded by Captain James McKay Rorty. (This native of County Donegal had originally been a member of the 69th New York State Militia and later of the Second Battalion of the New York Light Artillery, the little-known fifth regiment of the Irish Brigade.) That afternoon, as Confederate artillery supported Pickett's Charge against Cemetery Ridge, all the guns in Rorty's battery were damaged, three beyond use. Stripping down to shirtsleeves, Rorty helped his crew man their last remaining cannon. After observing Rorty's actions, Colonel James Mallon of the 42nd New York rushed up to the captain and cried out to him, "Rorty, you're the bravest man I have ever seen or heard of!"[134]

Sometime before the last futile Confederate charge up Cemetery Ridge, however, Rorty was struck dead. Although he was first buried near where he fell, his remains were later exhumed and reburied in Calvary Cemetery in Woodside, Queens, Long Island. Captain David Conyngham expressed the general sentiment by calling Rorty "one whose Spartan heroism would shed a lustre upon the brightest days of chivalry. . . . Rorty was not only a true soldier, but devoted heart and soul to the cause of Ireland." In 1993 Rorty's weather-beaten grave stone was replaced by a new one, engraved with the words of John Hazard, another artillery brigade commander at Gettysburg, describing the fallen Rorty as "a worthy officer, a gallant soldier, and an estimable man."[135]

Rorty was further immortalized in *"Captain O'Hay," a poem written by Michael Scanlon, a member of the Fenian Brotherhood, and published in 1887. Scanlon dedicated the poem to Rorty, "the gallant and patriotic soldier whom I had in mind at its first writing."

> The long day of battle and carnage was over,
> The Spirit of Silence came down with the night
> And spread her cool mantle of shadow to cover
> The wrath and the wreck of the day from our sight;
> The hour had passed nine and a truce had been sounded
> — Which smote, with its sweetness, our passion and pride —
> As we marched, sad and silent, to bring in the wounded,
> And bury the dead as they fell side by side.
>
> The new-risen wind swept the clouds from the night,
> And the stars, like the eyes of sad angels, look'd forth,
> And the field of the dead by the pale moon was lightened —
> Alas, for the moon-lighted homes in the North!

And full in the moonbeams a cannon seemed keeping
Its sentinel watch o'er the dead of the day,
And over it leaning a soldier seemed sleeping:
He raised up his head — it was Captain O'Hay!

Captain O'Hay was a soldier from Erin
Whose pulse beat unchanged in success or defeat;
His was a spirit which never knew fear in
The first in attack and the last in retreat;
His voice loud in fight like a trumpet's assailing
The red front of war with inspiring disdain,
Stole over the heart in sweet numbers bewailing
The days when his country was Freedom's domain.

His eye with its old battle fire gave us greeting,
But greeting which presaged sore travail of mind,
When he spoke we all knew that his brave heart was beating
Forced marches to leave some fond message behind:
Death had him at bay, but awaited surrender,
Nor sought that surrender by sudden assault;
The purpose which blazoned his soul's dying splendor
Had brought the grim despot lance-poised to a halt!

"I'm glad that you've come, for my spirit is pluming
Its wings for its flight to the grand camp above;
Ah, the long weary hours I have waited your coming
To leave you a soldier's last message of love!
The rage of the tempest which swept our position
Soon left me alone with my boys dead and true;
In sighting this gun I received new commission —
Already I hear the drums beating tattoo!

By the links which were forged in the furnace of danger,
Dear comrades, nay, brothers, baptized in the grand
Red font of Freedom, you'll think of the stranger
Who fought 'neath your banner and died for your land!
But know in the mess when his heart seemed the lightest,
And he sang those gay songs, had his soul been in tears,
When his spirits were wildest his eyes sparkled brightest!
'Twas the mem'ry and fire of the long vanished years.

How oft in the rattat of musketry's rattle,
When this cannon belch'd fire and death at his command,
Has he prayed that his life might go out in some battle

On his own native hills for his own native land:
When thro' the green valleys the war-cry is sounding,
And bugle blasts ring in the long-looked-for day,
And the men of my land down the hillsides come bounding[,]
Who'll answer the roll-call for Captain O'Hay?"

A dozen bright sabres flew out of their sheathing,
A dozen bronzed lips kissed them, each shouting, "I!"
He looked to the stars, but he looked there unbreathing,
His spirit had passed from the earth to the sky.
Tho' mustered for death — tho' we knew death had made him
A figure to shine 'mid his spirit compeers —
Tho' the red field was burdened with heroes — we paid him
The soldier's last honors in silence and tears.

We dug him a grave near his own shining cannon,
And laid him therein with his sword by his side,
Far away from his home by the fair flowing Shannon,
In the strength of his years and the flush of his pride;
Brave hearts and high souls shrined in song and in story,
Went out, Gettysburg, in thy fierce bloody fray,
But no spirit took wing from thy red tide of glory
More bold than the spirit of Captain O'Hay![136]

Twenty-five years later the nation's attention was once again focused on Gettysburg. On July 2, 1888, 126 veterans of the Irish Brigade gathered on the famous battlefield to dedicate a memorial to the Brigade's three New York regiments. The monument, in the shape of a Celtic cross, specifically honors the 63rd, the 69th, and the 88th New York regiments, which initially formed the Irish Brigade. The cross is made of green malachite emblazoned with a bronze front, which in turn is decorated with five medallions. Three medallions bear the emblems of the New York regiments in the Brigade, while the other two medallions represent Ireland (a sunburst) and New York (the state's coat of arms). The cross is also adorned with a harp guarded by two American eagles, and at the base of the cross lies an Irish wolfhound, the symbol of fidelity and courage. The monument was sculpted by William O'Donovan, who, ironically, had been a corporal in the Confederate army at Gettysburg and had seen earlier action against the Irish Brigade in engagements from Bull Run to Appomattox.[137]

A plaque on the reverse side of the monument describes the composition of the Brigade at Gettysburg: "The Brigade entered the battle under command of Colonel Patrick Kelly 530 strong, of which this contingent, composing three battalions of two companies each, numbered 240 men. The original strength of these battalions was 3,000 men. The Brigade participated with great credit to itself and the race it represented, in every battle of the Army of the Potomac in which the Second Corps was engaged, from Fair Oaks, June 1, 1862, to Appomattox Court House, April 9, 1865." Another plaque on the memorial honors Captain James McKay Rorty and the 14th Independent Battery, New York Light Artillery. Rorty had been a member of the 69th New York State Militia, and the 14th had

*The Irish Brigade Monument in Gettysburg National Military Park.*

originally been known as the Second Battalion of the New York Light Artillery, the Irish Brigade's little-known fifth regiment. At Gettysburg Rorty commanded the men of Battery B, First New York Light Artillery, by then consolidated with the 14th New York Independent Battery. Although at Gettysburg the 14th New York was no longer attached to the Irish Brigade, some of its men had once been part of that gallant unit.[138]

During the dedication, General Denis Burke, a native of County Cork and only twenty-two when he commanded the 88th New York at Gettysburg, spoke from a future perspective. He described the Irish Brigade Monument as "an emblem of Ireland, typical of faith and devotion, and the most appropriate that could be raised to hand down to posterity the bravery of our race in the great cause of American liberty. . . ." In the coming years, he predicted, the monument would tell "those who shall come after us how bravely their fathers battled and bled for the old flag and human liberty! And as the sympathetic ivy clings around it and the turf is worn by the footsteps of Freedom's worshippers who shall visit her, it will stand a shrine at whose footstool the patriot shall be buoyed with hope, and those who are yet slaves in their native land will be nerved with earnest and impassioned valor to meet the foeman [sic] who oppress them, as did the brigade and their comrades on this field of renown where the liberties of the Nation were saved and perpetuated for the glory and benefit of millions yet unborn."[139]

Following General Burke's oration that day, Father William Corby and Father Thomas Ouellet, the former chaplains, respectively, of the 88th and the 69th New York regiments, blessed the monument. Later during the dedication ceremony, William Collins and William Geoghegan recited the following poems of their own composition:

*"Our Fallen Comrades"
*In Memory of the Fallen Dead of the Irish Brigade*
by William Collins

Peace spreads her wings of snowy white
O'er Gettysburg to-day;
No sound is heard of coming fight,
No marshaling for the fray;
War's grim battalions dream no more
At morn the foe to greet;
The long, long, fitful strife is o'er,
And we as comrades meet.

We meet in love; and, hand in hand,
Above our brothers' graves,
We pledge true fealty to the land

O'er which our banner waves;
But while its folds in glory swell
And proudly flaunt the air
We think of those who fought and fell
To keep it floating there!

Of those who in their manhood died
To blot out Slavery's stain,
And rear aloft in all its pride
Fair Freedom's flag again!
'Tis ours to raise this cross on high
Above the Irish dead,
Who showed mankind the way to die,
When Truth and Freedom led.

They came from a land where Freedom was only known by fame;
Where Slavery's spell, like a breath of Hell, had banned and barred her
name;
Where the brave man moaned in fetters, and the patriot wept in thrall,
And red with the blood of martyrs the despot ruled o'er all!
But when on Freedom's soil they stood and saw her banner soar,
And heard the foeman's mustering shout re-echo on our shore,
They leaped, as leaps the lightning's flash athwart the storm-tossed sky,
For that old flag with bosoms bare, to triumph or to die!

This soil is the grave of heroes — it is not common mold!
Each foot is dyed and sanctified with the blood of the brave and bold;
And an incense rises from their graves to light us on to fame,
And mingles in each patriot soul and sets his heart aflame,
And nerves the veriest slave that e'er shrank from a tyrant foe
To leap to life with armed hand,  and give him blow for blow —
To strike the despot to the death though bulwarked round in steel,
And right, with fierce and desperate strength, the wrongs that brave
men feel!

Here, on the field of Gettysburg, where treason's banner flew;
Where rushed in wrath the Southern gray to smite the Northern blue;
Where'er that blue, by valor nerved, in serried ranks was seen
There flashed between it and the foe the daring Irish Green!
And never yet, on any land, rushed forth to Freedom's aid
A braver or more dauntless band than Ireland's brave Brigade.
Pause on their graves! 'Tis holy dust ye tread upon to-day —
The dust of Freedom's martyred dead, whose souls have passed away!

No more the ringing bugle blast
Shall fright the trembling air;
No more the squadron's hurrying fast
To meet the charge — perchance their last —
Amid the battle's glare;
Their pride, their strength — all, all are past.
In peace they slumber there,
And comrades true beside them lie,
Who oft, on field and flood,
Fought in the strife for Liberty
And sealed their faith in blood;
But never yet beat hearts as proud
As those which Ireland gave.
Night's sable mantle was their shroud,
The battlefield their grave!

But though from earth have passed away
Their spirits bold and true,
And tombed in cold and senseless clay
The hearts that bounded warm and gay
In war's wild wassail — every fray
Where men could dare and do —
Their deeds will shine in Freedom's ray,
While tyrants stand appalled;
Their name and fame shall last for aye,
And brighter burn from day to day
Till the sun sinks into eternity,
And the Judgment Roll is called![140]

---

*"The Irish Brigade at Gettysburg"
*Respectfully Dedicated to the Surviving Veterans of that Famous Corps*
by William Geoghegan

O comrades, step with reverent tread
Tow'rd this historic mound;
The soil that soaks the brave man's blood
Is always holy ground.
Here five and twenty years ago
An Irish phalanx stood.
And here they swelled the battle tide
With generous Celtic blood.

Thro' many a fierce, ensanguined fight

Two banners o'er them flew —
The emblems of the land they left
And the land they came unto;
No stain e'er fell on either's folds —
No foeman e'er could say
He'd plucked a tassel from those staffs
Or snatched a shred away.

Though rent and splintered, flags and staffs —
With foemen face to face —
Above the vanguard's fire-swept line
Those flags maintained their place,
And out of Stonewall Jackson's lips
The wrathful sentence drew:
"There goes that damned green flag again
Beside the Yankee blue!"

On Fair Oaks field, on Marye's heights,
Thro' Fredericksburg's dread days,
Well, well, the Southland's veterans knew
Those blended banner's blaze.
Where'er the fight was desperate
And spears struck fire from spears,
Those flags flashed out above the lines
Of the Irish Brigadiers.

The war drum's throb and bugle sound
Ye loved to hear is o'er —
The damp, cold earth is heaped above
Your hearts forevermore;
But memory of your gallant deeds
Enlivens, stirs, and thrills,
Like echoes of a clarion call
Around Killarney's hills.[141]

On a ridge not far from the Irish Brigade Monument at Gettysburg stand memorials to the 28th Massachusetts and the 116th Pennsylvania, the other two regiments associated with the Brigade. The 28th Massachusetts Monument was dedicated in 1886 to honor the largest unit in the Irish Brigade at Gettysburg. During that turning point in the war, the 224 men in this Massachusetts unit were commanded by Colonel Richard Byrnes. The monument incorporates an eagle, an Irish harp, and the Gaelic phrase *Faugh A Ballaugh* ("Clear the Way"). The memorial was created by

Austin Ford, whose father, Sergeant John Ford of the Ninth Massachusetts, was killed at Gettysburg. The 116th Pennsylvania Monument is the work of J. Henderson Kelly and was dedicated in 1889. This unusual memorial depicts a dead soldier lying near a shattered stone wall, his rifle and cap nearby. Commanded at Gettysburg by Major St. Clair Mulholland, the 116th Pennsylvania – with approximately sixty-six men – was one of the smallest infantry regiments in the Army of the Potomac.[142]

A historical marker near these two memorials summarizes the Irish Brigade's role at Gettysburg:

*Army of the Potomac • Second Corps*
*First Division • Second Brigade*
*Col. Patrick Kelly • 28th Massachusetts*
*63d (2 cos.), 69th (2 cos.), 88th (2 cos.), New York*
*116th (4 cos.) Pennsylvania Infantry*

*July 2: Arrived at 7 a.m. and took position on line from Cemetery Hill to Round Top at the right of First Brigade. Between 5 and 6 p.m. went with Division to left First Brigade on the left Third Brigade on right. Engaged the Confederate forces, including Brig. Gen. Anderson's Brigade, Major Gen. Hood's Division, in the Wheatfield and forced them through the field southerly into woods beyond, capturing many prisoners. The Fourth Brigade having advanced on the left, this Brigade held its position until the Division, being flanked on right and left, retired and resumed former position in line of the Corps. July 3: Constructed breastworks and remained entrenched until the close of the battle. Casualties: Killed, 1 officer, 28 men. Wounded, 4 officers, 105 men. Captured or missing, 2 officers, 60 men. Total 198.*[143]

Elsewhere on the battlefield is a statue of Father William Corby, sculpted by Samuel Aloysius Murray and dedicated in 1910. The statue depicts the chaplain of the 88th New York Regiment in the act of granting general absolution to the members of the Irish Brigade just before they went into battle on July 2, 1863. The famous Irish-American priest is the subject of the following two poems:

*"Father Corby" by James J. Creswell

All day, up Round Top's crested crown,
Two armor'd hosts are led;
Two banners wave, as night goes down,
Each over its soldier dead.
For far away, o'er ridge and slope,
The lone Palmetto tree
Still cheers those rebel lines to hope,
Their leader, gallant Lee.

Old Gettysburg to-day must stand,

The 28th Massachusetts
Infantry Monument
at Gettysburg.

The 116th Pennsylvania
Infantry Monument
at Gettysburg.

Or with the flag go down!
Thus vow'd our boys of Northern land,
To save that loyal town.
Our fathers' flag — to heroes given —
To-day shall wave *their* deed;
Shall wave each fold in sight of heaven!
Thus spoke our dauntless Mead [*sic*].

Fall in! the thundering guns sing loud,
Thro' morning's peaceful air;
Fall in! a soldier needs no shroud.
No time for soldier pray'r.
A moment Nugent's men may rest,
To jest or laugh the while,
Each folds upon a loyal breast
The Green of his loved Isle.

A moment — 'neath yon shelving stone —
Within that awful field —
Those heroes bend in deep atone,
While Death's dark shadows yield;
A soldier-priest, with hands extend
Absolves their sins! Forgiven —
Short shrift was theirs, Faith makes amend
Beneath approving heaven.

Forward! Thro' bristling lines of steel
Their gory work soon done,
The shattered columns backward reel
Our field to-day is won;
To-night the moon's pale rays shall rest —
Each in his narrow bed —
To-morrow flowers with perfume prest
We garland round our dead!

Old Gettysburg yet lives to tell
When night each star bends down,
How rebel hail of shot and shell,
Plow'ed thro' that loyal town.
And well hath Gettysburg relied
On soldier boys' brave deed
While little Round Top points with pride
To Corby's loyal creed.[144]

*Statue of Father William Corby at Gettysburg.*

\*"A Miracle of War" by Smith Johnson

Two armies stood in stern array
On Gettysburg's historic field —
This side the blue, on that the gray —
Each side resolved to win the day,
Or life to home and country yield.

"Take arms!" "Fall in!" rang o'er the line
Of Hancock's ever-valiant corps —
For to the left the cannons chime
With music terribly sublime,
With death's unceasing, solemn roar.

With spirits ardent, undismayed,
With flags uplifted toward the sky,
There stands brave Meagher's old brigade

Those noble laurels ne'er will fade
Upon the page of history.

"All forward, men!" No, pause a while —
Dead silence follows like parade
At "order arms," for 'long the file
There moves a priest with holy smile —
The priest of Meagher's old brigade.

All eyes were toward him reverent turned,
For he was known and loved by all,
And every face with fervor burned,
And with a glance his mission learned —
A mission of high Heaven's call.

Then spake the priest: "My comrades, friends,
Ere long the battle fierce will surge,
Ere long the curse of war descends —
At such a moment God commends
You from the soul all sin to purge.

"Kneel, soldiers; lift your hearts to God,
In sweet contrition crush the pride
Of human minds; kneel on the sod
That soon will welter in your blood —
Look up to Christ, Who for you died."

And every man, whate'er his creed,
Kneels down, and whispers pass along
The ranks, and murmuring voices plead
To be from sin's contagion freed
And turned from path of mortal wrong.

Across the vale the gray lines view
The priest and those who, kneeling now,
For absolution humbly sue,
And joining hearts, the gray and blue,
Together make the holy vow.

The smoke of battle lifts apace,
And o'er the field lie forms of men,
With glazen eyes and pallid face —
Dead — yet alive, for God's sweet grace.
Has saved them, from the death of sin.[145]

In 1903 St. Clair Mulholland expressed the feelings which Gettysburg ultimately aroused in Americans: "The field is fast becoming the National Mecca, and year after year the number of visitors to the ground increases until tens of thousands of Americans annually make a pilgrimage to the holy ground and worship at the shrine where so many noble men laid down their lives in defence of the State and cause.... Glorious Gettysburg! where five thousand of the bravest and best of the soldier-citizens sleep in honored graves on the field their valor won, is the National Sanctuary, the Pantheon, the Westminster of the Republic. No kings, princes or potentates lie here, but five thousand gallant men, greater than kings, more splendid in their deeds and in their death than any of the princes or great ones who slumber within the fretted walls of Europe's grand old cathedrals — fathers, brothers and kinsmen, men who came from eighteen states to shed their blood on Pennsylvania's soil in defence of the Union and human liberty. No wonder, then, that year by year thousands of Americans visit the field, linger on the long line of battle, dwell on the memories of the fight and meditate upon the heroism displayed in the battle."[146]

A week after the Union victory at Gettysburg, the nation's attention turned to the draft riots in New York City. The violence, which began on July 13 and lasted for three days, expressed the Irish community's opposition to two new developments. Many Irish perceived the new draft law as fundamentally unfair and resented the fact that the war to restore the Union had been transformed into a crusade to free the Southern slaves. The Irish particularly objected to a provision of the draft law which allowed wealthy conscripts to evade service by paying $300. In addition, Irish laborers feared that former slaves would flood the North looking for work and would quickly take their jobs. Just the previous spring, freed slaves had been used in New York to break a strike mounted by longshoremen and stevedores.[147]

The first drawing of names occurred in New York's Ninth Congressional District on Saturday, July 11, with the posting of 1,200 names, the majority of them Irish working poor. Though that event took place without major incident, when the draft resumed on the following Monday a mob attacked the draft office, burning the enrollment books and setting fire to the building. The mob prevented firemen from hooking up their hoses and fought with policemen — largely Irish — sent to restore order. The outnumbered police were forced to retreat, taking their badly wounded chief, Superintendent John Kennedy, with them. For three days several thousand rioters gave vent to their anger, burning hotels and private homes and capturing an armory. Throughout the city African-Americans were the special targets of the violence. The Colored Orphans Asylum on Fifth Avenue was destroyed (but only after 200 children had been evacuated), and hundreds of blacks were beaten, lynched, or shot at.[148]

Ironically, two of the mob's targets were well-known figures in the Irish-American community — Colonel Robert Nugent and Colonel Henry O'Brien. Nugent, who was recuperating from a wound sustained while leading the 69th New York at Fredericksburg, had the misfortune of being in charge of the draft in Manhattan and thus was a special object of the mob's anger. While trying to burn the colonel's house, the rioters noticed portraits of Nugent, Thomas Meagher, and Michael Corcoran on the premises. The trespassers slashed the likenesses of Nugent and Meagher but left the picture of Colonel Corcoran untouched. The mob also hurled the tattered battle flag of the 69th New York Regiment out the window and stole the sword presented to Nugent in 1854 by the Irish Fusiliers. The flag was picked up and saved by firemen from Engine Company No. 45, and two weeks later police discovered the colonel's sword in the possession of a boy (though its pearls and other ornaments were missing). Colonel O'Brien, meanwhile, was knocked down and trampled to death after the regiment of new recruits with which he tried to quell the violence allegedly shot a mother and her child. The *New York Times* described the obscene treatment which the mob accorded the colonel's corpse: "His body lay dead on the sidewalk for some time, and some of the more fiendish in the crowd amused themselves by firing several pistol-shots at his head, after which the body was strung up to the nearest lamp-post, where it remained for some time. It was afterward taken down and thrown again in the street  . . . ." A report in the *Times* the next day added details of the horrendous attack against O'Brien: "His murderers, after beating him in the most merciless manner with stones, bars of iron, bludgeons and stung-shots, stabbed him in several parts of his body and then dragged him through the gutters by a cord around his neck . . . ."[149]

Archbishop John Hughes helped bring the reign of terror to an end when he addressed a crowd of between 3,000 and 4,000 people at his residence. "Is there not some way," he asked, "by which you can stop these proceedings, and support the laws, of which none have been enacted against you as Irishmen and Catholics? You have suffered enough already. No government can stand or protect itself, unless it protects its citizens. Military force will be let loose on you, and you know what that is. The innocent will be shot down, and the guilty likely to escape." In fact, that same day twelve New York militia regiments arrived in the city from the Gettysburg campaign, and the governor assigned cavalry patrols to those parts of the city most affected by the violence. In the end, about 300 people were killed or wounded in the rioting. Although most of the atrocities were committed by Irish, others of that race did what they could to restrain the violence, some of them helping rescue the children from the Colored Orphans Asylum before it was torched.[150]

Following these anti-draft riots, Lieutenant Colonel Charles Halpine was assigned to the staff of General John Dix and charged with the task of winning back Irish support for the war. From his experiences with the 69th New York State Militia Regiment early in the conflict, Halpine had already written a series of burlesque pieces for the *New York Herald* under the pseudonym of a fictional private named "Miles O'Reilly." At first assumed by readers to be truthful accounts of their author's adventures, these and subsequent articles appeared in an 1864 edition entitled *The Life and Adventures, Songs, Services, and Speeches of Private Miles O'Reilly, 47th Regiment New York Volunteers.* A subsequent volume two years later was even more grandly named: *Baked Meats of the Funeral, a Collection of Essays, Poems, Speeches, and Banquets . . . Collected, revised, and edited, with the requisite corrections of punctuation, spelling, and grammar, by an Ex-Colonel [Halpine] of the Adjutant-General's Department, with whom the Private formerly served as Lance-Corporal of Orderlies.*[151]

Halpine's burlesques found a wide audience among Northern readers because of his title character and the stories' tendency to parody various aspects of the Irish themselves. In an episode that Halpine placed in the White House, O'Reilly is described as having the "usual type of Irish forehead — the perceptive bumps, immediately above the eyes, being extremely prominent." The brash Irish ingénue declares that "he and seventeen of his O'Reilly cousins, sixty-four Murphy cousins, thirty-seven Kelly cousins, twenty-three Lanigan cousins," together with a host of his other Irish relations, "would be both proud and happy to enlist or re-enlist for twenty years" if President Lincoln would oblige them by declaring war on England. General Meagher, who in the story presents O'Reilly to the president, addresses the chief executive with his usual rhetorical excess. Halpine expertly parodies the general's diction, syntax, and imagery: "[Meagher] wished to assure Mr. Lincoln that the bone and sinew of the army — his own countrymen in it not least — had eyes to see, and hearts to feel, and memories to treasure up the many acts of hearty, homely, honest kindliness, by which the Chief Magistrate of the nation had evinced his interest in their welfare. In the golden hours of sunrise, under the silver watches of the stars, through many a damp, dark night on picket duty, or in the red flame and heady fury of the battle, the thought that lay next the heart of the Irish soldier — only dividing its glow with that of the revered relic from the altar, which piety and affection had annexed, as an amulet against harm, around his neck — was the thought that he was thus earning a title, which hereafter no foul tongue or niggard heart would dare dispute, to the full equality and fraternity of an American citizen." Though his tone was humorous, Halpine had a serious point to make — one that he placed in these additional words from Meagher's imaginary speech: "By adoption of the banner [of the American flag], and by the communion of bloody grave-trenches on every field, from Bull Run to where the Chickamauga rolls down its waters of death, the race that were heretofore only exiles, receiving generous hospitality in the land, are now proud peers of the proudest and brave brothers of the best."[152]

In October 1863, the Confederate commander Robert E. Lee took the offensive against Union General George Meade in what is known as the Bristoe Station campaign. The objective was the capture of Washington, D.C., by means of a flanking movement against Meade's right. The Union general's response was to fall back and protect the capital from a new line in the Bull Run area of northern Virginia. Captain William O'Grady of the 88th New York described the Second Corps' rapid change of position: "A march of seventy-six miles in fifty-six hours, fighting two severe engagements in one day, and having to guard the entire baggage and reserve artillery of the army. This is unprecedented in the annals of war, beating the famous *march of the Fifty-second to Talavera." During the engagement at Auburn on October 14, Lieutenant Louis Sacriste of the 116th Pennsylvania saved the First Division's picket line from destruction. (Sacriste was the son of a French father and an Irish mother.) This rescue and Sacriste's earlier role in saving a gun of the Fifth Maine Battery from capture at Chancellorsville earned him the Congressional Medal of Honor in 1889. In the end, Lee failed to turn the Union right flank and retraced his steps to the Rapidan River. With the pressure now off, the Irish Brigade enjoyed the Indian summer by conducting horse races near Culpepper and entertaining a number of distinguished guests — General Meagher himself, Marshal Prim from Spain, and Captain Peel of the British army.[153]

At the end of the year the men of the Irish Brigade learned that they would receive a thirty-day furlough because at least 75 percent of each regiment had re-enlisted. The scheduled return home at Christmas was marred, however, by news of the death of Michael Corcoran, the commander of the Irish Legion and the revered former colonel of the 69th New York State Militia Regiment. Funeral services for Corcoran were conducted at St. Patrick's Old Cathedral in New York City on December 27. In noting the event in her diary three days later, Maria Lydig Daly took another swipe at Meagher, one of the pallbearers. Placing no stock in reports that Meagher had too much respect for the deceased to seek command of Corcoran's Irish Legion, Mrs. Daly wrote: "When I remember how useless he thought it in Mr. [John] Savage and the Judge [her husband] to do so much to release this brave Union prisoner two years ago and remember his [Meagher's] desertion of him on the field of Bull Run, I cannot but marvel. . . . [Meagher] wears a swashing and martial outside with an appearance of whole-soulness. His generosity and liberality are very taking, but he pays no one. He is the fox all over, as anyone might see by watching his small bright eye. . . . Now that Corcoran is gone, he is the representative of the Irish brave — what he has all the time been aiming at!"[154]

When the 63rd, the 69th, and the 88th New York regiments arrived in

New York City to begin their extended visit with family and friends, the men were disappointed by the extremely small turnout to welcome them. Despite this snub and the now widespread opposition to the war among the Irish in the Empire State, the regiments and their officers were determined to replenish their depleted ranks. (During the previous year and a half, the regiments had suffered 1,352 casualties, quite a loss from their original strength of 2,944.) To kick off this campaign, General Meagher organized a banquet at Irving Hall on January 16, 1864, for all the men who had ever served in the Brigade. There, amid the regiments' battle flags — both tattered and new — about 250 officers and men listened to speeches and toasts from the Brigade's icons. In all, ten toasts were made, among them tributes to President Lincoln, the "Irish Soldiers in the National Armies," and General Michael Corcoran. (The *New York Times* recorded the toast to the deceased Corcoran: "May the laurels for his grave be planted by his splendid old legion, and the shamrocks over it be the tribute of the land of his birth which he so deeply loved, and to the liberation of which he had hoped one day to give his sword, as he had already given it his heart.") Colonel Patrick Kelly proposed a toast to "Our Dead Comrades — Officers and soldiers of the Irish brigade; their memory shall remain for life as green in our souls as the emerald flag, under which, doing battle for the United States, they fought and fell." Colonel Robert Nugent of the 69th New York, meanwhile, concluded his remarks with a toast to "No negotiation, no compromise, no truce, no peace, but war to the last dollar and the last man, until every rebel flag be struck between the St. Lawrence and the Gulf, and swept everywhere, the world over, from land and sea." Colonel Brewster of the Excelsior Brigade closed his remarks with a toast to the Irish Brigade — "what there is left of it."[155]

In paying tribute to the Irish Brigade, Meagher drew upon the common memories of his guests and tugged at their heartstrings. He first recounted the privations which the men of the Brigade had so far suffered: "Having to endure the sunrays on the march, the blinding snows and chilling winds of winter, to plunge into the swollen torrent, or traverse the arid plains, nothing can possibly sustain him, unless it be a high and holy sense of the rectitude of the purpose in which he has taken up arms . . . ." Meagher then predicted that each man's wife would clasp him to her heart "with a love multiplied infinitely, multiplied by the dangers you have encountered, the labors you have heroically and resolutely performed, by the sacrifices of health and limb that you have endured for the country that has given you shelter, and has maintained for you a magnificent sanctuary . . . ." He ended his panegyric with what he regarded as his proudest boast: "[H]istory has no power to bestow upon me any higher distinction than that I have been the general in command of the Irish Brigade." After a toast by Sergeant Major O'Driscoll, Meagher tested his men's loyalty by asking them whether — as his enemies claimed — he had recklessly exposed them to danger (cries of "No, no") or not always been at their head when he led them into a dangerous situation ("Yes, yes").[156]

By spring the Brigade's recruitment effort had borne considerable fruit. Each of the three New York regiments had increased its strength to almost 600 men, the 28th Massachusetts had grown to 505, and the 116th Pennsylvania had added more than 600 new recruits, replenishing its four original companies and adding six new units. While Colonel Richard Byrnes was in Boston recruiting for the 28th Massachusetts, one of the founders of the regiment presented him with a traditional green flag, so dear to the hearts of Erin's sons. Byrnes replied on behalf of himself and his regiment: "I can promise no more, sir, than to assure you that it will be a fresh incentive to the brave men who are perilling their lives in defence of that flag which typifies Union and liberty, and beneath which the shamrock has ever bloomed. In a few days, sir, that flag will throw its emerald folds to the breeze, and the smoke of battle will encircle it; its freshness and beauty may be tarnished, but while there is an Irish arm to strike in its defence, its honor shall never, never be sullied nor impaired. . . . I thank you for the flag, and trust that one day we shall return it to the care of Massachusetts, crowned with the laurel of victory — of Union and liberty forever."[157]

Though the Brigade was now noticeably younger and less Irish in its composition, its new commander, Colonel Thomas Smyth, was a native Irishman. Born in 1832 in Ballyhooly, County Cork, he had acquired a rudimentary formal education before following in his father's footsteps as a farmer. Subsequent travel through England and Scotland, however, as well as extended stays in London and Paris, broadened his experiences. At the age of twenty-two he sailed for America, earning his bread by working in Philadelphia as a carver. After taking part in William Walker's filibustering expedition to Nicaragua, he settled in Wilmington, Delaware, in 1858. There he married Amanda Pounder and became an officer in one of the state's militia companies. When civil war split the nation, Smyth recruited and captained a company of enlistees which he offered to Delaware for three months' service. Impatient with the state's delay in accepting his offer, however, he took his recruits to Philadelphia, where they were enrolled as Company H in the 24th Pennsylvania Volunteers. During this brief service Captain Smyth won the accolades of his commander, Colonel Joshua Owen, for his bravery and prudence. When the 24th's term of service expired, Smyth joined the First Delaware Regiment, seeing action at Antietam, Fredericksburg, and Chancellorsville and serving in succession as major, lieutenant colonel, and colonel.[158]

From mid May 1863 to the end of the war, Smyth commanded various brigades in the Second Corps of the Army of the Potomac, including the Irish Brigade. On the last day of Gettysburg, he was wounded on the nose and the head by shell fragments. Although the wounds bled profusely and he was weakened by the loss of blood, he refused to leave the battle-field until General Alexander Hays ordered him to seek medical attention. When the wounded officer was told that his face was somewhat marred by the wound, he replied that he was perfectly willing to sacrifice his nose for the sake of his country and that the injury mattered little when compared to the Union victory at Gettysburg.[159]

When Colonel Richard Byrnes of the 28th Massachusetts went north to recruit for the Irish Brigade, Smyth took command of the latter unit from March 27 to May 17, 1864. Despite his regular drills and inspections, Smyth became a great favorite with his men, who appreciated his efforts to correct evils in camp more by "contrast and moral effect" than by punishment. For this reason, Smyth's camps were always remarkable for their cleanliness and his men were known for their "order, sobriety, and efficiency." In the middle of April, in fact, General Hancock wrote to Smyth saying that the Irish Brigade had never looked so good as at a recent review. David Conyngham expressed the general consensus of the Brigade when he wrote that "Smyth was not only a brave officer — in fact, heroically brave — but in every respect a thorough disciplinarian, as far as all the details and duties of a soldier are concerned. His modest, affable, and unassuming manners, combined and blended with his fine soldierly qualities and commanding appearance, soon rendered him so popular with the Brigade, so identified him with its fame and future aspirations, that no man could be found fitter to represent it, fitter to lead it to victory and glory."[160]

With the coming of April, the 69th New York looked forward to the third anniversary of its service in the Civil War. To commemorate the event, Colonel Charles Halpine, the former journalist who had briefly served with the 69th when it was still a militia unit, wrote an appropriate poetic tribute. The poem describes a reunion of surviving officers of an unspecified regiment. Of the unit's original thirty-seven officers, only eleven were alive to attend the commemorative banquet.

*"The Thousand and Thirty-Seven" (or "April 20, 1864")

Three years ago, to-day,
We raised our hands to Heaven,
And, on the rolls of muster,
Our names were thirty-seven;
There were just a thousand bayonets,
And the swords were thirty-seven,
As we took our oath of service
With our right hands raised to Heaven.

Oh, 't was a gallant day,

In memory still adored.
That day of our sun-bright nuptials
With the musket and the sword!
Shrill rang the fifes, the bugles blared,
And beneath a cloudless heaven
Far flashed a thousand bayonets,
And the swords were thirty-seven.

Of the thousand stalwart bayonets
Two hundred march to-day;
Hundreds lie in Virginia swamps,
And hundreds in Maryland clay;
While other hundreds — less happy — drag
Their mangled limbs around,
And envy the deep, calm, blessed sleep
Of the battle-field's holy ground.

For the swords — one night a week ago,
The remnant, just eleven —
Gathered around a banqueting-board
With seats for thirty-seven.
There were two came in on crutches.
And two had each but a hand,
To pour the wine and raise the cup
As we toasted "Our Flag and Land!"
And the room seemed filled with whispers
As we looked at the vacant seats,
And with choking throats we pushed aside
The rich but untasted meats;
Then in silence we brimmed our glasses
As we stood up — just eleven —
And bowed as we drank to the Loved and the Dead
Who had made us thirty-seven![161]

At the beginning of May 1864, the Confederate commander Robert E. Lee clashed with General Ulysses S. Grant in the battle of the Wilderness. This was the first of a series of engagements over the next six weeks in which Grant tried to outflank the Confederates and take up a position between them and Richmond. In each case, though, Lee was able to counter his opponent's move, and in the end the Union lost almost 55,000 men while the Confederates lost less than half that number. On the first day of the struggle at the Wilderness, the Irish Brigade participated in the Second Corps' offensive against the Southerners. According to Winfield Scott Hancock, the corps commander, the Irish unit "was heavily engaged and although four-fifths of its members were recruits it behaved with great steadiness and gallantry, losing largely in killed and wounded." When Sergeant John Cassidy of the 116th Pennsylvania was shot through the lungs, his noisy complaints about having to leave the field unaided caused a fellow soldier to cry out, "Why, Cassidy, there's a man with all of his head blown off and he is not making half as much fuss as you are!" Confederate fire also cut down two color guards of the 116th and wounded three more. As Captain James McIntire of the 28th Massachusetts dragged one of his wounded men to safety, he was hit by a Minié ball. After walking a half mile to a field hospital, the nineteen-year-old officer died of his wound later that night. The Brigade also lost Captain James Turner of the 88th New York, a writer whose reports of the Brigade's deeds had been printed in the pages of the New York *Irish American* under the pen name "Gallowglass."[162]

Late in the afternoon of the following day, Confederate troops attacked the Irish Brigade's breastworks, causing them to catch on fire and scorch some of the defenders. In the words of Corporal Samuel Clear of the 116th Pennsylvania, "The Irishmen stood their ground, firing blind volley after volley through the blazing barrier until the Confederates withdrew." After the battle Father Corby made one more round on the field, during which he came upon Private Daniel Lynch of the 88th New York, his body riddled with eight bullet wounds. The chaplain prepared the "brave, dutiful soldier" for death. Thirty years later, in his memoir of the war, Corby included an incident involving the hapless Lynch: "I remember on one occasion we secured some beans, which, with a limited quantity of pork, would be for us a genuine feast, as at that time we had no provisions. Instructed to cook them, he started to a farm-house to get water, but could find no pail to get water from the deep well, so he tied the black pot to a pole and let the pot down into the well. The beans were in the pot. The string broke and pot, beans, and all were lost."[163]

The bloody scenes from the battle of the Wilderness stood in sharp contrast to the atmosphere in the camp of the 116th Pennsylvania the following Sunday evening. As the men turned their thoughts to the divine while resting near Todd's Tavern, the scene prompted St. Clair Mulholland, the regimental commander, to reflect on the religious practices of his men. "[W]e must feel astonished at the high moral standard of the army that fought the War of the Rebellion, and the Regiment was second to none in that respect," he later wrote. "Seldom was an obscene word or an oath heard in the camp. Meetings for prayer were of almost daily occurrence, and the groups of men sitting on the ground or gathered on the hill side listening to the Gospel were strong reminders of the mounds of Galilee when the people sat upon the ground to hear the Savior teach. Ofttimes in the Regiment the dawn witnessed the smoke of incense ascend to heaven amid the templed trees where serious groups knelt on the green sod and listened to the murmur of the Mass. In the evening Lieutenant-Colonel {Richard] Dale or Captain Samuel Taggert would hold a meeting for prayer where the larger number of the men would gather in reverence and devotion, while others would kneel around the Chaplain's tent to count beads and repeat the rosary. Colonel Dale was a man of deep religious thought and feeling, and Captain Taggart was an ordained minister of the Gospel, both men of great devotion and sincerity, and by their example did much towards making others sincerely good."[164]

On May 12 General Grant made another attempt to outflank the Confederates by attacking Lee's new defensive position at Spotsylvania, Virginia. During the surprise assault Colonel Smyth's Irish Brigade charged into the Confederate abatis, giving, as Corporal Samuel Clear of the 116th Pennsylvania wrote, "such a yell as only the old Irish Brigade can give" and going in "like as if the devil had broke loose, over the works in among the Johnnies." That first assault netted for the Union eighteen field guns and 4,000 prisoners, including Confederate Major General Edward Johnson, captured in his tent by a private in the 28th Massachusetts. While awaiting a Confederate counterattack, Corporal O'Neill of the 63rd New York jumped atop the breastworks and challenged the enemy: "We have licked you before, you blankety, blanked Rebs, and we can do it again. Come on! We are ready for you!" Almost immediately this fiery native of Galway was knocked to the ground when a bullet struck him in the mouth. "I'll pay you for that some day!" cried O'Neill, shaking his fist toward the enemy line. A correspondent in the Brigade lauded Colonel Smyth unashamedly for his role in the initial attack: "The movement was eminently successful, and reflects lasting credit upon the intrepid, the gallant Colonel Smyth, whose name is already written in letters of gold on the scroll of military fame. Standing at the head of the column where the charge was made, he was slightly wounded, and taken from the field. . . . Colonel Smyth was born to command and be respected, and when he takes the lead, his valiant men follow his footsteps, no matter what impeding barriers rise up to impede their progress." When the Union troops pressed on to the Confederate reserve line, they were forced back by five Southern brigades, although Smyth's Irish Brigade continued to fight off repeated Confederate attacks. From their respective positions on either side of a log barrier, the two armies fired at each other until the bodies of the fallen became so numerous that they had to be removed from the trenches so the survivors could stand and fight. The Confederates withdrew at midnight. The Brigade's casualties included Lieutenant Richard Dale, commanding the 116th Pennsylvania, and Color Sergeant Peter Welsh, the famous letter-writer in the 28th Massachusetts.[165]

The battle resumed on May 19 when Hancock's Second Corps attacked the new Confederate position near Spotsylvania. As the Union troops advanced, they met heavy fire from the Confederate batteries and came up against a defensive abatis that covered the entire enemy line. The Irish Brigade came the closest of any unit to breaching the Confederate works, but many of the men became tangled in the brush and branches of the defense works and were shot in that exposed position. One sergeant from the 116th Pennsylvania did manage, however, to penetrate the abatis eight or ten feet farther than any of his comrades and was able to load and fire three or four times from inside the defenses. Captain John Blake of the 69th New York climbed up on the highest part of the works and from there rallied his men, waving the regimental flag and crying, "Come on, boys, and I will show you how to fight." Lieutenant King left an eyewitness account of what happened next: "Giving up the flag to the sergeant, he [Blake] then went in with any man he could find; and while a most infernal fire raged from both sides he fought conspicuously in the extreme front, till he was struck in the knee. I immediately got some help, and was in the act of carrying him off when he shouted out to me to save myself, that the enemy were upon us. I looked around and saw some a few paces from me, and as their firing had wounded one of the carrying party, and struck me on the back, which, however, was luckily shielded by my coiled up rubber-blanket, I had for the time to leave Blake, as he ordered, to avoid capture." Blake later died of his wound, as did Major Andrew Lawlor, commander of the 28th Massachusetts. Corcoran's Irish Legion, which had fought alongside the Brigade that day, suffered heavy losses.[166]

In the middle of May 1864, Colonel Richard Byrnes of the 28th Massachusetts learned that he would be named to replace Colonel Thomas Smyth as commander of the Irish Brigade. Soon later Byrnes shared with Father William Corby what seems to have been a premonition of his death (". . . he *felt* that he should get his 'discharge' that day"). After confessing his sins to the chaplain, the colonel gave Corby the following letter, asking him to send it to his wife, Ellen, in the event he was killed: "I am well. No fighting yesterday; but we expect some to-day. Put your trust and confidence in God. Ask His blessing. Kiss my poor little children for me. You must not give up in despair — all will yet be well. My regiment has suffered much in officers and men. I am in good health and spirits. I am content. I fear nothing, thank Heaven, but my sins. Do not let your spirits sink; we will meet again. I will write you soon again; but we are going to move just now. Good-bye, good-bye; and that a kind and just God may look to you and your children is my fervent prayer."[167]

Later in May, after the battle of Spotsylvania, Colonel Smyth was ordered to take command of General S. S. Carroll's Brigade in the Second Division. So attached had Smyth's men become to him that some of them wept at his departure and the officers presented him with a heartfelt testimonial. "You leave us after having led us on the battle field with a gallantry never surpassed, and delighted us in private by your frankness and cordiality," wrote the officers. "In you are combined the loyal American, the patriotic Irishman, and the high-minded Gentleman. You are called away from us, but our affections will follow you. You leave no fading memory in our hearts, and may the God of battles preserve you for the glory of this great land, the freedom of Ireland, and the happiness of your social circle." The Brigade's poet laureate, Dr. Lawrence Reynolds, once again called upon his muse, this time in praise of the self-effacing Smyth:

*"Tom Smyth, of the Irish Brigade"

Must friendship be strengthened by time?
Is the growth of affection so slow?
Ah! no; 'tis a feeling sublime,
Like the sun bursting forth in full glow.
Though few were the days you were here,
Your memory never shall fade;
No man on this earth is more dear,
Than "Tom Smyth" of the Irish Brigade.

Kind nature has marked on thy face,
The virtues that glow in thy soul;
She gave thee courage and grace,
The gallant to win and control;
The Irishman's laugh from the heart,
The tongue that no friend e'er betrayed;
Oh! the boast and the model thou art,
"Tom Smyth" of the Irish Brigade.

"Tom Smyth," proud Columbia can boast
Of no soldier more loyal or true;
No star from her flag shall be lost,
While she's guarded by heroes like you.
We grudge not our blood in her cause,
Nor her young men beneath her turf laid;
But we'll fight for her union and laws,
"Tom Smyth," and the Irish Brigade.

May come back sweet peace to this land;
May love o'er her gallant sons reign!
May the North and the South hand in hand
Sweep all foes from the land and the main.
And then may we free our green home;
May her tyrants forever be laid!
And then may fair liberty bloom,
"Tom Smyth" and our Irish Brigade.[168]

Despite the temporary Union setback at Spotsylvania, General Grant pressed on in pursuit of Lee's Army of Northern Virginia. Between May 22 and June 1, the Irish Brigade participated in the battles of North Anna, Pamunkey, and Totopotomoy, but now under its new commanding officer, Colonel Richard Byrnes. By June 3 the Irish Brigade had reached Cold Harbor in time to join the Union attack on Lee's defensive position there. Although the Brigade succeeded in reaching the Confederate rifle-pits, fierce rifle and artillery fire forced it to fall back and find protection in hastily dug trenches. When the Brigade tried to escape from its untenable position, the men were cut down by enemy cannon fire. The day's assault cost the Second Corps 3,000 men. Byrnes's former regiment, the 28th Massachusetts, barely survived the slaughter. Of the 310 men who went into action that day, only eighty came out whole. (The 28th counted fifty-three killed, 149 wounded, and twenty-eight unaccounted for.)[169]

Byrnes himself was mortally wounded after leading the Irish Brigade's attack and while trying to pull back his troops from the enemy's blazing batteries. He was wounded when a Minié ball struck him in the back and lodged in his spine after first passing through the chest and arm of his aide, Captain James Brady of the 63rd New York. The Brigade's commander was removed to a field hospital in the rear and then to a hospital in Washington, D.C., "where his loving, faithful, and weeping wife and children met him and embraced him before he departed for the unknown future" on June 12. The men of the 28th Massachusetts would have agreed with the words of praise which Captain David Conyngham later wrote about their former colonel: "Brave almost to rashness, he always led his men, who knew no fear under his eye; a strict disciplinarian, just to each and all in the exercise of his authority, he commanded the respect and esteem of those under him, and to his efforts is mainly due the high reputation for steadiness and discipline which the Twenty-eighth enjoyed." St. Clair Mulholland, the commander of the 116th Pennsylvania Regiment, remembered Byrnes as "strict, reserved and reticent[,] and one who did not know him would think him severe, but he was a man who did his full duty and expected everyone else to come up to the full measure of all demands. To those who knew him best he was kindly and lovable." A few days before Cold Harbor, Byrnes had had some harsh words with Captain Frank Lieb, then in command of the 116th Pennsylvania. After the battle, while lying wounded in the field hospital, Byrnes learned that Lieb was there also. Mulholland recorded that Byrnes then "had himself carried to where the Captain was lying and the dying officer apologized in the most courteous manner for anything rude that he might have said."[170]

---

The headstone on Byrnes's grave in Calvary Cemetery in Woodside, Queens, Long Island, contains the following information:

Richard Byrnes
Native of County Cavan, Ireland
Colonel, 28th Mass. Vol. Infantry • 1st Lieutenant, 5th U.S. Cavalry
Sergeant Major, 1st U.S. Cavalry • 1st Sergeant, 1st U.S. Dragoons
Mortally wounded leading the famed Irish Brigade in battle
at Cold Harbor, Virginia, June 3, 1864.
Died at the age of 31 years, June 12, 1864.

His devoted wife Ellen died January 12, 1911
Loving daughters
1862  Margaret  1900      1863  Catherine  1913

"Put your trust and confidence in God.
Ask His blessing. Kiss my poor little children for me.
. . . I fear nothing, thank Heaven, but my sins.
Do not let your spirits sink; we will meet again."
Richard[171]

*The grave of Colonel Richard Byrnes in Calvary Cemetery in Woodside, Queens, Long Island, New York. (Location number: Section 3, Range 23, Plot W, Grave 6)*

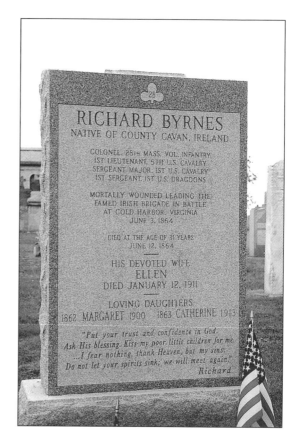

As the men of the Irish Brigade resumed their camp duties, many of them probably pondered the famous unit's fate over the past month. Since the battle of the Wilderness, the Brigade had suffered 973 casualties (killed, wounded, missing, or captured), the heaviest by the 28th Massachusetts (286) and the least by the 88th New York (98). (The 69th New York sustained 221 casualties.) In addition, Colonel Patrick Kelly, the former commander of the latter regiment, had replaced the ill-fated Byrnes as the Brigade's commanding officer. The ever-observant Captain William O'Grady of the 88th noted that Kelly's favorite charger was "probably the finest war-horse in the United States and would 'negotiate' the most formidable stone-wall, fence, or brook with his 'welterweight' master on his back like a colt — a frequent performance which never failed to start the Brigade cheering. It was the one thing where the light-heartedness of the boy showed in Col. Kelly, for he was habitually a grave man, a man of few words, gentle, kind, unassuming, feeling his responsibilities in fullest measure, and with a disciplined bravery that would send his men, himself at the head, to storm the very gates of hell, if ordered, and stay there til ordered back. After a battle he would grieve like a father."[172]

Despite its recent setbacks, the Irish Brigade went on to play a major role in General Grant's attempt to capture Petersburg, an important railroad center south of Richmond. Late in the day on June 16, the Irish Brigade captured the enemy's breastworks, but only after braving heavy fire and after fighting hand-to-hand with bayonets. Casualties in the 69th New York included Captain Bernard O'Neill (killed), Lieutenant Colonel James McGee (wounded), and Lieutenants Brennan, Clooney, and M. H. Murphy (wounded). Captains John Shea and Benedict O'Driscoll of the 88th New York also lay wounded. Over the next two days the Second Corps — and the Irish Brigade — attacked various positions along the Confederate line. Although a few men in the Brigade managed to get inside the enemy's defenses, they were either killed or captured. The Brigade suffered heavy losses at Petersburg and was ultimately pushed back. After casualties to the Corps numbered more than 10,000, Grant ordered a halt to the assaults and prepared to sit out a lengthy siege. The Brigade's losses for the second half of June amounted to another 248 men killed, wounded, captured, or missing.[173]

The most conspicuous fatality which the Irish Brigade suffered at Petersburg was its commander, Colonel Patrick Kelly, killed by a shot to the head on the first day. (The day before, Kelly had remarked about the loss of some old domestic pets and — in an allusion to his swarthy complexion — predicted his own demise: "I've lost my black horse, and my black dog, and now they'll have 'the little black man.'") A writer to the *Irish American* in New York lamented that over Kelly's lifeless body "strong old veteran soldiers wept like children and wrung their hands in frenzy," adding that there was no more "unblemished soul" in the Irish Brigade than "honest Colonel Patrick Kelly." Two years later David Conyngham succinctly captured the measure of the slain officer: "Gentle, brave, and unassuming, no truer man nor braver officer fell during the war."[174]

---

Colonel Kelly's grave in Calvary Cemetery in Woodside, Queens, Long Island, is marked by a headstone erected in 1998 and inscribed with the following words:

Patrick Kelly
Native of Castlehacket
Tuam, Co. Galway, Ireland
Commanding officer, Meagher's Irish Brigade,
Colonel and Lt. Col., 88th Reg't, N.Y.S.V.
Captain, Co. E, 69th Reg't, N.Y.S.M.
Killed while gallantly leading
the Irish Brigade on the enemy's works
at Petersburg, VA, on the 10th of June 1864
aged 42 years
Faithful to us here, we loved him to the last

". . . Colonel Kelly, has been mowed down by the
pitiless scythe of death far from the green fields
and loved home of his nativity; and like another
Irish hero expiring on the distant battle field
he no doubt regretted that his gushing life blood
was not shed for Ireland . . ."

His beloved wife
Elizabeth Kelly
who departed this life, November 22, 1858
aged 35 years[175]

---

Although events at Petersburg hit the Irish Brigade hard, the campaign produced some interesting anecdotes for future chroniclers to record. One such incident involved Daniel Duggan, an Irishman in the 116th Pennsylvania who mysteriously disappeared during the Brigade's initial charge. When he showed up the next morning and was accused of desertion in battle, he replied to his accuser, Captain Samuel Taggert: "Ah, then, Captain dear, sure it's many a poor fellow that's after bein' hit on the field lasht noight, an' here oi am shtill aloive!" "Well," replied Taggert, "if you had been killed you would have lived in the hearts of your countrymen." To this remark Duggan responded wittily: "Oh, thin, bedad [By God] but its [sic] a moighty hard place to live in. I'd sooner be livin' on Uncle Sam's hard tack!"[176]

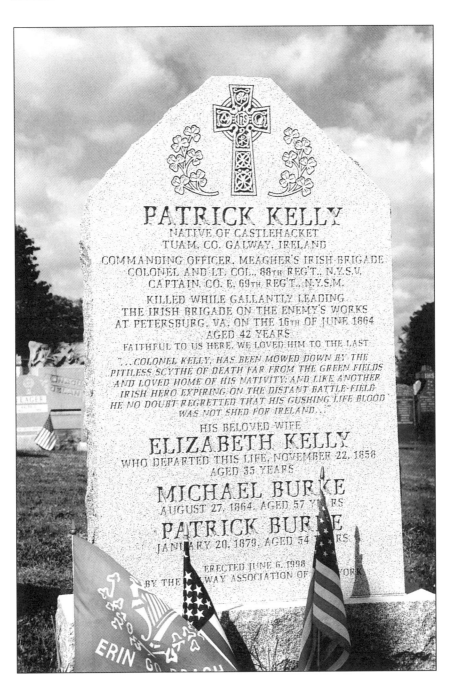

*The grave of Colonel Patrick Kelly in Calvary Cemetery in Woodside, Queens, Long Island, New York. (Location number: 4–5–H–14/16)*

Another tale which entered the Brigade's lore books occurred on the third day of the campaign, when, after enduring hours of Rebel taunts, Private Michael DeLacy of the 63rd New York, began to reply in kind. "Say Johnnies? You are a low-lived lot of spalpeens [rascals]," he cried out to the enemy in the nearest rifle-pits. "You face the Yankees in the open, and we'll knock the devil out of yees. We can lick yees every time." A Confederate voice replied: "Do you hear the Yankee-Irishman! Go soak your head, Pat! You keep still or we'll send a niggah after you!" DeLacy — his Irish by now definitely up — retorted: "I won't fight your nagur, but I will and can whip the best man in your measly gang. You infernal slave drivers; meet me half way and I'll show yees!" Jumping up from their opposing rifle-pits, the combatants charged each other with their bayonets but halted a few paces apart. After sizing up his opponent, the man in gray lunged at DeLacy, sure that he would strike his enemy's heart. The Irishman dodged the thrust and lodged the butt of his musket on the Confederate's chin. Major John Dwyer described the denouement: "Mr. Rebel staggered from the force of the blow, and fell full length on his back, his gun going into the air. In an instant DeLacy's foot was on his neck, his fixed bayonet pointed at his heart, where he held it for a moment.

'Now, Rebel, who is the best man, Yankee or Johnny?'

'You've won, Yank, and I give up.'

'Thin you larn to behave yourself, and remember a Yankee-Irishman can fight and be generous too. If you are not satisfied, send on your nagurs!'"[177]

One of the men captured during an engagement on June 22 was Captain Maurice Wall of the 69th New York. After three months in prison in Charleston, South Carolina, this native of Tipperary, Ireland, wrote home complaining that he had not heard from his brother all summer. The patient captain alluded to the horrors which other Union soldiers were suffering in Andersonville, Georgia, and thanked God that he had been spared that infamous hell hole. His own situation in prison was quite tolerable, and he had the good humor to joke about a recent experience with a needle and thread: "[A]s to tailoring, I have just completed an elaborate piece on the back of my unmentionables; for you must remember that this is the part most used to hardship among us prisoners. You can often see a black pants with a blue seat, and *vice versa*; but if you ask its wearer what is the reason of the change in colors, he will probably get off some joke by stating he belongs to the horse-marines, and he always has his headquarters in the saddle."[178]

Since early May 1864, when General Grant began his spring campaign, the Irish Brigade had been utterly transformed. Of the ten field officers who had started with the campaign, six had been killed and the other four severely wounded. Because of this lack of officers, command of the Brigade had been given to a captain, Richard Moroney of the 69th New York.

In addition, the 28th Massachusetts had been transferred to the First Brigade, and the 116th Pennsylvania sent to the Fourth Brigade. The remaining three New York regiments had become part of what was known as the "Consolidated Brigade," which also included units from the Third Brigade of the Second Corps. So angry were some of the men in the Irish Brigade about the reassignment of the 28th Massachusetts and the 116th Pennsylvania that they swore they would never charge again. According to Mulholland, the men of the 116th left the Irish Brigade with regret, having participated "in all the glories and triumphs of that famous brigade" for two years. Although the 116th was composed almost entirely of American-born citizens, its men had learned to love and esteem "the men of the Emerald Isle."[179]

Luckily, however, Colonel Robert Nugent and Lieutenant Colonel James McGee conducted a successful recruitment drive in New York to replenish the ranks of that state's three regiments in the Brigade. As part of the new "Consolidated Brigade," these regiments participated in the two Deep Bottom expeditions by the Second Corps that July and August. In the second expedition the Irish Brigade dislodged the enemy from his front line and, without firing a shot, rushed on to capture a line of Confederate rifle-pits, brandishing only bayonets and "a shout that completely drowned out the loudest din of shot and shell." In the eerie silence that followed, General Francis Barlow, the commander of the First Division and no favorite of the Brigade, jumped up to find the cause. Misjudging the reason, he shouted with glee, "That damned Irish Brigade has [been] broken at last!" Barlow was rendered speechless when his adjutant informed him that the Irish Brigade had taken the first line of the enemy's works.[180]

As part of his strategy to isolate Petersburg, General Grant attempted to cut the railroad lines that supplied the city from the southwest. Toward the end of August the Second Corps was ordered to Reams' Station, a point south of the besieged city along the railroad line that ran through Weldon, North Carolina, to Wilmington on the coast. On August 25, while the Second Corps — including the Irish Brigade and Corcoran's Irish Legion — was engaged in destroying the railroad, a Confederate force attacked the corps' entrenchments at Reams' Station. In the Union panic the Confederates captured more than 2,000 soldiers, including eighty-four officers and enlisted men from the three New York regiments of the Irish Brigade. The 69th lost six officers and men wounded and forty-five missing, most of the latter prisoners, including, again, Captain Maurice Wall. Adjutant James Smith was severely wounded.[181]

For the next two months the Irish Brigade spent much of its time in the trenches during the ill-fated siege of Petersburg. A break in the monotony occurred in early September, however, when General Meagher arrived in camp on a visit to General Hancock. To capitalize on the visit of the Irish Brigade's famed founder, a committee of officers drew up plans to celebrate the Brigade's third anniversary with a special celebration. The commemoration began on the morning of September 4 with a solemn high mass, at which Fathers William Corby, Thomas Ouellet, and Paul Gillen presided. The Brigade's various regiments attended under their respective officers, and Meagher himself served as master of ceremonies, at least in matters musical and *étiquette militaire*. In his *Memoirs of Chaplain Life*, Father Corby left a detailed account of this "military mass": "As soon as the priests are ready, the *Asperges me* is announced, and, instead of a grand choir, such as is heard in the royal cathedrals of Christendom, the bugles, followed by the report of numerous guns, announce the beginning. Then, under the direction of Gen. Meagher, at the *Introibo* various military bands discourse solemn music until after the *Credo*, when, again, by a sign from the Master of Ceremonies to the Officer of the Day, another discharge, a grand salute of guns, testify to *Credo in unum Deum* — I believe in one God. The bugle follows with its well-known notes, 'tara-taran-tara,' and again the bands play. Now their music is soft, low, and sweet, suitable to the devotion that immediately disposes the faithful for the more sacred portion of the Mass. The *Sanctus! sanctus! sanctus!* rouses all to a fixed attention and is accompanied by a sudden rattle of dozens of kettle-drums, with an occasional thundering sound from the bass drums. Shortly after this comes that moment of moments in the offering of the sublime mysteries. The preparatory is over, and now you see men bow down in deep devotion as the priest leans over the altar and takes up the *Host. Here, at a sign from the Master of Ceremonies, the bugle notes, 'tara-taran-tara,' ring out over the tented fields, and the same grand evidence of respect and faith is given by the sound of cannon and the roll of musketry, as the sublime words, full of power and purpose — the supreme *words of Consecration — are pronounced. Soft music is again in order at intervals, until the end, which is proclaimed in turn by guns, drums, and bugles that prolong a grand *finale*."[182]

After the religious service, Chaplain Corby spoke to the assembled men about the duties which the men of the Brigade owed their race, their creed, and their adopted country. The foremost obligation, he said, was to conduct themselves in an exemplary moral and Christian way. The popular priest concluded his remarks with the hope that the men would perform all their duties while in the military "in such a manner as to earn for themselves the approval of their own consciences, the esteem of their fellow-soldiers, and then return to private life, respected and useful citizens." In his later description of this anniversary celebration, Corby commented on the character of the Irish Brigade: "When all the rest of the army was more or less dormant or bewailing the situation and longing for 'the fleshpots of Egypt,' the Irish Brigade was making fun and cheer for itself and all the friends it could accommodate. Its hospitality was limited only by its purse, and sometimes it even borrowed or anticipated the salary of the coming 'pay-day.'"[183]

As the guests lingered at the luncheon tables, General Meagher addressed the Brigade in poignantly reminiscent tones. He expressed his pride that they and the thousands of men before them had never betrayed the trust which their adopted country had placed in them. On every battlefield, he said, the men of the Brigade had earned yet another laurel and in doing so had earned undying glory. Calling them the worthy descendants of their forefathers in valor and patriotism, Meagher said he was proud that no other country had contributed so much to the honor of the American flag as had Ireland. The general's exuberance turned to sorrow when he recognized but few faces among the men. He was consoled, however, by the belief that his earlier comrades had died in a noble cause. He ended his remarks by turning to General Hancock and calling for three cheers for the popular officer who had led the Brigade during some of its most glorious days.[184]

General Nelson Miles, one of the other guests, also praised the bravery of the Irish troops during the war, most recently at Reams' Station. There, he reminded his listeners, the Brigade had held off repeated enemy assaults and would have counted Reams' Station a victory had not reinforcements come to the enemy's aid. Miles singled out the gallantry of Captain Benjamin of the 63rd New York. Though Benjamin and his band of pickets had been driven back three times and cut off from their own lines, they managed to escape because of the captain's coolness and good judgment. Later in the battle Benjamin had rescued Sergeant McHugh (or McCue) and a boy belonging to the Seventh New York from their Confederate captors. General Philippe De Trobriand, one of the other guests at the banquet, added a bit of humor to the proceedings by pointing out that the Irishmen in his command claimed him as one of their own. His name, these men insisted, was originally Irish — O'Brien — and had been but slightly Gallicized. Late that evening the men of the Brigade were heartened by the return of Colonel Thomas Smyth. As the men gathered around their beloved former commander, the latter, who would "rather face a battery than make a speech," waved his hand "and retired with more precipitancy from his friends than he ever did from his foes."[185]

Although Colonel Smyth had been in command of various brigades since May 1863, his exploits had not yet been recognized with an appropriate promotion. That such recognition was not forthcoming was a source of resentment to his loyalists, particularly in the Irish Brigade. Dr. Lawrence Reynolds, the Brigade's poet laureate, gave expression to this feeling in the following poem:

"There's Not a Star for You, Tom Smyth"

Though stars are falling very thick,
On many a curious spot;
And warriors rising very quick,
Who never heard a shot.
Still though you periled limb and life,
And many a fight went through,
And laurels won in every strife,
There's not a star for you, Tom Smyth,
There's not a star for you.

'Tis true, when close the hostile lines,
The headlong charge you lead,
And your sword, glory's beacon, shines
In front of your Brigade;
But you can't like a courtier grin,
No little work can do,
So you perchance a ball may win;
But there's no star for you, Tom Smyth,
But there's no star for you.

Whene'er you tread the crimson sod,
Your form and soul expand;
In olden times you'd seem a god,
Not Hancock's self more grand.
But then your sword, a wily tongue,
Far greater deeds can do:
For while stars grace the gabby throng,
There's not a star for you, Tom Smyth,
There's not a star for you.

No coward in the ranks is seen
When gallant Smyth appears,
Men kindle at his voice and mien,
And move on with gay cheers.
Smyth's spirit moves the glowing mass,
Deeds past their power they do;
Yet while such things you bring to pass,
There's not a star for you, Tom Smyth,
There's not a star for you.

But by you for no selfish cause
Is battle's flag unfurled,
You fight to save our glorious laws,
To bless the future world.

> Brave Hancock owns you're skilled and brave,
> The army owns it too;
> Then the proud feeling you must have
> Is rank and star for you, Tom Smyth,
> Is rank and star for you![186]

When Smyth was finally promoted to the rank of brigadier general on October 1, 1864, the non-commissioned officers and privates of the 63rd New York Regiment addressed their former commander in the fondest terms. "We have no connection with you, as our Brigade is not now under your command," they wrote, "but the ties of affection still remain and will forever. We found in you a strict disciplinarian, but you had the singular felicity of combining mildness of manner with firmness of purpose, and we endured with pleasure every labor you commanded, for we knew your lofty motives and your love for us. Brave, courteous and humane, you bring before our eyes, a living portrait of the Irish hero of yore, and may the day come, when after preserving the glorious union of this land, you will lead us across the ocean to raise to independence and happiness our own dear, unforgotten Ireland."[187]

In the middle of October, Lieutenant Colonel Denis Burke, a native of Cork, was placed in command of the consolidated regiments of the Irish Brigade. Later that month the men of his former regiment — the 88th New York — presented him with a horse and accompanying trappings. On October 29 the new commander, with a party of a hundred men, attacked and captured a portion of the enemy's line opposite Fort Sedgwick, in the process taking some prisoners and holding the line until ordered to withdraw. Although Burke was later recommended for a brevet appointment for his role in this episode, the attack resulted in the death of Lieutenant Robert O'Driscoll, killed after mounting the enemy's works. According to Conyngham, O'Driscoll was one of the bravest and most courteous officers of the 88th New York.[188]

The next day the customary boredom of siege life was broken when a detail from the 69th New York was ordered to do picket duty opposite Confederate Fort Davis. During the night, however, a Confederate raiding party — pretending to be relief pickets — slipped past the Union line and captured 168 prisoners from the 69th New York. Before the Confederate raiders could return to their lines with their prisoners, though, Lieutenant Murtha Murphy noticed that his picket lines were unmanned and proceeded to sound the alarm. To Murphy's order to his men to commence firing, the enemy responded with spirit and fought off attempts to capture their prisoners. In the skirmish Murphy suffered a wound to the head. A subsequent investigation of the incident revealed that the Confederates had learned details about the positioning of the 69th's pickets from ten deserters from the regiment. Some of the deserters — whom General Miles claimed were actually Rebels — were later captured and executed.[189]

At the beginning of November 1864, the Irish Brigade was reconstituted as an identifiable unit, this time under Colonel Robert Nugent. The 63rd, the 69th, and the 88th New York regiments were removed from the Consolidated Brigade, and the 28th Massachusetts rejoined the reorganized unit. The Brigade was considerably enlarged when the Seventh New York Heavy Artillery, a new unit numbering 1,835 men, was added. At the time of the reorganization, the officers and the enlisted men of the 69th New York requested that Father Ouellet be restored as their chaplain. Although at the time the Jesuit priest was stationed at St. Francis Xavier College in New York City, he readily accepted the invitation. When each of the regiment's returning veterans received a $300 bounty, Father Ouellet lent his customary assistance to the men. For days on end he could be seen in the paymaster's office, writing letters for the soldiers to send home with their bonuses. Later, when the chaplain discovered that various "sectarian organizations" had distributed tracts among the soldiers in the regiment, he requested friends in New York to send him a supply of Catholic books for his men.[190]

The following February, during an operation at Hatcher's Run, the reorganized and re-energized Brigade encountered a Confederate division under General William Mahone. A large number of men in Mahone's force were Irish immigrants, and some of them may have been in the raiding party that had surprised the Union pickets opposite Fort Davis three months before. As often happened when Irish pickets from the opposing armies met, they put aside their differences and shared those coveted commodities that made military life bearable — tobacco, coffee, newspapers, and whiskey. Despite the camaraderie, such occasions sometimes elicited exchanges like the following between one of Mahone's Irish Confederates and a New York Irishman. "A fine bunch of Irishmen you are, coming into the South and burning our farms and acting worse than the English ever did in Ireland," charged the Southerner. The New Yorker retorted: "A fine bunch of Irishmen you are, trying to break up the Union that gave ye a home and fighting for the rich slave owners." But after sharing a sip of the *uisce beatha* (whiskey), the two men ended up toasting General Meagher of the Irish Brigade and Patrick Cleburne, an Irish-born Confederate general.[191]

As February gave way to March, the Irish Brigade made plans to celebrate the feast of St. Patrick with its accustomed mix of solemnity and revelry. By now the tradition had become well established, and officers from throughout the Army of the Potomac looked forward to receiving an invitation. The customary high mass, celebrated that day by Father Ouellet, was followed by horse racing and the Brigade's signature luncheon, at which its officers served sandwiches and whiskey punch to the guests. Among the nineteen generals in attendance were Meade, Miles, Meagher,

Smyth, and De Trobriand. On the racecourse Colonel Nugent's steed, "Harry," won once or twice, although the races were marred by two unfortunate accidents. Colonel Van Schaick of the Seventh New York was severely injured, while Lieutenant McConville of the 69th New York suffered a fractured skull, from which he died shortly afterward.[192]

A week later the Irish Brigade was with the Second Corps when it engaged the enemy at Skinner's Farm, near Hatcher's Run. During this attempt to retake Fort Steadman from the Confederates, General Meade inflicted heavy casualties while pushing the enemy back to its own lines. The Brigade's losses were also high, though. Captain John Mulhall of the 69th New York — a former member of the Papal Brigade — was severely wounded in the leg as he led a party of skirmishers. This native of Roscommon, Ireland, actually lay on the field for several hours as both sides fired away at each other before the Confederates withdrew. The 28th Massachusetts and the 69th New York each suffered seven dead and from thirty-three to thirty-five wounded.[193]

When April, the fateful final month of the war, arrived, the Irish Brigade participated in the general Union assault on the Confederates lines at Petersburg. On April 2 the Brigade charged the enemy's defenses but was forced to fall back. The Irish unit's second assault, however, was successful, resulting in the capture of 150 prisoners. The Irish Brigade paid dearly, though, losing another 124 men killed, wounded, or missing. Nevertheless, the Brigade joined in the pursuit of Lee's army. On April 4, at the head of the First Division, the Brigade reached the Danville rail line at Jetersville, between Richmond and Appomattox. Only two days before, Jefferson Davis and his cabinet had passed that way en route to an expected rendezvous with General Lee at Danville, near the North Carolina border. As the men of the Brigade entered Jetersville, they encountered the Union general Philip Sheridan, the son of Irish immigrant parents and a favorite with the Brigade. Sheridan ordered the troops to form a line of battle in a nearby wood and then await an attack by the enemy. As he rode away, "Little Phil" acknowledged the cheers of more than a thousand men in the Brigade.[194]

On April 7, during the Union army's pursuit of Lee in southwestern Virginia, General Thomas Smyth, the former commander of the Irish Brigade, was mortally wounded at Farmville. The last Union general to die in the war, Smyth was commanding the Third Division of the Second Corps when a sharpshooter's bullet entered the left side of his face and proceeded to his neck. There the missile fractured a vertebra and pushed a piece of bone against the spinal cord, paralyzing that part of the body. The wounded officer was at first treated at the corps' hospital, but the next day he was carried by ambulance toward Burkesville Station, a dozen miles away. Within two miles of the destination, however, the general took a fatal turn for the worse and passed his final hours in the home of a Colonel Burke.

Smyth's biographer recorded the scene as the general's life ebbed away: "At 4 o'clock on the morning of the 9th, he died as he had lived — a hero; he was perfectly resigned to his fate. Conscious within a very short period before his decease, he talked calmly. Not a groan or complaint had escaped him. He showed no emotion, but as a stoic endured the reflection that his once powerful, vigorous frame was but a complete wreck of humanity liable at any time to be engulfed. . . . He added, 'Now Doctor, you know that I am no coward, and that I am not afraid to die,' and throughout he spoke calmly about passing away." He was buried in Brandywine Cemetery in Wilmington, Delaware.[195]

Eulogists from both within and outside the ranks of the Irish Brigade expressed the high regard with which General Smyth was held. Dr. William O'Meagher, a surgeon in the 69th New York, described the Brigade's reaction to the death of one of its best and most beloved officers: "It would be impossible to picture the grief this unexpected calamity caused to his immediate command and to the Brigade, by whom he was almost idolized. Every thing else was forgotten, and even victory itself could not repay the survivors for the loss of such a gallant commander, and a noble specimen of a man and a soldier. Peace to his great soul, ever-increasing honor to his name, and to his widow and orphan the most heartfelt condolence of his companions in arms!" Another tribute in Captain Conyngham's history of the Brigade was especially poignant: "With the coolness and judgment of the scientific officer he combined a bravery almost amounting to rashness. He generally rode in front of his own picket-lines, along the outer posts, to make sure that all was right. It was a general remark among the men — 'Well, if General Smyth escapes he has a charmed life.' General Smyth was in every sense a credit to his race and his country. Like [Michael] Corcoran, he was thoroughly national, and joined every patriotic movement which had for its aim the liberation of Ireland. The greatest hope of his life was to strike a blow for her freedom, for, like most Irishmen, he felt the degradation of being a race without a country, and of winning renown on foreign battle-fields, while his countrymen at home were a starved, despised race. In him and General Corcoran, Ireland lost two of her noblest and purest patriots — England, two of her bitterest foes." Dr. D. W. Maull, a surgeon in the Second Division of the Second Army Corps, recalled Smyth's stoicism, force of character, modesty, and nobility of soul. Smyth's gentlemanliness drew his future biographer's special attention: "[H]is native refinement was so acute that he was seldom or never heard to utter a sentence that was calculated to offend the most fastidious . . . . [I]n all companies met together for sociality in the field where mirth reigned, he was, though genial as any, always dignified to a certain extent, and always the gentleman."[196]

On the night of the beloved Smyth's death, General Ulysses S. Grant sent his first communication to Robert E. Lee asking for his surrender.

Even in this penultimate act of the war, the Irish Brigade was involved, if only peripherally. Grant routed his letter to Lee through General Humphreys' Second Corps, and Humphreys in turn forwarded it through the Irish Brigade's sector. It was actually Colonel Robert Nugent, the Brigade's commanding officer, who carried the letter through the Confederate lines. The following morning the four regiments of the Brigade continued in pursuit of the Rebels, but not before losing nineteen men killed and ninety-four wounded.[197]

Six weeks later, on May 22, Colonel Nugent was in Washington, D.C., leading the remaining men of the Irish Brigade in a "Grand Review" of the Army of the Potomac. Many of the thousands of well-wishers lining the route no doubt noticed that each of the soldiers in the Brigade wore a sprig of boxwood in his hat, a reminder of the unit's heroism at the battle of Fredericksburg. On July 2, after about 200 convalescing soldiers and prisoners of war were returned to New York, the core of the Brigade — the 63rd, the 69th, and the 88th New York and the 28th Massachusetts — arrived at the Battery Barracks in Manhattan. On Independence Day the 700 marching heroes were escorted through the city by a unit of the New York State National Guard. The *Irish American* described the veterans as "strong and hearty; their faces, bronzed by the exposures of the field[,] were, along the march, wreathed with smiles, as cheer after cheer rent the air, welcoming them back to citizenship and their former homes." As the men of the 28th Massachusetts returned home to Boston, the 400 New York veterans proceeded to Irving Hall, where they cheered General Meagher and their other commanders. After paying tribute to the Brigade's dead, Meagher proposed the construction of "a round tower with a cathedral" to commemorate their glorious deeds.[198]

Meagher's suggestion was never implemented, and for a time the 69th New York had to be content with monuments in verse rather than in stone. Joseph I. C. Clarke, the journalist and poet, reviewed the Civil War service of the famous 69th — "Mother of Irish regiments" — from its early days under Colonel Michael Corcoran to its years as part of the Irish Brigade:

*"The Ballad of the Sixty-Ninth"

Clouds black with thunder o'er the Southern states;
North, East and West a sickening fear;
The Union on the dark laps of the Fates,
And nowhere sign the skies would clear.
Would hate haul down the flag we loved so well —
The star-flag that at Yorktown flew?
For answer came the hurtling of a shell,
With the Union cleft in two!

Never since out of chaos came the world
Sprang such resolve as took us then: —
"Thro' blood and fire, with that brave flag unfurled,
The Union shall be whole again."
At Lincoln's call men swarmed from towns and farms;
An ecstasy shook all the land.
Tramp! tramp! the people's bravest rose in arms.
With them the Irish took their stand.

For here their slave rags had away been cast,
Freedom had met them at the door,
To share such empire lovelit, rich and vast
As never fronted man before.
Our great Republic! Shall the kings behold,
Neath slavery's thrust, its overthrow?
Loud, righteous, quick our regiment's answer rolled: —
"The Irish Sixty-Ninth says, No!"

Tramp! tramp! At Corcoran's command they've swung
Down Broadway's length a thousand strong,
Their flag of green by grand Old Glory flung,
Their steps like music to the cheering throng,
The great Archbishop, blessing rank and file,
Bends o'er them — soldier, gun and blade,
On every face the bold-heart Irish smile
That looks in Death's eyes unafraid.
Mother of Irish regiments, march in pride;
No idle presage in your tread!
The way is long; the battle ground is wide;
High will be the roster of your dead.
Ever you'll find the battle's crest and front,
Then march to seek new fighting ground;
Ever, when shattered in the battle brunt,
Men for the gaps will still be found.

You'll be baptized in fire in Blackburn's Ford,
Bull Run shall see two hundred fall —
You facing south when north the rout has poured;
At Rappahannock like a wall;
You'll strike at Fair Oaks; clash at Gaines's [*sic*] Mill;
And ramp like tigers over Malvern Hill;
Stand and be hammered at Chancellorsville;
Antietam's corn shall redden at your name,
The while you deal the blow that stuns;

At Marye's Heights your men shall feed on flame
Up to the muzzles of the guns;
At Gettysburg fire-dwindled on you'll press,
And then remanned again seek fight;
All through the tangle of the Wilderness,
You'll battle day and night;
At Petersburg you'll spring to the assault;
*Only at Appomattox shall you halt!*

Let Nugent, Meagher, Cavanagh be praised,
MacMahon [*sic*], Kelly, Haggerty, Clark [*sic*],
But the thousands three that the regiment raised,
As surely bore the hero-mark.
Fame's darling child, the Sixty-Ninth shall shine: —
Never in Duty's honor to lag;
Forty-eight times in the battle line,
Never, never to lose a flag.

Tramp! tramp! You saw the Union split in twain,
Tramp! tramp! You saw the nation whole.
Your red blood flowed in torrents not in vain;
It fed the great Republic's soul.
Your drums still roll; your serried ranks still form:
From manhood's service no release.
Ready at call to ride the battle storm,
But best the pledge, the guard of Peace.[199]

After the war, when the statistics on the Irish Brigade were compiled, the figures confirmed the stature which popular opinion had accorded the famous unit. The brigade participated in no fewer than thirty-four battles throughout the war and enlisted in its organization a total of 7,715 men. Although the Brigade never numbered 4,000 men at any one time, it lost more than that number in total casualties (killed, wounded, missing, and dead from disease, accident, and imprisonment). Of that number, 961 were killed or mortally wounded in action, a statistic exceeded by only two other brigades in the Union army. Of the 2,000 regiments that fought for the North, the 69th New York and the 28th Massachusetts were ranked sixth and seventh, respectively, in the number of men killed or mortally wounded. (The 69th lost 259; the 28th, 250.) In addition, the 69th lost more men killed and mortally wounded in action than any other regiment from the State of New York. Viewed from another angle, the overall figures for the Brigade showed that those who died from direct war-related causes (disease and death or mortal wounds sustained in combat) numbered 1,494. These casualties were distributed among the five regiments as follows:

the 69th New York, 401; the 28th Massachusetts, 387; the 63rd New York, 249; the 116th Pennsylvania, 234; the 88th New York, 223. A closer examination of the record of the 69th New York reveals a more complete picture: total enrollment, 1,513; killed or mortally wounded, 259; wounded, 535; missing, 148; dead of disease or accident, eighty-six; died in Confederate prisons, fifty-six.[200]

Although complete in their own way, the statistics alone could not do justice to the legacy of the Irish Brigade and the 69th New York. In his report of the final days of the war, Colonel Nugent heaped praise on the Brigade, penning what he may have intended as its epitaph: "[I]t gives me sincere pleasure to add that the officers and men of my command behaved, under the most trying circumstances, with courage and fidelity, carrying out all orders to my complete satisfaction, they having now the proud satisfaction of seeing a stubborn enemy, whom they have combatted against for nearly four years, humbled, thereby adding their feeble mite to promote the life, prosperity, and independence of our nation." Perhaps with a similar intent, Frank Moore included in his collection of anecdotes an episode about the 69th New York: "Two gallant sons of Erin, being just discharged from the service, were rejoicing over the event with a 'wee taste of the cratur,' when one, who felt all the glory of his own noble race, suddenly raised his glass above, and said, 'Arrah, Mike, here's to the gallant ould Sixty-ninth: *The last in the field and the first to leave!*' 'Tut, tut, man,' said Mike, 'you don't mane [mean] that.' 'Don't mane,' said Mike, and he raised his glass high, and looked lovingly at it, 'Here's to the gallant ould Sixty-ninth — *equal to none!*' And so they drank."[201]

During New York City's tumultuous welcome to the returning Union veterans on July 4, 1865, Thomas Meagher was uncharacteristically inconspicuous, except for the civilian clothes he wore and the fact that he was on foot. To keen observers along the route, however, his humble — and humbled — appearance symbolized the eclipse which his life had suffered in recent years and which would characterize his life until his untimely death almost two years later. As far back as June 1863, Meagher had tried to convince the War Department and President Lincoln to reinstate him as a general and to allow him to reorganize the Irish Brigade. When no answer was forthcoming, he trimmed his request, asking only that his letter of resignation be withdrawn and that he be allowed to serve the government in some capacity. By the following fall, however, he was again talking about recruiting a corps of between 5,000 and 7,000 veteran troops. At about the same time, he confided to Captain James O'Beirne that military life was his "true life": "It is, perhaps, the only honest, generous, noble life we can lead — especially under the present circumstances in America, where Civil life has, for the most part, become so selfish and corrupt, owing to the vast amount of political patronage distributed through it . . . ." At the end of the year the War Department finally canceled his resignation as a brigadier general in the Volunteers, thereby reinstating him in the Union army.[202]

Not until the middle of September 1864, however, was Meagher given a command. At that time the War Department ordered him to proceed to Nashville, Tennessee, where he would receive an assignment from Major General William Sherman. In due course the Irishman was placed in command of some brigades of convalescents in the Army of the Tennessee. With these men Meagher guarded the railroad lines out of Chattanooga, an assignment that lasted about a month, part of which time he was in command of the Military District of Etowah. Sometime at the beginning of the new year, Meagher was ordered to embark with the Provisional Division, Army of the Tennessee, to Savannah to help Sherman. While Meagher and his troops made their way south, the War Department learned of charges that Meagher's officers were ill treating their troops. Although the Irishman and various of his officers denied the charges, additional claims that Meagher's command was in utter confusion and disarray led to his dismissal from command.[203]

As if this disgrace was not sufficiently detrimental to the advancement he craved, Meagher had alienated his natural constituency of Irish-Americans. In cozying up to the Lincoln administration in order to promote his military career, he had virtually abandoned the Democratic party. He seemed to seal his fate when he imprudently criticized Irish Democrats in print. His letter, which appeared in the *Irish American* on October 15, 1864, read in part: "To their own discredit and degradation, they [Irish Democrats] have suffered themselves to be bamboozled into being obstinate herds in the political field, contracting inveterate instincts, following with gross stupidity and the stoniest blindness certain worn out old pathways described for them by their drivers . . . ." He gratuitously added that to be a Democrat was to be a partisan of "a selfish and conscienceless faction." In reply, the *Irish American* pronounced his political obituary: "Between him and the people who loved and trusted him once he has opened a gulf he never can bridge over." But it was Meagher's endorsement of Lincoln's reelection that November which caused the *Irish American* to fulminate: "In General Meagher's fall from the high position he once held in the esteem and affection of his countrymen, we see only a subject for regret; our indignation at his unprovoked attack upon our people has long subsided into contempt, and we have no desire to add a deeper tint to an act that has gone so far to darken the whole record of his life, of which the promise was once so fair."[204]

Thus frustrated in his military ambition and virtually a pariah to his countrymen, Meagher turned his thoughts to beginning a new life in the Far West. On August 2, 1865, while in Minneapolis, he received word from President Andrew Johnson asking whether he would accept the secretaryship of Montana, at the time still a territory. The general needed no time to ponder his reply and immediately set out by stagecoach to Virginia City, then the capital of the expansive future state. En route he was met by Montana's territorial governor, Sidney Edgerton, who summarily turned over his executive duties to Meagher before departing for a visit to his home in Ohio. The general lost no time in informing William Lyons, his friend at the *New York Herald*, of his sudden good fortune, referring to himself as the "Acting Governor of the richest territory of the Union." Meagher also asked Lyons to publish the news in the New York press so the local Irish would know of his sudden ascendancy.[205]

Despite its auspicious beginnings, Meagher's tenure as acting governor was marked by conflict on a variety of fronts. The territory had been created under a Republican administration and was governed by Republicans, although Southerners and Democrats made up most of its population. When Meagher bowed to requests to order elections for a new legislature, the resulting assembly was overwhelmingly Democratic. In response, the Republican-appointed officials virtually declared war on Meagher, arguing that he had had no authority to call for new elections (an argument later upheld by the Radical Republicans in Congress). To these political attacks was added a campaign of extremely vile personal epithets, part of what Meagher called a conspiracy by his enemies to "disable me by slander." The acting governor even became the victim of death threats, most notably when he pardoned James Daniels, who had been sentenced to three years' imprisonment for killing another man in a quarrel during a card game. When a group of vigilantes hanged Daniels from a tree, they attached to his coat a warning: "If our acting governor does this [i.e., grant such a pardon] again, we will hang him too."[206]

Much of Meagher's time was taken up with trying to obtain for the territory military protection against both real and imagined threats from local Sioux. Thus it was that on July 1, 1867, the acting chief executive arrived at Fort Benton, Montana, expecting to pick up 2,500 guns sent up the Missouri River from St. Louis for a regiment he had raised against the Indians. The arms had not arrived by steamboat, however, but were instead 120 miles away at Camp Cook. According to I. G. Baker, the proprietor of the store in Fort Benton where Meagher spent several hours that afternoon, the general had been suffering from a severe case of diarrhea for the previous several days. Meanwhile, Johnny Doran, the pilot of the *G. A. Thompson*, the steamboat which had just arrived from St. Louis, found Meagher at Baker's store. Learning that Meagher had made no plans for the evening, Doran invited his fellow countryman to dine and to spend the night aboard the boat. There they spent the rest of the afternoon smoking cigars, reading, and no doubt catching up on events since their last meeting. Suddenly, according to Doran, his guest put down his book and said excitedly, "Johnny, they threaten my life in that town." Although Doran tried to allay the general's fears, Meagher asked to check the pilot's pistols. After seeing that Doran's two weapons were loaded and capped, he handed them back to their owner and retired to his berth. Sometime during the night, however, Meagher mysteriously disappeared. Doran and others on board heard a splash in the water that night and then two agonizing cries, the first one very short, the last prolonged. The would-be rescuers realized that to jump into the river in search of a body would be suicidal, given the darkness and the depth of the river and its rushing current. Instead, Doran and his companions ran down river to one of the other steamers, from which they hoped to save the presumably drowning man by throwing him lifelines. But these efforts were to no avail.[207]

Additional light was shed on Meagher's disappearance by Captain Patrick Condon, one of the general's trusted friends and a former officer in the Irish Brigade. In the fall of 1868, Condon happened to meet the soldier who had served as sentry aboard the steamer the night of Meagher's disappearance. In a letter to Michael Cavanagh, one of Meagher's biographers, in 1892, Condon wrote that the sentry's sworn testimony "was substantially as follows: While on duty during the night, pacing the deck, I heard a noise stern-ward; on looking in that direction I saw somebody moving in white clothing (underclothes) toward the left rear of the stern, where I knew the temporary accommodation place [privy?] of the vessel was. Of course I about faced and marched the other way, thinking some one of the officers had a 'short call,' and re-pacing my round about midway, I heard a shout and then a splash — that was all. I shouted 'man overboard.' In a moment the deck was alive; floating life buoys were flung out — boats and lights on the water. . . . but all to no purpose."[208]

On August 14, 1867, a month and a half after Meagher's disappearance, the officers of the Irish Brigade memorialized their famous leader at two special events. The first, a requiem mass, was celebrated at St. Francis Xavier Church in New York City, while the other was a gathering that night at the Cooper Institute, during which Richard O'Gorman eulogized the friend of his youth. In an exceptionally long oration, O'Gorman recalled the excitement which rippled through Ireland on the eve of what was hoped would be a national uprising against British rule in 1848. "He did not shrink from the ordeal," O'Gorman said of his subject. "He deemed himself in honor bound — himself to take for weal or for woe the risks he had invited others to assume. He threw himself among the people, ready to lead or to follow, as they pleased, going forth to face fearful odds with a heart as light as if he thought there was merry-making before him, and not the harvest of death. Remember he had nothing to gain and everything to lose — an honorable social position, the prospect of wealth, the reputation of distinguished ability — all the advantages that give to youth sure promise of a brilliant and prosperous future." But, of course, the uprising was not to be, and instead Meagher was arrested and sentenced to death. After reciting Meagher's speech during his trial at Clonmel,

O'Gorman challenged the condemned man's later critics: "[T]ell me if you could have raised your souls to so grand an eminence as his who that day set the prisoner above the judge who tried him, and dignified the felon's dock till it became, in the eyes of the world, a temple of freedom." O'Gorman continued with a summary of Meagher's civilian and military life in America and reached a climax by including him among the pantheon of Irish martial leaders: "Never did *Clare, or Dillon, or Sarsfield more gallantly lead on gallant men on *Landen, on Cremona, on Fontenoy, than did Meagher, when he cheered on the boys of his Irish Brigade at Fair Oaks, Malvern Hill, Antietam, or, when at Fredericksburg, he obeyed the fatal order that doomed the Irish Brigade to hopeless slaughter in the attack on Marye's Heights. Aye! Be proud of the Irish Brigade. Be proud of him who led it. Preserve his memory, ye who served with him in these days of fire and death. Three thousand men were in that Brigade when it went into the war; *five hundred were all that left it. Yet it never disobeyed an order, never lost a flag, never lost hope, or heart, or cheerfulness." Near the end of his lengthy eulogy, O'Gorman spoke what could serve as a fitting epitaph on Meagher's watery grave: "Never forget this; he gave all, lost all, for the land of his birth. He risked all for the land of his adoption, was her true and loyal soldier, and in the end died in her service."[209]

---

*"Thomas Francis Meagher" by James J. Bourke

As rolls Montana's tideless wave,
Far westward out where sinks the sun,
It sweeps above a nameless grave
Where sleeps a Tribune bright and brave;
A soldier whose campaigning's done —
A soldier on whose conquering sword
Both gods and men might look with pride;
An orator whose lightning word
Could flash like meteor of the Lord —
Who loving lived and loving died.

The regal sun, the watching stars,
The moon when in its rounded crest,
Fling forth in rays of slanting bars
Deep through the rush of watery wars
A cross of silver o'er his breast,
Down where his whitening bones are strewn
Beneath the river's ceaseless roll;
And sobbing winds that night or noon,
His wailing mourners hymn their tune,

And sigh soft dirges for his soul.

Full many a stately galley speeds
In gleam of glory o'er the place,
Where, far below the throbbing reeds
And shrouded by the water weeds,
Lies stark his pale, uncoffined face;
And travellers list with bated breath
While pilots tell the tale of doom —
How he who wore the victor's wreath
Sank battling here with night and death,
And found an unanointed tomb.

But, ah, no trophy crowns the spot
Where cold and pulseless wastes the heart
That dared of yore, when youth was hot,
The hangman's rope, the felon's lot,
To act for Eire a true man's part;
The waters seethe with hurrying dread
Above the dull and lampless brain,
The tongue of fire is mute and dead,
And sands are round the God-like head,
And all but prayer for him is vain.

Yet had he, when his sands were run,
Been laid to sleep in hallowed clay,
The land for whom his work was done,
Beneath whose flag he'd fought and won
Would strew his grave with flowers to-day,
The marble pile they'd upward rear
Till flame-like it would flaunt the skies,
And many a broken lance and spear
They'd place around the warrior's bier
And shattered drum and banner-prize.

They mourn him in the land he loved,
His priceless worth, his conquering arm,
They miss him where in grace he moved —
For camp and council both have proved
His master mind to guide or charm.
And many a tale will yet be told,
By camping fires in future wars,
Of him who with his clansmen bold
Shook out the old green banners fold

To fight beneath the Stripes and Stars.

And hosts will whisper listening guests
The Southern foeman's wild refrain,
When glared he o'er the green-plumed crests,
And sprigs of green on Irish breasts —
"Here comes that damned Green Flag again!"
And hearts will fire and pulses bound
At thoughts of Antietam's day;
When hemmed by fire and foeman round,
The Irish stormed the vantage ground —
And claimed the glory of the fray.

And Fredericksburg's hard foughten field,
Where men were mown like autumn grain,
Shall prove, though oft it broke and reeled —
That Irish valor could not yield,
Though wheel-deep lay the mangled slain.
What time that Meagher with glance of pride,
Points out the range of belching guns —
"Go take them now," he laughing cried;
And while the storm of death rung wide,
They straight obeyed like duteous sons.

Oh, these are memories that evoke
The noblest traits that stamp our race,
For through the rift of fire and smoke,
Where wild the Irish slogan broke,
When foe met foeman face to face,
We know that each day's battle close
Though fierce and bloody'd been the fight,
Saw wounded soldiers tend the foes,
Heard pitying words that heavenward rose,
And prayers above the dead at night.

But we, with whom the chieftan [sic] grew
Who proudly led this bold brigade,
Whose voice, whose form, whose face we knew,
Whose fiery soul, whose courage true,
Are with us dreams that will not fade;
Who've heard his glorious burning words,
Like Him the Roman chief of old,
Who bade the slaves gird on their swords,
And smite to doom their tyrant lords,

And Heaven would aye them guiltless hold.

And we within the circling bound
Of this proud city of the Gael,
The rebel Emmet's camping ground,
The scene of Edward's martyr wound,
The throbbing heart of Innisfail —
Shall we erect no storied urn,
Or marble statue carven fair,
To him whose God-like words could burn,
Who never more may now return,
Like wearied child her breast to share.

Oh, pile the stone and heap the cairn,
And carve the likeness of his face,
And twine at foot the oak and fern,
That coming nations yet may learn
He lived the Isaiah of our race.
But if you'd fill your glorious part,
And glance upon your work with pride,
And image true of Meagher impart,
Oh, place a shamrock o'er his heart —
For it he lived, for it he died![210]

On July 4, 1905, thousands of spectators gathered outside the west entrance to the capitol building in Helena, Montana, to witness the unveiling of a huge equestrian statue in honor of Thomas Francis Meagher. The artwork depicts Montana's acting territorial governor in a martial stance astride a charger and brandishing an uplifted sabre. Sculpted by Charles Mulligan and cast by William Burns of the American Bronze Company of Chicago, the statue was erected through the efforts of the Meagher Memorial Association, chaired by Marcus Daly, the Irish-born "Copper King" of Butte, Montana. An account of the event in the *Helena Independent* pointed out that the statue captured the contrasts in Meagher's character: "The strong features, the deep sunk eyes, the strong mouth, covered by a drooping mustache, everything about the figure suggests the man of melancholy and of courage, of gentle thought and fiery action, the eyes of the dreamer and the mouth of the stern man of affairs. It suggests the alluring contradictions of the man's character, the versatility which made him the leader of his party in his youth, the 'Meagher of the Sword' and the Meagher of the spoken word."[211]

One of the onlookers at the unveiling was a Civil War veteran from New York who was believed to be the last survivor of Meagher's original company of Zouaves. (This unit was later incorporated into the 69th New York State Militia as Company K.) The *Montana Daily Record* referred to the veteran as "William Burns" — perhaps confusing him with the name of the individual who cast the statue — while the *Helena Independent* identified the former soldier as "Thomas J. Byrne." Neither name, however, is found in the *Roster of Union Soldiers* as a member of Company K of the 69th New York, although a veteran named "Thomas Burns" is so listed. Whatever the man's identity, "Burns" was unwilling to talk to the press about his connection with General Meagher, although he did describe the creation of the Zouaves. Burns, in fact, attended the unveiling of Meagher's statue dressed in his old Zouave uniform: blue jacket faced with red, green tunic bordered in red, green sash, gray trousers, canvas leggings, and blue cap. Referring to one of the consequences of the Civil War, Burns said that it gave the Irish "the opportunity to show what we were and to break down the prejudice that obtained against us because of our race and religion. . . . It was on the field of battle [that] those who misunderstood us learned to know Gen. Meagher and the men of his race, and there has since been no misunderstanding."[212]

As was the custom of the time, several lengthy speeches accompanied the dedication of the Meagher statue. R. R. Purcell, the mayor of Helena, praised the famous general as one "who never raised his voice or sword except in behalf of honor, the interest and the prosperity of the people of the land of his birth, as well as the people of the land of his adoption." Lieutenant Governor Edwin Norris sounded a similar theme but added that "Wherever there has been a meeting in the name or cause of liberty, wherever a sword has been raised for freedom, an Irishman has been found there." The principal oration of the day, however, was delivered by Colonel John Finerty, a native of Galway and a well-known journalist and congressman from Illinois. The colonel reminded his audience of how Ireland lost her political independence when the Act of Union was passed in 1801: "The strong-arm of a greater power and [the] genius of an unscrupulous minister and the treason of men who thanked God that they had a country to sell, but who, thank the lord of freedom, were not men of the old Celtic race, handed over to the power of England cheerfully and unscrupulously the native land of 20,000,000 of the American people." Finerty continued with a review of Meagher's life and career, especially as "the compeer of the greatest among the orators of the world." "The speeches of Thomas Francis Meagher are the gospel of freedom," Finerty went on. "They come to us as a precious heritage which we will always treasure here in this great free country which he helped to unify: here in this country all of which he loved, for Gen. Thomas Francis Meagher was a nonsectarian; he loved the south as well as the north, and when he drew that sword [pointing to the monument] it was with no hatred of the south, which had so hospitably received him, but with a full sense of citizenship

*The Thomas Francis Meagher equestrian statue in Helena, Montana. During the Civil War Meagher was captain of Company K in the 69th New York State Militia Regiment and later organized and commanded the Irish Brigade.*

that he entered into the army of the union." In his concluding words Finerty expressed his hope that some day the liberty enjoyed by Americans will "be borne on the mountain breezes of Montana across the sea and give to Ireland the liberty of which England has rapaciously deprived her."[213]

The base on which the statue of Meagher stands is adorned with several bronze plaques — two summarizing his life, three containing excerpts from his speeches, and one containing a tribute from Richard O'Gorman:

*Irish patriot and orator; born in the city of Waterford, Ireland, August 3, 1823; sent to Paris in 1848 by the Irish Confederation and the citizens of Dublin to present an address of congratulation to the French people on the establishment of the Republic; indicted and tried at Clonmel, Ireland, September, 1848, for active participation in the Irish insurrectionary movement against English rule, and sentenced to be hanged, drawn and quartered; sentence commuted to transportation for life to the convict colony of Van Dieman's Land.* [Some sources give Meagher's birthdate as August 23.]

*American soldier and statesman; brigadier general United States Army; raised and organized the Irish Brigade in the Army of the Potomac, and personally com-*

manded it in the battles of Fair Oaks, Mechanicsville, Gaines' Mill, White Oaks [sic] Swamp, Malvern Hill, Fredericksburg, Antietam and Chancellorsville; appointed to the command of the Etowah District as acting major general in November, 1864; acting governor of Montana from September, 1865 to July 1, 1867, when he was drowned in the Missouri River, at Fort Benton, Montana.

"Abhor the sword, stigmatize the sword; no, my lord, for at its blow a giant nation started from the waters of the Atlantic and by its redeeming magic, and in the quivering of its crimson light, the crippled colony sprang into the attitude of a proud republic prosperous, limitless and invincible." From speech at Conciliation Hall, Dublin, July 28, 1846.

"If in the vicissitudes to which all nations are exposed, danger should fall upon the great Republic, and if the choice be made to us to desert or befriend the land of Washington and Franklin, I, for one, will prefer to be grateful to the Samaritan, rather than be loyal to the Levite." From speech on American Be-

The Thomas
Francis
Meagher
equestrian
statue
in Helena,
Montana.

nevolence–Irish Gratitude, Rotunda, Dublin, 1847.

*"My heart, my arm, my life are pledged to the National cause, and to the last it shall be my highest pride, as I conceive it to be my holiest duty and obligation to share its fortunes."* From speech at Jones' Wood, New York, 1861.

*"The true American knows, feels, and with enthusiasm declares, that of all human emotions, of all human passions, there is not one more pure, more noble, more conducive to good and great and glorious deeds, than that which bears us back to the spot that was the cradle of our childhood, the playground of our boyhood, the theatre of our manhood."* From address delivered in Virginia City, Montana, March 17, 1866.

*"To the end, I see the path I have been ordained to walk, and upon the grave which closes in that path, I can read no coward's epitaph."* From speech on the transportation of Mitchel, 1848.

*"In Ireland, in America, he invited no man to danger he was not ready to share. Never forget this: he gave all, lost all for the land of his birth. He risked all for the land of his adoption, was her true and loyal soldier, and in the end died in her service."* [From Richard O'Gorman's eulogy of Meagher, August 14, 1867.][214]

On March 4, 1914, almost nine years after the dedication of the Meagher statue in Helena, the Irishman's life was again at the center of a commemorative event. This time the occasion was the presentation of the famous general's sword to the University of Notre Dame. In making the presentation, Senator Thomas Walsh of Montana referred to Meagher as "the gifted orator, the zealous patriot, the redoubtable warrior, the genial and cultured gentleman" and explained how the sword had come into the possession of the university. After Meagher's untimely death, the great Irishman's widow entrusted the sword to Andrew O'Connell, whom Meagher had appointed justice of the peace at large for Montana Territory. O'Connell, it seems, had shown such kindness to Mrs. Meagher in her grief after her husband's disappearance that she left the treasured relic with him when she returned to her parents' home in New York City. In turn, O'Connell bequeathed the sword to his niece, who, like him, had lived as a youngster in Terre Haute, Indiana, but had migrated to Montana. It was at the direction of that lady — Catherine Young of Kalispel, Montana — that Senator Walsh entrusted Meagher's sword to the university.[215]

After accepting the prized gift on behalf of Notre Dame, Father John Cavanaugh explained why it was fitting that the sword should finally rest there. Noting that "the fairest fruit of true education is to hunger and thirst after justice, to admire nobility of soul and strength of character and unselfish devotion to an unpopular but worthy cause, and to cherish dearer than life the ideals of Christian chivalry and Christian civilization," the priest described Meagher as one of the best types of the "rightly educated man." After alluding to Meagher's education in Ireland  — at a school which Cavanaugh compared to Notre Dame — the priest went on: "From such academic groves [Meagher] emerged the idealist, the patriot, the lover of human freedom, . . . dedicating his eloquent tongue and his brave heart to the service of religion and liberty. Let his sword be a perpetual reminder, to the youth of America, of a patriot, the story of whose life is as thrilling as *Emmet's; of an orator as magic as *O'Connell; a scholar whose biblical and classical lore would adorn the most learned lecture hall; and a soldier whose courage, dash and brilliance are unsurpassed in the history of modern war. . . . To no man of Irish birth or Irish blood does America owe more than to Thomas Francis Meagher, the orator who rallied the people of his race to the support of the nation, the intrepid leader who dashed at the head of his troops into the deadliest danger in every battle. It is well that the symbol of such a soldier should find its final resting-place in a great school which has always cherished the twin-ideals of religion and patriotism."[216]

Father Cavanaugh offered three more reasons that Meagher's sword should repose at Notre Dame. One was the fact that during the Civil War the founder of the university, Father Edward Sorin, had sent to the seat of war seven of his "ablest and noblest" priests as chaplains. Among the seven, Cavanaugh reminded his hearers, was Father William Corby, "the friend and confessor of Meagher" and a chaplain in the famous Irish Brigade. In addition, the university already possessed the Brigade's original Green Flag as well as the sword of another great Irishman, General James Shields, who had urged the appointment of Meagher as the Brigade's first commander.[217]

At the conclusion of Father Cavanaugh's remarks, Father Charles O'Donnell read a poem of his own composition celebrating the reunion of Meagher's sword with the Irish Brigade's battle-scarred green flag. In his imagination the poet conceived a host of Irish heroes come to celebrate the marriage of the "sun-bright sword and the sea-bright flag":

*"A Hosting of the Gael"

This is a marriage feast today,
A wishèd anniversary
Of union and reunion; Emmet, Meagher, all
True sons of Irish blood for honor dead,
With lifted head,
Hearken to this most jocund muster call;
Their ships are on the sea, —
From ancient Donegal
They come, from Kerry,
Ah, and from Tipperary,
Yea, rather, say

From Dublin to Cathay,
From Belgian battlefields, from Spain,
From snowed Saskatchewan, from Afric sand,
From Flodden Field, and Fontenoy,
From every field and every land,
Come man and boy
To keep with us this day a sacred trust,
For the earth is starred with work of Irish brain
And rich with Irish dust.
Behold, of heroes hosting here today,
In the farthest fore
Stand men whose eyes
Are blue and gray
Like Irish skies
And like the coats they wore.

No party festival of North or South
By us is kept,
And on our mouth
No vaunting of a single patriot name
To envied fame;
But in one man stands glorified the race.
Their brow we grace
With crown of laurel and with olive leaf,
And in proud grief
That has no tongue and keeps its tears unwept,
We greet the splendid host of Irish dead,
Leaving their age-old shroud,
Gaunt witnesses, a cloud,
By every wind increased,
Ghostly battalions led by greater ghosts
That round us troop, with measured, noiseless tread —
O God of Hosts,
We bid them welcome to our marriage feast.

Should any answer come
Whence stand they ranked and dumb?
A sudden thunder of a shout
Their throats give out
As if these long dead bones
Yet kept remembrance of old trumpet tones;
The dense, straight ranks are stirred
And rises one great word —
"Fredericksburg" is heard,

While comes this chorus forth:

"We are the men that followed, followed after
The sun-bright sword and the sea-bright flag,
With a faith in our hearts that rose like laughter
Most in the straits where the craven lag;
We are the men no danger daunted,
Following Freedom like a star,
Hot after glory, honor-haunted,
With our flag of green and our sworded Meagher.

"We are the men and these our brothers
Who held the heights and threw us back;
Over them, too, these thousand others,
A green flag waved through the war cloud black.
And Fredericksburg is an open story,
It was Irish blood both sides outpoured,
For they, too, followed honor and glory,
A green flag theirs, but not our sword.

"And we are come from the peace of slumber,
Nor North, nor South, by division sharp,
But Irish all, of that world-wide number
In all times mighty with sword and harp;
To lift once more, from the dust, our voices,
In one last cheer that may echo far —
Fredericksburg in the grave rejoices,
Now the Flag of Green weds the Sword of Meagher."

So sang they, pale dead men,
Risen from their cold dream
To follow still the Gleam;
And in their hollowed eyes
Were what with mortals pass for tears
As after many years
They saw again the frayed and faded fold
That was their Cloth of the Field of Gold;
And a flash as of a star
When they saw the shining length
Of the blade that in his strength
Girt the dauntless Meagher.
Lo! flag and sword together pressed,
By all their eyes caressed.
Then like a breath of prayer

They melted on the air.

Learn we from these our dead
The meaning of this day,
And be not lightly led
From our fathers' way.
Not what our hands may hold —
Few threads of green and gold
And storied steel —
Not by these tokens may we feel
Sons of our laurelled sires,
Save that the same pure fires
Burn all our souls within,
And heart to heart, the quick heart to the dead, be kin.
Keep we the Faith sword-bright
By day, by night,
Our fathers' meed shall never suffer loss
But know increase.
The sword itself is likened to the cross
That is our peace.[218]

The Honorable W. Bourke Cockran concluded the presentation ceremonies at Notre Dame with a final tribute to "Meagher of the Sword." Warning his audience that it would be a mistake to think that Meagher had earned this sobriquet because of a blood-thirst for glory earned by the sword, the speaker stressed Meagher's belief in the right of resistance to British oppression in his native Ireland. Meagher boldly proclaimed, said Cockran, "that there was but one position which a freeman could hold in the teeth of tyranny and alien oppression, and that was resistance — resistance by peaceable means while there was a hope that it would be effective, but when the eyes of the tyrant were closed to remonstrances of a whole suffering people, that then it was not merely the right, but the unescapable duty of every freeman to draw the sword, no matter what the odds against him, no matter how powerful the forces of the oppressor."[219]

# Chapter 3

## The 69th New York National Guard Regiment in the Spanish-American War

When the United States declared war on Spain in the spring of 1898 over events in Cuba, the 69th New York National Guard displayed the same readiness to serve which earlier members of the regiment had shown at the outbreak of the Civil War. Major General Charles F. Roe, the commander of the New York National Guard, was eager to ascertain how many members of the state regiments would be willing to volunteer for service outside the boundaries of the state. At the time, the 69th counted in its ranks thirty-one officers and 529 enlisted men. In response to Roe's inquiry, Lieutenant Colonel Edward Duffy, the regimental commander, reported that the men in the famous regiment would volunteer as a unit and could be counted on to serve anywhere the nation might ask it to. In order to make his offer official, Duffy accordingly issued General Order No. 47, dated April 1, 1898: "The Commanding Officer, mindful of the record and traditions of the regiment, rests assured of the enthusiastic support and cooperation of every member, and takes occasion to impress upon all the necessity for the vigorous recruiting of the different companies, so that our ranks may be swelled to full numbers. The example of our heroic predecessors of 1861 should be always before us, and it should be our pride to emulate their glorious conduct if called upon to vindicate the nation's honor and defend in any quarter the flag of our country."[1]

Despite this lofty wish, several unfortunate incidents during the next few days reflected poorly on the famous 69th New York Regiment. At a caucus of officers gathered to discuss the question of a candidate for colonel, angry words were hurled and violence almost broke out. The caucus — attended by twenty of the regiment's officers — had been called at the suggestion of Father Patrick Daly, the regimental chaplain. In a letter to the officers, the priest had expressed his belief that the regiment's reputation would be enhanced if the caucus was unanimous in the selection of its colonel during the upcoming regimental election. Captain Edward McCrystal immediately jumped to his feet to protest against the letter, arguing that the chaplain should not have interfered in a matter that was strictly military. Further disagreement arose over whether the chaplain's letter meant that the vote of the caucus should be binding on the final vote. Tempers reached the boiling point when Captain Charles Healy, the presiding officer, accused McCrystal of hypocrisy. The latter officer, Healy charged, now supported the candidacy of Lieutenant Colonel Duffy but four years earlier had argued that that officer was incompetent and unfit to lead the regiment. When McCrystal denied that he had made such remarks about Duffy, Healy called his fellow captain a liar. The two appeared headed for a fist fight until several other officers interposed themselves between the antagonists. During the caucus balloting, Duffy won eleven votes to his two opponents' nine. A second ballot gave Duffy two more votes. The following evening the official election showed that Duffy was the choice of fourteen officers, although many men in the ranks greeted the news with hisses. In fact, his principal opponent, Major Thomas Lynch, received loud cheers from the men, and his friends and supporters carried him through the hall on their shoulders.[2]

On April 28 Colonel Duffy received authority to recruit the regiment to twelve companies of three officers and eighty-one men each. This task was accomplished so quickly that on May 2 the regiment left for Camp Black in Hempstead Plains, Long Island. The names of the regiment's chief officers reflected its overwhelmingly Celtic composition. Besides Colonel Duffy, the roster included Lieutenant Colonel Joseph Donovan, Major Thomas Lynch, Adjutant Granville Emmet, Quartermaster James Cronin, Chaplain William Daly, and company captains Michael Lynch, Peter Maguire, John Kennedy, James Plunket, Michael Ryan, Anthony Griffin, John Duffy, Daniel Devlin, Charles Healy, Daniel McCarthy, Hugh Barron, and John Roche.[3]

When the 69th was mustered into the service of the United States less than three weeks later, it was the only regiment sworn in with a full complement of officers and men. As the 1,030 men of the regiment formed in battalions, an immense crowd of visitors from Manhattan gathered on the edges of the mustering ground to witness the ceremony. Volleys of cheers echoed from the onlookers after the soldiers raised their hands to take the oath as members of the United States volunteer army. Although the regiment had as yet received no information about its destination, the rumor that a good New York regiment was to be sent to the Philippines had heightened the recruits' expectations that they would see active duty sooner than their comrades. The only thing that marred the men's enthusiasm was the fact that not all the recruits had been provided with their uniforms and equipment.[4]

Following the mustering-in ceremony, a committee of the Friendly Sons of St. Patrick presented the 69th New York with a stand of national, state, regimental, and Irish flags. Judge James Fitzgerald of the Court of General Sessions of Manhattan made the presentation speech, to which Colonel Duffy replied. Joseph I. C. Clarke, the well-known journalist and poet, described the scene: "The deeper notes in the diapason of history vibrate in us, and Irish brigades of other centuries and other lands seem once more enacting their outlined braveries beneath many skies, under many banners fluttering in a breeze as fresh as that blowing cool and damp in our faces now. In a good round voice a civilian orator, Judge Fitzgerald, is telling without oratorical paraphrase what the gathering means. His sentences tell clearly that the thousand men before him love the great land of their adoption, the great State that sends them forth and the land that gave them or their fathers birth — a Shamrock of love, he says poetically. As he speaks, flag after flag is unfurled — first the red, white and blue of the Stars and Stripes, eagle crowned; next the white figured flag of the State of New York, and last the green sunburst flag of Ireland, surmounted by a gold pikehead, all brave and beautiful, and each one flapping and whipping from its staff like a great tropical bird first trying its bright wings upon the wind. Cheer upon cheer rises from the crowd, and rolls back as in echo from the regiment. Colonel Duffy salutes, and says briefly that his regiment thanks the Friendly Sons of St. Patrick for their silken gift, and says for his men that they will carry the flags to the war with pride and bring them home without stain. It is all very simple and in proportion touching."[5]

By May 24 the 69th New York had received orders to leave Camp Black and to report to General John Brooke of the United States Army in Chickamauga, Georgia. Although the two battalions of the regiment were not scheduled to arrive in Manhattan before noon, a crowd began to gather at the ferry landing near East 34th Street at 9 a.m. By 2:15 in the afternoon, when the first battalion — under Colonel Duffy — landed, a crowd estimated at 10,000 filled the streets leading to the ferry. Ten minutes later the second battalion arrived under the command of Lieutenant Colonel Joseph Donovan. As Colonel Duffy wheeled his men into First Avenue, the regimental band started to play "The Star-Spangled Banner," but its notes were all but drowned out by the enthusiastic cheers of the well-wishers in the streets. The volunteer soldiers proceeded along 34th Street, their senses reeling from the continued cheering, the sight of American, Cuban, and Irish flags everywhere, and the melody of *"The Wearing of the Green." Just before the column of soldiers reached Second Avenue, a girl sprang from the crowd and rushed to the side of Drum Major Frank Evans, her father. Her arm around his shoulder, and tears streaming down her face, she marched for almost a block before melting back into the crowd along the curb. Elsewhere along the route, so the New York Times reported, "Men rushed at the soldiers, offering them flasks, cigars, and even money, and women pressed forward with slices of pie and huge chunks of cake. Other women, carrying babies, held the little ones aloft, so that the husbands and fathers in the ranks might see them. Others, again, parted temporarily with their children, that the fathers might carry them for a block or two."[6]

At the last minute the regiment's route was changed, and the columns of volunteers marched north along Park and Fifth avenues to St. Patrick's Cathedral. There a half dozen priests stood on the steps and responded to the cheers and salutes of the recruits, waving, in particular, to Father William Daly, the regimental chaplain. The troops then circled the cathedral, visiting en route the residence of Archbishop Michael Corrigan. As the cleric blessed the regiment from his doorstep, the music and the cheers of the crowds were momentarily hushed. At 22nd Street a tobacco firm showered the men with packages of their product wrapped in red, white, and blue colors. At Madison Square about 20,000 people greeted the regiment from a large reviewing stand, while farther along 24th Street 700 school children saluted the troops with a rendition of "Glory, Glory, Hallelujah!" All along the route, but especially on Broadway, the men were showered with roses by the women in the streets and from the windows above. At Union Square the regiment halted while the band again played "The Star-Spangled Banner." Elsewhere along the route, when the men saw a British flag hanging from one of the residences, some of them cried out, "Take that in!" As if to make amends for her neighbor's insensitivity to the Irish-American troops, a "buxom ironing girl" waved a bright green shirt toward the soldiers, who replied with a cheer. When the line of march approached the ferry building, a crowd of 10,000 blocked the entrance, and it was only with great difficulty and patience that the soldiers pushed their way through the wall of humanity. In the meantime, women clung desperately to their uniformed sons, while the latter, "staggering under the weight of their heavy packs and rifles, could only nod their heads or perhaps throw a free arm out to clasp the weeping women." The band again struck up "The Wearing of the Green" as the men filled the two boats that would take them across the Hudson to Jersey City. When the vessels moved into the river, a British steamer saluted them by blowing her whistles and lowering her flag, and when the ferries carrying the 69th Regiment passed the memorial to General Grant along the shore, the whistles were sounded and the men bowed their heads as the chaplain recited a prayer. After disembarking at Jersey City, the men boarded the Baltimore & Ohio Railroad for Chickamauga National Military Park in Georgia.[7]

The following day the *New York Times* reported the 69th's march through New York City with the obligatory reference to the regiment's glory days. "Not since the stirring days of '61 has New York so thrilled with patriotic fervor as it did yesterday, when the Sixty-ninth . . . marched through the city on their way South. . . ," the *Times* journalist proclaimed. "If they had been battle-scarred heroes of a hundred fights, the boys of the Sixty-ninth regiment could not have received a more enthusiastic welcome than that which greeted them yesterday. From east to west through the city they marched amid a blaze of flags, and the tramp of their feet was lost in the cheers that roared from tens of thousands of throats. Fifth Avenue and Tenth Avenue united in enthusiasm. Truck drivers and longshoremen did not shout louder than bankers and club men, and the fluttering flags in Fifth Avenue were not less numerous than the banners that waved from factories and tenements." Rhetoric like this would later stand in sharp contrast to the fact that the 69th never saw action in Cuba.[8]

While en route to Chickamauga, the 69th New York Regiment made brief stops in Cincinnati, Ohio, and Lexington, Kentucky. The troops arrived in Cincinnati in the early hours of May 26. If the train had pulled into the city the night before as expected, it would have been greeted by a distinguished array of Irishmen headed by General Michael Ryan, the assistant United States treasurer. As it happened, though, only Ryan and a few sleepy sentries were on hand to welcome the troops early the next morning. So that rations could be more easily issued to the soldiers, the regiment was laid over in the train yards, while Colonel Duffy and the officers were the guests of honor at a breakfast at the Grand Hotel. Later that afternoon, the regiment arrived in Lexington, to the welcome of 10,000 people, more than half of them women. About a hundred of the "handsomest young women" rushed into the train coaches and pinned freshly cut flowers on the coats of the officers and men. After dining at the Phoenix Hotel, the officers marched with their men to the opera house, where the day's hosts planned to give the soldiers some of Kentucky's best bourbon. Fearing that such an opportunity to imbibe would prevent the troops from returning to the train station on time, Colonel Duffy marched them off to the trains forthwith. The city's hosts accommodated the soldiers, however, by bringing the bourbon and other refreshments to the trains and distributing them on board.[9]

When the regiment arrived at Chickamauga, it was attached to the Second Division of the Third Army Corps. Three days later the regiment proceeded to Tampa, Florida, where it reported to General Carpenter and was assigned to the Second Brigade, Second Division, Fourth Army Corps. A final reassignment occurred on June 5, when the New York regiment was placed in the Second Brigade of the Third Division. By the middle of that month, however, the New York soldiers apparently had not yet received their pay. To relieve the regiment's urgent needs, the Friendly Sons of St. Patrick collected approximately $2,000. In a letter to John Crimmins, the organization's treasurer, Colonel Duffy expressed his appreciation: "It gives me much pleasure to write you and express my own and also the thanks of my whole regiment for your very kind work in their behalf. The money sent by the Friendly Sons was spent for fresh meat, which was needed very much by my men. Their appreciation was marked, and their gratitude will be indeed lasting. We are in very good health now, and with God's help I hope we all will continue so." In comments to the *New York Times*, Crimmins laid bare additional grievances about the current situation: "While we are willing and ready to do all we can for our boys in the field, there should be no occasion for calling on individuals for aid. It is a burning shame that the troops cannot get their pay from the State, and a still greater shame that they must come under the ban of a lot of incompetent men such as are in charge of the War Department."[10]

At the end of August the 69th was transferred by train from Florida to Camp Wheeler in Huntsville, Alabama. The regiment was split up into two sections as it left the "Sunshine State," but at Montgomery, Alabama, the railroad company decided to divide it into three sections because of the steep grades over which the train would have to travel. The first five cars of the first section were occupied by Companies E and G and were eight miles west of Birmingham, Alabama, when the cars, which were traveling at a high rate of speed, left the rails. The cars were thrown against the side of a "cut" with such force that they shot high into the air and landed upside down. Private Peter Farley of Company G was killed instantly, while twenty-six other men were hurt. The injured were sent back to Birmingham for treatment, but Sergeant Frank Glennon of Company G died en route. One of the first members of the regiment to volunteer when the call for troops was made, Glennon was a nephew of Colonel Duffy and was survived by his parents and four sisters and two brothers. The injured, meanwhile, were not considered in serious condition and received spiritual aid and comfort from the regimental chaplain, Father Daly. The men in the ranks blamed the train's engineer for the accident, claiming that he had sacrificed their safety by running the train at an excessive speed.[11]

By the fall the 69th had been drilled and molded into such an impressive force that it attracted favorable comment from its superiors. When Secretary of War Russell Alger took part in a general review of the Fourth Corps at Huntsville at the end of September, he thought the troops of the 69th were regulars rather than volunteers. Even the brigade commander congratulated Colonel Duffy for his regiment's "efficiency" on the parade ground that day, adding that the "Sixty-ninth is certainly a fine example of the volunteer soldier." Duffy himself was even more effusive, remarking to the press that "A finer command never drew breath. They would do honor to Napoleon or Grant. They are 50 per cent. better than when they went away."[12]

In mid October Colonel Duffy reported on other aspects of the regiment's situation. He noted that forty-five men were in either the regimental or the divisional hospital, victims of the typhoid fever which they had contracted in Tampa. In addition, he had granted 220 furloughs, explaining that he regarded them as one of the best ways to overcome homesickness. About Huntsville itself, Duffy said it was a "singularly salubrious place," boasting an abundance of spring water and such fine red clay that sinks could be dug to the depth of fifteen feet, a convenience to which he attributed the camp's cleanliness and healthfulness. The officer also reported that he had given discharges to about eighty of his men because they had families dependent upon them back home. As to reports that the regiment would be sent to Cuba or Puerto Rico, Duffy said that the men "display no aversion to going, and are — as the Sixty-ninth always is when called on — ready to do their duty."[13]

To the men the notion of "doing their duty" meant participating in military action on the battlefield. As a result, when it appeared that the 69th might be assigned to garrison duty in Cuba or Puerto Rico, more than 700 of the men signed a petition in protest. While home on leave, a private in Company D reported that all but a few noncommissioned officers in Huntsville were among the signatories. He added that no effort had been made to obtain signatures from Company G because its captain was Colonel Duffy's son and that the petition drive had been stopped when the colonel learned about it.[14]

In the middle of December, another incident occurred which tarnished the image of the 69th New York. In a lengthy letter from Huntsville, a prominent member of the regiment charged that the unit as then constituted was unfit for service and should be immediately disbanded. While chiefly blaming Colonel Duffy for the condition of the regiment, the complainant added that the 69th had suffered "from the gross ignorance and bad habits of those at the head of the regiment." To support his charge, the author appended a long list of particulars. He first complained that the regiment could have seen action during the fighting at Santiago, Cuba, if it had been properly equipped. Similarly, he seemed to say, the 69th lacked proper military training, having had a chance to practice rifle shooting only once since leaving New York. The author scoffed at an incident at Huntsville when the colonel gathered his officers together to show them how to handle a sword — "something, by the by, which he never learned himself." The episode was called "all around the mulberry bush" because the officers had to walk around him, saluting as they passed, "like a lot of d—— fools!" The letter-writer also informed his readers that the men had collected $4,000 to buy for themselves some "little luxuries to vary Uncle Sam's monotonous menu." Of that amount — and of the money contributed earlier by the Friendly Sons of St. Patrick — only $900 had so far been divided among the companies, and the whereabouts of the balance was unknown. The irate author also complained that the men who suffered from typhoid while the regiment was still in Florida were inadequately supplied with medicine and cots. At one of the camps in Florida, he charged, 30 percent of the men fell sick, and fifty soldiers eventually died, "almost as much [sic] as if we had gone into an action."[15]

The "prominent member" of the regiment who made these charges saved his most vitriolic remarks, however, for Colonel Duffy. Now that the war was virtually over and all danger removed — the letter-writer noted sarcastically — the colonel and some of the other "holders of sinecures" began to show the "most ardent courage" and expressed their hope of being sent to Cuba. On October 1, however, the colonel was so drunk at the Huntsville Hotel that he fell off his horse twice. The complainant seemed to take special delight in the fact that Duffy was subsequently charged not only with drunkenness but also with misapplying funds, misrepresenting the number of sick in the regiment, and showing disrespect to both superior and inferior officers. According to the letter-writer, all the men in the regiment and three-quarters of the line officers wanted the charges to be tried, and a petition requesting an early trial was drawn up. Our complainant again dipped his pen in acid: "The men who don't sign are the men who owe him [Duffy] all they amount to in the regiment. Naturally they should be grateful, because he violated in their favor every rule of military precedence and every dictate of conscience and justice. They were all promoted over the heads of men of longer experience, and, as far as I can see, of superior ability."[16]

The 69th New York Regiment was never sent to the front during the war and remained in the service of the United States until January 31, 1899. At that time it resumed its former status as a unit in the state National Guard. When the officers and the men were paid off and discharged in New York City, new charges against Colonel Duffy came to the surface. The men, it seems, had learned that by being mustered out of service in New York rather than in Huntsville they had forfeited an average of $30 apiece. The explanation for this loss lay in the fact that War Department regulations allowed each of the men and officers a transportation allowance per mile for the distance between the place of discharge and the place of enrollment. But this allowance would be given only if the transportation was not supplied by the government to the whole regiment. In other words, the men would receive the allowance only if they found transportation from Huntsville on their own. The controversy arose because Duffy had decided that the regiment be transported to New York en masse and thus at direct cost to the government. It was for this reason that Colonel Duffy and his adjutant, Granville Emmet, were charged with deceiving the regiment, sacrificing the allowance due the men for the pomp of a welcoming parade.[17]

These grievances were aired publicly, however, only after the men had been discharged and received their service pay and clothing allowance. First Sergeant John Walsh of Company F was the first to vocalize the general complaint that the men would have preferred their extra pay to a parade. "There are men in the command who gave up positions to go to the front and who have since lost their places; and $30 would be a big help to some families," he said. "We were told by the Adjutant that the difference in pay to us would amount to not more than $5 a man, and it was on that account that the men decided to forego this trifling sum to have the little honor that a parade would bring them. When they found out what the difference would really be to them, they voted almost solidly to be mustered out in the South, but it seemed that it was either too late or that the officers had arranged matters to suit themselves. At all events, we were not consulted further, but told to come North for muster out." Major

Harrison, the mustering officer, responded to the charges by agreeing that the men had not been asked their preference while they were still in Huntsville. He denied, however, that the situation had not been properly explained to the men.[18]

While the soldiers in Company C were receiving their pay, an argument broke out between Major Edward McCrystal and Sergeant Felix Hagan. The former officer claimed that the will of the regiment had been followed in bringing the men north for mustering. Hagan countered by saying that all but three of the men in Company C had voted to be mustered out in the South, adding his belief that three-quarters of the regiment had voted the same way. When confronted with the allowance issue in person, Colonel Duffy sarcastically asked whether the men had lost the $30 or whether the shopkeepers in Huntsville had lost it. Duffy also defended himself by saying that his accounting of the regiment's funds had been audited and found to be in order.[19]

Another disturbance almost occurred during the mustering out of Company D. When Private William Carey looked at the back of his discharge paper, he saw the notation "Services not faithful, character not good" written on the back of it. With an oath the outraged Carey jumped toward Captain Tuite, shouting that he would kill him. Only the timely intervention of some policemen prevented Carey from carrying out his threat. While Carey admitted that his record was not perfect — he had been fined for being absent without leave on two occasions — he insisted that he had done nothing worse than many other men who had been honorably discharged. He went on to claim that his dishonorable discharge was due to Tuite's animosity toward him. This dislike, Carey claimed, arose from his earlier call for permission to investigate the captain's disposition of the company's funds. In his defense Tuite said that an examination of his accounts had shown no irregularities. He added that Carey had been a disturbing element in the company and that the private's case had been decided by a board of at least two other officers.[20]

The streets in midtown Manhattan teemed with people on October 21, 1900, when funeral services for six members of the 69th New York were held at St. Patrick's Cathedral. The bodies of the men, who had died in Southern training camps during the war, had actually been interred in the South but were to be reburied in Calvary Cemetery in Woodside, Queens, Long Island. John Burke, Henry Murray, William Pyne, and John Riley had first been buried in Huntsville, Alabama, while Daniel Crawley and William Ray had been laid to rest in Newport, Kentucky. The night before the funeral, the bodies of the men had lain in state in the old regimental armory at Third Avenue and Seventh Street. At the head of the procession to the cathedral the next day was Colonel Duffy, followed by the regimental band, the main body of the regiment — about 700 strong — and members of the 69th Regiment's veteran corps. Father William Daly,

*Memorial to the men of the 69th New York who died during the Spanish-American War.*
*(Calvary Cemetery, Woodside, Queens, Long Island, New York)*

the regimental chaplain, delivered a sermon before the requiem mass for the men.[21]

Four years later, on April 23, 1904, the cornerstone of the regiment's new armory on Lexington Avenue between 25th and 26th streets was laid. By design the date of that event marked the forty-third anniversary of the regiment's departure from New York City for the seat of war soon after the surrender of Fort Sumter. Two hundred members of the Friendly Sons of St. Patrick were the first to arrive at the site, while members of the Ancient Order of Hibernians escorted the regiment from Great Jones Street. Major General Martin McMahon, a former colonel of the regiment, acted as the presiding officer during the ceremonies, and Father Daly offered the opening prayer. In his oration that day, Thomas Fitzgerald, a state supreme court justice, noted that the new armory "will constitute the future home of one of our historic city regiments, the gallant old Sixty-ninth, the record of whose past glory is the best pledge of its fidelity and efficiency for the future." After reviewing the history of the regiment through the Civil War and the war with Spain, Fitzgerald continued: "With your glorious past — with the bright example furnished by a long line of illustrious predecessors — with the abundance of material from which a careful selection can be made — with a thoroughly equipped armory situated in a central location, a superior type of young men should become at-

tracted to your ranks, whose glory and pride it should ever be to keep
alive the spirit and traditions that won renown for the regiment almost
from its infancy, and that are characteristic National traits of the brave
people from whose sons its ranks have been at all times so largely recruited."[22]

William Clarke then read a poem composed for the occasion by his
father, Joseph I. C. Clarke. In its account of the day's events, the *New York
Times* printed four stanzas from the *poetic piece:

> A home for the brave, the warm, the true,
> Who love the old, and who love the new;
> Whose blood has so oft divinely sealed
> Devotion's uttermost gift of life
> On the long, red ridge of the battlefield,
> In the tortuous aftermath of strife,
> Content in the pride of the fearless soul,
> To lengthen the regiment's golden roll.
>
> And long already that roll of fame,
> Which caught its gold from the battle-flame.
> Antietam reaped them amid its corn,
> Gettysburg under its orchard shades;
> At Vaughan's Pass they were bullet-torn;
> On Petersburg crest they reddened their blades;
> And up at the wall on Marye's Hill [sic]
> They piled their dead with an Irish will.
>
> Eight times were the warworn lines refiled,
> Nor faltered to measure the blood outspilled.
> To the front, to the front marched man and boy,
> While the great Republic's need loomed large.
> And eighty and eight were their days of joy,
> When the bugles rang for a headlong charge.
> As the regiment honored its fighting vow,
> Be it welcome here in its glory now.
>
> * * * * * * * * * * * * * * * * * * * * * * * *
>
> Then here let the deathless Celtic race,
> In rank and file, take their fathers' place.
> And prouder their spirit, since longer here
> They've drunk the strong air from Freedom's hills;
> And stouter their hearts that their blood runs clear,
> From the fount that Freedom's bosom fills.
> And their souls on stronger wings shall soar,
> And glory shall wait by the open door.[23]

On St. Patrick's Day the following year, the 69th New York escorted President Theodore Roosevelt to the 121st Annual Dinner of the Friendly Sons of St. Patrick. In his remarks on that occasion, the president acknowledged in a special way both Colonel Duffy and his officers and men. At the time, it should be noted, the colonel was marking his thirty-eighth year as a member of the regiment, having enlisted as a private in Company E in June 1867. By the end of the decade he had reached the rank of major, and in 1896 he was named a lieutenant colonel and two years later a colonel. Despite the criticism against Duffy during the Spanish-American War, he was breveted brigadier general in 1903 for his long and otherwise meritorious service. He retired six years later, after forty-two years of continuous service in the 69th New York.[24]

The regiment's new armory was completed in 1906, and on October 13 of that year the men of the 69th proudly took possession of the new facility. As its band played "Home, Sweet Home," the regiment marched from its old armory at Seventh Street and Third Avenue. Immediately following as an honor guard was the Seventh New York, whose presence revealed that the old rivalry between the two regiments had been put aside. When the line of march arrived at the new armory, the band of the Seventh New York struck up *"Garry Owen," soon followed by *"The Wearing of the Green" from the band of the Ninth Massachusetts Volunteers. Drawing up the rear was Brigadier General Alexander Hamilton, the

*The armory of the 69th New York National Guard Regiment, New York City (on Lexington Avenue between East 25th Street and East 26th Street).*

ninety-one-year-old grandson of the famous Revolutionary War soldier. The interior of the new armory was bedecked with American flags and streamers of Stars and Stripes as well as at least one green Irish ensign. After the bands played "The Star-Spangled Banner," flag-bearers unfurled for the first time in many years the riddled and torn flags which some of the veterans had brought to the event. These historic banners were then transferred to the custody of the 69th for perpetual care. Instead of answering "Amen" to Archbishop John Farley's invocation, the assembled soldiers added their "So be it" by pounding their rifle butts on the armory floor. Colonel James Smith, who had received a gold medal for bravery at Gettysburg, then asked that the veterans' torn flags be paraded once a year to tell their story of patriotism to future generations of American soldiers. A poem by Joseph I. C. Clarke was then read, two stanzas of which were printed in the *New York Times* account of the event:

> Enter in[,] ye leal and tried,
> Enter[,] stout sons of the Gael;
> Here where only shall abide
> Faith and love that never fail.
>
> Enter[,] ye[,] with Valor's lamp
> Lighting up each soul and face;
> Enter with the ringing tramp,
> Challenge of our fighting race.[25]

# Chapter 4

## The 69th New York National Guard Regiment in the 1916 Punitive Expedition

As the year 1914 opened, the United States found itself embroiled in a diplomatic crisis of its own making vis-a-vis Mexico. A year before, Victoriano Huerta, a brutal spokesman for the propertied groups in Mexico, had seized power. President Woodrow Wilson, suspicious of the moneyed interests that backed Huerta and fearful that the new Mexican leader would inaugurate a bloody regime, refused to grant diplomatic recognition to his government. Then, in February of that year, Wilson lifted the arms embargo against Mexico in the hope that the resulting flow of weapons into the country would help Huerta's chief opponents, Venustiano Carranza and Francisco Villa. As a result of the subsequent military struggle, Huerta fled to Spain in July and was succeeded by General Carranza. Not for more than a year, however, did Wilson recognize the Carranza regime as the de facto government of Mexico.[1]

The expected improvement in relations between the two countries failed to materialize. Hoping to discredit Carranza by provoking war with the United States, Francisco Villa launched a bloody campaign against Americans. On January 11, 1916, he and his followers killed eighteen American mining engineers at Santa Isabel, Mexico. In March he and 1,500 Villistas crossed the border and killed seventeen more Americans in Columbus, New Mexico. In response Wilson and Carranza agreed to allow either nation to pursue outlaws across the border. Although the American "punitive expedition" under General John Pershing ultimately numbered about 12,000 men, it failed to capture Villa and his fellow bandits. When Pershing's cavalry advanced more than 300 miles into Mexico, Carranza's followers demanded an end to the *Yanqui* presence, and another war between the two countries looked imminent. Bloody incidents between Mexican and U.S. soldiers followed, one clash resulting in the death of twelve Americans and the capture of twenty-three more. As calls for war became shriller in the United States, Wilson strengthened the defense on the border by beginning a call-up of the National Guard. In mid June Guard units from Texas, New Mexico, and Arizona were the first to be mobilized, but eventually the entire National Guard was called up. The Guard's primary function was to patrol the border so as to free up Pershing's regular army troops for possible military action.[2]

Although the 69th New York was one of the National Guard units to be called into service, voices from various quarters charged that the famous regiment had been the victim of politics. In an editorial on July 5, the *New York Times* noted that the 69th had hoped to be the first or among the first to be sent to the U.S.-Mexican border. Instead, the newspaper said, echoing the men's complaint, the 69th had been "left behind to do dull work in absolute safety and comparative comfort." While the *Times* congratulated the 69th for its spirit — especially in contrast to the "miserable chatterings of the avowed pacifists" — the newspaper advised the disgruntled men that "even in a military emergency the country needs service elsewhere than on the firing line, and that there may have been adequate reason in their special abilities for delaying their departure for the South." From the regiment's complaint the *Times* took heart for the future of the country, concluding that it is far better that the men "should be too eager to go than that they should be too glad to stay behind."[3]

A few days later the 69th New York seemed to be the victim again. This time many men in the regiment complained that they had not received the pay promised them by their employers before they were mustered in the federal service. In addition, because the regiment had finally gotten its wish to be sent to the border, it appeared that many of the men would be leaving New York before knowing whether their families would be adequately provided for. Over the following few days, the regimental chaplain, Father Francis Duffy, interviewed several of the employers charged with reneging on their promise. When the priest returned to Camp Whitman in Beekman, New York, he said that progress had been made on the issue, but he refused to reveal the names of the employers to whom he had spoken. He did say, however, that he would make public the names of any employers who failed to keep their promises to family men who could not otherwise afford to serve in the recent call-up. Among the complaints by members of the 69th New York were those against the New York Central Railroad and various municipal departments. The assistant general manager of the railroad indicated his company's willingness to keep its commitments and said that the complaints were probably based on some misunderstanding about the pay day rather than on the promise itself. Tim Kennedy and J. J. Sullivan, meanwhile, charged the street cleaning department with not forwarding their wages to their families. After the Active Service Auxiliary investigated twenty-six complaints by National Guardsmen and their families, it was determined that all but three of the cases were groundless.[4]

As it turned out, the departure of the 69th New York for the Mexican border was at first delayed and then marred by subsequent developments. A few more days were needed to equip the regiment properly and to await the arrival of replacements after sixty soldiers and one lieutenant were rejected because of overweight. The regiment's strength was brought to 1,300 with the addition of about 160 men from the 14th Infantry and the First Cavalry. A more serious threat to the regiment's morale occurred on July 11 as the 69th New York was about to leave Camp Whitman on trains bound for the Texas border. At literally the last minute, Major General

Leonard Wood relieved Colonel Louis Conley and Lieutenant Colonel John Phelan of command of the regiment on the grounds that they were physically unfit for military duty. The anger and despair which the regiment felt on hearing the news was temporarily stayed, however, when Wood allowed Conley to accompany his men to the border. There he was to turn over command to General Frederick Funston.[5]

Immediately upon hearing the news of Colonel Conley's removal, Senator James O'Gorman of New York and nine congressman from that state lodged a protest with Secretary of War Newton Baker. Following a meeting with President Wilson, Baker ordered an investigation into the circumstances of the two officers' dismissal. It was speculated that the removals were in response to the desire of regular army officers that the state militia organizations sent to the border be under the command of army officers. It was also revealed that the War Department might reinstate Colonel Conley if his disability — heart trouble — proved slight. Reliable sources at the time added that Lieutenant Colonel Phelan's condition was more serious and that his removal from command would probably be approved. Other early reports indicated that Conley would now remain with his troops on the border, but as the regiment's lieutenant colonel. The reason for Conley's earlier dismissal from command became more problematical when it was revealed that Major Wadhams, the regular army surgeon who had examined him, had made a favorable report. A possible explanation lay in the suggestion that the phraseology in Wadhams's medical report could have been altered as it made its way to General Wood's staff and to the general himself.[6]

Later press accounts indicated that both the 69th's surgeon and an army medical officer had reported that Lieutenant Colonel Phelan was suffering from hernia. In contrast, the army surgeon reported that Colonel Conley had a slight heart affliction, even though the regimental doctor had given him a clean bill of health. As to Conley's earlier statement that he would not be displeased to remain with the 69th New York as its lieutenant colonel, high officials in the War Department said that if Conley were reinstated it would be as a colonel. Secretary of War Baker, meanwhile, expressed his belief that Conley would be reinstated if it could be shown that his infirmity would not interfere with his ability to command according to the best interests of his men. Major Wadhams even stated that Phelan could be made fit for service after a ten-day leave of absence for a slight operation. Whether Conley would be reinstated became a moot point, however, when it was announced that Captain William Haskell of the regular army would take his place.[7]

As the 69th New York sped across the country en route to the Southwest, the *New York Times* reported on life "on the rails." One account described the provision and supply system on the train as "little short of perfect." From Camp Whitman the men had brought rations for ten days

— a veritable cornucopia of groceries: ham, bacon, beans, turnips, potatoes, canned goods, tomatoes, soups, eggs, coffee, preserves, fruit, tea, and milk. With some embarrassment Lieutenant Michael Carroll of the general mess described the culinary situation on board: "We're supposed to be soldiers, but it looks more like a picnic train as far as food is concerned. We have every sort of food from peaches to turnips." When the train arrived in Buffalo, New York, Red Cross volunteers distributed sandwiches to the men, and the officers were driven to a local club to make use of the steam room, the showers, and the swimming pool. En route to St. Louis the train stopped at Easton and Sayre, Pennsylvania, where members of the local Irish organizations met Colonel Conley at the station and provided refreshments to his men. In return for gifts of cards, stamps, cigars, and tobacco, the men gave three cheers for the Knights of Columbus and the Friendly Sons of St. Patrick in both cities. The next morning the officers ordered the men to erase a particularly boastful bit of graffiti that had been chalked on one of the train cars: "This car is owned and operated by a model company, Company B of the Fighting Irish Sixty-ninth Regiment. We are regular guys." As for more prosaic matters, the cars were policed three times a day, tanks were kept ready for frequent sponge baths, and tanks were filled at every stop with ice water.[8]

The regimental train arrived outside Vermilion, Ohio, on the morning of July 13. To the great delight of the men, Colonel Conley allowed them to bathe in Lake Erie just across the track. If there were any onlookers near the site, they must have been surprised at the sight of 600 militiamen splashing about in the water. When the train stopped at Bellevue, Ohio, one of the men raced to a drugstore near the station, probably to purchase an item not found in the regiment's mess. The soldier, Melvin Sheppard, was a well-known middle-distance runner and at first eluded the guards placed around the train. But on his return he was pursued by two officers of the guard — James Archer, the holder of two of the world's running records, and Thomas Reilly, a former Yale football player. Although Sheppard won the race, the officers followed him to his train car, where he defended his actions by saying that he had never been ordered to stop. Later in the afternoon a poker game in the Company F car was broken up when it was learned that the mascot — an Irish terrier named "Buffalo" — had swallowed an ace of spades.[9]

At 3 p.m. the train pulled into Continental, Ohio. While the men visited the town, some of the officers tried to obtain cots for use on the border but discovered that other regiments passing through had already bought up the town's supply. Some time that afternoon, when the troop train stopped in Cleveland, soldiers from the 69th New York were among the 700 recruits and militiamen who raided grocery stores for food and merchandise and destroyed what they could not carry away. Local police were called to the scene, and the soldiers were driven back to their trains by a detachment of twenty armed men called out by Major Timothy Moynahan, who commanded the train. The next day, however, the non-commissioned officers and men of the 69th New York denied newspaper reports that they had been without food for thirty-six hours before their arrival in Cleveland. In a public letter the soldiers stated emphatically that the commissary department had been satisfactorily providing meals for almost 700 men (300 of them from units other than the 69th): "[O]ur meals are being served to us regularly and in a sufficient quantity to satisfy our appetites." The next day the train arrived in St. Louis at 5 p.m., much later than scheduled. As a result, the many Irish delegations which had planned to greet the men had already left the station. When the militiamen returned from sightseeing, they were delighted to find that electric fans had been placed in their Pullman cars.[10]

When the train carrying the 69th New York Regiment passed through Texarkana, the men knew that their long journey would soon be over. After arriving at Longview Junction, Texas, early on July 16, the regiment fell in and marched five minutes to an open field, where Father Duffy celebrated mass around his portable altar. As almost the entire population of the town looked on, and as Mexican laborers were visible nearby, the chaplain asked the soldiers to live up to the regiment's traditions in the event it was broken up and the men were brigaded with regular army troops. As the men resumed their journey, across increasingly barren plains, the troopers learned the meaning of the saying "The sun has riz, the sun has set, and here we is in Texas yet." But by then the men's spirits were noticeably subdued. Major Thomas Maguire, the regimental surgeon, attributed the downcast mood to the heat, the monotony of the journey, and a feeling of homesickness experienced by the older troops. A newspaper report filed from Dodge, Texas, on July 16, however, gave another reason for the gloom. Some of the men were still mourning the loss of "Mike," an Irish terrier owned by Adjutant Felix Donnelly and honored as the regimental mascot. It seems that after the train had left Prescott, Arkansas, Donnelly noticed that the dog was missing. The mascot was soon spied 300 feet behind the moving train — "racing and panting for dear life and home" — but it was soon outdistanced by the "Iron Horse." At the next stop Donnelly wired back to report his missing pet. When the troops arrived at Palestine, Texas, they were delighted to hear that a dog had been sent ahead by express from Prescott. Though it was an Irish terrier, it was not Mike.[11]

On July 18, after a sometimes grueling 2,600-mile journey, the 69th New York arrived along the Texas-Mexican border. The men had expected to detrain at Pharr, about 225 miles south of San Antonio, but as the train approached that village about midnight the conductor received an order to proceed nine miles farther to the town of Mission. Not until 9 the next morning did the men actually complete the "detrainment," at which time they began the mile-long march to their camp. When the regiment — headed by its fife and drum corps — reached the camp, it was greeted with cheers by the other two units of the brigade already there. At the entrance to the camp Colonel James Andrews of the Second Infantry met Colonel Conley, and the band of the Second moved to the head of the parade, playing "The Wearing of the Green." His mission accomplished, Conley prepared to say goodbye to the men he had led for more than six years and — as ordered — to begin the long journey back to New York.[12]

Although most of the Guardsmen had expected to see military action soon after their arrival on the border, they instead spent their time drilling, improving their marksmanship, and "hiking." Before long, the men in the 69th New York were what Captain Rupert Hughes, a journalist in civilian life, called "dirty, bored, and disheartened." According to the captain, this mood changed for the better, however, when Colonel Haskell told the men of his ambition to make the regiment the model of efficiency for the whole Guard. Hughes emphasized that Haskell had "talked to us of our ideal state, of our duties to the regiment and ourselves, of the divinity of service, the pride of subordination, the high privilege of saluting, the economy of promptness and precision . . . ."[13]

Despite the usually pleasant associations with the word "hike," in military parlance it meant a practice march. In a magazine account of one such march by the 69th New York, Captain Hughes defined the hike as "an imitation of a desperate advance or retreat without the inspiration of rescue or escape." The eleven-day march began on Sunday, August 27, with an early mass celebrated by Father Duffy on the dark Texas prairie. Since General John O'Ryan had forbidden the use of intoxicants, the marching men fell prey to various sutlers en route who tempted them with lemonade, grape juice, and ice cream. ("I drank enough Mexican lemonade there to equip a camel for a Sahara crossing," Hughes confessed — or boasted.) The irony of such scenes prompted Hughes to confide to his readers: "Down at the border warriors did evil deeds for the sake of root beer, and strong men wept when the freezers went dry." The suffocating heat made the march unbearable, especially for unpracticed citizen-soldiers carrying a hefty pack, and the average three-mile-an-hour gait was broken only by a ten-minute halt each hour. Laboring under such conditions himself, Hughes noted that Isaac Newton had failed to realize that things grow heavier and heavier the farther one carries them. At first Hughes envied the cavalrymen whose feet were spared the cruel blistering that he and his men suffered, but he eventually learned that though the mounted men had no blisters on their feet, they still had blisters. As Hades continued to hold his grip on southern Texas, water became the god of the men's idolatry, prompting Hughes to write that the "blessed privilege of drinking quarts of water atones for much." But when some of the men were overcome by the heat, they invariably fell in the more pleasant spots along the way: "They could keep going across the unbroken wastes of sun-beaten road, but at the sight of a mesquite tree they were apt to be suddenly overcome. It was puzzling." Before the "Big Hike" was over, the 69th New York had suffered 130 "casualties" — men who fell by the wayside, exhausted from the heat. The regiment recovered from its embarrassment, however, upon learning that 340 men from another New York regiment had broken ranks to rest along the road.[14]

About his own role on a typical march, Captain Hughes was both candid and ironically humorous. Pointing out that a "captain nowadays is more of a chambermaid and a chiropodist than a fearless warrior," he observed that his leadership experience so far extended no further than to teaching a man how to trim his toenails, puncture a corn between his toes, and dig through a callus into a blister. Such duties, he quickly added, had future career possibilities: "Foot inspection is a captain's duty after every important march, and he must study underwear and hosiery as well, not to mention shoe science, so that if one has patriotism enough to persist in the service until his own business is entirely ruined, he will know enough about bunions and bookkeeping to be qualified as a buyer for a small haberdashery in any village or as a chiropodist in a second-class barber shop." Like his men, Hughes experienced a predictable psychological pattern during a march: an initial euphoria giving way to a sullen quiet punctuated by the rhythmic tramp of boots and the occasional curse at a cactus followed by murmured complaints. In the end, though, Hughes concluded that "even resentment grew too much of an effort, and we subsided into walking machines, donkey engines, mere trudgers." He confessed that toward the end of each hike he was tormented by the same thoughts: "I don't see how I can stand it another hundred yards! . . . My watch must have stopped! . . . That's all tommyrot about its being bad to drink on the march. I tell the men that, but it doesn't count for me! . . . It would be a shame to fall out and have the whole regiment see me sitting at the roadside. . . . I'm getting too old for this. . . . I'm straining my heart . . . . And for what? It's only pretend. We're not getting anywhere to help anybody. Nobody is in danger. The rest of the country is laughing at us. . . ."[15]

Another New York Guardsman listed his complaints to friends in the East. "They are working us very hard to get us in shape," he wrote." Thank God, we didn't go straight into Mexico, for half of us would have been dead by this time." About Texas itself he griped: "This is the most forsaken country the Lord ever made. We ought to clean Mexico up, and for punishment make them take back this part of Texas." In addition, the size of the food rations prompted another complaint: "I read in the newspapers of the wonderful things we have to eat. I wish some of those reporters were living here for a week. They don't give us half enough. This noon, after working all morning in the sun, having had at six o'clock a piece of bacon and bread, they gave us one piece of bread with maple syrup on it and a cup of lemonade."[16]

Though the 69th New York spent most of its time on the border training rather than fighting, all was not quiet on the southern front. On October 11 a potentially disastrous incident occurred near the Mission pumping station along the Rio Grande. At midnight, while a squad of men from Company E were guarding the pumping facility, Private Kelly noticed what he thought was a boatload of Mexicans crossing the river toward the American side. Hearing the shot of a gun and believing that he was under fire, he dropped behind a bank and began to shoot toward the sand bar from which the boat had departed. When the other men in the squad heard the gunfire, they rushed to the river bank and began shooting. From along the river the American sentries opened fire also. While Captain John Patrick Hurley ordered his men into formation, Lieutenant William Patton telephoned the nearby signal corps to report that Mexicans had fired on the 69th and that the Americans had returned the fire. The regiment remained under arms all night, and in the morning the sentries found an abandoned boat along the American shore. Although Sergeant McKirnan told officers that he was sure he had seen boats the night before, the commander of the Mexican garrison across the river said that no party had set out from the southern side of the Rio Grande.[17]

In response to this episode, General O'Ryan took steps to assign various New York infantry regiments to posts along a twenty-five-mile stretch of the Rio Grande. Besides protecting the pumping stations along the river, the regiments were charged with preventing all persons from crossing the Rio Grande except at the immigration station at Hidalgo, where the 69th was posted. Although it was believed that the newly established patrol posts would not be attacked, the men were ordered to erect barricades and dig trenches. The soldiers were informed that the threat of danger came not from the Mexican side of the river but from the American side, where Francisco Villa's agents had been actively recruiting bands of marauders.[18]

Although the 69th New York saw no significant military action during its months along the border, its officers and men gained valuable experience for what was soon in store for them in France. When the United States declared war on Germany only a few months later, almost all the men who had served under Colonel Haskell in Texas went overseas with the regiment. One of the men who had accompanied the 69th to Texas and who would later accompany it to Europe was its chaplain, Father Duffy. Born in Cobourg, Ontario, Canada, in 1871, Francis Duffy was one of eleven children of an Irish father and an Irish-Canadian mother. He completed his university education in Toronto and New York City and attended St. Joseph Seminary in Troy, New York, before being ordained to the priesthood in 1896. At the outbreak of the Spanish-American War, he volunteered to minister as a chaplain to the soldiers stationed at Montauk Point,

Long Island, but he fell victim to typhoid fever and could not serve. He was subsequently assigned to St. Joseph Seminary in Dunwoodie, New York, where he taught a variety of liberal arts subjects to more than 500 future priests. His reputation for scholarship led him to write numerous articles for the *Catholic Encyclopedia* and other scholarly publications. The *New York Review*, which he cofounded, attempted to present Catholicism as compatible with such American values as democracy, tolerance, and religious freedom, but the journal's tone conflicted with Vatican policies at the time against "modernist" thought. As a result, in 1912 Duffy was transferred to parochial work, his first assignment being to establish a new parish — the Church of Our Savior — in the Bronx. (There the innovating pastor set aside a room where mothers could leave their infants while they attended mass. "If you can check a suitcase," Duffy asked, "why not check a baby?") The priest's association with the "Fighting 69th" Regiment of the New York National Guard dated from November 1914, when he was appointed that unit's chaplain by Cardinal John Farley. It was in that capacity that he had accompanied the 69th to the Mexican border.[19]

Toward the beginning of the new year, on February 17, 1917, the 69th New York was ordered home from the border. In issuing the order, Secretary of War Baker announced that the 75,000 National Guardsmen in Texas had completed their work and could be spared from the federal service. The 50,000 seasoned regulars who were to remain on the border were considered sufficient to cope with the situation. On its way home from Texas the 69th New York marched in the presidential inauguration parade in Washington, D.C., and arrived in Jersey City on March 6. Later that afternoon Colonel Haskell and the regiment were ferried across the Hudson River to West 23rd Street, where they were greeted and escorted by the Seventh New York Regiment. The "Fighting 69th" received its first ovation from a group of Catholic school children before being convoyed up Tenth Avenue by the Friendly Sons of St. Patrick. As the men moved up the avenue, they were cheered by crowds standing eight deep on the sidewalks and were serenaded by strains of "The Rocky Road to Dublin." At St. Patrick's Cathedral the regiment was greeted by Cardinal Farley and other prominent Catholic clergy, while Governor Whitman reviewed the troops as they passed the Public Library. The *New York Times* account of the stirring event pointed out that the men's faces were bronzed from eight months on the Mexican border and that their uniforms were the color of Texas dust.[20]

# Chapter 5

## The 69th New York (165th Infantry) Regiment in World War I

March 6, 1917, was a memorable day for the Irish in New York City. In scenes reminiscent of the welcome which the 69th New York Volunteers received on their return from the Civil War, the 69th New York National Guard made its way down Fifth Avenue — home at last from the Texas border. To the strains of *"Garry Owen" and the cheers of an enthusiastic crowd, the 69th turned east and arrived at its armory, where it was mustered out of service. Almost immediately, though, its 783 men and officers lost almost 300 of their number — victims to a law that men with dependent relatives must be discharged from the service. In addition, soldiers who had completed three years of active service were ordered furloughed.[1]

To restore the regiment to full strength, staffing officers began a major recruiting effort. But this campaign was more than just a quest to refill the ranks. It was, as Joyce Kilmer, the regiment's poet-historian, wrote, a drive "to enlist strong, intelligent, decent-living men, men whose sturdy Americanism was strengthened and vivified by their Celtic blood, men who would be worthy successors of those unfortunate patriots who at *Bloody Ford and on *Marye's Heights earned the title of 'The Fighting Irish.'" By the end of May the regiment numbered 2,002 men, many of them from the Irish county societies and the Catholic athletic clubs of New York City. Of this number, according to Father Francis Duffy, the regimental chaplain, only about 5 percent were not of Irish ancestry. (He said they were, instead, "Irish by adoption, Irish by association, or Irish by conviction.") By May, of course, the United States had entered the great European war, and the men of the 69th were ready to join the conflict. Their desire to be sent overseas came closer to fulfillment when, on July 15, the National Guard throughout the country was called into federal service.[2]

Exactly two weeks later, on July 29, the 69th New York marched to St. Patrick's Cathedral, where the men attended mass and heard Father Duffy extol the regiment's traditional loyalty to the United States. While pointing out that the regiment was overwhelmingly Irish and Catholic, the chaplain stressed that the men of the 69th were going into the war "as patriotic, loyal Americans, fighting for America and American ideals." The well-known priest also hinted at the hoped-for effect of the war on Ireland, stressing that the war was being fought to preserve the rights of small nations: "[W]e all cherish the hope that the interests of Ireland . . . will be represented after the war by America and we trust that America will see to it that the rights of the Irish and other small nations are safeguarded." On August 5 the regiment was drafted into the regular army of the United States. Ten days later the 69th was selected as the first New York National Guard unit to be sent to the war as part of the American Expeditionary Force. According to Kilmer, the 69th was chosen because its service in the recent Mexican border campaign had shown it to be the "best trained and equipped fighting unit" that the United States possessed.[3]

That summer the 69th was incorporated into the new 42nd Division and was redesignated as the 165th Infantry. This "Rainbow Division," as it was also known, had been formed from the National Guard organizations in twenty-six states and the District of Columbia and was so named because, as General Douglas MacArthur said, it was "spreading like a rainbow across the country." (Father Duffy said that his predominantly Irish unit had been added "to put green in the rainbow.") Together with the 166th Ohio Infantry and the 150th Wisconsin Machine Gun Battalion, the 165th made up the 83rd Infantry Brigade under the command of Brigadier General Michael Lenihan. Serving with Colonel Charles Hine, the 165th regimental commander, were Majors William Donovan, William Stacom, and Timothy Moynahan, the respective commanders of the First, Second, and Third battalions. Father Duffy, who had served with the 69th along the Mexican border only a year before, became chaplain of the 165th with the rank of first lieutenant.[4]

In his memoir of wartime life with the 69th New York, Father Duffy wrote movingly and humorously of the many recruits who went on to become some of the regiment's finest soldiers. When two young men who before the war had been Jesuit novices enlisted, the priest commented wryly that "they were exercising the traditional religious privilege of seeking a higher state of perfection by quitting the Jesuits and joining the 69th." The chaplain also recalled Private Michael Donaldson of Company I, formerly one of his altar boys. Before the war Donaldson had enjoyed a career as a prizefighter, becoming, as Duffy said with false modesty, "much more widely and favorably known to his fellow citizens than I can ever hope to be." When one day in camp the young Donaldson gave the priest an opponent's battered boxing gloves, Duffy at first did not know what to do with them. But so earnest were the pugilist's words of presentation that the chaplain decided to suspend the gloves "reverently from the rafter of my chapel like the *ex voto* offerings of ships that one sees in seaport shrines." Father Duffy left some of his finest words of tribute, however, for Captain John Patrick Hurley of Company K, whom he described as "an argument for the continued existence of the Irish as a people." About Hurley's idealism the priest noted that the young man was "willing to die for what he believes in. He would find that much easier than to live in a world of the cheap and commonplace." Duffy even compared him to Patrick Pearse, Joseph Plunkett, and Thomas MacDonagh, three Irish patriots executed by the British for their role in the Easter Monday uprising in Dublin in 1916. The chaplain added that Hurley was a wartime volunteer "because he feels that it is a war against the tyranny of the strong, and a fight for the oppressed peoples of the world."[5]

Besides Father Duffy, no other man would become so linked in the public's mind with the fortunes of the 165th Infantry as Major William Donovan. The grandson of Irish immigrants, he was a native of Buffalo, New York, and had initially attended Niagara University with the intention of pursuing the priesthood. After completing his undergraduate work at Columbia College (now University) and obtaining a law degree, he returned to Buffalo to practice law. In 1912, although the young lawyer had never ridden a horse before, he joined Troop I, First Cavalry Regiment, a newly formed unit of the New York National Guard. With his usual determination, Donovan mastered horsemanship and occupied his evenings by studying cavalry tactics. Later that year he was elected captain of Troop I. In 1916 he and his cavalry unit were sent to the Mexican border as part of President Wilson's response to the killing of Americans by Mexican marauders. While stationed with his men in Texas, the young captain earned a reputation for drilling them mercilessly, part of his plan to prepare them for what he regarded as America's inevitable entry into World War I. (Troop I's regimen included long rides, some of 250 miles, and twenty-five-mile dismounted hikes.) When the United States declared war on Germany the following year, Donovan asked to serve in one of the four volunteer divisions which his hero, former president Theodore Roosevelt, had proposed to raise. When President Wilson refused Roosevelt's proposal, Donovan accepted an assignment as assistant chief of staff in the 27th Division. He longed, however, to transfer to the 69th Regiment of the New York National Guard, a unit that seemed to fit his temperament and whose *esprit de corps* he had witnessed along the Mexican border. Though he was offered the colonelcy of the 27th Division, Donovan threw in his lot with the Irishmen of the Old Fighting 69th. Father Duffy wrote that Donovan was attracted to the 69th because it was to be among the first regiments sent to Europe and because "he would rather be Major than Colonel, for in battles, as now conducted, it is Majors who command in the actual fighting."[6]

On August 20, less than six months after its tumultuous welcome back from the Mexican border, the 69th New York Regiment — now known as the 165 Infantry — was greeted even more enthusiastically as it moved to its temporary camp at Mineola, Long Island. During its two-and-a-half-mile march through midtown Manhattan, the Old 69th numbered about 2,100 men and ninety-five officers, making it the largest infantry regiment ever seen in the streets of the city. The grand march began at the regimental armory, where Bishop Patrick Hayes called down God's blessing on them and wished them good luck. As the men waited for the order to march, their company officers informed them that Colonel Delanzier, the commander of the 69th Regiment of the French army, had cabled them a greeting, expressing his belief that "from the common effort will arise a decisive victory." It was also announced that Private Martin had been recommended for a special award in recognition of his rescuing an unknown child from the East River earlier in the month.[7]

When Drum Major John Mullens led the column into Lexington Avenue, the men were greeted by the shouts of the awaiting crowds. The regimental band began to play "Hail, Hail, the Gang's All Here" and followed it with "Garry Owen." The welcoming onlookers cheered even more loudly as Sergeant O'Shea of Company F carried a flagstaff bearing the Stars and Stripes and the regimental honor rings glistening in the sun. At points along the route where members of the regiment's families were waiting, some of the women and children rushed into the street and seized the sleeves of the men's uniforms. Father Duffy frequently broke ranks to speak to the weeping women on the sidewalks, telling them that they would have another chance to see their sons and husbands at camp. Trying not to be distracted by the throngs of people and the flags they proudly waved, the soldiers continued up the avenue to the familiar music of "Erin Go Bragh," "Columbia, the Gem of the Ocean," and "The Harp That Once Through Tara's Halls." As the regiment approached the 34th Street ferry along the East River, Colonel Edward Duffy's escort of veterans broke ranks and divided on each side of the street, standing as a kind of honor guard for the troops. Despite the press of the crowds, the men successfully boarded the boats, while the band played *"The Wearing of the Green," "I Want to See Old Ireland Free Once More," "Put Your Troubles in Your Old Kit Bag," and "The Girl I Left Behind Me." As the ferryboat left the pier, a group of soldiers in the stern serenaded their well-wishers with "Goodbye Old New York, Farewell America, Hello France." When the regiment landed at Long Island City, it was met by more large crowds and escaped only by boarding the train for Mineola. The men marched the last mile to Camp Albert Mills, where Colonel Hine waited to take command.[8]

Martin Hogan, who had signed up with the 69th after hearing a speech by a recruiting agent, later recorded his emotions as he marched with the regiment along Fifth Avenue that day. "The strong impressions that we men got from this march, however, were not those of the large triumphant sort, of the cheering, of the affectionate calls of friends, of martial pride to know that we were on our way into a great, and probably glorious, adventure for home and country, but rather humbler impressions of a chastening sort, impressions of heartbroken mothers, wives, and sisters who tried to force their way by [i.e., past] the police to kiss their 'boy,' a comrade in our ranks, good-bye, of fathers who gulped out some choking word of love as their boys swung by with us. Seeing these heart-heavy dramas all along our line of march, I somehow missed the exultant spirit of the crowd and was mostly near to tears myself."[9]

Soon after Colonel Hine had been placed in command of the 165th, orders came down that the regiment's numbers were to be increased to 3,500, primarily by additions from other New York National Guard units. As a result, the Seventh New York Infantry was joined with the Old 69th, with whom it had previously served on the Mexican border. When Colonel Willard Fisk and the 332 men of the Seventh New York reported to the 69th's armory, they were welcomed as brothers by their former comrades. The ranks of the 165th grew to about 3,700 with the later addition of men from the 12th, the 14th, the 23rd, and the 71st New York regiments.[10]

By all accounts, Major Donovan put the First Battalion of the 165th Infantry through a grueling regimen at Camp Mills. Reveille was at 4:50 a.m., and from then until mess at 6 p.m. the men went through the same daily routine. Although the soldiers did plenty of formation drilling and bayonet practice (*sans* dummies, however), they had almost no shooting practice. (Ironically, the camp had no rifle range.) Sometimes the men played sports — boxing, baseball, or football — or went on the cross-country runs that Donovan, now in his mid 30s, especially liked to lead. One day Sergeant Michael Donaldson, the former boxing champion, gently challenged his commanding officer to a few rounds. At first Donovan hesitated to accept the invitation, but rather than disappoint his men he relented. The sergeant was apparently unaware of Donovan's boxing skills, honed as a youngster when he and his brother Tim had sparred in the family barn back home in Buffalo. As one witness to the bout between the sergeant and the CO said, "Donaldson couldn't touch him." When Donovan finally struck the sergeant on the jaw, the subordinate sank to his knees.[11]

Father Duffy was an unabashed admirer of the young Donovan. The major, wrote the priest, was "very attractive in face and manner, an athlete who always keeps himself in perfect condition. I like him for his agreeable disposition, his fine character, his alert and eager intelligence. But I certainly would not want to be in his battalion." When Donovan's daughter was born near Camp Mills before the men left for Europe, Duffy baptized the infant — with water from an army canteen. The chaplain had already dedicated the 165th to St. Patrick, and the men under Donovan's command approved when their CO named his daughter Patricia. His men adopted her as the daughter of the regiment.[12]

Training with the 165th Infantry at Camp Mills was the 167th, formerly known as the Fourth Alabama Regiment. The men in the two units got along well at first, at least until some of the men began to receive hometown newspapers. Besides informing their readers that the Fourth Alabama and the Old 69th had fought each other in several important engagements in the Civil War, these journals lamented the fact that the two regiments were now part of the same division. Consequently, according to Albert Ettinger, a private of Irish and German extraction in the 165th

Infantry, the soldiers from Alabama became unfriendly to the New York-ers, and the former rivals resumed their historic rivalry with occasional fist fights at taverns in the nearby town of Hempstead. Ettinger pointed out, however, that the two regiments' common experiences in France made them finally appreciate and count on each other. In fact, one unit usually fought on the other's flank, or they often relieved each other. (Ettinger recalled that at postwar reunions of the Rainbow Division the Alabamians usually sought out veterans of the 69th New York with whom to drink and socialize.)[13]

When the 69th New York sailed for France in 1917, it went without Captain Rupert Hughes. The famous author had served with the more famous regiment on the Mexican border and had written about its experiences there. But because of a slight hearing impairment he was not allowed to go overseas with the 69th. In a short story entitled "The Murphy That Made America," Hughes conveyed his empathy with the story's main character — a young Irish boy in New York who longed to join the Old 69th. At first the boy's mother would not allow him to enlist, but at last she relented: "Thady boy, you're more Murphy than I am. I'd give you the veins of my heart for to make you happy, and there's only one way, that's certain sure, so go you and be a soldier, and the lovin' grace of the saints shield you round, O my *maneen [little man?], O Thady *avic ["Oh, son"]." Another of Hughes's stories — "Except He Were a Bird" — revolved around Shane O'Mealia, an Irish immigrant who had risen to a second lieutenancy in the 69th New York Regiment, National Guard. Shane's modesty prevented him from boasting of his rank to his employer. Instead, the young officer waited for the proper time to make the announcement: "He [the employer] was a foreigner, anyway, and would have to be educated up to the meaning of the Sixty-ninth in the history of the nation, the achievements of its child, the Irish Brigade, in the Civil War, and other matters that have given the regiment a place all its own." After the United States entered World War I, these and other Irish short stories by Hughes were published under the title *Long Ever Ago*. Hughes dedicated the volume of ten stories to "The Fighting 69th, now the 165th Infantry, with homage and with envy. 'The 69th in France and I not with them.'"[14]

About two weeks before the 165th Infantry was scheduled to sail for Europe, Private Albert Ettinger requested a two-day pass to visit his parents in New Jersey. When his platoon commander denied the request, and instead assigned him to do extra guard duty, Ettinger left camp without permission for what he later called "a wonderful weekend" with his parents and friends back home. Upon his return to camp on Monday morning in time for reveille, however, he was arrested as soon as his platoon commander laid eyes on him. About Ettinger's appearance the next day before a court-martial presided over by Major Donovan himself, the young private recalled that Donovan had eyes like blue ice that drilled straight through him. During the proceedings the major listened to Ettinger's version of events and then lamented the fact that the accused had blemished an otherwise perfect record. After reminding the soldier that the most important thing in the army is to obey orders, Donovan sentenced the offender to a month at hard labor and a fine of two-thirds of his monthly pay. Contrary to Ettinger's expectations, "hard labor" turned out to be a few hours every day picking up paper in camp, and the "prisoner" whiled away his time playing cards and shooting craps with several other prisoners. The worst part of the experience was the embarrassment he felt when his father and Father Duffy appeared at the entrance of the "guard tent" and found him gambling on the first Sunday of his confinement. After his father and the chaplain gave him "a good talking to," Ettinger, by now thoroughly shamed, was released.[15]

By the end of October the three battalions of the 165th Infantry were ready to sail for Europe. According to Kilmer, "The feeling of the officers and men was one of stern delight, of that strange religious exhaltation [sic] with which men of Celtic race and faith go into battle . . . ." On the night of October 25–26, the 1,200 soldiers of the First Battalion left Camp Mills and traveled by train to Montreal. En route Father Duffy passed from car to car hearing confessions and giving absolution, and the men said the rosary by squad, platoon, and company. In Canada the troops boarded the *Tunisian*, which set sail on October 27 and landed at Liverpool, England, two weeks later. In short order they entrained for Southampton and on November 11 crossed the English Channel to Le Havre. Major Donovan described the latest experiences: "Neither moon nor stars. Boat so crowded that it was like walking on a floor of faces to get through the ship. Then the landing. Marching through a strange city with queer names in an unknown tongue on all the shop windows. And our men truly overwhelmed. They seemed stunned with the new tongue and quite at a loss." Donovan himself, however, gloried in his position, writing to his wife that the rank of major is the "best job of the war," allowing him to be in touch with his men while still requiring him to use his mental powers.[16]

The second and third battalions, meanwhile, departed from New York harbor on the night of October 29 aboard the *America* (formerly the *Amerika* of the Hamburg-America line). One of the sailors on board — an old hand at transporting soldiers across the Atlantic — marveled at the apparent lack of concern about the dangers ahead shown by the men of the 69th. In his memoir of the war Kilmer tried to explain the psychology involved by quoting a verse from G. K. Chesterton's poem "The Ballad of the White Horse": "For the great Gaels of Ireland / Are the men that God made mad / For all their wars are merry / And all their songs are sad." As the ship approached England, the men of the Third — or "Shamrock" — Battalion spent hours trying to catch a glimpse of Ireland, but the ship was too far to the south, and, according to one of the men in the battalion, "their patience was not rewarded."[17]

On board the *America* the men of the 165th made the best of cramped quarters, the prohibition against smoking, and the need for constant vigilance against submarine attack. But spirits remained high, with concerts on deck or in the mess hall every night (when the ship was outside a danger zone) and singing and laughter in the holes. Kilmer humorously noted that "If there is left in the Atlantic a mermaid who cannot now sing 'Over There,' 'Goodbye Broadway, Hello France,' 'Mother Machree,' and "New York Town,' it is not the fault of the 69th New York." Yet the men's minds always returned to weightier thoughts, as they studied their military manuals and wondered when they would be sent to the front. The soldiers' underlying concern was evident on the main deck every afternoon and evening when long lines of men waited their turn to confess their sins to Father Duffy. And every morning, not just on Sundays, a large number of men again gathered around the regimental chaplain as he celebrated mass on an altar resting on two nail kegs.[18]

After the *America* finally anchored in the harbor of Brest, France, an even more unpleasant journey was about to begin. The men first unloaded their baggage and supplies from the ship and then piled into open box cars whose capacity was designated by the French as "Hommes 36-40, Chevaux 8" (Men 36–40, Horses 8). Not being linguists, the men called these box cars "Pullmans for forty hommies (*hommes*) and eight chevoos (*chevaux*)." With blankets, hard tack, and corned beef, between forty and fifty men settled down into each car for an unbearably cold three-day ride to Savoie in Lorraine. About the only comfort was cigarette smoking: "The moment the lucky possessor of a cigarette lighted it, a dozen crowded around him and asked for a turn at its soothing vapor. One never appreciates the value of tobacco until one is forced to pass hours of consistent and unrelieved discomfort."[19]

From Savoie, where the Second and Third battalions arrived on November 21, the troops marched to Naives-en-Blois, the village which would serve as their regimental headquarters. (The troops in the First Battalion had already arrived and were quartered in several other villages nearby.) There the men were introduced to the life of a billeted soldier — European style — sleeping in barns, stables, and other outhouses owned by the locals. Kilmer described the conditions during that "winter of unprecedented severity": "A freezing wind blew through the great holes in the tumble-down shed where the men slept, covering them, night and day, with snow. They learned many soldierly things. How to make blouse and overcoat supplement the thin army blankets, for instance. How to keep shoes from freezing in the night by sleeping on them. How to dress and undress in the dark — for lamps were unknown and candles forbidden." The countryside had been so devastated by the war that one of the American soldiers asked, "If this is what they are fighting for, why not give it to them and call it off?"[20]

Soon after the 165th was settled in Naives-en-Blois, Major Donovan was ordered to attend a field officers' school to learn about trench warfare. When he returned, he resumed the usual drilling and conditioning regimen for his men. By now some of the soldiers in his battalion had begun calling him "Galloping Bill" or "Hard-Boiled Bill." "Wild Bill," the nickname that was destined to stick, began to be used after a particularly grueling three-mile run that took the men down embankments, through barbed wire, and over walls and trenches. When the men returned exhausted, Donovan asked what was the matter with them, adding, "I've got the same fifty pounds on my back as you men, and I'm ten years older." Anonymously from within the ranks came the remark, "But we ain't as wild as you, Bill." It was perhaps after this run that Father Duffy overheard three of the men discussing their commanding officer. While two of them stressed Donovan's positive qualities, even insisting that he should be king of Ireland, the third man described him as a "son of a bitch." In the ensuing argument the two defenders maintained their ground, pointing out that the CO held himself to the same standards as he did the men. The dissenting soldier finally moderated his view, saying that Donovan was still a son of a bitch "but he's a game one." When the chaplain passed on the gist of this conversation to Donovan, the latter man laughed and said to the priest, "that's what I want on my epitaph."[21]

Because Naives was near the front, where a possible German offensive was feared, the 42nd Division was replaced by more seasoned French troops. The men of the 165th accordingly relocated to the town of Grand, an easy two-day hike away. As the regiment entered that historic town on December 13, the men learned that it had once been a Roman encampment and settlement, as evidenced by the ruins of an amphitheater. A heavy snow blanketed the town the day before Christmas. "It was as though a kindly disposed Fate was to make this last Christmas that many among us should know a good old-fashioned one," wrote Corporal Martin Hogan of Company K of the Third ("Shamrock") Battalion. "The white Christmas snow and the turkey dinner next day made everything quite complete."[22]

It was here that Father Duffy, the "friend, adviser and guide of very man in the regiment," celebrated midnight mass. Kilmer again recorded the details: "[A]ll the town came to see these strange, gentle, brave, mirthful, pious American soldiers, who, coming from a new land to fight for France, practiced France's ancient faith with such devotion. The Regimental colors were in the chancel, flanked by the tricolor. The 69th was present, and some French soldier-violinists. A choir of French women sang hymns in their own language, the American soldiers sang a few in English, and French and American joined in the universal Latin of *'Venite, Adoremus Dominum.'" At Christmas breakfast the first mail to reach the men was distributed. "I received a letter from my sister, which I read and re-read that morning until I knew it by heart," recalled Corporal Hogan. "Each time I saw a pal reading his letter from home I took mine out and proceeded to read it again. I wanted to impress on him that I, too, had not been forgotten." At dinner the men enjoyed traditional American fare — turkey, chicken, cranberries, mashed potatoes, carrots, bread pudding, nuts, figs, and coffee — a feast which made Hogan declare the army "a first-rate caterer."[23]

Early the next morning the 42nd Division left Grand en route to a new assignment. For four days and nights the men of the 165th endured the most appalling privations of food, covering, and warmth as they trudged through the Vosges Mountains, sometimes in the eye of a blizzard. Father Duffy noted that the supply wagons became stuck on the steep, icy roads. To get the wagons over the hills, the men had to hitch their best mule teams to each of the stalled vehicles, repeatedly driving the animals over the same ground and at times pushing and pulling the wagons themselves. For three days the men in the Third Battalion had no food, and when the supply wagons finally arrived the rations were meager: a raw potato and a slice of bread one day, and coffee and a bacon sandwich the next. According to Kilmer, though, the soldiers were never dispirited or too cold or hungry or weary to teach the French villagers along the way "strange bits of New York slang." In fact, although many in the 69th New York fell down during the excruciating trek, not one of them "fell out" during the ordeal. In other words, despite exhaustion or injury, not one of them broke ranks and waited along the road to be picked up. Those who arrived at their destination with the help of truck drivers or the ambulance corps did so only because they had fallen into the snow and become immobilized. Many observers remarked that the men reminded them of General Washington's heroic soldiers at Valley Forge, while one of the medical officers commented that "That hike made Napoleon's retreat from Moscow look like a Fifth Avenue parade." As if to prove that their spirits were still intact, upon arriving at Longeau on December 29, the regiment's band — as well as the rank and file — ironically broke into a hearty rendition of "The Good Old Summertime." Major William Stacom, who commanded the 165th Infantry's Second Battalion, reported that the men in the division had walked 117 kilometers and that more than 700 men — 200 from the 165th — had suffered from exposure during the ordeal.[24]

Life in the regiment's new home in Longeau was unlike anything the men had so far experienced in France. The billets in which they were housed while awaiting the construction of barracks were warm and comfortable, and their energies were now taken up in training for the trench life they expected soon to encounter. Besides incessant bayonet drill, the men got a "thorough working out" on the rifle range several times a week and practiced digging trenches and "going over the top." Father Duffy objected when the British bayonet instructors taught the men to curse while lunging their pointed weapons into stuffed mannikins. The chaplain admitted that cursing would not be so objectionable in the heat of battle — he did not think that God would even notice it — but its use in training was "organized blasphemy." He added that the men "will do more in battle by keeping their heads and using the natural cool courage they have than by working themselves up into a fictitious rage to hide their fears." In contrast to the chaplain's seriousness, Corporal Hogan joked that with the return of better times the "cooties" (body lice), which had become "mighty scrawny" on the rationless hike, returned with a vengeance. "They had their own systems of intensive drilling," he wrote, "and they practiced all things upon us during the night, which they had learned with us in the day." While at Longeau, the men witnessed the arrival of Colonel John Barker, the new regimental commander, who had replaced Colonel Hine.[25]

To Colonel Barker fell the task of reorganizing and training the regiment according to the latest thinking about military effectiveness. He and his staff formed and trained a series of specialized platoons, from which the most competent enlisted men were culled for additional instruction by officers who had served in actual combat. In addition, every man was issued grenades, a steel helmet, and two gas masks (one French made, the other English). In February officers and men received instruction in grenade throwing and trench warfare from a crack French unit known as the 32nd Battalion of Chasseurs. It was also at Longeau that the 165th Infantry organized an intelligence section, the first in the 42nd Division. The officers of this new unit successfully trained a group of scouts, observers, snipers, and map makers who could expertly detect and hinder the enemy's movements. Some of the members of this corps were so talented that they were assigned to division headquarters.[26]

For the first six weeks of 1918, the men of the Third Battalion were billeted in a village a few miles west of Longeau. One of the village's attractions was a distillery, which, quite naturally, was placed off limits to the American doughboys. However, for a fee the local parish priest occasionally made the distillery's products available to the soldiers. On January 20 Private Tom Shannon, a native of Ireland and lately a brick mason and pugilist from Boston, was drinking with his buddy, Private Francis Hays, in their billet near the still. Having exhausted their supply of liquor, Shannon sent Hayes to procure another bottle of liquor from the cleric. When Hays tried to pay for the contraband with a twenty-franc note, however, the priest refused to sell because he did not have change. Angered that his buddy returned empty-handed, Shannon loaded his rifle and walked over to the rectory, where he allegedly threatened the priest's life with particularly offensive language. A sentry at the distillery and another soldier who saw the incident hustled the priest into his house, where the three men remained just long enough to hear a shot fired in the street. When the sentry looked outside to find the source of the shot, he saw Shannon walking back to his billet. Presuming that the Irishman was the culprit, the sentry accosted the drunken Shannon, took his rifle away, and found one round missing from the clip. (Undeterred, Shannon returned to the rectory, where the priest gave him what he wanted.) Although no one had seen Shannon fire the shot, and although the priest was not in Shannon's line of vision at the time of the shooting, the soldier was charged with firing a weapon at the cleric with intent to do bodily harm. Shannon was found guilty and was to be punished by a dishonorable discharge and six years imprisonment at hard labor. When the findings and the sentence were reviewed on the division level, however, they were disapproved, although Shannon may have suffered some other kind of punishment.[27]

At the end of January, when Father Duffy visited Company H at Cohor, he found that the men were angry because the French had asked them to wear British uniforms. Expressing the anti-British sentiment of the typical Irish recruit, Private Martin Higgins said he would rather be hanged than put "won of thim rags on me back." To Colonel Barker's question whether the men would object to wearing English boots, the chaplain probably spoke for the men when he wittily replied, "No. They'd have the satisfaction of stamping on them." But to assure the colonel that the Old 69th would not let its anti-British feelings undermine the Anglo-American war effort, Duffy turned serious: "If you put our fellows in line alongside a bunch of *Tommies [British soldiers], they would only fight the harder to show the English who are the better men . . . . There are soldiers with us who left Ireland to avoid service with the British Army. But as soon as we got into the war, these men, though not yet citizens, volunteered to fight under the Stars and Stripes."[28]

In mid February the 42nd Division was ordered to Lunéville, in Lorraine, for further training and actual duty with French troops in the trenches. Donovan's First Battalion arrived first, and Companies B and D were the first from the 165th Infantry to take up positions in the trenches along the front line, in the process relieving some French Chasseur units. When Company D arrived at its post on February 27, the men were surprised by the serenity which pervaded the area, officially known as the Rouge-Bouquet-Chausailles subsector. Within a half hour, however, the men of Company D had "started something." In the ensuing gun fire Corporal Arthur Trayer and Private John Lyons were hit by fragments when a high explosive shell burst after striking the roof of a shack in which they were resting. Though not seriously wounded, the two men spent a few weeks in hospital — the first of the regiment's casualties in Europe.[29]

Life in Lunéville occasionally allowed the men a welcome break from the rigors of camp. When one of the girls in town would invite some of them to her home, this meant "home folks, a cloth upon a table, a pleasant-faced motherly head of the table for a treat, a kindly, fresh-eyed girl, a rare treat, though we could not understand her; and it meant cheese and bread and *vin rouge*, the singing of French songs after supper and the roaring forth of American ragtime." Almost two years later Corporal Hogan recalled nostalgically: "These were evenings of genuine American-French *entente cordial*, and they are good to look back upon, the pleasantest memories which our mission gave to us."[30]

French domestic scenes like these inspired Sergeant Joyce Kilmer to write a short story mysteriously entitled "Holy Ireland." The tale describes a heartwarming incident involving a dozen Irish-American soldiers billeted for the night in the home of a French widow and her children. As the widow and Sergeant Reilly attempt to communicate in front of a roaring fire in the widow's Spartan home, Kilmer draws the reader into the wartime scene:

"A spirited conversation it was, too, in spite of the fact that she knew no English and the extent of his French was *'du pain,' 'du vin,' 'cognac'* and *'bon jour.'* Those of us who knew a little more of the language of the country acted as interpreters for the others. We learned the names of the children and their ages. We learned that our hostess was a widow. Her husband had fallen in battle just one month before our arrival in her home. She showed us with simple pride and affection and restrained grief his picture. Then she showed us those of her two brothers — one now fighting in Salonica, the other a prisoner of war — of her mother and father, of herself dressed for First Communion.

"This last picture she showed somewhat shyly, as if doubting that we would understand it. But when one of us asked in halting French if Solange, her little daughter, had yet made her First Communion, then Madame's face cleared.

"*'Mais oui!'* she exclaimed. *'Et vous, ma foi, vous êtes Catholiques, n'est-ce pas?'* ['But yes!' she exclaimed. 'And you, to be sure, you are Catholics, right?']

"At once rosary beads were flourished to prove our right to answer this question affirmatively. Tattered prayer-books and somewhat clingy scapulars were brought to light. Madame and the children chattered their surprise and delight to each other, and every exhibit called for a new outburst."[31]

On March 1 two officers and fifty men in the First Battalion of the 165th Infantry earned the distinction of being the first American troops in France to advance into and hold a German defensive position. Although four Americans were killed and three were wounded, the detachment drove out the defenders and held its position against counterattack. (For this bit of history making, the regiment earned twenty *Croix de Guerre*.) On a subsequent night the enemy attacked the First Battalion's trenches seven times and was successively repulsed. During one of the forays Tim O'Rourke killed an enemy sniper and announced to his companions in the trenches that he had gotten his first German. O'Rourke's exaltation was quickly snuffed out when a grenade landed in the trenches and killed him.[32]

Four days later the Second Battalion relieved Major Donovan's men, who returned to Camp New York, the regiment's support area three miles behind the trenches. Corporal Hogan of the Third ("Shamrock") Battalion referred to the new training camp as the muddiest in France and described the muck almost onomatopoetically: "It oozed, slopped, quivered and trickled. It slipped down our backs, matted our hair, got into our eyes and savored our food. We floundered and splashed and chunked through its wallows. We reveled in mud like turtles and ground hogs." Probably because of the muddy conditions, the regular gas mask drill was conducted inside the barracks, and some of the men became so proficient that they could get their masks on in about four seconds, the difference of a second or more being "the difference between life and death on occasion at the front . . . ." While the First Battalion "enjoyed" life in Camp New York, its commanding officer, Major Donovan, remained in the front lines to give support to Major Stacom's Second Battalion. Thus it was that Donovan was on hand when the Second Battalion underwent its baptism of fire and the regiment suffered its first major tragedy.[33]

This unfortunate episode took place at Rouge Bouquet, an area of the Lunéville subsector, on March 7. At 3:20 p.m. the enemy launched a barrage of shells into the Second Battalion's position for about an hour. One of the projectiles smashed into the roof of a dugout in Rocroi occupied by First Lieutenant John Norman and twenty-one other men of Company E. Some of the Americans were killed instantly, and all were buried in the mass of collapsing earth and beams. When it appeared that Major Stacom was not going to rush to the scene of the incident to survey the situation, Major Donovan determined to go in his stead. But first he made sure that the frontline defense was in good order. After reassuring each of the men, he put his arm around seventeen-year-old Eddie Kelly. To Donovan's question whether the young man would let the Germans "get his goat," the private replied in the negative and held on to his weapon with extra determination. Almost immediately, though, a bombardment forced the major and his party of ten men to return to the command post. Still determined to reach the men trapped under the roof of the dugout in Rocroi, Donovan set out again. En route he passed through the same trench where only minutes before he had given encouragement to the men. But this time he found the lifeless corpse of Eddie Kelly, shot in the head with shrapnel.[34]

Finally arrived at the collapsed dugout, Donovan himself jumped into the hole and began digging for the trapped men. At last a rescue crew unearthed the bodies of seven men — two alive and five dead. The voices of other survivors — including Lieutenant Norman — could be heard from the crater, and several times these men were able to pull themselves to the surface. But, each time, shells rained down on the ill-fated men, and they were again cast down into the pit. Rescue work was finally halted, but only after heroic efforts by the men of Company E and the pioneer platoon of Headquarters Company. Kilmer described the tragedy's denouement: "The bodies of fourteen men and one officer still lay in that ruined dug-out — it was unwise, in view of the constant bombardment of it, to risk the lives of more men in digging for them. So a tablet was engraved and erected above the mound, the last rites of the church were celebrated by Father Duffy, and the place where the men had fought and died became their grave." To memorialize the men killed in the dugout that day, Kilmer wrote the poem "Rouge Bouquet," and Corporal Hogan mused what a pity it was that "these men were killed without a chance to come to grips with the enemy, without even catching sight of him."[35]

In his account of this demoralizing incident, Corporal Alf Helmer, one of the survivors, recalled the cries of the trapped men and guessed that about half of them had died within thirty minutes of the explosion. He himself had been buried up to his chin in dirt and had managed to survive by using his tin hat to scoop away the dirt from near his mouth. Even after rescuers arrived, it took them twelve hours to clear away the dirt down to Helmer's waist. Once unearthed, Helmer moved along the trenches toward company headquarters, dropping to the ground when he heard whistling shells and thinking how ironic it would be if he were killed by incoming fire after eluding a suffocating death in the dugout. After reporting to headquarters, he noticed that he was shaking like a leaf and that tears were streaming down his face. Nevertheless, he insisted that he be allowed to return to the site of the explosion to help in the continuing rescue effort. In his memoir he explained his motivation: he could not abandon his buddies, it was his duty as an American soldier, and he feared the disgrace if he did not follow his conscience.[36]

The rescue operation at Rouge Bouquet was assisted by the pioneer platoon under Sergeant Abram Blaustein, one of the between sixty and eighty Jewish members of the 165th Infantry. Despite the shellfire which continued during the rescue effort and the danger of being buried himself, Blaustein helped haul out the dirt and the timbers that had fallen into the dugout. His heroic action received extensive coverage in the *Brooklyn Eagle* of March 25. Upon the recommendations of Major Donovan and Major Stacom, the sergeant was awarded the *Croix de Guerre* for his competence and courage. John O'Keefe expressed the regiment's appreciation for their Jewish comrade with a poem entitled *"Blaustein of the Irish":

You talk about your melting pot,
The crucible of man —

Where Celt and Saxon, Slav and Scot
Are made American.
But oh! 'tis war makes strangers one
To face a foe defiant
Like Sergeant Abey Blaustein,
The scrappy, happy Blaustein,
The hustlin', bustlin' Blaustein in
The Irish Sixty-Ninth.
Sure, foolish prejudice some took
At first in racial pride,
When Danny's pug and Solly's hook
In line ranged side by side.
But what's a nose when, mid the din,
Its owner is reliant
Like Sergeant Abey Blaustein,
The scootin', shootin' Blaustein,
The mighty, fighty Blaustein in
The Irish Sixty-Ninth.
O'Connell, here's a *slainthe* lad
And Donovan, here's two.
I wish an open tube I had
To share the drink with you.
And next I lift a Yiddish *boak*,
Far bigger than a pint,
To Sergeant Abey Blaustein,
Untirin', firin' Blaustein,
To Abey Blaustein, one in soul
With all the Sixty-Ninth.[37]

Despite the disastrous interlude at Rouge Bouquet, the regiment held the line, in no small part because of Major Donovan. After extricating himself from the shattered dugout, he and three of his sergeants had gone up and down the line, telling the men what to do and calming their nerves. Finally, at 2 a.m. the major felt free to return to his own lines. But having neither rifle nor revolver — having nothing, in fact, but what he called a "fancy cane" — he needed a guide. After latching on to a "husky youngster," Donovan and his companion headed toward headquarters, at times crawling on the ground and at others crouching under enemy fire. At one point Donovan's "guide" became so terrified that the major had to take the lead himself. Two hours later the two finally reached their lines. But Donovan's mission was not yet complete. He hiked another four miles to regimental headquarters to report to the colonel and then walked back to the Second Battalion's command post. In a letter to his wife the major mused about the recent night's events: "[Y]ou would be surprised at the fear of the dark that men have, and you would wonder how the mere fact that a man is an officer and is standing with them has a guiding effect upon an enlisted man. These men did not know me. I was not their battalion commander, but all they needed was someone to talk to them." Donovan's devotion to duty that night earned him a brace of commendations. The Rainbow Division cited him as "an example of bravery, activity, and remarkable presence of mind" during a violent bombardment, while from the French authorities he received the *Croix de Guerre*. To the French he protested his unworthiness, saying that his rank required him to do more than was expected and that "I did only what I should have done." He relented only on condition that the medal also be given to the lieutenants and the sergeants who had worked under his direction.[38]

On St. Patrick's Day that year the 165th Infantry celebrated as the Old 69th had always done. Father Duffy said mass for each of the three battalions, the afternoon was given over to sport, and the evening to music and entertainment. The chaplain noted in his memoir that the mass for the Second Battalion was held in a grove of birch trees on a hill, with the men scattered over the slope. Duffy told the soldiers that their presence there that day made them the envy of every man back home. "The leading men of our country had called us to fight for human liberty and the rights of small nations," he recalled telling the men, "and if we rallied to that noble cause we would establish a claim on our own country and on humanity in favor of the dear land from which so many of us had sprung, and which all of us loved." During the concert that evening, Sergeants Robert Frye and Tom Donahoe provided the music for a medley of both funny and serious songs, while Privates McManus and Quinn played the fife for Irish dances.[39]

The entertainment turned literary when Lieutenant John Prout recited John Locke's poem "O Ireland, I Bid You the Top of the Morning" (also known as *"Dawn on the Irish Coast"):

> TH' ANAM THO' DIAH! but there it is,
> The dawn on the hills of Ireland!
> God's angels lifting the night's black veil
> From the fair, sweet face of my sire-land!
> O Ireland, isn't it grand you look,
> Like a bride in her rich adornin',
> And with all the pent-up love of my heart
> I bid you the top o' the mornin'.
>
> Ho — ho! upon Cliona's shelving strand,
> The surges are grandly beating,
> And Kerry is pushing her headlands out
> To give us the kindly greeting;

Into the shore the sea-birds fly
On pinions that know no drooping;
And out from the cliffs, with welcome charged,
A million of waves come trooping.

O, kindly, generous Irish land,
So leal and fair and loving,
No wonder the wandering Celt should think
And dream of you in his roving!
The alien home may have gems and gold,
Shadows may never have gloomed it,
But the heart will sigh for the absent land,
Where the love-light first illumed it.

And doesn't old Cove [*sic*] look charming there,
Watching the wild waves' motion,
Leaning her back against the hills,
And the tips of her toes in the ocean?
I wonder I don't hear Shandon's bells!
Ah, maybe their chiming's over,
For it's many a year since I began
The life of a Western rover.

This one short hour pays lavishly back
For many a year of mourning;
I'd almost venture another flight,
There's so much joy in returning —
Watching out for the hallowed shore,
All other attractions scornin';
O Ireland, don't you hear me shout?
I bid you the top o' the mornin'.

For thirty summers, *asthore machree*,
Those hills I now feast my eyes on
Ne'er met my vision, save when they rose
Over Memory's dim horizon.
Even so, 'twas grand and fair they seemed
In the landscape spread before me;
But dreams are dreams, and my eyes would ope
To see Texas' skies still o'er me.

Ah! often upon the Texan plains,
When the day and the chase are over,
My thoughts would fly o'er the weary wave,

And around this coast-line hover;
And the prayer would rise that, some future day,
All danger and doubting scornin',
I'd help to win my native land
The light of young Liberty's mornin'.

Now fuller and truer the shore-line shows —
Was ever a scene so splendid?
I feel the breath of the Munster breeze;
Thank God that my exile's ended.
Old scenes, old songs, old friends again,
The vale and cot I was born in!
O Ireland, up from my heart of hearts
I bid you the top o' the mornin'![40]

But, as had often been the case during the 69th's celebrations in the Civil War, the day's festivities belied a recent sorrow. For on that feast Father Duffy read aloud for the first time Joyce Kilmer's tribute to the men killed at Rouge Bouquet. In his diary the chaplain recorded the drama that surrounded the recitation: "The last lines of each verse are written to respond to the notes of 'Taps,' the bugle call for the end of the day, which is also blown ere the last sods are dropped on the graves of the dead. Sergeant Patrick Stokes stood near me with his horn and blew the tender plaintive notes before I read the words, and then from the deep woods where Egon was stationed came a repetition of the notes."

*"Rouge Bouquet"

In a wood they call the Rouge Bouquet
There is a new-made grave to-day,
Built by never a spade nor pick
Yet covered with earth ten metres thick.
There lie many fighting men,
Dead in their youthful prime,
Never to laugh nor love again
Nor taste the Summertime.
For death came flying through the air
And stopped his flight at the dugout stair,
Touched his prey and left them there,
Clay to clay.
He hid their bodies stealthily
In the soil of the land they fought to free
And fled away.
Now over the grave abrupt and clear

Three volleys ring:
And perhaps their brave young spirits hear
The bugles sing:
"Go to sleep!
Go to sleep!
Slumber well where the shell screamed and fell.
Let your rifles rest on the muddy floor,
You will not need them any more.
Danger's past;
Now at last,
Go to sleep!"

There is on earth no worthier grave
To hold the bodies of the brave
Than this place of pain and pride
Where they nobly fought and nobly died.
Never fear but in the skies
Saints and angels stand
Smiling with their holy eyes
On this new-come band.
St. Michael's sword darts through the air
And touches the aureole on his hair
As he sees them stand saluting there,
His stalwart sons;
And Patrick, Brigid, Columkill
Rejoice that in veins of warriors still
The Gaels' blood runs.
And up to Heaven's doorway floats,
From the wood called Rouge Bouquet,
A delicate cloud of bugle notes
That softly say:
"Farewell!
Farewell!
Comrades true, born anew, peace to you!
Your souls shall be where the heroes are
And your memory shine like the morning-star.
Brave and dear,
Shield us here.
Farewell!"

At Father Duffy's wise suggestion, the band followed up his recitation with a "medley of rollicking Irish airs." The chaplain ended the tearful scene with a typically Irish sentiment: "We can pay tribute to our dead, but we must not lament them overmuch."[41]

In the Third Battalion, meanwhile, St. Patrick's Day was celebrated in a more martial manner. Major Timothy Moynahan, a native of Ireland, summoned Sergeant Howard Emerson and told him that it would be a fitting way to celebrate the day if he and his snipers went out and brought back a "bagful" of prisoners. After dark, Emerson took his detail out toward enemy lines. When they found the first and second lines deserted, Emerson sent his men back, but he and Private Edward Dittman pushed on farther into enemy territory. Around midnight they saw the crouching figure of a man, toward whom Emerson alone crawled until he came within easy range. Taking careful aim, he fired. He saw the figure hunch upward and then lurch forward out of sight. But the shot, of course, echoed though the hills, and a machine gun began to sweep the field. Emerson turned and crawled rapidly back toward Dittman, whom he could not find, however. Although Emerson got back to his lines safely, he never reported his encounter with the enemy. Nevertheless, the story got around, and thus it was that he received the credit for being the first man in the Shamrock Battalion to kill one of the enemy.[42]

After recounting this episode in his wartime memoir, Corporal Hogan mused that the technology of modern warfare had made it more and more painful for the soldier to season himself for his task. "Somehow the guns, the gas, the crackling automatics, the liquid fire, the deviltry of modern warfare etches its [sic] way into his spirit like a biting acid until callous[ness] comes, until apprehension and the feeling of self-preservation deadens, and the soldier becomes intent alone upon his mission of enemy destruction." Hogan concluded that soldiers "stunned past fear" like this are known as "shock troops." "The Rainbow Division, our Division," he wrote, "soon qualified as shock troops."[43]

Three days after St. Patrick's Day, on the night of March 20, the 165th Infantry pounded the enemy with a surprise attack — what the French call a *coup de main*. When the regiment sallied forth to the trenches, the men must have been heartened by the sight of a green banner fluttering from the bayonet of one of their comrades. The banner — a green one marked with the traditional golden harp and the motto *Erin Go Bragh!* [Ireland Forever!] — had been given to Sergeant Evers of the regimental band by an elderly woman before the men went to Camp Mills. Sergeant Kilmer boasted that the green flag went "over the top" twice that night and added that the name "Rouge Bouquet" was later embroidered on it. As to who had given Evers the green banner, Kilmer thought it might have been *Kathleen ni Houlahan herself.[44]

The Germans retaliated at nine the next night with a barrage of high explosives, gas shells, shrapnel, and machine-gun bullets. In describing the inferno, Corporal Hogan wrote that "There was a winged fury breaking over us, tearing the earth up in chunks and amid frightful pandemonium showering us with earth, stones and debris . . . The air above us hissed and roared and snapped. . . . The gas flooded unaware over the trenches, chlorine, tear and mustard gases. The shrapnel pieces flew thick among us. And then the high explosives rained down and tore our trenches up in masses. It was an awe-inspiring baptism into the cult of modern war that our Shamrock Battalion had! . . . All stayed with the drum fire until gas or shell got them or until they were relieved." By morning only thirty men were left on their feet, and most of them needed the attention of doctors.[45]

In the retaliatory bombardment from the Germans, the men of the 165th learned the value of precaution. The French had previously questioned why the Americans so conscientiously wore their gas masks in the trenches. Surely, said the French, the enemy could not send cloud or projector gas through Rocroi Woods, and their last gas shell attack had been three years before. In the ensuing gas attack, the Germans hurled shells filled with mustard gas, which blinded the men and poisoned their clothing, blankets, and food. Only two Americans were immediately killed by the gas, and of the 400 others who were taken to the hospital only three died — of bronchial pneumonia caused by the gas. The French casualties were far greater.[46]

Among the victims of the night's gassing were Corporal Hogan and Private Harry McCoun. "The gas takes its victim unawares," Hogan later wrote. "The first that I noticed in my excitement was that the water was streaming from my eyes almost as though they were hydrants. I could not see my hand before my face. A gray, impenetrable mist closed thickly around me and I fell upon my knees to steady myself. Crawling I knew not in what direction, I was starting to feel my hands and knees stinging as though they had been burned. I had crawled into mustard gas. . . . I was blind." When McCoun complained of a frightful burning in his shoulder flesh, the surgeon knew that the soldier would die. McCoun asked for a drink of water, and then he pressed his lips together and fought the pain off silently until the end came. "He died a soldier's courageous death," concluded Hogan, "and, though the end came slowly and most bitterly, no whimper passed his lips while he lay waiting."[47]

The heroism which the 165th Infantry had displayed during these two days and nights of intense bombardment became part of the regiment's glorious tradition. For their bravery two first lieutenants were awarded the *Croix de Guerre* by the French. One of the men, George Patton of the Sanitary Department, had removed his mask during the gas attack in order to give medical attention to a wounded soldier. When the other first lieutenant, Thomas Martin of Company K, noticed that every other officer in the company had been taken to the hospital, he took command of the unit and held the sector during the two-day attack.[48]

One of the most famous members of the 165th was Sergeant Joyce Kilmer, the well-known poet and a member of the *New York Times* staff.

Kilmer had enlisted in the war effort only seventeen days after Congress declared war against Germany. (Ironically, Kilmer's poem "The White Ships and the Red" — in which he expressed his outrage at the German sinking of the *Lusitania* — may have moved the United States closer to entering the war.) He had originally joined the Seventh Regiment, New York National Guard, but transferred the following August to Headquarters Company of the 165th. Although Kilmer was at first assigned to the regimental adjutant's office, he soon chafed under the monotony of doing statistical work and openly longed to go to the front. After his arrival in France, he transferred to the Old 69th's intelligence staff, and by the spring of 1918 his work had attracted the attention of Major Donovan. On April 5 Kilmer wrote to Father James Daly, a friend of his, that he had been made a sergeant: "I'll never be anything higher. To get a commission I'd have to go away for three months to a school, and then — whether or not I was made an officer — I'd be sent to some outfit other than this. And I don't want to leave this crowd. I'd rather be a Sergeant in the 69th than a Lieutenant in any other regiment in the world." Rather than give up a chance to work with Donovan, Kilmer even refused an offer to work on *Stars and Stripes*, an Army publication. According to Father Duffy, Donovan in turn placed great reliance on Kilmer's coolness and intelligence and kept him by his side. The chaplain explained that this relationship suited Kilmer

*The birthplace of Joyce Kilmer, 17 Joyce Kilmer Avenue, New Brunswick, New Jersey.*

well, "for to be at Major Donovan's side in battle, is to be in the center of activity and in the post of danger." Duffy also ventured a description of what Kilmer's new role meant to the young soldier: "To be in a battle, a battle for a cause that had his full devotion, with a regiment he loved, under a leader he admired, that was living at the top of his being."[49]

Kilmer seems to have been attracted to the Old 69th New York by its camaraderie and its Irish roots. In September 1917, he had written to Father Daly from the front that "The people I like best here are the wild Irish — boys of 18 or 20, who left Ireland a few years ago, some of them to escape threatened conscription, and travelled about the country in gangs, generally working on the railroads. They have delightful songs that have never been written down, but sung in vagabonds' camps and country jails." The following April, in a letter to his wife, Kilmer explained his comment to a fellow editor that he was "half Irish." "The point I wished to make," the poet told his spouse, "was that a large percentage — which I have a perfect right to call half — of my ancestry was Irish. For proof of this you have only to refer to the volumes containing the histories of my mother's and my father's families. . . . I have the good fortune to be able to claim, largely because of the wise matrimonial selections of my progenitors on both sides, Irish blood." Indeed, Robert Holliday, one of Kilmer's earliest biographers, claimed that his subject had a natural affection for Ireland and for her literature, her people, and her traditions. Holliday even went so far as to say that everything "chivalrous and sacrificial" appealed to Kilmer's instincts and that it was not improbable that "had he been an Irishman born and resident in Ireland he would have been among the *martyrs of Easter Week."[50]

In his new assignment Kilmer became what Lemist Esler, the supply sergeant at the time, called "a perfect trial." According to Esler, Kilmer always reconnoitered closer to the enemy's location than his orders called for: "Night after night he would lie out in No Man's Land, crawling through barbed wires, in an effort to locate enemy positions and enemy guns, and tearing his clothes to shreds. On the following day he would come to me for a new uniform." On his days off, however, Kilmer invariably went to visit Father Duffy, and together they talked until midnight and sometimes beyond. The priest referred to these sessions with obvious relish: "Books and fighting and anecdotes and good fellows and things to eat and religion; all the good old natural human interests are common to us, with a flavor of literature, of what human-minded people have said in the past to give them breadth and bottom."[51]

In March and April, meanwhile, various rumors about the fate of the Old 69th had appeared in the press. On March 18 the *New York Times* reported that Father Duffy had been killed in France. The priest's sister, Mrs. Michael Bird, said she thought the rumor was false, adding that it might have started when a speaker at a Catholic war drive rally in the Bronx told his audience that Duffy had been wounded. Mrs. Bird indicated that she had received a letter from her brother three weeks earlier. In it he had assured her that she would be notified immediately in the event of his death. In a December letter he reported having a cold and joked that a rumor of his death had quickly arisen: "I was [reported] dead before the story [of my cold] had gone the rounds of the regiment." On April 20 a Liberty Bond salesman told his listeners that virtually the entire 69th New York had been wiped out on the battlefield, a statement later found to be untrue.[52]

On April 12 a *New York Times* story reported that the Americans had suffered 234 casualties in recent fighting on the western front. Among the wounded were many members of the 165th Infantry. One of the best-known of the wounded was thirty-one-year-old Patrick Dowling of Company K. This Irish native had attended the preparatory department of the University of Dublin before coming to the United States at the age of sixteen. He had served with the 69th New York during the 1916 mobilization along the Mexican border and attended the officers training camp in Plattsburgh, New York. One of the missing, meanwhile, was twenty-two-year-old Private Thomas Connely, who had been a machinist before enlisting in the 69th. After learning of his disappearance, his mother described him as a "real fighter" and said that he was "a happy-go-lucky sort of boy, but in a fight I feel certain that he would give every ounce of him toward the defeat of the enemy."[53]

Because news about Father Duffy was always "good copy" for the newspapers, he continued to be the subject of numerous rumors. So persistent were they that in some quarters the conflict in Europe was known as "Father Duffy's War." When anyone brought this designation to his attention, he would good-naturedly reply, "Oh, yes, I won the war!" and then change the subject. On one occasion he joked that he intended to name his book about the conflict *Alone in Europe*. (The actual title — *Father Duffy's Story: A Tale of Humor and Heroism, of Life and Death with the Fighting Sixty-Ninth* — was more characteristic of the man, focusing as it did on his beloved regiment rather than on him.) About the more serious rumors that he was dead, wounded, or crazy, he wrote home: "I hate to contradict so many good people, but I must say that I know I am alive and that I never felt better in my life. As to the third count, perhaps I had better leave it to others to testify, but I'm no worse than I always was."[54]

Like the Civil War chaplains who had preceded him, Father Duffy often reflected on his role in wartime and on the practical effect which religion had on the Irish Catholic soldier. On one occasion he described the 165th as an itinerant parish of approximately 3,000 souls — "generally scattered through five or six French villages, when *en repos* [at rest], and more scattered still through trenches and abandoned towns when in line." But, unlike parish priests back home, he took up no collections, a "breach of rules" for which he expected some day "to be put out of the Pastor's Union." He also pointed out that the local French curés were impressed by the way his men practiced their religion. Elsewhere in his memoir Father Duffy noted that non-Catholic officers always provided opportunities for their Catholic men to go to confession. The officers did this, he explained, not only to accommodate the men in their religious practice but to reap the practical military benefit attached to it. As an example of the latter value, the chaplain recorded the sentiments of some men who had just come from confession. "You can put my name down for any kind of a job out there [in the trenches]," said one such penitent to his first sergeant. "I'm all cleaned up and I don't give a damn what happens to me." Turning to a related topic, Father Duffy described a "striking" characteristic of the Irish soldier's Catholicism: "They make the Sign of the Cross with the right hand, while holding the left ready to give a jab to anybody who needs it for his own or the general good. I cannot say that it is an ideally perfect type of Christianity; but considering the sort of world we have to live in yet, it [is] as near as we can come at present to perfection for the generality of men."[55]

In the meantime, toward the end of March the Germans had begun a major offensive in the north. To allow the 128th French Division to meet that challenge along the Somme, the 42nd ("Rainbow") Division was ordered to take over the Baccarat sector, about forty miles west of the Rhine. On May 2 French and American artillery poured a destructive fire against a German stronghold in the Bois de Chiens near Ancerville. At the end of the next day a battalion of the 166th Ohio penetrated the entire salient with virtually no losses. Two mornings later, on May 5, Lieutenant Cassidy of the 165th led a raiding party behind the German outpost at Ancerville in hopes of bringing back some prisoners from whom the Americans could obtain needed information. In the surprise attack the doughboys killed two Germans and captured four. Private Charles Cain of Company D, one of the thirty men in the raid, later described the operation in a letter to a friend in New York City. Because of the bright moon that night, Cain wrote, the raiders blackened their faces before starting to crawl a thousand yards toward the enemy lines. "At last we got to the boches' [blockheads', i.e, Germans'] wire. Then came the ticklish work, cutting the line and hugging the ground whenever a star or flare went up. It seemed hours, but at last we cut through. Once a fellow away back coughed, and then and there we said a prayer to ourselves. Then, just to the right of us, a machine gun opened up, and everybody stopped dead still, but Mr. Boche must have been just sweeping in front of him[self], for he did not get us." After finally arriving at the German lines, one of the Americans hurled a grenade into the dugout, while Lieutenant Cassidy boldly flashed a pocket lamp before firing at one of the Germans. With their prisoners in hand, the raiders set out to recross the "No Man's Land" from which they had come, but heavy machine-gun fire from the enemy forced them to hit the ground every few yards. The Americans returned to their lines safely, to be congratulated by General Lenihan. The German prisoners gave the staff at headquarters the information it wanted, wrote Cain, concluding his letter, "and Company D was the real berries in the strawberry dish for some days thereafter."[56]

In May the 165th Infantry received a change in command when Colonel Barker was replaced by Colonel Frank McCoy, former aide-de-camp to General Leonard Wood and former military aide to President Roosevelt. When the colonel visited the Old 69th in the lines, he was delighted with the regiment's Irish spirit. At Father Duffy's request Tom Kelly welcomed the new commanding officer by singing "O'Donnell Aboo" and "The Wearing of the Green." In his memoir the chaplain described the officer's reaction: "Colonel McCoy's face was beaming. He evidently likes things to have their proper atmosphere. I can see the old Irish 69th is just what he expected it to be, and what he wanted it to be. I see there is no worry in his mind how these singers of [Irish] rebel songs will do their part in the war." The men readily accepted their new commander when they learned of his friendship with Father Duffy and of his service with the 69th along the Texas border in 1916. In his recollections of the war, McCoy noted Duffy's ability to preach to the men not only the Gospel but also the rules of military discipline. In fact, McCoy often expressed his belief that the popular chaplain should be made a colonel of the regiment, although not right away, since McCoy was not ready "to go to Blois or Hades just yet." In reply, Father Duffy good-naturedly told the colonel not to mock his priest, since "I'll be saving you from Hades yet."[57]

On June 10 the 165th took over from a French regiment an area known as Rendezvous des Chasseurs in the Baccarat sector of Lorraine. But later that month the regiment withdrew from Chasseurs when it accompanied the 42nd ("Rainbow") Division to the Champagne front to the west. (According to Father Duffy, when the men of the 165th Regiment heard that they would be fighting in the Champagne region, they expected to find bottles of the Widow Cliquot's sparkling "bubbly" hanging from every tree.) This redeployment was designed to meet the expected onslaught of 200,000 Germans massed on the western front for a last offensive. (On the morning of the 42nd Division's departure from the Baccarat sector, Major General Charles Menoher, the division commander, noticed that a "most beautiful rainbow" appeared directly over the area.) The 165th traveled by train to the province of Champagne but made the final leg of the trek to Chalon-sur-Marne by foot. There the regiment became part of General Henri Gouraud's Fourth French Army.[58]

As part of their strategy against the German threat, the French planned to use the newly arrived Americans as bait in a trap. The Gallic commanders believed that the Americans would put up only token resistance against the expected German onslaught and then retreat. And when the Germans followed in pursuit, they would fall into the hands of the waiting French. Such was the French plan — at least until General Douglas MacArthur became aware of it. The American commander told his regimental officers to assign a small number of men to the first trench, intentionally making it vulnerable to the expected attack. Most of the Americans were to be placed in the second line.[59]

On July 15 the Germans finally began their attempt to break through to Paris. From about midnight until 4:30 a.m., German artillery pounded the American position mercilessly. After a suspenseful silence, the barrage resumed, heralding the first wave of the German attack. As the French expected — and as MacArthur had planned — the 42nd Division fell back, abandoning its trenches to the enemy. At first the assailants thought the victory was theirs, but they were proved wrong when American artillery rained fire on their position. Although some of the Prussian Guards were able to reach the second line, they were eventually repulsed in hand-to-hand combat. At 5 a.m. that morning the Shamrock Battalion was moved up to reinforce the First and Second battalions. As the men waited in the trenches, Father Duffy passed along the lines, stopping to say a few words to each man. Martin Hogan described the chaplain's effect on the troops: "One look into Father Duffy's face was good for jaded nerves; for his face radiated a cheerful calm which made the hell around us seem unreal. He might just as well have been walking down the silent aisle of some majestic cathedral for all his face told of heeding danger or of wrought-up nerves. He spoke little personal things to each of the men, as though his thoughts were not on the battle, as though no battle were going on."[60]

On the morning of July 16, a German battalion launched a furious attack against one of the positions defended by the 165th Infantry. When the Germans got into the trench, Joe Daly snatched up a rifle and, after whirling it over his head like a shillelagh, hurled it at one of the enemy. Another American, Michael Tracy, was wounded while trying to get a better vantage point from which to demonstrate his marksmanship. Privates Finnerty and Fitzgerald, meanwhile, successfully used hand grenades to destroy a group of Germans but at the cost of their own lives. And John O'Connor of Company O flushed out an enemy machine-gun nest, forcing the gunners into the American line of fire.[61]

Although the Germans hurled twenty-five divisions against the Rainbow Division's ten, the Americans at Champagne pushed back the enemy time and time again. Corporal Hogan graphically recounted the gruesome scene on the trench line: "Clubbed rifles were splintered against skulls and shoulder bone; bayonets were plunged home, withdrawn and plunged home again; automatics spit here and there in the line; grenades exploded . . . ." Hogan grudgingly admitted that the endless bayonet training which the men had received had saved many a life that day: "We had growled a lot about this bayonet work, . . . for, we argued among ourselves, in modern war one never has occasion to use a bayonet; why, one seldom sees the enemy, it's just a question of being shot at and shooting with big guns, with much use of rapid-firers and machine guns and, now and then, long-distance rifle practice. . . . [But] it was the good old-fashioned knife that won the day in the battle of the Champagne. And the many hundreds of dead Germans before our trenches and deep in the field bore bayonet marks and not bullet holes."[62]

From the recent campaign emerged an episode similar to at least one which occurred during the Civil War. In the Champagne sector, one of two brothers, both first sergeants in the 165th, was hit in the left shoulder. Despite his wound he managed to obtain an automatic weapon, with which he opened fire into a German trench. He continued his barrage until he was finally hit in the right hand. After shifting his weapon to his other shoulder, he resumed firing and was stopped only when an enemy bullet killed him. Although the soldier's death quickly became known to headquarters, the officers there decided not to inform the dead man's brother until the next morning, preferring to use the latter soldier on a special mission that night. As the sergeant and a lieutenant started off on their reconnaissance, they found themselves along the trench from which the Germans had been driven earlier that day. "Here's one of our men," said the sergeant after seeing an American soldier lying face down. "I'll see who it is — if there's anything we can do." When the sergeant turned over the body — and recognized the face as his brother's — he let out a barely audible exclamation. He put aside his grief for the moment, however, and resumed his reconnoitering mission.[63]

Another casualty during the campaign was Corporal John Finnegan, who had run into battle to avenge the death of Lieutenant Thomas Young. After a shell burst near him, Finnegan was hurled into the air and fell to the ground deaf and wounded in the leg. Apparently undismayed, the soldier bandaged the wound himself and waited to be rescued. Later at the first-aid station, medics ripped his pants in order to bandage his leg wound properly. There Finnegan exclaimed to Father Duffy: "There's nawthin' the matther with me, Father, exceptin' that I'm deaf. They got the Lootenant[,] and I haven't squared it with thim yet. I'm goin' back." After the chaplain had left to attend to more pressing duties, Finnegan sat up in bed and demanded a knife — but at the moment with no other intention than to cut holes in his pants and to sew them up with a shoe string. Seeing that no one around him would oblige, he said, "All right. I have the tools God gave me." With that remark he proceeded to use his teeth to tear a few holes in the breeches and to stitch them up with the shoe lace. He then demanded to know where his gun was. Told that he should wait for Father Duffy to return, Finnegan said that the chaplain would be the last man to "keep a well man out of a fight." Seizing a stray rifle nearby, he warned those around him to stand clear: "Keep out of me way, now, I don't want to fight with the Irish excipt for fun. This is business." Father Duffy concluded the tale with words that could have aptly served as an epitaph: "So wounded, bruised, half dead, John Finnegan returned to battle. Immortal poems have been written of lesser men."[64]

On July 19 the 165th Infantry withdrew from the Champagne sector and traveled by train toward the Château-Thierry district, fifty miles east of Paris. At Epieds, en route to the front lines, the men of the Old 69th came upon the unburied dead of the 26th Division lying in the wheat fields, a sight that must have reminded them of the battle of Gettysburg. While advancing to the Forêt de Fère to relieve a French division, the Americans passed ambulances carrying wounded Alabamians from a fight at Croix Rouge Farm. Arrived at their destination, the 165th took over the French foxholes. The next morning the regiment began its advance to the Ourcq River. Dubbed the "O'Rourke" by the men, this tributary of the Seine was no more than a stream at that time of year — twenty feet wide and twenty inches deep — but its banks were very steep. At the nearby village of Sergy, the men came under heavy machine-gun fire and explosives as the Germans tried to cover their retreat. Since the First Battalion was to lead the attack, Major Donovan and four company commanders reconnoitered the German lines. After returning, though, the five officers came under attack, and Donovan himself was gassed. He nevertheless recovered sufficiently to carry out General MacArthur's order to advance when it finally came. Donovan and his adjutant, Lieutenant Oliver Ames, led the pursuit of the enemy. Although the Germans were thrown back across the Ourcq, they dug in their heels for an expected lengthy defense. From the safety of trees and bushes, the "Boche" [Germans] poured a rain of bullets upon the Americans on the opposite shore. The men of the Third "Shamrock" Battalion replied by shooting the Germans out of the trees with rifle and revolver fire, though the battalion's own ranks were somewhat thinned. As the Shamrock's officers advanced to the river bank, the Germans opened with another "frenzy of fire."[65]

At three o'clock on the morning of July 28, German explosives and shrapnel raked the men of Company D as they waited in the streets of Villers-sur-Fère. Most of the officers, it turned out, were away on various assignments at the time, and as the numbers of wounded from the shelling began to mount, two corporals searched for someone in higher authority. Although they found no officer, they came upon Sergeant Tom O'Malley sitting against a stone wall and puffing away on his pipe. Father Duffy recounted the initial exchange and used the outcome of the episode to make a point about the Irish:

"'Where's the officers, Tom?'

"'Oi don't know where th' hell they are,'" says Tom, between puffs of his pipe, and in the slow, soft speech of the West Coast Irish. "'If ye were in camp and ye didn't want to see thim, ye'd be thrippin' over thim. But now whin ye want t' know what ye got to do in a foight ye can't find wan of thim.'

"'Well, Tom, we'll elect you Captain and you take charge of the men until some of the officers get back, or they may be getting out of hand.'

"'No, lads, Oi don't fancy meself in a Sam Brown belt. Dick O'Neill here is a noice young fallah, so we'll elect Dick Captain, and Oi'll make ye fellahs do what he tells ye.'

"So Sergeant O'Neill, a youth of twenty-one, took charge of the situation, got the men together in small groups under their non-coms, and in places of comparative safety, and had them all ready when Lieutenant Cook came back from the conference to issue their orders to cross the Ourcq.

"It is something that we call typically American that a number of men under a stress and in an emergency like this, should get together, choose their own leaders and obey them implicitly for the common good. These four men are Americans of the type we are proudest of. Yet is worth noting that three out of the four were born in an island whose inhabitants, we are often told, are unfit for self-government. As for Dick O'Neill, he is one hundred percent American, but it would take a braver man than I can claim to be to tell Dick O'Neill that he is not Irish, too."[66]

(Later in the war, after a battle during the Argonne offensive, Father Duffy came upon the same Sergeant O'Malley mentioned in the story above. Seeing that the soldier was wounded, the chaplain asked: "Tom, what did you want to get yourself hit for? We're short of officers as it is, and it's only men like you that can put this thing through." "Well, Father," Tom replied with his Connemara brogue, "you see it's like this: a sergeant stands an awful fine chance of gettin' hit as things are goin' now. We got a lot of new min that he's got to take care of to see that they don't get kilt; and whin the line moves forward, there's some of thim nades a bit of coaxin'.")[67]

As planned, the Rainbow Division began to cross the Ourcq at 4:30 a.m. on July 28. The Americans were unaware, however, that enemy machine-gunners were hidden in the woods and fields opposite them. As the three battalions of the 165th Infantry advanced, the Shamrock Battalion led the way. Captain John Hurley of Company K stepped out in front of his men to give the order: "Come on, boys, we're going in. We're going to pull off a thing here that the Germans ain't tried yet. We're goin' to give 'em a bellyful of Uncle Sam's cold steel." According to Corporal Hogan, Lieutenant Patrick Dowling jumped into the river, "with a broad grin on his face and his automatic in his hand" and started over "in a gale of bullets." His platoon sergeant, Frank Doughney, however, was killed in mid stream. Dowling and Corporal James McGovern were the first to pull themselves out on the opposite bank, and with the help of Private Thomas Lydon they routed a machine-gun nest and facilitated the crossing of hundreds of other American troops. When Dowling learned that Captain Hurley, his superior officer, had been wounded, he took over command of the company and led the men into a "murderous fire" coming from a thickly forested hill. It may have been during this sequence of events that there appeared the rainbow which Major General Charles Menoher reported seeing when the 42nd ("Rainbow") Division became engaged on the Ourcq.[68]

On July 28 Captain James Finn of Company H was wounded while he lay in a ravine along the river trying to catch some sleep. As shells began to fall around him, one of them struck his right leg, crushing it so badly that a bone-grafting operation was necessary to restore its use. In an account of the Ourcq campaign after the war, Finn noted that the 165th had no artillery support and was forced to march right up to the enemy's machine guns. But the lack of food — and the need to eat on the run when food was available — drew his special attention. "We had had no food for three days, and it was raining hard — mud everywhere," he recalled. "We hadn't been able to get our kitchens set up, because we were so busy fighting; and there was always the trouble in getting provisions up to the lines. Finally, after these foodless days, we did get the kitchen set up one night, the call went out for a real mess, and everyone was jubilant. The men all were ready with their mess kits, and about ten of them had got some food — but had not had time to eat it — when an order came: 'Hurry up! March at once!'"[69]

After the war Captain Finn told a story of an episode which may have occurred during the Ourcq campaign. One day a man who had just been sent to Company H approached Finn with his gun in his hand. After announcing that he was a "motor transport repairman," the newcomer confessed that he had never fired a shot in his life and that the weapon in his hand was useless to him. Restrained by the needs of the battlefield, Finn could spend no time trying to verify the man's story. Instead, he said, "If you've never handled a gun, this is a good time to learn; go on out and they'll show you." Finn later learned that the repairman had been telling the truth and that the man's corporal had had to load his gun for him. But what surprised Finn even more was that the "unwilling soldier" made no further objection but simply took his gun and went where he was ordered to go. Within minutes, though, the recruit was hit in the leg. As he tried to crawl to safety, he was struck twice in the right arm. Finn concluded his tale succinctly: "That ended his fighting experience. He wasn't killed; he's all right again now. But he had a short and sad term as a warrior!"[70]

Colonel Frank McCoy, who commanded the 165th Infantry, reported that the Third Battalion had crossed the Ourcq and reached its objective without great loss. But when the men's "fighting Irish got the better of them" — as McCoy expressed it — they charged the hill in an attempt to capture the German machine guns. The Third Battalion was "soon finished," however, and its commander, Major James McKenna, was among the fatalities in the assault that day. The next morning, July 29, Major Donovan was ordered to go to the relief of Company K. As his troops crossed the river, which at that point was only a stream, six of the men were killed. One of them, Jack Finnegan, was comforted by Father Duffy as he lay dying along the river. When the priest offered Finnegan a canteen of water, the stricken man told him to give the water to the Ourcq. "It needs it more than I do," the soldier quipped. While Company L prepared to make the crossing at another point, its commander, Captain Van Merle-Smith, observed that the Ourcq looked relatively deep. After the war he confessed that he had not relished the prospect of leading his men across the river, never having liked a cold bath in the morning. When he jumped from the bank into the river, he had expected to swim, but his feet touched a muddy bottom and the water was not as cold as he had feared.[71]

Just less than a year before Major McKenna's death, while still at Camp Mills, New York, the young soldier had expressed his hope that he would get a chance to fight six Germans "one after the other or all in a bunch." Though the future officer claimed that American soldiers were superior to their enemy — because the former thought as well as fought — he believed that he himself would not return alive from the war. But he was optimistic about the future record of the 69th: "We are going into the fiercest kind of fighting the world has ever known and the boys of the Sixty-ninth are bound to live up to the traditions of the regiment, which means they will be in the thick of the scrimmage and court death over and over again for their country's flag." In subsequent letters from the front, McKenna boasted that his men kept their cool under fire, although he admitted that the 69th had no monopoly on the military virtues. "As for our regiment — well, we thought we were the best," he confessed, "but as we look the facts in the face we are bound to admit there is no best — all are wonderful and what one does depends solely on the opportunity. Bravery is taken for granted, and the greatest acts of heroism are looked upon as 'in the line of duty.'" Nevertheless, ten days before he was killed McKenna stressed to Father Duffy the special obligation of the Irish-American soldier: "We must show the whole world where Irishmen stand . . . We must show that we are in this fight for liberty with heart and soul."[72]

After establishing a foothold across the Ourcq, the 165th Infantry dug in on the side of the hills less than seventy-five feet from the Germans, who by then had taken a position on the heights at Bois Colas and Meurcy Farm. On July 29 the Old 69th began its assault on the latter position, in what Lieutenant Harold Allen, the regimental intelligence officer, called the "most terrific fight of the war" up to that time. For seventy-two hours German machine-gun fire pounded the Allies, while the enemy attacked the Allied dressing station at Villers-sur-Fère with gas and explosives and fired from their planes onto the ambulances below. During this bombardment the battalions on Donovan's right and left fell back until he and his men were left alone, dug in on the crest of the hill and almost completely surrounded by machine gunners.[73]

Although the two other battalion commanders refused to advance without artillery assistance, Donovan resumed the attack. His First Battalion successfully charged up a steep hill at Bois Colas and routed its German defenders. To prevent the enemy from setting up a machine-gun nest there, Donovan stationed automatic riflemen and sharpshooters in a nearby wheat field to harass the Germans. Despite Donovan's initiative, the enemy established a machine-gun post behind the stone buildings at Meurcy Farm. From there they directed their fire on the American infantry in Bois Colas. As Donovan and his adjutant, Lieutenant Oliver Ames, advanced up the river bed ahead of companies A and C, the adjutant was hit in the head by a sniper's bullet. Although another bullet hit Donovan on the hand, the major continued to hold the dead youth in his arms. Ames was buried near where he had been killed, and on the wooden cross over his grave was inscribed the epitaph "A courteous kindly gentleman and a true soldier."[74]

Donovan and his slain adjutant had long held each other in the highest regard. Oliver Ames had been a member of the Harvard University Regiment, had attended officers' training school in Plattsburgh, New York, in May 1917, and had reported for duty with Donovan's battalion the following September. When the major made Ames his adjutant in January of the new year, the young lieutenant described the promotion to his parents as "the greatest honor I've ever had." Ames soon learned, however, that being Donovan's adjutant was not going to be easy. "After the first four days, I was really all in," the young man wrote. "I was so unused to the speed. Donovan has a wonderful mind, the result of years of training, has energy, is untiring, his personality is the strongest I've ever come in contact with, and with it all combines the most consummate tact." To criticism that Donovan should have been a colonel by now if he was as good as Ames claimed, the lieutenant replied that general headquarters had been trying to get Donovan on its staff for at least two months but that the major had succeeded in "ducking it." Donovan had, in fact, sent Ames to see General Douglas MacArthur at division headquarters to try to prevent the transfer. Father Duffy attested to the young lieutenant's solicitude for the major by recording that Ames periodically asked the chaplain to "boss the Major into taking care of himself." Ames insisted that "I [Duffy] must tell him that he is doing entirely too much work and taking too great risks and must mend his evil ways." After Ames's death Donovan felt as if he had lost his right hand. The major tried to soften Mrs. Ames's grief by obtaining for her husband the Distinguished Service Cross. In a letter to the widow explaining the circumstances of her husband's death, Donovan said that the young adjutant had insisted on following him as he ran into machine-gun fire: "I told him to go back. He said, 'no,' that he was going to take care of me." Donovan closed the letter with the ultimate compliment: "More than my feeling of respect and admiration for his qualities as a soldier and a gentleman, there was between us an even deeper relation. To me he was like a younger brother."[75]

On the next day, July 30, the 165th participated in the drive to take Brulé Wood. In describing his company's movement in that strike, Sergeant Richard O'Neill said his men got about a thousand yards ahead of the two flanking units that accompanied them — the French on the right and the 167th on the left. After his company had captured a ravine, O'Neill stumbled into a machine-gun nest occupied by twenty-five Germans. Having lost his rifle, the Irish-American officer used his revolver to put three of the enemy out of action but not before being hit three times himself. For whatever reason, the Germans retreated toward the woods, and O'Neill was struck another three times after pulling himself out of the machine-gun pit. Despite his wounds he insisted on bringing his report to Major Donovan in person, but en route he suffered four additional wounds. After recovering at a hospital near the Spanish border, O'Neill rejoined his regiment for the Argonne campaign. During this offensive a wound to the right hand partially paralyzed his arm, bringing to eleven the number of wounds he sustained during the war. Nevertheless, he was in good enough shape to accompany the Americans on their march into Germany, and he remained with the 165th until it returned to the United States.[76]

In July 1921, O'Neill received word that he had been awarded the Congressional Medal of Honor. The official citation read as follows: "In advance of an assaulting line he attacked a detachment of about twenty-five of the enemy. In the ensuing hand-to-hand encounter he sustained pistol wounds, but heroically continued in the advance, during which he received additional wounds, but, with great physical effort, he remained in active command of his detachment. Being again wounded, he was forced by weakness and loss of blood to be evacuated, but insisted upon being taken first to the battalion commander in order to transmit to him valuable information relative to the enemy positions and the disposition of our men." In addition, O'Neill received six other awards for his bravery: the Conspicuous War Cross from the United States, the *Medaille Militaire* and the *Croix de Guerre* from France, the Belgian *Croix de Guerre*, the Italian War Cross, and the Montenegrin War Cross. In 1922 he was unanimously chosen the most conspicuous World War hero from New York by the first convention of disabled American veterans held in that state.[77]

On the same day that O'Neill performed his heroic feat in Brulé Wood, Edward Geaney of the 165th Infantry won with his own bravery the Distinguished Service Cross. Seeing that the company commander, Captain Edward Connelly, lay dying out in front of the unit's position, First Sergeant Geaney risked death to bring him to safety. But, in performing this heroic act, the rescuer was shot through the left arm. Undeterred, Geaney carried Connelly 300 yards to the rear. Following his recuperation, the sergeant participated in the battle of Château-Thierry, but the wounds which he sustained in that engagement disabled him for life.[78]

On July 31 Major Donovan led the First Battalion in a successful attack against Meurcy Farm, although the cost was considerable. Bloody fighting continued the next day, but early on August 2 all enemy resistance seemed at an end except near Moreuil-en-Dole. Although the American Fourth Division was on its way to relieve the Rainbow Division, Colonel MacArthur wanted his troops to make one last effort. After learning from various regimental commanders that their men were exhausted, MacArthur called on Colonel McCoy of the 165th. The latter officer in turn contacted Captain Martin Meaney, then in command of what was left of the Shamrock Battalion, and asked him to report on the condition of his men. Meany replied memorably: "My men are few and they are tired, sir, but they are willing to go anywhere they are ordered, and they will consider an order to advance as a compliment." As the Shamrock Battalion took its position at the head of the Division, MacArthur exclaimed, "By God, McCoy, it takes the Irish when you want a hard thing done." By the end of the day German resistance in the area was broken and the vaunted Fourth Prussian Guard Division had pulled back to the Vesle River.[79]

On both a statistical and an emotional level, the battle of the Ourcq reflected mixed results for the 165th Infantry. The regiment suffered 1,750 casualties (250 dead, 1,250 wounded, and 250 missing), a large number relative to its original complement of about 3,000 men. Although Donovan's First Battalion — of approximately 1,000 soldiers — lost 600 men (killed, wounded, and missing), it could brag that it had participated in every day's fighting, had gone the farthest, and had stayed the longest. Donovan summed up some of the other statistics: During eight days of battle, the Rainbow Division had crossed the Ourcq, captured prisoners from six German divisions, and routed and decimated three divisions (including the crack Prussian Guard). But it was Father Duffy who recorded the battle's emotional toll: "Back came our decimated battalions along the way they had already traveled. They marched in wearied silence until they came to the slopes around Meurcy Farm. Then from end to end of the line came the sound of dry, suppressed sobs. They were marching among the bodies of their unburied dead. In the stress of battle there had been but little time to think of them — all minds had been turned on victory. But the men who lay there were dearer to them than kindred, dearer than life; and these strong warriors paid their bashful involuntary tribute to the ties of love and long regret that bind brave men to the memory of their departed comrades." He described the "heartbreaking task" of burying the dead as particularly hard on himself "because I knew these men so well and loved them as if they were my younger brothers. It has been the saddest day in my life. Well, it is the last act of love I can do for them and for the folks at home." After the war Colonel McCoy predicted that the battle on the Ourcq would always be the "proudest remembrance" of every man in the 165th Infantry who had participated in it. He added that in forty years of military service he had found no soldiers more loyal and devoted than those in that regiment.[80]

One of the most devastating losses which the 165th Infantry suffered during the last days of the Marne campaign was the death of Sergeant Joyce Kilmer on July 30. As part of the Intelligence Department, he had been put in charge of a patrol sent ahead of the First Battalion to locate enemy guns and enemy units. When the men of the battalion caught up to the patrol's advance position, Sergeant Major Esler noticed Kilmer lying on his stomach on a bit of sloping ground, as if looking over the top of the incline. After the calls of Esler and his companions failed to draw Kilmer's attention, they perceived that the thirty-one-year-old journalist was dead. Turning him on his back revealed that he had been shot through the brain. "What had happened was obvious," Esler reported to the *New York Times*. "He had crawled ahead of his patrol to scent out the guns and had reached this ridge of ground behind which he held himself concealed from the German gunners until, no longer able to resist the temptation, he stuck his head over the ridge to get a better view of the enemy. In that position the bullet found him." Privates Edwin Stubbs and Walter Collins, snipers in Donovan's First Battalion, carried Kilmer's body off the battlefield. The dead intelligence officer was buried next to Lieutenant Oliver Ames, not far from the Ourcq River. Private Stubbs drove a wooden stake into the soil over the grave and placed one of Kilmer's identification tags on it. The stake was later replaced with a cross. Among the other members of the 165th Infantry who joined Kilmer in death that day were Sergeants Joseph O'Rorke and Bernard Finnerty, Corporals Thomas Fitzgerald and Edward Mulligan, and Privates Patrick Farley, Patrick Morrissey, and Patrick Joseph Grimes. About losses like these Donovan wrote his wife: "It just makes me shiver when I think of the devotion and loyalty of these men and young officers immediately about me who have given freely to me in spite of my strictness and sometimes irritability with them."[81]

Once the Germans had finally pulled back, the 165th took a rest from the bloody business of war and paid an appropriate tribute to its fallen favorite, Sergeant Kilmer. During a service at his grave, a bugle sounded taps and Father Duffy again recited "Rouge Bouquet," the dead poet's earlier tribute to fallen comrades. According to eyewitnesses, every man in the regiment — including Major Donovan — wept at the heart-wrenching scene. A few days later Alexander Woollcott, who had resigned as drama critic for the *New York Times* to join the staff of the army newspaper *Stars and Stripes*, visited Kilmer's grave. Although Woollcott had brought a spray of cypress to lay on his fellow journalist's burial place, he found that his offering added little to the dignity which had already been accorded the site: "The sod was so trim, the green cross of sod across its surface shaped and patted with such painstaking care." A simple wooden cross bore Kilmer's name, the designation of his company and regiment, and the notation "Killed in Action — July 30, 1918." Woollcott was moved most, however, by the affection and admiration with which Kilmer's comrades spoke of him: "The captain under whom he had been serving for several months, the Major [Donovan] at whose side he fell, stray cooks, doughboys, runners — all shook their heads sorrowfully and talked among themselves of what a good soldier he had been and what an infinite pity it was that the bullet had to single him out. . . . Death is too common to distinguish any one. So the glowing praise and admiration I heard for Joyce was real — every word of it. I should be proud if any one ever talked of me as I heard dozens talk of him."[82]

In tribute to the slain Kilmer, the *New York Times* printed in its August 25 edition a variety of eulogies submitted by its readers. Whether penned in verse or prose or filled with religious or secular images, the tributes acknowledged the apparent irony in the life and death of the soldier-poet. Alter Abelson, one of Kilmer's colleagues on the staff of the *Standard Dictionary*, described him as "a fascinating prose writer and melodious versifier" but added that "no one ever dreamed that this modest, kindly youth had down deep in his heart the instincts of a heroic soldier — who loved world liberty and died for it." Joseph Rethy, another friend, attributed to Kilmer the essence of the poetic art: "For the authentic wand of the real poet illuminates the humblest object as well as the most grandiose. And Kilmer was a genuine poet, deeming his profession a sacred one, and scalding the poetasters with the contempt of his satire." Rethy also stressed Kilmer's rare mix of earthiness and sublimity: "If he liked you he loved to drink wine with you . . . . Nothing disgusted him so much as unmanliness. He hated the prude as well as the degenerate. . . . He was a genius, a man whose soul soared above this commonplace world. Yet when his country called for men, he forthwith responded. He was among the first to go. He went as a private, although he could, no doubt, have got a commission."[83]

For Eleanor Rogers Cox, Kilmer's death evoked a flood of imagery and sentiment that the famous writer would have appreciated:

*"Joyce Kilmer"

Dead! with that golden splendor all about you
Of high and pure and selfless sacrifice,
Dead! and for us, the legioned friends who loved you.
Deep Sorrow's veil enshrouding heart and eyes.
For us the loss — the thought that no tomorrow

Shall bring back the poet-friend we knew —
The soul to all nobility responsive,
The spirit gallant, valorous, and true.
The knightly hand that Truth's bright fashion wielded
St. Michael-wise, undaunted, and serene,
The song that brought new glories to the worship
Of Christ our Lord and Mary Virgin-Queen.
The friend so leal to Friendship's fairest meaning,
The poet chaunting down triumphant ways.
Yet turning still to cheer his wearied brother
With words of strength-enkindling cheer and praise.
The soldier who at Freedom's holy calling
His splendid all laid freely on her shrine,
And in far France with Eire's lines advancing,
Poured out his life's bright sacrificial wine.
The kindly human man whose very presence
Has blessed and bettered wheresoe'er he trod,
The Saint whose face already shines upon us
A star to light us to the courts of God.[84]

One of the members of the 165th Infantry who were wounded during the recent campaign was Captain Henry Bootz. A native of Germany, he stood about six and a half feet tall and had four brothers serving in the German army. Bootz had immigrated to America at the age of eight and seven years later joined the U.S. Army. He saw his first combat in the Philippines, became a first sergeant in the 13th Cavalry, and served with General Pershing in Mexico in 1916. After attending officers' training school, he was assigned to the 69th New York as a second lieutenant. At Camp Mills he was placed in command of Company D, composed almost completely of Irish longshoremen and notorious for its lack of discipline. To the assembled company Bootz laid down the law, reciting — in his heavy German accent — his impressive military experience and throwing down the gauntlet: "I iss da Papa and you iss da kids, and if da kids don't do vat da Papa says, da Papa knocks da hell out of dem! Remember dot! Und if any of you tink da Papa can't do dot, I vill take off my blouse anytime, and you can try me out." According to an eyewitness, the unruly men roared their approval and from then on worshipped their new leader.[85]

Bootz had been one of the first officers of the 165th to lead raiding parties with the French soon after the American arrival in France. On one of those early raids he carried a wounded French officer back in his arms, a fete that won for the American the *Croix de Guerre* and an honorary membership in a French regiment of chasseurs. On the next raid Bootz rescued a sergeant in his own company whose leg had been almost completely severed above the knee. Because the wounded man weighed about 190 pounds, Bootz knew he could not carry the sergeant with his leg in such a condition. As a result, Bootz used his jackknife to sever the remaining bit of skin on the sergeant's leg and then placed the wounded man on his shoulder. But the sergeant's weight forced Bootz briefly to lay down his burden while he removed his own heavy equipment — all as shells were falling around him. After carrying the sergeant to relative safety at a first-aid station, Bootz rushed out the door, prompting some of the men to ask, "You're not going out again?" "Of course I am," Bootz replied. "I'm going back for my stuff. Do you think I'm going to leave it there and let the Germans get it?" About two weeks after he himself was wounded at the Ourcq, Bootz was traveling by train to a new hospital when he noticed that the train was preparing to stop at a village just south of Neufchateau. As he looked out the window, he noticed small Irish flags on some of the pup tents in a field outside the village. "Is this the 69th?" the surprised Bootz called to a group of American soldiers who had come to meet the train. When informed that it was and that the Third Battalion of the 165th was encamped nearby, he began to cry and immediately exited the train. After being escorted to headquarters, Bootz reported for duty to Colonel McCoy. Noticing that one of Bootz's arms was in a sling, the colonel said that Bootz would be useless in combat. But when Bootz insisted that there was nothing wrong with him and that the sling would be off in a week, the colonel allowed him to stay. Months later, while recovering stateside from the wound he sustained at Château-Thierry, Bootz was permitted to watch an unusual surgical operation at the hospital. In contrast to his earlier composure under fire, Bootz emerged from the operating theater trembling and in an agitated state. "Oh, that's awful!" he exclaimed. "It almost finished me. I don't think I could stand another experience like that!"[86]

Meanwhile, on September 7, 1918, in France, newly named Lieutenant Colonel William Donovan and other officers and men of the First Battalion received from General Pershing the Distinguished Service Cross. Honored for his actions at the Ourcq River, Donovan was cited for being "in advance of the division for four days, all the while under shell and machine-gun fire from the enemy, who were on three sides of him, and he was repeatedly and persistently counter-attacked, being wounded twice." To rumors that Donovan would be named colonel of the entire 165th Regiment, he replied that he preferred his present rank: "As lieutenant Colonel, I can get into the fight, and that's what I'm here for." Donovan confided to his wife his belief that his men — many of whom had once thought him too strict and demanding — now appreciated the high standards he had set for them. They were now convinced, he believed, that he would ask of them nothing he would not do himself. His men's realization of this fact, he concluded, was "greater than any honor my superior officers can give me."[87]

The next day the *New York Times* reported that Father Duffy had also been awarded the Distinguished Service Cross for his bravery during the battle of the Ourcq. All day he had directed the work of the stretcher bearers and personally carried wounded men to shelter under heavy machine-gun fire. In presenting the award, General Pershing noted that Father Duffy had devoted himself to the care of the wounded and dying in Villers-sur-Fère from July 28 to July 31 and that, "despite constant and severe bombardment with shells and aerial bombs, he continued to circulate in and about the two aid stations and hospitals, creating an atmosphere of cheerfulness and confidence by his courageous and inspiring example." Edwin James, the *Times* reporter, added that the chaplain was so loved by the men of the 165th that "they wouldn't trade Father Duffy for the Kaiser, as much as they would like to have Wilhelm." In the same report the *Times* noted that two other Irish Americans from the 165th received the Distinguished Service Cross that day: Private Martin Higgins (who helped Duffy save wounded American soldiers along the Ourcq) and Corporal John McLaughlin (who, after rescuing a severely wounded comrade, cleared out a farmhouse, killing four Germans and capturing one prisoner single-handedly.) In an editorial the next day, the *New York Times* lavished praise upon Father Duffy, describing him as a "hero whose flame of valor burns luminously, steadily, inspiringly, wherever death confronts men and there is need of the stout heart and soul that loves its kind." The editorialist went on to call the priest a "hero of a regiment of which heroism is always expected . . . oblivious of danger, thinking only of those in danger, tireless in helpfulness, spending his strength in good deeds — lion-hearted, tender FATHER DUFFY!"[88]

A week before receiving the Distinguished Service Cross, Father Duffy learned that the corps commander had promoted him to the rank of major. Aware that Colonel McCoy had recommended him for both the award and the rank, the famous chaplain wrote to his friend — thanking him, on the one hand, and requesting a favor, on the other. "The British reward their military heroes with a peerage, a pension, and a tomb in Westminster Abbey," the priest wrote, setting his reader up for a mock request. "You have gotten me the American equivalent of them — the distinction and the emoluments — and it only remains for you to fix it up so that I can have a tomb in St. Patrick's Cathedral. All that is necessary to give me a right to that is to make me Archbishop of New York; Cardinal, if you insist. I never knew you to fail in anything you went after so I shall consider this matter as settled."[89]

Toward the middle of September, Lieutenant Colonel Donovan and his First Battalion were assigned a role in the vanguard of another American offensive. The Germans' control of the St. Mihiel salient blocked any Allied invasion of southern Germany and cut off communications between the Lorraine region on the east and Paris and Verdun on the west. To overcome this obstacle, the Allied commander primed an attack force of 450,000

Americans. The 42nd ("Rainbow") Division was to be in the vanguard of this assault, and quite naturally the 165th Infantry was placed at its head. In turn, Donovan and his First Battalion were to lead the regiment's attack against the southeast corner of the St. Mihiel salient, thirty miles from Verdun. As they waited for the planned night assault to begin, Donovan must have been concerned that 75 percent of his officers and 65 percent of his men were replacements, brought in to offset the severe losses which the First Battalion had suffered on the Ourcq. Thus it was a relief as well as a surprise when the German guns did not reply to the Allied barrage that started at 1 a.m. that night. The Germans, as it turned out, had decided to abandon the salient and had already begun to remove their troops. At 5 a.m. the First Battalion began to push ahead, for the most part still advancing despite German machine-gun fire. At the village of Maizeray, Donovan led thirty men behind the enemy's flank and opened fire. The German infantry and gun crews there quickly surrendered. The Americans were amazed to find that some of the German dugouts were almost luxurious, fitted out with running water, electricity, and dining and recreational facilities. Over the next two days the regiment advanced nineteen kilometers, liberating five French villages and capturing 350 prisoners. Within three days after Donovan had led the first skirmish line into battle, the Rainbow Division, along with other American divisions, had cleared the St. Mihiel salient. Patrols sent out by the 165th later pushed forward to the Hindenburg Line opposite the fortified area of Metz.[90]

As the 165th Infantry continued its advance, Donovan set up new headquarters in each of the newly gained areas. At his post at Haut-Mont he questioned a German prisoner brought in by Sergeant Moore of Company B. At first the lieutenant colonel was suspicious of the prisoner's offer to lead the Americans to his machine-gun post, where, he promised, all but two of the nine men in it would surrender. Donovan finally agreed to let the prisoner lead a patrol back to his post, but with the proviso that the German be collared with a rope. When the Americans and their "guide" arrived at their destination, all the enemy gunners except the officer surrendered. On another occasion, when Donovan's headquarters was near Hassavant Farm, an orderly prepared a sandwich and a cup of coffee for Lieutenant Richard Allen, who had just finished a patrol assignment. Before he could eat the food, however, a soldier brought in two prisoners — one an elderly German and the other a teenage Romanian boy. To the lieutenant's surprise, Donovan offered the food to the enemy prisoners. When Allen reminded his superior officer that it was against regulations to feed prisoners before they had been questioned, Donovan told him he should be ashamed of himself. "This poor little boy has been wandering around in the woods for two days with nothing to eat," he added.[91]

During the next two weeks the 165th Regiment helped defend the Essey-Pannes sector. At 1 a.m. on September 23, the Allies began a terrific barrage against the Germans that did not let up until 7 that morning. The First and Second Battalions of the 'Fighting Irish' then set off with a speed that amazed the Allies. In the words of Martin Hogan, the two battalions "ran over the first opposition before the enemy had opportunity to catch its breath after the terrors of the tremendous battering by our guns. They continued to overrun all opposition throughout the day, to romp over nerve-shattered and demoralized Germans." After inspecting the battle-field later that day, some of the men found a treasure trove in the abandoned German dugouts: iron crosses, boots, writing paper, postcards, beer, sausages, wines, and pumpernickel. One soldier returned loaded down with medals, officers' belts, side arms, and knicknacks. "It was the richest field over [which] the 'Rainbow' ever prospected," Hogan reported.[92]

Six weeks earlier, on August 8, meanwhile, the British had launched a major offensive of 300,000 soldiers, 1,000 aircraft, and 2,000 tanks against the Germans in Flanders. This attack was so threatening to the German position that General Erich Ludendorff began to withdraw his troops into the Hindenburg Line. This impressive system of defenses was punctuated at its most vulnerable points by a series of fortresses, the most formidable of which was the Kriemhilde in the Argonne. On September 26, in an attempt to open the way to Sedan, General Pershing ordered a massive assault of 1,250,000 men against the Kriemhilde. Although one of the three American corps succeeded in penetrating the line, that unit's advance was stopped at a fortress known as Kriemhilde Stellung near the village of Landres-et-St. Georges. Still determined to take the line, Pershing ordered seven veteran divisions — including the 42nd — to prepare to launch another assault, this time at the Kriemhilde Fortress near Sedan.[93]

At the beginning of October, the 42nd Division received orders to relieve the First Division, which had suffered heavily during an engagement a few days earlier at the Kriemhilde. Donovan now prepared to lead the 165th Infantry in a follow-up attack scheduled for dawn on October 14. But instead of making himself less conspicuous to the enemy's rifle sights, he did just the opposite. So his men could see him more easily, he dressed in a Sam Brown belt with double straps, completely indifferent to his increased personal danger. Just before giving the signal to attack, he roused the men with a threat to the Germans — "Come on, we'll have them on the run before long!" To a frightened young soldier he added the boast, "Come on, old sport, nobody in this regiment was ever afraid." The men finally charged from the trench amid a shower of machine-gun bullets, until the colonel signaled his troops to take cover in shell holes around them. He himself, however, remained standing, reading a map and completely exposed to enemy fire. "Come on now, men," he cried. "They can't hit me, and they won't hit you." Although some of the men reached the barbed wire at the top of the hill, they were subsequently killed or wounded.[94]

(In his account of the fighting that day, Father Duffy added paren-
thetically that the motto of the Donovan clan must be "Come on." The
priest also described the colonel as "one of the few men I know who really
enjoys [sic] a battle. He goes into it in exactly the frame of mind that he
had as a college man when he marched out on the gridiron before a football game, and his one thought throughout is to push his way through.
'Cool' is the word the men use of him and 'Cool' is their highest epithet of
praise for a man of daring, resolution and indifference to danger.")[95]

The following morning Donovan made the rounds in his old First Battalion, exhorting the men to the attack. But just as he and the battalion
sallied forth, he was hit in the knee by a machine-gun bullet. Though now
on the ground dangerously close to the German position, Donovan continued to direct the attack. He first called for artillery support, but the fire
was insufficient to allow his men to break through. Then, after realizing
that the First Battalion was in an untenable position, he ordered its commander, Major Michael Kelly, to retire. In the meantime an officer had
given Donovan medical attention, and soon two other officers arrived,
intending to carry him to safety. Prevented from doing so by continued
enemy fire, one of the newly arrived officers seems to have jumped into
Donovan's foxhole, while the other found shelter in a nearby depression.
Soon later a shell exploded in yet another foxhole not far from Donovan's,
blowing the two men in it to pieces and raining their remains down on the
colonel. At last, weakened by loss of blood and the smell of poisonous gas
wafting across the battlefield, Donovan allowed himself to be carried out
of danger. When a shell burst nearby, he ordered his carriers to take cover
and leave him. The men ignored his order and instead brought him to the
regimental aid station, where his wound was finally treated properly. There
he teased Father Duffy: "Father, you're a disappointed man. You expected
to have the pleasure of burying me here." Playing along with the joke, the
chaplain replied, "I certainly did, Bill, and you are a lucky dog to get off
with nothing more than you got." Lieutenant Allen later described this
battle as the hardest fought by the Old 69th while it was in France. According to Anthony Cave Brown, the American line would have collapsed
had Donovan not remained on the battlefield to encourage his men and
direct the mortar shelling that broke the attack.[96]

Meanwhile, the heroics of Sergeant Michael Donaldson of Company I
earned for the former pugilist a place in the annals of the 69th New York.
Father Duffy's erstwhile altar boy captured Hill 288 at Landres-et-St.
Georges from soldiers of the Prussian Guard and held it despite counterattacks. The lengthy citation accompanying his congressional medal —
issued five years after the war — described more of the particulars: "The
advance of his regiment having been checked by intense machine-gun
fire of the enemy, who were entrenched on the crest of a hill before Landres-
et-St. Georges, his company retired to a sunken road to reorganize their

position, leaving several of their number wounded near the enemy lines. Of his own volition, in broad daylight and under direct observation of the enemy and with utter disregard for his own safety, he advanced to the crest of the hill, rescued one of his wounded comrades, and returned under withering fire to his own lines, repeating his splendidly heroic act until he had brought in all the men, six in number."[97]

During the Argonne campaign an episode involving Captain Michael Walsh of the Third Battalion's Company I illustrated a particularly tragic and ironic side of the war. Prior to the battle of the Argonne, Walsh had served twenty-seven years in the U.S. Army and the National Guard. Because of this earlier experience, he had been assigned jobs in the rear echelons of the 165th Infantry since the time of its arrival in France. An expert rifleman, he longed for service in the front lines and chafed under the yoke of a less conspicuous role. When finally granted permission to join the Third Battalion at the front, he said gleefully: "I'm coming to join the army now. I am no longer in the boy scouts. After twenty-seven years I am finally in the war." As Walsh and a young soldier named Roberts advanced with Company I, they were almost hit by an enemy sniper. It took the two Americans a while to find their antagonist's position about 600 yards away, but once they did they kept firing until they saw him run, drop his weapon, and fall to the ground. "I'm in the army now," Walsh repeated. "I'm out of the boys scouts at last." Later during the fighting, however, Walsh was hit in the arm and lay in a sunken road when Major Thomas Reilly found him. The major tried to comfort the stricken man with the promise that he would now get a nice rest with plenty to eat until his arm was healed and he could then rejoin the conflict. Walsh protested that he could not leave his men in the front and only relented when the major ordered him to seek medical attention. That night Walsh was found dead — the back of his head caved in — about 150 yards from where he had fallen earlier in the day.[98]

Toward the end of his wartime memoir, Father Duffy tallied up the heavy cost of the Argonne victory for the 42nd Division. Of the Rainbow's 4,309 casualties, 758 were men killed or dead from wounds. Of that larger number, 1,321 belonged to the 165th Infantry, fully 44 percent of its overall complement. In fact, of the survivors in the Old 69th, only about 600 were men who had left New York with the regiment just over a year before. One can imagine the chaplain's grief as he summarized the fate of "his boys": "The great bulk of the old regiment is in hospitals, convalescent and casual camps; some of them promoted, some transferred, hundreds invalided home, a great many, alas! buried on battlefields or in hospital cemeteries."[99]

At the beginning of November, the American forces launched what would be the final act of its European military adventure. On November 1 the 165th Regiment participated in the third American assault, this time in the direction of Sedan. A week later the Second Battalion, under Major Henry Bootz, seized the heights of the Meuse River dominating Sedan, and the unit's advanced patrols forced from Sedan the last German troops west of the river. A week after the armistice, the 165th marched into Belgium on its way to Germany. Contrary to Father Duffy's belief that news of the victory would fill him with delight, the armistice turned his thoughts to the men who had made the supreme sacrifice. "I knew that in New York and in every city at home and throughout the world men were jubilant at the prospects of peace," he wrote. "But I could think of nothing except the fine lads who had come out with us to this war and who are not alive to enjoy the triumph. All day I had a lonely feeling and an aching heart. It would be a lesser thing to have been killed myself than to go back to the mothers of the dead who would never more return."[100]

While the 165th Infantry was in Luxemburg, the regiment spent Thanksgiving Day at Useldingen Castle, where Father Duffy preached at a solemn mass and where Lieutenant Colonel Donovan made a surprise appearance — to the cheers, naturally, of his former charges. After Donovan told his chaplain-friend that he wanted to be back with his old outfit, Duffy recorded in his diary his expectation that the lieutenant colonel would be rejoining the regiment in a very short time. The 165th finally entered Germany at Bollendorf on December 3, crossing the bridge into the village to the tunes of "Garry Owen." Father Duffy noted that a rainbow framed the sight and that "nothing more hostile greeted us than the click of a moving-picture camera." Again his thoughts stood in sharp contrast to those of the men: "Every soldier in the line was glowing with happiness except myself, perhaps. On occasions like this of glory and excitement my mind has a habit of going back to the lads that are gone." During the next two weeks, as the regiment made its way to the Rhine, Donovan caught up with his beloved former 69th and again took official command. The regiment arrived in Remagen-am-Rhein in the middle of December.[101]

In his postwar memoir Father Duffy headed his description of the Christmas feast in Remagen that year with the exclamation "Christmas Mass on the Rhine!" Other men in the regiment no doubt recalled with him the previous two years' celebrations in Texas and France: "In 1916, our midnight mass was under the open sky along the Rio Grande; in 1917, in the old medieval church at Grand in the Vosges; and now, thank Heaven, in this year of grace, in 1918, we celebrated it peacefully and triumphantly in the country with which we had been at war." As the regimental band played "Onward, Christian Soldiers" and "Adeste Fideles," the men marched to the parish church in Remagen for the service. In his sermon Father Duffy examined the question of whether the recent war could be ascribed to a failure on the part of Christianity. (In his memoir he seems to have answered his question by citing G. K. Chesterton's observation that "Christianity has not been tried out and found wanting; Christianity has been tried — a little — and found difficult.") After the mass the soldiers sang the hymn of Thanksgiving, "Holy God, We Praise Thy Name," while the local Germans in attendance praised the Lord with "Grosser Gott wir loben Dich."[102]

Lieutenant Colonel Donovan's reassignment to the Old 69th New York was the result of a well-orchestrated effort by Father Duffy, who wanted to guarantee that the regiment returned home with its Irish and Catholic identity intact as much as possible. At the time of the armistice, Donovan was working in the provost marshal's department, responsible for the discipline and inspection of all the American units at the front. Although the breakdown in discipline in many American ranks after the armistice necessitated such a position, Donovan disliked the assignment. In addition, the original ethnic and religious composition of the Old 69th had changed by the end of the war, due to the tremendous losses it had suffered and the infusion of replacements into its ranks. To make matters worse — in Duffy's eyes — the new regimental commander, Colonel Charles Howland, had had no previous connection with the regiment and was taking steps to ensure that he — and not Donovan — would be at the head of the 165th upon its return to New York. The situation changed dramatically, however, when Donovan inspected the regiment and found its morale at an all-time low. After General MacArthur was informed of this state of affairs, he relieved Howland and reassigned Donovan — now a full colonel — as the regiment's commanding officer, effective February 15, 1919.[103]

Not satisfied with Donovan's return to the regiment, Father Duffy launched a successful campaign to win for his friend the Congressional Medal of Honor for his heroism in the Argonne. The official citation explained that, as the American troops were suffering heavy casualties, Donovan "encouraged all near him by his example, moving among his men in exposed positions, reorganizing decimated platoons, and accompanying them forward in attacks. When he was wounded in the leg by machine-gun bullets, he refused to be evacuated and continued with his unit until it withdrew to a less exposed position." The longer citation entered into the Congressional Record detailed his courageous deeds and concluded *summa cum laude*: "Officers and men of this battalion say that it would have been impossible for them to have made the advance they did had it not been for the cool resolution, indifference to danger, and personal leadership of Colonel Donovan. It is the general opinion that his conduct on this occasion was of the highest type of courage witnessed by anybody in this regiment during the four major actions in which it has been engaged." Donovan also received two Purple Hearts and a bronze oak leaf for his Distinguished Service Cross, as well as additional honors from France, Italy, Britain, Belgium, Poland, and Norway. (He received more awards than any other American in the 42nd Division.) Even former president Theodore Roosevelt, one of Donovan's heroes, took note, adding that his sons regarded the colonel as "about the finest example of the American fighting man." Donovan later earned the Distinguished Service Medal for reorganizational work with the provost marshal's department.[104]

While the 165th Infantry was in Remagen, it did garrison duty and administered the city's civil affairs. Now billeted in hotels and private homes, the men enjoyed a new-found social life, both attending and hosting dinners in the city's hotels. To some of these repasts Colonel Donovan invited officers from among the other occupation forces in the area, treating them to what Father Duffy called "our Metropolitan Hibernian hospitality." On March 16 General Pershing arrived to review the Rainbow Division. Noticing the silver battle furls on the flag staff of one particular regiment, he asked to which unit the honors belonged. When informed that it was the 165th Infantry, he inquired what the unit's designation had been before the war. Told that it had been the 69th New York, the general owned, "I understand now." The next day the famed regiment celebrated St. Patrick's Day with the usual mix of piety, feasting, and athletic competition. From an altar set up in a field along the Rhine, Father Duffy addressed the men on "the debt that the world owes to the sons of Saint Patrick for their fight for civil and religious liberty at home and abroad, with the prayer that that debt might now be squared by the bestowal of liberty on the Island from whence we sprung."[105]

At Remagen Father Duffy and Colonel Donovan amused the men with their feigned competitiveness and savored a friendship built on mutual admiration. It seems that if either of the two men was mentioned in the press — presumably for his courage or devotion to duty — one of them would brandish the newspaper clipping in the other's face. Father Duffy recorded an incident of this playful sparring: "The other day Captain Ryan gave Donovan an editorial about him from a paper in Watertown, New York. It was immediately brought to mess, and Donovan thought he had scored a triumph, but I countered with a quotation from a letter which said that my picture, jewelled with electric lights, had a place of honor in the window of a saloon on 14th Street. Donovan surrendered." Writing about the spectacular view along the Rhine which the two men shared one evening, Duffy recorded in his diary that the panorama was all the more attractive because of the companionship. He continued with unabashed praise for Donovan: "This young Buffalo lawyer who was suddenly called into the business of war, and made a name for himself throughout the American Expeditionary Force for outstanding courage and a keen military judgment, is a remarkable man. As a boy he reveled in Thomas Francis Meagher's *'Speech on the Sword[,]' and his dream of life was to command an Irish brigade in the service of the Republic. His dream came true, for the 69th in this war was larger than the Irish Brigade ever was. But it did not come true by mere dreaming. He is always physically fit, always alert, ready to do without food, sleep, rest, in the most matter of fact way, thinking of nothing but the work in hand. He has mind and manners and varied experience of life and resoluteness of purpose. He has kept himself clean and sane and whole for whatever adventure life might bring him, and he has come through this surpassing adventure with honor and fame. I like him for his alert mind and just views and ready wit, for his generous enthusiasms and his whole engaging personality. The richest gain I have gotten out of the war is the friendship of William J. Donovan."[106]

The men of the 165th Infantry remained in Remagen for about four months, adjusting to a less bellicose life and savoring the impressive wartime record that the regiment had compiled. During its eighteen months in Europe, the 165th had participated in five major operations and the defense of four sectors. In addition, it had fought with the American army in every great battle in France and had been engaged with the French in an additional one. In its 180 days of actual contact with the enemy, the 165th had suffered 3,501 casualties (644 killed and 2,857 wounded). And to its regimental battle flag it had added nine new furls for action in the following sectors or campaigns: Lunéville, Baccarat, Esperance-Souain, Champagne-Marne, Aisne-Marne, St. Mihiel, Essey and Pannes, and Argonne-Meuse (first and second phases). A breakdown revealed the following casualties: one officer and thirty men at Lunéville, eight men at Baccarat, forty-eight men and one officer at Champagne, thirteen officers and 268 men in the Aisne-Marne sector, one officer and forty-six men at St. Mihiel, and five officers and 194 men in the Argonne sector. Colonel Donovan himself had been wounded in the left hand at Baccarat and again by a machine gun bullet in the Argonne. In addition, sixty-two officers and men received the French War Cross, and sixty were awarded the Distinguished Service Cross by General Pershing.[107]

Early the following spring the *New York Times* began to carry reports about the return of the 165th Infantry from Europe. On March 30 the paper announced that the Old 69th had sailed from Brest, France, en route home to New York City. Plans for a fitting reception were immediately begun, and Major Thomas Reilly of the 165th called on recuperating members of the organization to gather at the 69th New York's armory to prepare to march with the returning veterans when they arrived. The next day the *Times* reported that 250 convalescent wounded from the 165th had just arrived aboard the Cunard liner *Aquitaine*. Two days later the *Leviathan* arrived, carrying among its 14,426 returning men 190 wounded and sick from the 165th. Many of the latter men had been decorated for their heroism at Château-Thierry, St. Mihiel, and the Argonne. On April 5 six more noncommissioned officers and men from the 165th arrived aboard the *Frederick*: Colonel Charles Knowles (Company M), Sergeants Joseph Ward (Company B) and Frank May (Company M), Corporal Dennis Richardson (Company B), and Privates Patrick Dowling (Company K) and

Edward McCreary (Company L).[108]

Later that April the *New York Times* printed extracts from letters written from Remagen by two members of the 165th. In missives to his parents the previous December and January, Private Walter Phillips of Headquarters Company wrote almost chattily about the good food that the company occasionally enjoyed and the souvenirs that he planned to bring home. About his accommodations with a local family, he was almost ecstatic: "When we first moved in, it was a bare room with beaucoup straw on the floor, but the owners took a liking to us, and each day their improvements showed, until one day we came in and found beds. Real beds with white linen, but, thank God, no smell of chloroform, which usually goes with hospital beds." He limited his nostalgia to saying that he missed New York's "tall buildings and the paved streets, and most of all the women and children who understand my language." The other letter-writer, Lieutenant J. Langdon Leslie of Company L, painted less pleasant scenes. Writing after the fighting of the previous summer, this winner of the *Croix de Guerre* informed a friend in New York: "There have been thousands of shells falling everywhere and millions of bullets in the air. You would say no one can live in that fighting, but many do! Plenty of gas was given us, too . . . . We stopped the Fourth Prussian Guard, which is the best German shock troops under the Crown Prince. This was the first time since 1914 that they were stopped in an attack without advance. Ten times they attacked without any advance." Leslie's pen recorded other experiences all too familiar to his comrades: "[N]o shelter, just boche [German] planes giving us hell all the time; no food, no sleep, no water — just taking it. All of a sudden the offensive by the French. We were ordered out at 1 a.m., and marched and rode in autos, only to get into it again just as bad, with no food available and no rest, sleeping in the woods and being shelled all the time."[109]

Other newspaper stories that spring reported that the battlefield exploits of soldiers like Henry Bootz had gone far in winning for the Americans the admiration of the French. Early on, the Rainbow Division had trained with the French and had gone into battle side by side with the "Frogs." But before the Americans had shown their mettle, the French military, as well as the French population, had not expected much from the American war effort. "I've heard a good deal about how the French people threw flowers in the paths of the American soldiers, and all that sort of thing," said a captain in the 165th Infantry, "but I never saw anything of that sort until after we had done some hard fighting and they had come to realize that we were there to fight. There is no question but that the French felt, in the beginning, that America was not going to do much in the way of actual battling with the Boche [Germans]." The American captain noticed the difference especially after the Champagne fighting: "Those little Frenchmen were just falling all over themselves in their eagerness to give us all their funny little salute. They couldn't do it enough. . . . And, of course, after that there was nothing they couldn't do to show their faith in us."[110]

On April 21, after almost eighteen months of service in France, 1,962 men of the 165th Infantry arrived in New York City's lower bay aboard the transport *Harrisburg*. As the ship came up the bay, it was greeted by cheering crowds at the Battery and by other well-wishers on excursion boats or ships chartered for the occasion. On some of the welcoming craft were members of the city's various Irish organizations, including the Friendly Sons of St. Patrick, the Ancient Order of Hibernians, the Irish Counties Association, and the Sons of Irish Freedom. From the bands on board almost every boat came the strains of such tunes as "The Wearing of the Green," "Come Back to Erin," and "The Bard of Armagh." At the foot of 23rd Street, meanwhile, the members of the new 69th New York Regiment had gathered aboard the steamer *Grand Republic*, as had wounded members of the 165th and Spanish-American War veterans of the 69th. From aboard the steamer Colonel John Phelan of the new 69th New York ordered a signaler to wigwag a welcome to the commanding officer of the 165th on the *Harrisburg*. When Colonel William Donovan returned the greeting by waving from the ship, the crowd of spectators on the *Grand Republic* roared their approval. The *Harrisburg* proceeded up the Hudson River and docked at Hoboken, New Jersey, in mid afternoon. From there the men were ferried around the Battery to Long Island City en route to Camp Mills. The remaining 800 men of the regiment were scheduled to arrive the next day aboard the *Prinz Frederich Wilhelm*.[111]

While the 165th was still in Hoboken, Colonel Donovan informed port officials that 1,400 of the men who had originally sailed to France with the regiment were still alive. Of the original 108 officers, twenty-seven were still "with us," the rest having been transferred to other regiments during the war or sent home because of injuries or sickness. Donovan then alluded to the special character of his command: "The morale of the regiment has never been better than it is today. Formerly 85 per cent. of its strength were [sic] of Irish descent, and now it is only 50 per cent., but the spirit of the Old Fighting 69th is stronger than ever. The replacements, whether they are Jews, Italians, or any other foreign descent, have imbibed the right spirit and are more Irish now than the Irish." (Donovan later pointed out that at one time during the Argonne fighting the adjutants of the First, Second, and Third Battalions were all Jews.) About his own plans, now that the war was over, the colonel said that his only ambition was "to get back to private life, live once more with my family, and return to the practice of law."[112]

When asked whether it was true that Father Duffy had been in the frontline trenches during the fighting, Colonel Donovan said that only officers and men on duty were allowed in such positions. Instead, Donovan explained, the chaplain had typically been at the dressing station in the rear, where the wounded were brought for immediate treatment before being sent to the field hospital. With heartfelt words of admiration, the soldier paid tribute to the priest: "I would rather you pictured Father Duffy as we saw him doing his great work for humanity and never shirking it no matter how late or how early the hour was. Here was this doctor of philosophy, doctor of divinity, a student of nature, taken away from his flock and transplanted amidst the scenes of devastation and bloodshed in Europe. This man of wonderful opportunity went there and was an inspiration to the officers and men of the 165th Regiment. His was the dirtiest and yet the most important work from the humanitarian standpoint, and so necessary to keep up the morale of the men. After we came in at night and laid [*sic*] down on the ground tired as dogs, Father Duffy, [who] was tired too, with his long hours under shellfire at the dressing station, had to go out and bury his dead."[113]

During the week following the arrival of the 165th Regiment, its officers and men were hailed at a round of public events. On April 23 Colonel Donovan, Father Duffy, and the other officers of the regiment appeared at City Hall to receive from Mayor John Hylan the keys of the city. The mayor expressed the city's appreciation: "Colonel Donovan: what you and the men of the 69th Regiment did under your command will be one of the brightest pages of our history. You are not only the idol of your regiment, but of all New York. Your courage and vigor in all the situations confronting the regiment are known to all of us. In congratulating you on your remarkable achievements, I know that I express the gratitude of every race as well as the Irish people in this great metropolis. What a glorious record the 69th has!"[114]

Later that afternoon the officers of the 165th were the guests of the directors of a benefit fund created for the regiment. There Father Duffy expressed the men's appreciation for the welcome they had received from the city. He also explained how he had often reminded the men in the trenches that they were much appreciated by the people back home. "When the boys were in the dumps, with mud everywhere and cold rain pouring down, with a hard fight finished and another harder struggle just ahead," he said, "I crawled from shell hole to shell hole preaching sermons and trying to cheer the lads up by telling them just how much the old city thought of them, how it loved them." Though his words had the desired effect, neither he nor the men were prepared for the tumultuous reception they received upon their return. "[N]ow that we are home again they are accusing me of being a poor prophet," he said. "[T]hey say I did not tell them half of what the city and the folks 'back home' thought of them."[115]

The regiment was still being feted three days later. On Saturday, April 26, most of the men in the 165th attended a dinner-dance in their honor at the 69th New York's armory, while their officers enjoyed a repast hosted by the Mayor's Committee. In his toast to the regiment at the latter event, Mayor Hylan briefly sounded a somber note: "We cannot forget in the midst of our gladness the hundreds of brave men of the 69th who freely offered their lives on the altar of patriotism. But the dead of the 69th, martyrs of liberty, were worthily honored by their living comrades who carried to victory the battles which they had begun." When Colonel Donovan rose to thank the chairman of the event for the silk flag presented to him on behalf of the city, he was roundly cheered. He proudly accepted it for the 69th and promised that it would remain among the cherished trophies of the wars in which the regiment had fought. Father Duffy entertained his listeners with humorous stories about his life with the 69th and ended the evening with a prayer for the 615 men of the regiment who had died in the recent conflict.[116]

Monday, April 28, was an official holiday in New York City so its residents could properly greet the members of the 165th Regiment as they paraded up Fifth Avenue. The men left Camp Mills at about 10 a.m. and were transported by ferry to Pier 45 along the Hudson River at West Tenth Street. The current 69th New York Regiment of the State National Guard escorted the returning soldiers to Washington Square, where they enjoyed a cold lunch while awaiting the start of the parade. Of the 2,700 men of the 165th Infantry who marched that afternoon, about 1,400 of them were members of the original regiment at the time of its incorporation into the 42nd (Rainbow) Division. Of this latter number of men, 800 had served with the Old 69th on the Mexican border. When someone suggested that Colonel Donovan ride in an open car over the five-mile parade route at the head of the 165th, he replied brusquely, "It was good enough to go on foot in Europe. It's good enough now." The humorist Will Rogers made a more practical suggestion: "If they really want to honor the boys, why don't they let them sit in the stands and have the people march by."[117]

The regiment marched in four battalions under the command of Majors Michael Kelly, Van Merle-Smith, Martin Meaney, and Henry Bootz. In addition, about 700 wounded men who had returned to the United States at various intervals during the war paraded as a battalion under the command of Major Thomas Reilly, himself a casualty of the conflict. (One of the officers in Reilly's group was Colonel Charles Hine, who had taken the 165th Infantry overseas.) Other wounded veterans unable to march were allowed to sit in one of the reviewing stands. At the head of the regiment was its sixty-piece field band, playing its usual repertoire of music: "The Wearing of the Green," "Killarney," "The Harp That Once Through Tara's Halls," and "Garry Owen." In what was a novelty for the regimental band, twenty trumpeters marched at the forefront. From each of their trumpets hung a small green banner emblazoned with the traditional golden Irish harp.[118]

The regimental band included in its repertoire that day a new musical composition entitled *"When the Sixty-Ninth Comes Back." The words to the piece had been written as a poem by Joyce Kilmer shortly before he was killed in France. At the request of Colonel Donovan's brother, Father Vincent Donovan, the poem had been set to music by Victor Herbert, the famous Dublin-born composer and president of the Friendly Sons of St. Patrick. Herbert assigned the royalties from the new musical piece to Kilmer's widow, Aline, who was in the reviewing stand near St. Patrick's Cathedral as the regiment passed by.[119]

The Sixty-ninth is on its way — France heard it long ago,
And the Germans know we're coming, to give them blow for blow.
We've taken on the contract, and when the job is through
We'll let them hear a Yankee cheer and an Irish ballad too.

Chorus:
The Harp that once through Tara's Halls shall fill the air with song,
And the Shamrock be cheered as the port is neared by our triumphant throng.
With the Potsdam Palace on a truck and the Kaiser in a sack,
New York will be seen one Irish green when the Sixty-ninth comes back.

We brought back from the Border our Flag — 'twas never lost;
We left behind the land we love, the stormy sea we crossed.
We heard the cry of Belgium, and France the free and fair,
For where there's work for fighting-men, the Sixty-ninth is there.

The men who fought at Marye's Heights will aid us from the sky,
They showed the world at Fredericksburg how Irish soldiers die;
At Blackburn Ford they think of us, Atlanta and Bull Run;
There are many silver rings on the old flagstaff but there's room for another one.

God rest our valiant leaders dead, whom we cannot forget;
They'll see the Fighting Irish the Fighting Irish yet.
While Ryan, Roe, and Corcoran on History's pages shine,
A wreath of laurel and shamrock waits the head of Colonel Hine.[120]

The regiment marched the eighty blocks from Washington Square to 115th Street in less than two hours. Although the 1.2 million people along the route were enthusiastic in their welcome — calling out the names of Colonel Donovan and Father Duffy, in particular — they complied with the colonel's request not to throw cigarettes and fruit to the soldiers. Instead, the onlookers showered flowers upon the men, many of whom caught them and tucked them into their shirts or belts. The crowds responded wildly to the sight of the flags and banners that accompanied the troops. Besides the regimental colors and a tattered American flag, the standard bearers carried an immense service flag covered with more than 600 gold stars (for the men who had made the supreme sacrifice). Careful observers along Fifth Avenue noticed that the staff of the national flag bore several new silver battle rings. To the emblems of the Civil War battles in which the Old 69th had fought were added ten new trophies for its heroism during the various campaigns of the recent war. Many of the men wore on their uniforms the emblems of their own personal bravery — the *Croix de Guerre*, the Distinguished Service Cross, or stripes on their right arm (indicating their wounds).[121]

Along the route up Fifth Avenue, many of the veterans were no doubt reminded of episodes from the earlier history of the Old 69th New York. When the men approached Archbishop Patrick Hayes and about 500 priests and 1,800 leading Catholics in front of St. Patrick's Cathedral, the officers paid their respects by saluting the archbishop while the men marched with "eyes right." Archbishop Hayes acknowledged the salute by waving his biretta. From the steps of the church, groups of girls paid tribute to the dead by throwing flowers on the star-spangled service flag. Farther up the Avenue, at 105th Street, the troops passed grandstands filled with Civil War veterans who had fought with the 69th or with other regiments of the Irish Brigade under the command of Brigadier General Thomas Meagher. One of the onlooking veterans, in fact, was Patrick Tumulty, uncle of Joseph Tumulty, President Woodrow Wilson's secretary. The older Tumulty had served in Company D of the 69th New York during the last year and a half of the Civil War and still remembered the regiment's homecoming parade in New York on July 4, 1865. After the 165th Regiment completed its own homecoming march, the troops were honored at a dinner at the Hotel Commodore sponsored by the trustees of the regiment's benefit fund, all of whom were members of the Friendly Sons of St. Patrick.[122]

The day's pomp and ceremony prompted different reactions from some of its participants. For Colonel Donovan, possibly the proudest day in his life ended anticlimactically. After the parade Donovan and his priest-brother returned to Camp Mills, where the colonel had taken command of the First Battalion eighteen months earlier. Weeping, the colonel told Father Vincent, "I can't forget the men we left behind." In contrast, Martin Hogan approached the end of his chronicle of the Shamrock Battalion's exploits with an explanation for its writing: "I regarded my company [K] as a shade better than all others; my regiment, the 165th, as the greatest regiment in France, and my division, The Rainbow, as the finest fighting organization produced in the whole World War." He concluded his memoir with characteristic pride: "This parade closed the latest chapter of the regiment's service, and throughout that chapter the old organization was true to its proud tradition, a tradition that reaches back to the founding of the Sixty-ninth in 1851, and that was maintained in fifty battles of the Civil War and forty-four battles of the World War — 'It never disobeyed an order; it never lost a flag!'" After the war Father Duffy expressed his belief that the welcome accorded the soldiers that day was a fitting tribute to men who had played such a "manful part" on behalf of their country. While stressing that he was not a militarist, the former chaplain praised the ideal of the citizen-soldier. "[A]s long as liberties must be defended, and oppression or aggression put down," he wrote, "there must always be honor paid to that spirit in men which makes them willing to die for a righteous cause. Next after reason and justice, it is the highest quality in citizens of a state."[123]

Even before the men of the 165th Infantry returned from Europe, plans had been made to raise an endowment fund for them and to erect monuments to the memory of their fallen comrades. "The appreciation of New Yorkers for the deeds of the Fighting Sixty-Ninth in this war is not going to end with the stirring welcome home and the cheers and applause when the men parade," said Lieutenant Colonel Charles Healy, commander of the Veteran Corps, 69th New York. "This time the boys are going to be taken care of after they return to civilian life. It will not be like the aftermath of the civil war, when many of the men were without means of livelihood and, at times, in dire financial straits." The regiment's supporters also took steps to erect a granite monument in Calvary Cemetery (honoring the men of the 69th fallen in service) and a shaft in Greenwood Cemetery (bearing the names of the battles of the Civil War and of the Great War in which the 69th Regiment had fought).[124]

The list of decorations which various men of the 165th Infantry received both during and after the war stands alone in the annals of U.S. regimental history. Besides three winners of the Congressional Medal of Honor, the 165th boasted 160 recipients of seven other major honors. The awards and the names and/or the number of the honorees follow:

Distinguished Service Cross with Palm: Colonel William Donovan.

Distinguished Service Cross: Lieutenant Colonels Timothy Moynahan and Charles Dravo; Majors James McKenna, Michael Kelly, Thomas Reilly, Van Merle-Smith; two captains; three first lieutenants; four second lieutenants; three chaplains; thirty-six sergeants; nine corporals; one wagoner; and eight privates.

Distinguished Service Medal: Father Francis Duffy.

Legion of Honor: Brigadier General Frank McCoy, Colonel William Donovan, Lieutenant Colonel Timothy Moynahan, Major Michael Kelly, and First Lieutenant William Maloney.

*Medaille Militaire*: Sergeant Michael Donaldson, two corporals, and one private.

*Croce di Guerra*: Colonel William Donovan and Sergeant Michael Ruane.

*Croix de Guerre*: Brigadier Generals Frank McCoy and John Barker, Colonel William Donovan, Lieutenant Colonels Charles Dravo and Timothy Moynahan, Majors Henry Bootz and Michael Kelly, five captains, three first lieutenants, four second lieutenants, forty sergeants, fourteen corporals, one cook, and one private.[125]

During his first public lecture in Carnegie Hall after the war, Father Duffy was both playful and somber. While stating that there had been little drinking among the men of the 165th New York in the service, he added that what little there was did them good. "When they came out of the trenches, dirty and muddy and grouchy," he said, "I thought many times the money of the Trustees' Fund could have been put to no better use than in rolling a keg of wine down every company street. And the song the soldiers sang was this: 'We'll all go home / And drink up bottles of pop, / For the slackers voted the country dry / While we went over the top!'" The famous chaplain also praised the regiment's bravery but poignantly reflected on the heavy price of war: "War is bad business. . . . It is a heavy price that has been paid. It rests on my mind more than I care to talk about. Armistice Day was a sad day for me, thinking of the good lads who had passed out; and these days of welcome home are sad with thinking of the mothers whose sons didn't come back. And yet I don't know — it is better to go that way than to hang on till fifty or sixty and rot away. And when the Sixty-ninth paraded up Fifth Avenue yesterday there was something they passed on to the young lads who watched, the lads of six and sixteen — God bless them all. There is nothing too good on earth or in heaven for those we left behind us."[126]

After returning to America, Father Duffy resumed his parochial duties. He briefly served at his former parish — the Church of Our Savior — in the Bronx, but in 1920 Archbishop Hayes gave him the pastorate of Holy Cross parish on West 42nd Street. The famous priest soon found that many Catholics worked the late shift in the hotels, restaurants, and newspaper plants in the Times Square section of his parish. Concerned that their late hours made it difficult for these workers to attend regular Sunday morning masses, he polled these men and women as to a time more convenient for them. When the workers voted for the "ungodly" time of 2:15 a.m. — when many of them got off their shift — Duffy accommodated them by establishing a predawn liturgy. In 1921 Father Duffy was the guest of honor at a public event recognizing the twenty-fifth anniversary of his ordination. To the tributes paid him on that occasion, he replied with his usual humility: "If I have helped any one to be a better man, and he loves me for it, that's my D.S.C. [Distinguished Service Cross]."[127]

In recollecting his wartime experiences with the 165th Infantry, Albert Ettinger spoke at great length and with great admiration for the former chaplain. Ettinger believed that Father Duffy's speaking voice was the most beautiful he had ever heard and that the priest's memory for the names of most of the men in the regiment — as well as of their wives and children — was remarkable. Whether in the trenches or on the open battlefield, Ettinger recalled, the chaplain was everywhere, appearing like a "gigantic apparition," unmindful of bullets, giving absolution to the dying, and attending the wounded. Even for men not of his own faith, Father Duffy showed the greatest solicitude: For the seriously wounded Jew, he said a prayer in Hebrew; for the Protestant, a Protestant one. And for the dead he would arrange a proper burial and then write what Ettinger called "a very personal and lovely letter" to each man's parents. (For both living and dead soldiers, Duffy wrote some 100,000 letters from the front lines to relatives back home.)[128]

When Father Duffy died on June 26, 1932, after suffering from colitis and a liver infection, tributes to the legendary priest poured in. General Douglas MacArthur, the commander of the Rainbow Division in France when Father Duffy was one of its chaplains, revealed that he had recommended the priest for the colonelcy of the 165th Regiment. "This is one of the few occasions in the history of the American Army when the suggestion was made that a minister of the gospel be converted into the commander of a fighting unit," MacArthur was quoted as saying. Colonel William Costigan, the commander of the 165th Infantry, described the fallen priest as "a man in a class by himself. . . . He was a busy man but always had time to do something to help others. He was the idol of all the soldiers who knew him, no matter what their religion." The Reverend Samuel Trexler, a Lutheran minister who served with Father Duffy in Europe, said that the famous Irish American "had a warmth of heart and a tolerance that made him loved by churchmen of every faith. Whether in Holy Cross parish or on the Ourcq, his heart responded to the needs of every one. Even in the trenches the military title yielded. He was always 'Father Duffy.'" Rabbi Benjamin Tinter, a chaplain in the U.S. Army Reserve, recalled that Father Duffy was the only priest he ever knew who participated at the funeral of a Jewish soldier — by delivering the eulogy for "one of his boys." The *New York Times* joined in the chorus of hosannas for Father Duffy: "His interest was not limited to his own faith, devoted son of his church though he was. He had a warm heart for the religious life wherever he found it. His genial and generous nature led him to volunteer for every good service which he could render to the people of this city. In public gatherings to consider public needs he was a constant and welcome aid by his presence and speech." Elsewhere it was said of him that "he understood the faults and failings of human nature, made allowances for them and always found and developed the good he was sure existed in everyone, even the seemingly unregenerate."[129]

A poem in the *New York Times* the day after his death lauded the famous priest and implored the Almighty with the traditional refrain, *"Dona ei requiem!* ("Grant him rest!")*:

"The Fallen Chaplain" by Clifford J. Laube

Dead our soldier chaplain lies;
Peace is sealed upon his eyes.
God, Who gave the light to them,
*Dona ei requiem!*

Gallant to the war he went
With a gallant regiment.
Christ, his only stratagem,
*Dona ei requiem!*

By a Sign his men were steeled,
Though red Death rode down the field
With an onset none could stem.
*Dona ei requiem!*

Hark! A Voice above the drums:
"To the Faith that overcomes
I will give a diadem."
*Dona ei requiem!*[130]

On the day of Father Duffy's funeral, a thousand members of the Old 69th New York Regiment escorted his body from his parish church to St. Patrick's Cathedral. They had come to bid farewell to a man with whom many of them had served on the Mexican border and in France and whom Cardinal Hayes once described as "the ideal army chaplain and the ideal parish priest." The regimental orders issued two nights before contained a fitting eulogy: "Father Duffy represented everything good, true and upright that constituted the soldier. He was a priest of unusual abilities, and these, coupled with his soldierly qualities, went far to establish the basis for the great morale extant in this regiment today. . . . He brought back many honors for himself, but that indefinable something that he gave his beloved Sixty-ninth Regiment will remain his lasting monument." Among the cortege were Father Duffy's sister, Mrs. Michael Bird, his brother, Hugh, and Colonel James Fitzmaurice, the famous transatlantic flier who was there to represent the Irish Free State. During the requiem mass Father Michael Lavelle reminded the mourners that Father Duffy's name had become a household word "because of the nobility of his life and the valor of his deeds." "Every citation that could be given to a gallant, self-sacrificing officer was bestowed upon him," continued the eulogist. "The Protestant and the Jew and those of no religious faith loved him and loved to come to him for help. When Chaplain Duffy came home, he met with laudations on every side, but he remained the humble priest."

As Father Duffy's body was laid to rest in St. Raymond Cemetery in the Bronx that afternoon, a fleet of army airplanes circled over the burial site.[131]

The *New York Times* writer Alexander Woollcott perhaps best expressed what the popular priest meant to the people of his beloved New York: "This city is too large for most of us. But not for Father Duffy. Not too large, I mean, for him to invest it with the homeliness of a neighborhood. When he walked down the street — any street — he was like a *curé* striding through his own village. Everyone knew him. I have walked beside him and thought I had never before seen so many pleased faces. The beaming cop would stop all traffic to make a path from curb to curb for Father Duffy. Both the proud-stomached banker who stopped to speak with him on the corner and the checkroom boy who took his hat at the restaurant would grin transcendently at the sight of him. He would call them both by their first names, and you could see how proud they were on that account. Father Duffy was of such dimensions that he made New York into a small town. . . . One woman I know saw an unused bit of pavement [outside St. Patrick's Cathedral on the day of the funeral] and asked a huge policeman if she might not stand there. He told her the space was reserved. 'But,' she explained, as if offering credentials, 'I was a personal friend of Father Duffy's.' The policeman's answer was an epitaph. 'That is true, Ma'am,' he said, 'of everyone here today.'"[132]

*Statue of Father Francis Duffy,*
*Father Duffy Square,*
*West 47th Street between*
*Broadway and Seventh Avenue,*
*Midtown Manhattan.*

In 1933 friends and admirers of Father Duffy began a campaign to erect a memorial to the famous chaplain of the 69th New York Regiment. The following year the sculptor Andrew O'Connor was offered the commission to design a suitable monument. In a letter of inquiry about the memorial, O'Connor had expressed his willingness to undertake the project. As he explained to Colonel William Donovan, the chairman of the memorial committee, his reason for doing so was purely sentimental — out of gratitude for some type of kindness shown to his son, Owen, by Father Duffy. About a year later, however, in July 1935, it was announced that Charles Keck would take over the commission following O'Connor's resignation from the project for reasons not entirely clear.[133]

When Keck's memorial was unveiled on May 3, 1937, approximately 30,000 spectators attended the event. Besides scores of Father Duffy's former associates on hand were 1,100 officers and men of the 165th Infantry, who participated as a unit. The monument, which is located at the intersections of Broadway, Seventh Avenue, and West 47th Street, at the north end of Times Square, features a nine-foot-high statue of Father Duffy standing in front of a twelve-foot Celtic cross. The figure is dressed in a military uniform and holds a breviary. The statue was unveiled by Agnes Bird, one of Father Duffy's nieces, and was blessed by Father Joseph McCaffrey, the chaplain of the 69th New York at the time. A sense of visual irony pervaded the precincts around the statue that day: Surpliced altar boys with candles and a crucifix contrasted with the theaters, dance halls, and closed burlesque houses in Times Square.[134]

Among the political luminaries who spoke at the dedication were Postmaster General James Farley, former governor Al Smith, and Mayor Fiorello LaGuardia. "In the large sense, Father Duffy needs no monument," said Farley, reading from a letter from President Franklin Roosevelt. "His true monument is in the heart of every Legionnaire who called him friend, among whom I am proud to be numbered, and in the lives of those made better by his counsel and example. As long as there is one survivor of the 165th Infantry Regiment of the Rainbow Division, successor to the old Sixty-ninth, his memory will be blessed, priest and patriot, comforter of all in sorrow, father of the poor." Farley paid his own tribute by describing Father Duffy as "a swell guy," "unique in our generation," and "the apostle of toleration," whose service to humanity had been recognized by citizens of all creeds and denominations. Former governor Smith said he thought Father Duffy's death was due largely to his having been gassed in France, adding that the priest had died for his country as "heroically and as valiantly" as any soldier who fell on the battlefield.[135]

In commemoration of the unveiling, Father John Kelly, the chaplain of the Catholic Writers Guild, wrote the following poem:

*"The Rainbow's Shepherd: Father Francis Patrick Duffy, Ph.D."

The Church Triumphant hails with cheers
The Rainbow's priest, where saints abide.
The hosts of darkness find new fears
Beholding him at Michael's side.

Times Square is bathed in Rainbow's light,
The sign of Heaven's deathless peace
Reflected in a priestly knight
Who warred with Hate that wars might cease.

St. Francis with St. Patrick bows
Acknowledgment to him whose name
Shed luster on their laureled brows,
Reflecting Christ who fled acclaim.

His fellow Veteran, Heaven's Lord,
His blessing breathes on troops who chose
The Sign of Peace and Love's accord
To scatter Light's infernal foes.[136]

Almost three years later, on January 24, 1940, the annual reunion of
veterans of the 69th New York paid a special tribute to Father Duffy. Besides the regiment's current commander — Colonel John Mangan — three
of its former commanding officers were also present at the event — Colonel William Donovan, Major General Frank McCoy, and Major General
William Haskell. After praising Father Duffy as "a brave and kindly priest
who placed duty to God and man above all else," Governor Herbert
Lehman of New York alluded to the new world war raging in Europe at
the time. "Contemplating the heart-rending spectacle of suffering and force
and paganism overseas," he said, "we Americans have a special reason
for thankfulness. It is our blessing that we live in a land whose essential
doctrine is spiritual freedom and opportunity for all of its citizens, irre-
spective of race or creed."[137]
    But it was to the remarks of General Douglas MacArthur, broadcast
by radio from Manila, that the assembled veterans responded most enthusiastically:
    "No greater fighting regiment has ever existed than the One Hundred
and Sixty-fifth Infantry of the Rainbow Division, formed from the old Sixty-
ninth Regiment of New York. I cannot tell you how real and how sincere a
pleasure I feel tonight in once more addressing the members of that famous unit. You need no eulogy from me or from any other man. You have
written your own history and written it in red on your enemies' breast,
but when I think of your patience under adversity, your courage under
fire, and your modesty in victory, I am filled with an emotion of admira-

tion I cannot express. You have carved your own statue upon the hearts of your people, you have built your own monument in the memory of your compatriots.

"One of the most outstanding characteristics of the regiment was its deep sense of religious responsibility, inculcated by one of my most beloved friends — Father Duffy. He gave you a code that embraces the highest moral laws, that will stand the test of any ethics or philosophies ever promulgated for the uplift of man. Its requirements are for the things that are right and its restraints are from the things that are wrong. The soldier, above all men, is required to perform the highest act of religious teaching — sacrifice. However terrible the results of war may be, the soldier who is called upon to offer and perchance to give his life for his country is the noblest development of mankind. No physical courage and no brute instincts can take the place of the divine annunciation and spiritual uplift which will alone sustain him. Father Duffy, on those bloody fields of France we all remember so well, taught the men of your regiment how to die that a nation might live — how to die unquestioning and uncomplaining, with faith in their hearts and the hope on their lips that we might go on to victory. . . ."[138]

The annual reunion also featured a preview of *The Fighting 69th*, the new motion picture about the famous regiment's World War I exploits. Actors Pat O'Brien, Jeffrey Lind, and Jimmy Cagney were on hand to lend their "star power" to the evening's festivities. Much of the plot of this Warner Brothers film revolves around the fictional character Jerry Plunkett (played by Cagney), a streetwise tough whose cockiness leads him to think he can take on the Germans single-handedly. During his first taste of combat, however, he proves to be a coward. When he inadvertently reveals his regiment's position, his companions are killed and he is held responsible for their deaths. Although he is to be executed by a firing squad, before the sentence can be carried out a bomb destroys the stockade in which he is imprisoned. Thus saved to fight another day, he redeems himself and his honor on the battlefield by sacrificing himself for his comrades. In remarks at the reunion, Pat O'Brien, who played the role of Father Duffy in the film, acknowledged the great honor it was to portray the beloved chaplain. Jeffrey Lind reprised his film role as Joyce Kilmer that night by reading "Rouge Bouquet," a tribute by the famous soldier-poet to some of his fallen comrades. Cagney, meanwhile, expressed what he described as the cast's sense of responsibility to portray "the gallant Irish" justly. Major Donovan, whose role in the film was played by George Brent, also said a few words to the assembled veterans, many of whom had served under his command. He included a warning to representatives of the film industry to use the power of their medium to advance the cause of truth and not to be used by those in authority to manipulate public opinion.[139]

Despite the hoopla in the Irish-American community surrounding the release of *The Fighting 69th*, a review of the film in the *New York Times* was decidedly mixed. The reviewer, Frank Nugent, proclaimed the picture a success in terms of its battlefield scenes, "doughboy humor," and depiction of the 69th. But the storyline about Private Plunkett and "How He Became a Hero" was judged "embarrassingly unconvincing." Nugent gave this latter assessment despite what he called Cagney's "vivid performance of the swaggering recruit who turned yellow in the trenches." All in all, Nugent advised, the picture is "better if you can manage to forget the plot, with all its obvious theatrics, hokum and unoriginality, and think of it instead as the human, amusing and frequently gripping record of a regiment's marching off to war."[140]

# Chapter 6

## The 69th New York (165th Infantry) Regiment in World War II

By the time *The Fighting 69th* made its film debut in January 1940, Germany had invaded Poland, and Europe was again about to be engulfed in a world war. Within six months the Nazis controlled Denmark, Norway, the Netherlands, Belgium, and France, and in August Hitler began to prepare an invasion of Britain. In response to these developments, President Franklin Roosevelt began to turn the United States from "neutrality" to "non-belligerency," a shift that moved the country toward openly helping the Allies without going to war against the Axis Powers. On September 16, 1940, President Roosevelt signed a selective service act requiring men between the ages of twenty-one and thirty-five to register for military training, the first step toward the first peacetime draft in American history. On October 29 the first draftees were selected.[1]

To accommodate the growing numbers of men called to serve, several National Guard units were activated, among them New York State's 27th Division. At the time, the 27th was composed of four regiments, the most famous being the 69th New York, known since World War I as the 165th Infantry. Members of the Old 69th were especially pleased to see that the 27th Division was commanded by Major General William Haskell, the regiment's commanding officer when it served along the Mexican border in 1916. Using the permission granted him to select New York draftees for the 27th Division, Haskell assigned to the 165th Infantry as many of the drafted officers and men with Celtic surnames as he could find.[2]

The 165th Infantry was called to active duty with the 27th Division in October 1940. The famous regiment, numbering about 1,700 men, was inducted into federal service on October 15. About 70 percent of the men in the regiment — which still bore the title "Fighting Irish" — were of Irish ancestry, down about 10 percent since 1917. One of the new recruits in the 165th was Private Christopher Kilmer, the twenty-three-year-old son of the famous poet, Joyce Kilmer. Private Kilmer had been ten months old when his father was killed in 1918 while fighting with the 69th in France. (Among the private's fellow doughboys in Company D were two men who knew his father well — Corporal Charles Knowlton and Bugler Edward Brady.)[3]

Before heading south to Fort McClellan in Anniston, Alabama, the 165th Infantry participated in several events reminiscent of former times. On October 20, 1,200 men and officers of the regiment attended a field mass in New York City's Central Park. The mass was celebrated by the regimental chaplain, Captain Thomas Egan, who, symbolically, wore vestments that once belonged to Father Francis Duffy, the regiment's famous World War I chaplain. In his brief sermon Father Egan quoted Duffy's description of the regiment as "an institution offered to the nation by a people grateful for liberty." The chaplain pointed out that the chalice used during the mass had belonged to the regiment ever since it was presented by Archbishop Hughes to Father Thomas Mooney, chaplain of the 69th New York during the early months of the Civil War. Father Egan concluded his remarks with an allusion to the regiment's past heroes: "One of the responsibilities of having such ancestors is the duty of living up to them, of representing them as best we can." Three days later, on October 23, the 165th Infantry and about 10,000 onlookers participated in ceremonies at the statue of Father Duffy in midtown Manhattan. During the gathering Mayor Fiorello LaGuardia expressed the city's best wishes for the regiment. That night 500 men and twenty-five officers of the Second Battalion of the 165th Infantry left New York for Fort McClellan. The next morning the regiment's other two battalions emerged from the regimental armory and turned down Lexington Avenue. While the regimental band played "Come Back to Erin," thousands of spectators cheered and broke through the police lines to say good-bye to their friends. Once on board the ferryboat that transported them across the Hudson, the soldiers provided the words as the band struck up the familiar strains of "Harrigan."[4]

Once arrived at Fort McClellan, the 165th Infantry began its military training in earnest. Within six weeks more than 66 percent of its inductees qualified as expert sharpshooters and marksmen in the use of the army rifle, and of the men assigned to the machine-gun companies 87 percent achieved the expected competence. The 165th Regiment also participated in various army maneuvers, some in Tennessee in May and June 1941 and others in Louisiana the following August and September. In October, at its encampment at Fort Polk, Louisiana, the 165th marked the first anniversary of its activation. Shortly, however, the ranks of the 27th Division were depleted when the War Department authorized the discharge of all men over twenty-eight years of age, of men whose continued service posed hardships for their families, and of members of the army who had served for more than a year. It was for this reason that the division was below strength by about 3,000 men when the Japanese attacked Pearl Harbor on December 7, 1941.[5]

Within a week after the disaster at Pearl Harbor, the 27th Division was placed under the command of Brigadier General Ralph Pennell and was sent to California. After arriving in Los Angeles in as many as seventy-two trains, the regiments in the division were stationed throughout the state to support regular army units and the California National Guard in the event of a Japanese attack on the West Coast. The 165th set up regimental headquarters at the Los Angeles Municipal Airport in Inglewood, and troops provided around-the-clock protection for all vital defense installations in that suburb. On December 27 Lieutenant Gerald Kelley requisitioned 7,852 enlisted men and 196 officers to bring the division up to full strength. In January 1942 the Division was sent to Fort Ord, eight hours from San Francisco, the port of embarkation for expected overseas service. On February 1 the division was told that it would be sent out of the country, although the men were not informed of their final destination. Over the next three weeks the division received almost the full number of requisitioned troops, thus bringing its total strength to 21,719.[6]

From the end of February to April 7, the various elements of the 27th Division sailed from San Francisco for Hawaii. The 165th Infantry was thus part of the first combat infantry division to be deployed overseas in World War II for what would become the longest wartime overseas service of any National Guard division in the American army. As the disparate units of the 27th Division arrived in Hawaii, they were assigned to help defend the islands from a possible Japanese invasion. After the troops arrived in Honolulu, the men of the 165th were shipped to the island of Kauai, where they were temporarily detached to the 40th Division. In October the various units throughout the islands were recalled to Oahu to begin training for an invasion of the Gilbert Islands, the first American offensive in the Pacific.[7]

The specific objective in the Gilbert Islands was the Japanese seaplane base on Makin, a small coral atoll 2,000 miles southwest of Oahu. Makin's dominant land feature was Butaritari Island, a narrow landmass roughly shaped like a crutch and extending thirteen miles in length and facing northward toward a lagoon. At the time of the planned invasion, the island was defended by about 800 Japanese and Koreans (evenly divided between combat troops and laborers) armed with machine guns, howitzers, and field guns. The invading American force, meanwhile, totaled about 6,500 men, drawn principally from the 165th Infantry and the Third Battalion of the 105th Infantry. This assault unit was named the Northern Landing Force and was commanded by Major General Ralph Smith of the 27th Division. Because of feared air strikes from two Japanese bases between 200 and 250 miles away, the American assault team was backed up by eight battleships and cruisers, thirteen destroyers, and planes from four carriers — all under the command of Rear Admiral Richmond Kelly Turner.[8]

The invasion plan called for three landings on Butaritari Island. Assault troops from the First and Third Battalions, 165th Regimental Combat Team, would land on the Red (western) Beaches, the Second Battalion would attack from the north against Yellow Beach, and divisional artillery would take up a position on Ukiangong Point (south of the Red Beaches). The Japanese were expected to mass their defenders against the American invaders at the Red Beaches and then be trapped there as the invaders from Yellow Beach on the north moved to the west. The Japanese commander, however, probably foresaw the American strategy and decided to keep his troops along the strip of land facing Yellow Beach.[9]

At 6:01 a.m. on November 20, 1943, six American transports arrived off the Red Beaches, and two minutes later one of them began to lower its LCVPs filled with soldiers. Carrier planes soon began a twenty-minute air bombardment, followed by a gun barrage from the American armada's cruisers and destroyers. At 8:13 all thirty-two of the transports' LVTs headed for the landing beaches, while cruisers and destroyers fired behind the Red Beaches and fighter planes strafed the beach. The first amphtracs landed at 8:32, and within thirteen minutes two tanks and several machine-gun and rifle companies had touched shore. But because there was less water in the approaches than had been expected, further landings were slowed down, so that only forty-nine landing craft (of a possible 278) actually got ashore on the Red Beaches — an average of only five landing craft per hour. In addition, because the Japanese had preferred to remain in relative safety at Yellow Beach, the Americans encountered no opposition at the western end of the island.[10]

To the surprise of the American invaders, the few score natives still on the western part of Butaritari were extremely friendly. The aborigines were intrigued by the landing vehicles and gave the Americans valuable information about the Japanese. One native chief welcomed Lieutenant Clarence Selden, the Navy beachmaster, with a mouthful of a greeting uttered in a single breath: "I-am-so-glad-you-have-come-we-have-waited-many-months-we-are-happy-you-have-come-may-I-get-your-men-coconuts?" After spotting Lieutenant Colonel James Roosevelt, who had landed on the island in 1942 and who was now accompanying the 165th as an observer, another native exclaimed, "Welcome back, Mr. Roosevelt!" In return, the Americans offered the natives Spam and K rations.[11]

At 10 o'clock Lieutenant Colonel Joseph Hart of the Third Battalion, 165th RCT, reported that the western beachhead was secured. By 1 p.m. the Americans had fortified Ukiangong Point with 105-mm guns with which they intended to protect troops as they advanced east toward the Japanese position near Yellow Beach. As the men of the First Battalion, 165th, moved in that direction, their progress was stopped by a tangle of jungle undergrowth. In addition, several hundred of them were stopped by about fifteen Japanese riflemen and one machine gun. Although a few American tanks were nearby, their drivers refused to take orders from anyone other than their commander back along the beach. Since the 165th had no way of communicating with the beach, one of its officers, Colonel Gardiner Conroy, decided to make a personal appeal to the tank drivers, presumably to help clear the road. By the time the colonel returned at the head of four light tanks, enemy fire had erupted in the area. Despite warnings to take cover, Conroy walked out into the clearing and proceeded to direct some infantrymen to move forward. As he turned to motion the four tanks into position, however, he was killed by a rifle shot between the eyes. Deprived of their leader, the 165th became pinned down by enemy snipers and failed to cross the western tank trap until 10:30 the next morning. Conroy was succeeded in command of the 165th by Colonel Gerard Kelley, who went on to led his men in the Saipan and Okinawa campaigns.[12]

Leif Erickson, a *New York Times* journalist accompanying the 165th on Makin, described Colonel Conroy's death and the events immediately preceding it. "When snipers' bullets began ringing through the trees I dropped behind a coconut trunk," he wrote. "About twenty paces to my left was Lieut. Col. James Roosevelt, son of the President, who also took cover behind the trunk. Colonel Conroy, after standing behind the tree, grew impatient and walked out about twenty-five yards to order a light tank in the road to proceed. As he walked past Colonel Roosevelt a sniper's bullet clipped the bark off a stump between Colonel Roosevelt and Colonel Conroy. Colonel Conroy paid no heed, and shortly thereafter a bullet got him squarely between the eyes as he stood up and waved his arms in ordering the tank to go ahead."[13]

Conroy, fifty-four years old at the time of his death, had been a member of the National Guard since 1911 and had served on the Mexican border in 1916 and 1917. He had received command of the 165th Infantry in August 1940. An editorial in his honor appeared in the *New York Times* a week after his death:

"A lawyer, successful in his profession, he loved the soldier's hard life, outdoors, adventure and the chances of the fight. He loved his country greatly. He began soldiering in the National Guard when he was 22. He served in the First World War and came out a captain. When this Second World War began he was over 50. He might well have thought that he had done his full share of service and that he wasn't called on to fight by the side of boys of another generation.

"But his invincible gallantry forbade him a life of ease. In more than twenty years he had learned the military art. His commands were always noted for their efficiency and spirit. . . . Such a death as his after such a life touches sorrow with a noble pride and leaves not only to those who were nearest to him in blood and affection but to his country an inheritance of honor."[14]

Another victim of the enemy fire which killed Colonel Conroy was Captain Stempen Meany, a chaplain with the 165th Regimental Combat Team. The thirty-nine-year-old Jesuit priest and former editor of the Jesuit magazine *America* was struck in the chest while going to the aid of a wounded man from Company C. Unlike Conroy, however, Stempen was only wounded but lay without aid for three hours before a patrol unit could reach him. The priest later claimed that the religious medal he wore had saved his life by deflecting the bullet so that it only glanced his chest and arm.[15]

Meanwhile, on the northern flank of the island, along Yellow Beach, the Second Battalion Landing Team of the 165th Infantry was brought by transport to a point outside the lagoon. There they were transferred to LCVPs and amphtracs. The landing vehicles were unable to come closer than 250 yards from shore because the water over the shelving reef was not as deep as had been expected. As a result, the infantrymen had to wade ashore in water that was sometimes up to their necks while heavy automatic fire came from the right flank. All the equipment was soaked, and three men were killed and twelve wounded in Companies E and F. Although these landing troops under Lieutenant Colonel John McDonough outnumbered the enemy, they took until noon to secure a continuous line across the island. On the eastern flank of Yellow Beach, the 105th Regimental Combat Team suffered a few casualties from heavily protected dugouts. That night the Japanese harassed the American troops by shouting curses and threats in English, throwing lighted firecrackers, and attacking them with grenades and sniper fire. When the U.S. soldiers shot off their weapons indiscriminately, they revealed their positions and drew a fiery response from the enemy.[16]

In the *New York Times* account of that first day's action, two of Colonel McDonough's men received special recognition. When McDonough encountered heavy fire just after landing at Butaritari village, he realized that he would need tank support. He was unable to call for it, however, because the tank radios were not working. Unwilling to let this communications breakdown doom the landing, Captain Wayne Sikes of the tank battalion took matters into his own hands. While enemy bullets flew past him, he ran to each tank, got the driver's attention by rapping on the window, and told him what to do. In another situation Staff Sergeant Michael Thompson of New York City responded with similar initiative. As Thompson led his platoon west from Butaritari along the lagoon shore, they encountered a well-fortified machine-gun nest blocking their advance. Concluding that only a tank could handle this inconvenient obstruction, the sergeant called for one. But the only tank nearby had just been ordered elsewhere and could be seen heading off in another direction. Since the terrain near the machine-gun nest offered no covering for a flanking movement, Thompson waited until the gun was pointing inland at the flank opposite him. He then raced toward the emplacement and shot two Japanese who were firing the weapon inside. Thompson rewarded his efforts by taking the saber and the pistol he found on the body of one of the slain soldiers.[17]

On the next morning, November 21, a U.S. trooper ran along the beach shouting "There's a hundred and fifty Japs in the trees!" This warning set off a "wave of shooting hysteria" by the Americans that took the officers many minutes to bring under control. Later in the day three U.S. soldiers were killed and several others wounded when a plane from the *Enterprise* dropped a 2,000-pound "daisy-cutter" bomb on the western tank trap rather than on the eastern one, which was still in enemy hands. Early the next day Colonel Hart's Third Battalion, 165th Infantry, took up the fighting at the front line near a tank trap west of Butaritari Village. The men pushed 600 yards to the tank barrier despite heavy rifle and machine-gun fire. The Third Battalion then advanced within three miles of the eastern end of the island. In the meantime, a company of the First Battalion had landed on the lagoon side of the tip to support them. The day's fighting brought the Japanese casualties to 400 killed, with some prisoners and an undetermined number of wounded. By the close of the day on Butaritari, the Third Battalion had established a skirmish line across the island within 150 feet of enemy positions.[18]

Later that night, however, as the men in the Third Battalion lay in their foxholes, a sentry outside Colonel Hart's command post heard the sounds of children crying and people advancing on foot. After issuing a challenge to the shadowy figures in the dark, he learned that they were about thirty natives with infants trying to make their way home. Although the group at first refused an officer's invitation to stay the night at the command post, the natives changed their minds and proceeded into the compound. As they did, however, sentries heard sounds of stealthy movement in the dark. When the Americans received no answer to their challenge, they opened fire with a machine gun, killing four Japanese and forcing an unknown number of their companions to take cover. Foiled in their attempt to sneak into the command post, the Japanese sniped at the Americans for an hour and a half. When the U.S. soldiers revealed their locations by firing back, the enemy opened fire with machine guns. At 10:30 groups of three and four Japanese — numbering sixty in all — rushed toward the center of the command post with hysterical laughter and shouts of "Banzai!" (The Americans theorized that the attackers were drunk, fortified for the charge with *sake*.) Eight of the attackers got within fifteen yards of the command post tent itself, while others captured an American machine gun and turned it on the GIs. When the Japanese tried to flank the Third Battalion from the left of the command post, Colonel Hart's men ignited a flare, using its light to mow down the enemy with machine guns.[19]

Shouting "Banzai!" or laughing hysterically, the Japanese again charged the American lines, coming face to face with outpost guards from the Third Battalion. Private First Class George Antolak was on watch when he saw three Japanese running toward his trench, one of them swinging a saber wildly. Although Antolak aimed his rifle and pulled the trigger, the weapon failed to fire. The American then grabbed a carbine belonging to one of his sleeping trench mates and hit the saber-wielding enemy in the head. As the two struggled in the trenches, Antolak grabbed the saber in both hands and, despite the cuts to his palms, succeeded in throwing his attacker to the ground. Antolak's two mates, now fully awake, began to beat the Japanese over the head with their helmets. Seemingly impervious to the pummeling he was getting, the enemy soldier continued his wild laughter as he wrestled with the three GIs. Antolak stabbed him in the chest after finally wresting the saber from him. Before the night's wild attacks were over, the Third Battalion had lost three dead and twenty-five wounded, compared to 103 Japanese dead found in front of the perimeter position and another hundred who managed to drag themselves off into the jungle before dying.[20]

By mid morning on November 23, the Third Battalion reached the eastern end of the island, and at 1 p.m. General Ralph Smith signaled to Admiral Turner, "Makin taken." During three days of fighting, the 27th Division lost fifty-eight killed in action, eight dead of wounds, and 185 wounded. Over 700 enemy soldiers were killed. For their roles in the invasion of Makin, Colonel Kelley, Lieutenant Colonel Hart, and Colonel McDonough were each awarded a Silver Star.[21]

The capture of Makin Atoll in 1943 involved considerable irony for the men of the 165th Infantry. Before the Japanese seized Makin in December 1941, it had been a British protectorate. When Makin was recaptured by a force that included men from the 165th Infantry (the Old 69th), the irony was not lost on the men of that famous New York Regiment. In 1860, it will be recalled, the 69th New York State Militia Regiment had refused to march in honor of the Prince of Wales when that future king of England visited New York. On April 18, 1946, Britain acknowledged its debt to the 165th Infantry for its role in retaking Makin by awarding the Distinguished Service Order to Colonel Gerard Kelley, the regiment's commander at the time of the invasion. The honor was bestowed on the colonel by the British consul-general in New York during a ceremony at the Waldorf-Astoria Hotel in that city.[22]

After taking Makin and Tarawa, the U.S. navy continued its campaign across the Pacific with an attack on the Mariana Islands. The first objective of this island-hopping strategy was Saipan, an island about 1,385 miles south of Tokyo. The Americans particularly desired Aslito Air Field on the island as a base from which to launch air strikes against the Philippines and the islands closer to the Japanese mainland. For three and a half days before the land invasion, the American navy bombarded Saipan, destroying most of the Japanese airpower and seapower in the area. The bombing did little damage, however, to the island's defensive works, which were manned by almost 30,000 enemy troops.[23]

By June 1944 the U.S. Marines' Second and Fourth Divisions were ready to invade Saipan. The 27th Infantry Division was to play a supporting role and was held in reserve on transports. As at Makin, the 27th Division was composed of the 165th Infantry and the 105th Infantry, but this time it included the 106th. When the Marines landed on the western side of the island on June 15, they encountered stiff resistance, suffering 2,000 casualties that first day. On the 16th, however, Marine tanks and naval gunfire stopped an enemy attack, leaving 700 Japanese dead.[24]

Faced with staggering Marine losses, Admiral Raymond Spruance decided to call in the 27th Division. Commanded by Major General Ralph Smith, the 27th landed on Saipan at 1:15 a.m. on June 17. The honor of being the first army unit ashore went to the 165th Regimental Combat Team under Colonel Gerard Kelley. Although their first assault was beaten back by heavy artillery fire, by nightfall the Second Battalion, 165th, had reached the southwest corner of Aslito Airfield, defended at the time by between 1,200 and 1,500 troops. The First Battalion, meanwhile, continued to fight for control of a ridge between the airfield and Cape Obian.[25]

On the next day, June 18, the Marines' Fourth Division crossed the island to Magicienne Bay on the east coast, and the 165th captured the airfield without opposition. The 165th then joined the 105th Infantry to begin clearing out the southeastern end of the island, at Nafutan Point. The task proved extremely challenging, primarily because the enemy found refuge in caves. On June 22, however, all army units except the Second Battalion, 105th Infantry, were withdrawn from Nafutan Point. This redeployment left the Second Battalion with the task of crushing about 500 enemy troops, the former defenders of Aslito Airfield. The effort went badly, and on June 27 the Japanese broke through the lines of the Second Battalion and reached the airfield before being repulsed.[26]

In the meantime, beginning on June 22, the two Marine divisions began their steady advance up the lower slopes of Mount Tapotchau in the center of the island. The next day the 165th Regimental Combat Team prepared to attack an elevation that became known as Purple Heart Ridge. The 106th Infantry, meanwhile, was to advance up a high plateau between that ridge and Mount Tapotchau. (Tellingly, the ridge became known as "Death Valley.") Despite devastating flanking fire from the enemy, by June 27 Purple Heart Ridge had been all but cleared off. Of the units that had borne the brunt of the fighting in Death Valley, the 106th Infantry had suffered the most. The Second Battalion, 165th Infantry, was next in number of casualties, having lost two commanders in two days. But by the time Marine units captured the heights of Mount Tapotchau on June 27, the Japanese had lost about 80 percent of their combat strength.[27]

The last formidable objective in the "Death Valley Campaign" was Hill Able. But before the Second Battalion, 165th Infantry, could attack that obstacle in the drive north, it had to clear off Hill King to the south. When Company E scrambled up the crest of Hill King, it found that Company K, 105th Infantry, was already engaged with the enemy. Company E lent its support to the struggle, and within a half hour all the Japanese had been killed. As Company E mopped up the hill, it found 125 freshly killed enemy. All that night the Second Battalion pounded Hill Able with mortar, so that on the next day, June 29, Company G moved up the slopes with little resistance. In the following days the Third Battalion, 165th Infantry, and the First Battalion, 105th, pushed to the northwest. They reached the west coast of the island near Tanapag Harbor on July 4, thereby fulfilling the men's hope of spending Independence Day on the beaches there.[28]

The day before, as the 165th pushed on northwest from Charan Danshii Mountain, an unexpected event had broken the monotony of the advance. Because the Third Battalion had by now left all roads behind, its support vehicles had to make their way across an expanse of sticky volcanic ash. By the end of the day's march the infantry had far outstripped the resupply vehicles, and at dinner the men had to make do with a dwindling food supply. If the support vehicles did not arrive in the morning, breakfast would be even smaller. During the night the northern part of the island was visited by a heavy shower, which made the red clay impassable by any type of motorized vehicle. Although carrying parties were sent back to Charan Danshii Mountain for supplies early the next morning, they were not expected to return until almost noon. The hungry men had resigned themselves to the situation when a deer suddenly appeared to the front. Captain Edmund Love described the outcome of the serendipitous event: "The animal obligingly headed straight for the L Company perimeter where he was shot. It was only a matter of minutes before the experts in all three 3d Battalion companies sat down to a venison breakfast. It was the 'best meal we had on Saipan.'"[29]

Although the American drive to take the island went on apace, it was temporarily stopped by the biggest banzai attack of the war. The 27th Division was unprepared when at least 3,000 screaming Japanese — some unarmed and others carrying bayonets tied to bamboo sticks — attacked at 4:45 a.m. on July 7. The First Battalion of the 105th was completely overrun, although its commanding officer, Lieutenant Colonel William O'Brien, refused to retreat. Despite suffering a serious wound, he manned a .50-caliber machine gun mounted on a jeep. The Japanese onslaught was slowed down by Marine artillery, and close-quarter fighting at the 105th command post resulted in the death of all the Japanese. The early morning's banzai attack cost the Americans 406 lives.[30]

Later that day the 165th Infantry was ordered to attack in the direction of the coastline in order to secure the village of Makunsha. The advance from the cliffs above the plain proved difficult because the steep and rugged terrain was heavily fortified by the Japanese. Another obstacle to the advance was the fact that some companies of the First Battalion had to clean out a number of caves where enemy stragglers had taken refuge. As a result, only the Second Battalion reached Makunsha by nightfall on July 8. The First Battalion still had two companies on the cliffs and one company below them, and the Third Battalion had reached the ground at the head of Paradise Valley, where it dug in for the night.[31]

The last fighting in the official battle of Saipan involved Companies A and C of the 165th Infantry and one platoon from L Company — all under Lieutenant Robert Dennington. At that officer's command, a squad under Staff Sergeant Harry Harkbearth destroyed several enemy machine-gun nests. Unknown to "Hairbreath Harry," though, Private First Class John Stein Jr. ventured into one of the cleaned-out caves in search of a souvenir. As Harkbearth passed by the cave, the staff sergeant saw movement inside. Drawing his pistol, "Hairbreath Harry" took aim and fired, hitting Stein's helmet and temporarily stunning him. (The bullet had gone inside the helmet's liner, spun around, and come out the back.) When the staff sergeant saw a hole in the helmet, he concluded he had killed a Japanese soldier. Harkbearth began to proceed up a cliff when Stein came rushing out of the cave, crying, "Harry! Harry! For God's sakes, there's still a Jap in that goddam hole and he just shot me in the head." Harkbearth, still unaware that it was his bullet which had struck Stein, entered the cave and shot every one of the Japanese again.[32]

Saipan was declared secured on July 9, but resistance continued for more than a year. By the time the last elements of the 27th Division left the island on October 4, its men had killed an additional 1,972 enemy soldiers and captured almost 3,300 civilians. Although 14,500 civilians on the island gave themselves up, hundreds of Japanese committed suicide rather than surrender. In some cases, men, women, and children cut each others' throats and parents dashed their children's brains out before hurling themselves and their offspring off the cliffs at the northern end of the island. These grisly casualties were added to the final tally: about 24,000 Japanese killed in the struggle for Saipan (versus 16,525 American casualties). The 27th Division, which went into action with 16,404 men, suffered 3,566 casualties (1,034 killed and missing and 2,532 wounded).[33]

The following spring the 27th Infantry Division was attached to the Army XXIV Corps when that command was part of the American invasion of the Ryukyu Islands off Japan. Although most of the XXIV Corps was among the invasion force that hit the western beaches of Okinawa on April 1, 1945, the 27th Division was held as a floating reserve. When the Division was finally deployed, it was used in a sweeping action along the southwestern end of the island. On April 19 the 165th Infantry was ordered to take over the right of the Division line as it advanced toward Machinato Airfield. To take this target, however, the 165th would have to overcome a system of Japanese defenses known as "Item Pocket." This formidable obstacle was composed primarily of three main ridges, two minor ones, and four gullies. The principal ridges came to be called Ryan's Ridge (for the captain of F Company, which captured it), Charlie Ridge (for C Company, which tried for several days to take it), and Potter's Ridge (for the captain of I Company, which eventually occupied it from April 22 to April 26).[34]

By April 20, as ordered, Colonel Gerard Kelley had moved two battalions of the 165th Infantry into position on the Division line. The First Battalion, commanded by Lieutenant Colonel James Mahony, was on the left, and the Second Battalion, under Lieutenant Colonel John McDonough, was on the right. Companies A and G were to knock out enemy positions along the crest of Charlie Ridge, while the rest of the battalion was to make its way across the bottom lands and rice paddies to Potter's Ridge and then move farther to the southwest. By the end of the day the crest of Charlie Ridge had been largely cleared out, and the First Battalion had advanced as far south as Gusukuma, despite deadly flanking fire from somewhere in the Pocket. Along the west side of the Charlie Ridge divide, meanwhile, the Second Battalion pushed forward to Potter's Ridge without opposition. But when G Company moved onto the ridge, it became engaged in a heavy fire fight with enemy dug in on the east nose of the ridge. Over the next two hours Company G cleaned out these positions and gained possession of a network of dugouts and tunnels. As G Company prepared to make contact with the First Battalion on the left, though, the battalion came under intense flanking fire from the rear, again out of the Pocket. Some time later, enemy positions on the top of Ryan's Ridge opened fire with mortars. In the meantime, F Company under Captain Bernard Ryan, had pushed across the open ground to Fox Ridge, where it waited for G Company to arrive.[35]

The next day, April 21, when the Second Battalion failed to improve its position, Colonel Kelley withdrew the battalion to Division reserve near Machinato to the northeast. Captain Ryan and Company F were now left to hold the right flank of the Division line west of the Pocket. For the next three days he and his men held this area virtually alone. During that time Captain Ryan witnessed the unsuccessful attacks against various Pocket positions made by Companies E, G, K, and I. As he had expected, Ryan was called upon to lead F Company in an attack on the Pocket on April 25. Although he had originally planned to launch his assault at 2 o'clock that morning, headquarters changed the time as well as the plan of attack. With only an hour's notice, Ryan was expected to attack at 8:30 p.m. on April 24. Almost immediately F Company came under the enemy's regular evening artillery barrage, which knocked out Ryan's communications and pinned his men in their foxholes. To make matters worse, the already disorganized company was attacked by marauding Japanese patrols, and fighting continued until daylight.[36]

Not until that morning was Ryan able to launch an assault against the ridge that came to bear his name. After signaling his mortars, antitank guns, and machine guns to commence firing, he sent two platoons to make the assault. Within minutes thirty-one men reached the top of the ridge, but they were soon attacked by Japanese emerging from the cover of caves, tunnels, and pillboxes. The band of men from F Company fought like wild cats, finally using their rifles as clubs when they ran out of ammunition. Although five Americans were killed and two seriously wounded, the close-quarter encounter cost the enemy thirty-five dead. At least forty-five more Japanese were chased off the ridge, and an undetermined number were killed in their caves. After only twenty minutes, F Company had secured the top of Ryan's Ridge, achieving what other units of the 165th Infantry had failed to do for five days.[37]

Although F Company had established a foothold, its control of Ryan's Ridge was far from secure. To reinforce his men, Captain Ryan led a force of twenty-one men to the top of the crest, losing two men killed and three wounded, however. Some of the soldiers cleaned out a few Japanese positions and widened F Company's base to about 150 yards along the crest, but Ryan knew he still needed more men. He and two volunteers managed to reach K Company, which, with the rest of Company F, reached the top of Ryan's Ridge by 11:30 that night. The crest was now securely in the hands of more than a hundred Americans.[38]

The following morning, April 26, Companies F and G tried to expand their area of control on the ridge by sweeping down its sides in two directions. By 10 a.m. units from Company F had advanced almost 800 yards to a point just opposite the north end of Machinato Airfield. Despite this advance, F Company remained on Ryan's Ridge for two more nights. Under cover of darkness on April 26, Ryan led a carrying party of men from Companies F and K down from the ridge to the beach, where they made a prearranged meeting with landing vehicles loaded with supplies. When the men of F Company were given food the next morning, it was the first they had received for almost fifty-four hours.[39]

For their endurance over the previous week under the most trying conditions, Company F and Captain Ryan later received a Distinguished Unit Citation: "*Company F, 165th Infantry Regiment*, is cited for conspicuous valor and outstanding performance of a combat mission against the Japanese military forces in the Okinawan phase of the Nansei Shoto Operation during the period 20-25 April 1945. On April 20, during the drive south toward Machinato Airfield, *Company F* held an isolated position along the west coast. All supplies had to be brought by amphibious cargo carrier M29c (known as the 'weasel') for a distance of almost 2,000 yards, and it was necessary to evacuate wounded by the same method. When the tide conditions were unfavorable, rations had to be carried in and wounded evacuated by hand for over 2,000 yards. During the night of 20-21 April, men not engaged on the outpost line voluntarily sacrificed their sleep in order to hand carry five antitank guns, broken down, which they assembled in the darkness and used against the enemy the following day with devastating effect. On 24 April, *Company F* was ordered to conduct a night attack on Mike Ridge, west of Gusukuma Village. They ate a meal at 1700, filled their canteens, and drew ammunition. This was the last food, water, or ammunition they were to have until the morning of 27 April. At 1920, the enemy laid an intense artillery barrage on the company's positions, but at 2230 the attack was launched toward the ridge. Hardly had it got under way before the company ran headlong into a Japanese counterattack. This they beat off, reorganized, and at 250200 launched another attack. Again they ran into a counterattack, which they beat off. After engaging in a heavy fire fight for the remainder of the night, the company assaulted at 1900 the ridge which four other companies had previously failed to capture in their turn. The company commander pushed his men to within 40 yards of the impact area of his supporting artillery, whose axis of fire was parallel to his front line, and, by following the fire at that distance, placed his two assault platoons atop the ridge within 20 minutes. When they reached this point, there were only 31 men left in the two platoons, and within 10 minutes, 5 of these were killed and 2 wounded. However, in gaining this objective, this small group had killed or dispersed an enemy force estimated at 150. Their medical supplies exhausted and with little ammunition and water left, these men held off, without food, a series of four enemy counterattacks in force, during the ensuing 6 hours. At 1600, the company commander again took up the attack. He called for supporting artillery fire between the remnants of his two platoons atop the ridge and the support platoon at the bottom. Following the friendly artillery fire closely, he succeeded in getting 20 men of his support platoon and company headquarters to the top of the ridge, bringing his strength at that point to 46 men. Again, he launched an attack, which increased his foothold on the hill to a width of 150 yards. After darkness, the remainder of the company joined those on the crest of the ridge. Stripping machine-gun belts of ammunition, the company commander had it redistributed among the riflemen, and, at dawn, launched a determined attack, which by 261000 eliminated all enemy resistance for a distance of 1,200 yards to the south. When he reported the success of his mission, he was ordered to return to his starting point of the morning and to eliminate the enemy still to his flanks on the ridge. At this time the men of *Company F* had slept for only 2 nights out of 6 and had not eaten for over 48 hours. Intelligence estimates place the number of well-armed and determined enemy soldiers manning the defense sector which *Company F* breached at being over 500. The area captured by this greatly outnumbered force was considered such a skillful piece of enemy defensive engineering that the methods of construction and defense became the subject for study by Headquarters Tenth Army. *Company F, 165th Infantry Regiment*, overcame this elaborate system of enemy defenses through dogged determination, disregard for the privations suffered by lack of food and water, and individual heroism on the part of every member of the command. (General Orders 53, Headquarters 27th Infantry Division, 20 July 1945, as approved by the Commander in Chief, United States Army Forces, Pacific.) [*General*

*Memorial to the 69th New York Regiment in Calvary Cemetery, Woodside, Queens, Long Island, New York. The monument bears the names of the engagements in which the regiment participated during the Civil War, World War I, and World War II.*

*Orders No. 100, War Department, Washington, D.C., 7 November 1945.*]"[40]

Company F finally dislodged the enemy from the western side of Ryan's Ridge on April 27. The eastern side of the ridge was not cleared, however, until nightfall of the following day. But this achievement was accomplished not by F Company but by Company A, which had relieved Ryan's men that morning. For his amazing exploits during that day's struggle, Private First Class Alejandro Ruiz was later awarded the Congressional Medal of Honor. The citation that was issued in June 1946 detailed the young man's heroism: "Sergeant *Alejandro Renteria Ruiz* (Army serial No. 38,442,412) (then Private First Class), Company A, 165th Infantry Regiment, Army of the United States, on 28 April 1945 at Okinawa, when his unit was stopped by a skillfully camouflaged enemy pillbox, displayed conspicuous gallantry and intrepidity above and beyond the call of duty. His squad, suddenly brought under a hail of machine-gun fire and a vicious grenade attack, was pinned down. Jumping to his feet, Private Ruiz seized an automatic rifle and lunged through the flying grenades, rifle and automatic fire, for the top of the emplacement. An enemy soldier charged him and his rifle jammed. Undaunted, he whirled on the assailant and clubbed him down. He then ran back through the bullets and grenades, seized more ammunition and another automatic rifle, and again made for the pillbox. Enemy fire was now concentrated on him, but he charged on, miraculously reaching the position and, in plain view, climbed to the top. Leaping from one opening to another, he sent burst after burst into the pillbox, killing 12 of the enemy and completely destroying the position. Private *Ruiz'* heroic conduct, in the face of overwhelming odds, saved the lives of many comrades and eliminated an obstacle which would have long checked his unit's advance. [*General Orders No. 60, War Department, Washington, D.C., 26 June 1946.*]"[41]

# Chapter Notes

## Introduction

### Page 11

**Bull Run, Antietam, and Fredericksburg:** famous Civil War battles. At Bull Run, Virginia, on July 21, 1861, Colonel Michael Corcoran's 69th New York State Militia Regiment fought valiantly but suffered heavy losses (38 killed, 59 wounded, and 95 missing), about 16 percent of its strength. (Jones, *Irish Brigade*, p. 88) During the battle of Antietam, Maryland, on September 17, 1862, the 69th New York Volunteers suffered 194 casualties, or 61 percent of its men. (Boyle, *Party of Mad Fellows*, p. 193) Three months later at Fredericksburg, Virginia, the 69th New York suffered a 68-percent casualty rate: 128 of its 189 officers and enlisted men killed or wounded. (Nugent, "Sixty-Ninth at Fredericksburg," p. 198) **Somme, Meuse, and the Argonne:** famous World War I offensives. **Saipan, Makin, and [Okinawa]:** Pacific islands captured by American forces during World War II. **Mount Surabachi [sic]:** actually Mount Suribachi, an extinct volcano on Iwo Jima Island off Japan. About 20,000 Americans were killed or wounded in the month-long fight for the island. (Bailyn, *Great Republic*, p. 766)

### Pages 12–13
#### From "The New 69th Veteran" by Victor Olney

**Pearl Harbor:** the American naval base in Hawaii that was attacked by the Japanese on December 7, 1941. **Gettysburg, Fredericksburg:** famous Civil War battles. On the second day of the battle of Gettysburg (July 1–3, 1863), the Irish Brigade suffered heavy casualties while escaping through the Wheatfield: 202 killed, wounded, and missing — almost 40 percent of its strength. (O'Brien, "Irish Brigade," p. 109) Six months earlier at Fredericksburg, Virginia, the 69th New York had listed among the killed and wounded 112 of its 173 enlisted men and each of its sixteen officers (68 percent). (Nugent, "Sixty-Ninth at Fredericksburg," p. 198) **West Street:** a thoroughfare along the Hudson River in Manhattan marking the western boundary of the World Trade Center area. **Makin, Okinawa and Saipan:** Pacific islands captured by American forces during World War II. **Baptiste's sacrifice:** an allusion to Gerard Baptiste, one of the more than 300 New York firefighters reported missing after the terrorist attack on the World Trade Center on September 11, 2001. Besides being a fireman with Ladder 9 in the SoHo district of lower Manhattan, he was an officer in the 69th Infantry — first lieutenant of Company A, First Battalion. (*New York Times*, December 8, 2001, p. B8)

## Chapter 1
### Michael Corcoran, the 69th New York State Militia, and Corcoran's Irish Legion

### Page 22

**Michael Doheny** was born near Fethard, County Tipperary, Ireland, in 1805, the son of a small farmer. He was self-educated until the age of twenty-one, when he briefly came under the tutelage of a celebrated classical and mathematical scholar named Maher. The eager student became well versed in the Irish language and exhibited a talent for writing poetry and songs. From his youth he was well aware of the oppression which British rule imposed on the Irish people, and he firmly believed that nothing beneficial to Ireland could come from the British Parliament. Hoping that legal training would allow him to play a role in the emancipation of his country, he studied law in London, where he may have supported himself as a parliamentary reporter. After returning to Ireland to practice law in Cashel, he earned a reputation for defending the poor and for serving as legal advisor to the Borough of Cork. In 1842 he joined the movement to repeal the political union between England and Ireland, and in this cause he was a frequent contributor to the *Nation*, the organ of the Young Ireland movement. (He signed his prose and verse with his initials and with the pseudonym *Eiranach* — Irishman.)

For taking part in the abortive uprising of 1848, Doheny became the object of a £300 reward and a police pursuit. The British authorities' description of the fugitive painted a motley picture that is accurate in some respects, prejudicial in others, and at odds with his reputation as a very effective public speaker: "Barrister; forty [*sic*] years of age; five feet eight inches in height; fair or sandy hair; grey eyes; coarse red face like a man given to drink; high cheek bones; wants several of his teeth; very vulgar appearance; peculiar coarse unpleasant voice; dress respectable; small short red whiskers."

After escaping to the United States, Doheny continued the practice of law and wrote *The Felon's Track: History of the Attempted Outbreak in Ireland*. Like other Irish exiles, he became a member of various military organizations in New York City, including the Ninth, the 69th, and the 75th New York regiments. In 1858, with fellow emigrés James Stephens and John O'Mahony, he founded the Fenian Brotherhood in America and was a member of the delegation that accompanied the remains of the Fenian hero Terence Bellew MacManus to Ireland for burial in 1861. Doheny died in April 1863 and is buried in Calvary Cemetery in Woodside, Queens, Long Island, New York.

Besides describing Doheny's efforts to evade police after the 1848 uprising, *The Felon's Track* gives glimpses into the conditions of the Irish peasantry. The author vividly depicted the scene inside a hut that gave him shelter in the mountains of Glengariff: "The cabin was ten feet square, with no window and no chimney. The floor, except where the bed was propped in a corner, was composed of a sloping mountain rock, somewhat polished by human feet and the constant tread of sheep, which were always shut up with the inmates at night. The fire, which could be said to burn and smoke, but not to light, consisted of heath sod, dug fresh from the mountain. A splinter of bog-wood, lurid through the smoke, supplied us with light for our nightly meal. The tea was drawn in a broken pot, and drunk from wooden vessels, while the sheep chewed the cud in calm and happy indifference. They were about twelve in number, and occupied the whole space of the cabin between the bed and the fire-place." Surprisingly, Doheny's statement that eggs and potatoes were regular fare in the cabins stood in contrast to the "Great Hunger" ravaging other parts of the country. Even in "the most filthy cabin" above Killarney, where "the dung of the cattle had not been removed for days, and half-naked children squatted in it as joyously as if they rolled on richest carpets," Doheny was treated to "the finest trout I ever saw," with "boiled new milk, slightly curdled." The next morning there were "excellent new potatoes, butter, new milk, and a slice of the flesh of fried badger."

In addition to *The Felon's Track*, Doheny is best known for a history of the

American Revolution (published in Dublin in 1846) and for the poems "The Outlaw's Wife" and "*A Cushla Gal Mo Chree*" ("Bright Vein of My Heart"). (For the latter poem, see Brook and Rolleston, *Treasury of Irish Poetry*, pp. 175–176.)

(Cavanagh, *Memoirs of General Meagher*, pp. 231–233; Hickey and Doherty, *Dictionary of Irish History*, p. 133; Brady and Cleve, *Biographical Dictionary of Irish Writers*, p. 62; O'Donoghue, *Poets of Ireland*, p. 111; Crimmins, *Irish-American Miscellany*, p. 396; Boylan, *Dictionary of Irish Biography*, p. 93; Corkery, *Hidden Ireland*, pp. 11–12; Foster, *Modern Ireland*, pp. 330–331)

### Pages 22–23

**Patrick Sarsfield:** a leader in the Irish Catholic resistance (1689–1691) to William III and a supporter of the failed cause of the Stuart king James II. After the Williamite victory in Ireland, Sarsfield and about 12,000 Irishmen went into exile in France. (Lydon, *Making of Ireland*, p. 216) **Landen:** the site in the Austrian Netherlands (modern Belgium) where the French army and its Irish regiments defeated William of Orange (William III of England) in 1693. The Irish exile Patrick Sarsfield was killed during the engagement and was buried on the battlefield. (Hennessy, *Wild Geese*, pp. 35, 42) **Cremona:** the Italian city in which a French garrison of about 4,000 men recovered from a surprise attack by Austrian troops under Prince Eugene of Savoy on February 2, 1702. The garrison included 600 Irish soldiers commanded by Walter Bourke and Daniel Mahoney. The Irish suffered 364 casualties (killed, wounded, and captured). (O'Callaghan, *Irish Brigades*, pp. 197, 214) **Fontenoy:** the site in the Austrian Netherlands (modern Belgium) where the six Irish regiments of the French army turned the tide for Louis XIV by helping defeat a British and Allied force of 60,000 on May 11, 1745. During the battle the Irish regiments numbered 3,870 of the 60,000 French troops and suffered 656 casualties. While smashing through the Allied right flank, the Irish troops shouted, "Remember Limerick!" — a cry to avenge the surrender of that Irish city to the army of William III in 1691 and the English betrayal of the subsequent peace terms. (Hennessy, *Wild Geese*, pp. 64–65, 68–69) **One hundred and eighty thousand:** actually about 120,000. (Hennessy, *Wild Geese*, p. 64) **Lord Edward Hay:** actually Lord Charles Hay (d. 1760). (*Dictionary of National Biography*, s.v. "Hay, Lord Charles") **Sir Arthur Dillon:** actually Colonel James Dillon, one of five sons of Arthur Dillon (1670–1733). (O'Donnell, *Irish Abroad*, pp. 188–189; *Dictionary of National Biography*, s.v. "Dillon, Arthur") **Sassenach:** a term used, often disparagingly, by the Scots and Irish to refer to the English.

### Page 25
*From "The Two Unions" by F. D. B.*

**The Two Unions:** the American Union created by the Constitution of 1789; Ireland's political union with Great Britain in 1803. **Hibernia:** the Latin name for Ireland, derived either from Ivernia — the name of a people in the south of Ireland — or from Heber (Iber) — the first Milesian king of the southern half of the island. (MacManus, *Story of the Irish Race*, p. 19) **Sunburst:** a favorite symbol of the Fenians, Irish revolutionaries who sought the establishment of an independent Irish republic. The sunburst was a feature of the flags used by many of the Irish regiments in the Union army during the Civil War. (Kelly, "Green Flags," p. 197) **Erin's green soil:** Ireland (from a literary name for the island).

## Page 26

**Remember Fontenoy:** a slogan derived from the name of the site in the Austrian Netherlands (modern Belgium) where the six Irish regiments of the French army turned the tide for Louis XIV by helping defeat the British and Allied forces on May 11, 1745. During the battle the Irish regiments numbered 3,870 of the 60,000 French troops and suffered 656 casualties. While smashing through the Allied right flank, the Irish troops shouted, "Remember Limerick!" — a cry to avenge the surrender of that Irish city to the army of William III in 1691 and the English betrayal of the subsequent peace terms. (Hennessy, *Wild Geese*, pp. 64–65, 68–69)

**Father Thomas Mooney** was born in England about 1824 and immigrated to the United States at an early age. He completed his theological studies at Fordham College in New York City and was ordained by Archbishop John Hughes in 1852. After two years as curate of St. Bridget Church in Tompkins Square in New York City, in 1854 he was named pastor of that parish, a position he held until his death in 1877. He served as chaplain of the 69th New York State Militia Regiment from April 20 to August 3, 1861, and accompanied the regiment to Washington, D.C., and Virginia at the start of the Civil War. Because of pressing business in his parish, however, he returned home before the first battle of Bull Run (July 21, 1861). In the report of his death from a carriage accident, the *New York Times* eulogized the popular cleric: "Father Mooney was full of energy and kindliness. He wrought an immense amount of good in his parish, which is the abode of a great many poverty-stricken people. Father Mooney was a patriotic citizen, and proved his devotion to his adopted country by many good deeds during the late rebellion. . . . He labored hard to suppress the riots of July, 1863, by appealing to the turbulent in his parish, and at the conclusion of the troubles he recovered a good deal of plunder from the tenements therein." (*New York Times*, September 14, 1877, p. 2; *New York Times*, September 6, 1877, p. 12; Phisterer, *New York in the Rebellion*, vol. 1, p. 686; Bayor and Meagher, *New York Irish*, p. 199)

## Page 27

**Charles Graham Halpine** was born in 1829 in County Meath, Ireland, and studied medicine and law at Trinity College, Dublin, before taking up journalism in the Irish capital. In 1851, however, he sailed for America, where he initially found employment as private secretary to P. T. Barnum. That same year, in Boston, he began to co-edit a humorous publication called the *Carpet-Bag*, but his satires on the public's taste for trashy novels and on its "spread-eagle" patriotism led to the magazine's early demise. After taking up residence in New York City, he made his debut as a writer for the *Herald* with a poem protesting the use of federal troops to return a fugitive slave. As Nicaraguan correspondent for the *New York Times*, he reported the filibustering expedition of William Walker in the mid 1850s, and he later became the paper's associate editor. By the time of the Civil War, six of his novels about Ireland had been serialized in the Irish American, and he had become editor and co-owner of the *New York Leader*, which used its editorial pages to oppose New York's Tammany Hall political machine. At the beginning of the war, he enlisted as a private in Company D of the 69th New York Militia, but after three months' service he was promoted to the staff of General David Hunter, in whose service he spent most of the remainder of the war. The Irishman continued to work as a writer, though, sending to Northern newspapers letters highly critical of their lukewarm support for the war. On other occasions he wrote poetic or prose pieces in the persona of an ignorant but likable Irish private named "Miles O'Reilly." After Hunter issued the first order for the enlistment of an African-American regiment, Halpine wrote "Sambo's Right to be Kilt," a satirical poem intended to overcome the unpopularity of the move among the Northern troops (by arguing that every time a black soldier was killed or wounded a white one was spared). Following his untimely death in 1866, his remains were accompanied to Cypress Hill Cemetery in Brooklyn by the 69th New York Regiment. (*Dictionary of American Biography, American National Biography*, s.v. "Halpine, Charles Graham"; Boatner, *Civil War Dictionary*, p. 367; *New York Times*, August 9, 1868, p. 8)

### Page 28

**John Savage** was born in Dublin, Ireland, in 1828. While attending the art school of the Royal Dublin Society, he was awarded prizes for watercolor drawings and studies in oil. Although he matriculated at the Jesuit college in Clongowes-Wood in Kildare, he soon left that institution to join the "Young Ireland" movement and its revolutionary activity against British rule. Beginning in 1848, he contributed verse to the *United Irishman*, a newspaper operated by the revolutionary John Mitchel. (It may have been at this time that the *Patriot*, an inflammatory publication co-authored by Savage, was suppressed.) When the authorities banned Mitchel's paper, Savage became an owner of its successor, the *Irish Tribune*, which likewise soon fell victim to the censorship laws. (Almost four decades later David Conyngham, the chronicler of the Irish Brigade, placed Savage in the pantheon of Irish writers who gave "poetical inspiration" to the revolutionary movement and who "poetized and deified the new gospel of physical force.")

After fleeing to the south, Savage joined John O'Mahony, the head of the Fenian Brotherhood, near Carrick-on-Suir. Savage participated in the unsuccessful uprising of 1848, rallying the people in Tipperary, Waterford, and Kilkenny. With other Young Irelanders John O'Leary, Joseph Brenan, and Fintan Lawlor, he organized an attack on the police station in Cappoquin, County Waterford. (Seven police killed two of the seventy assailants, who were armed mainly with pikes.) Of the young man's role in that uprising, O'Mahony wrote in 1856: "John Savage never flinched from the post of danger, nor was any duty left dependent upon him left undone. . . . He shared with me the *bivouac* upon the bleak hills, and partook of my hard bed in the rock-bound grot of Ballyquirkeen; or, as we laid [*sic*] side by side in some fragrant meadow by its banks, we listened to the Suir's wild lullaby singing us to sleep." Savage's memory of the incident was probably less romantic, and it may have been about the aborted uprising that he said, "The Irish are always ready for revolution, but they never make ready."

Having made his escape to New York City, Savage resumed his career in journalism, first as proofreader for the *New York Tribune* and then as literary editor of the *Irish Citizen*, a newspaper founded by John Mitchel, who had also sought refuge in America. In 1857 Savage moved to Washington, D.C., to became the leading editorial writer for — and later the owner of — the *States*, the political mouthpiece of Stephen A. Douglas. When the Civil War broke out, Savage's Southern friends urged him to move the newspaper to one of the Confederate states, but he refused. He resigned as assistant editor of the *New York Irish News* to join the 69th New York Regiment, serving on Colonel Corcoran's staff with the rank of captain. He later aided in the formation of the Irish Brigade and was both a member of the executive committee and a secretary of the Brigade's civilian support group. In a diary entry early in 1864, Maria Lydig Daly, the wife of Judge Charles Daly of New York, described Savage as "the best specimen I have yet met of a native Irish character. He has less of the desire of display and the conceitedness of the race than the other prominent men I have met." That same year Savage accepted a position as an editorial writer for the *New Orleans Times*.

The Irish-born journalist subsequently became an active spokesman for the Fenian movement, serving between 1867 and 1870 as chief executive of the Fenian Brotherhood in America. He recognized the failure of the Fenian invasion of Canada in 1867 but held out hope that the movement's fate would change. The official report of the Fenian Congress that year summarized Savage's sentiments, perhaps in his own words: "The world judges causes by results — measures the character of attempts by their issues, but time, to use a journalistic simile [*sic*], was a careful proof-reader, a sedulous emendator, and revised the erroneous impressions left by contemporaneous judgments, often proving — what it will again prove — that failures are but the openings to success." The next year Savage ran for Congress on a third-party ticket (as a Fenian) against Fernando Wood, a Democrat, and Francis Thomas, the Republican candidate. The *Irish American* accused the Republicans of financing Savage's campaign in order to draw off enough votes from Wood to enable Thomas to win. In August 1870, soon after one of the periodic "Orange Riots" between Irish Protestants and Catholics in New York City, Savage addressed a large group of Irish Catholics at a picnic at Jones' Wood. He lamented that the two groups continued their religious animosity in America and contrasted this state of affairs with that in Ireland, where the cause of Irish unity was bringing the two sides together. (Many of his listeners apparently did not share his lament, and his remarks were greeted by loud jeers.)

Savage's major works were *Lays of the Fatherland*, *'98 and '48: The Modern Revolutionary History and Literature of Ireland*, *Our Living Representative Men*, *Campaign Life of Andrew Johnson*, *Life and Public Services of Andrew Johnson*, *Fenian Heroes and Martyrs*, two collections of his verse (*Faith and Fancy* and *Poems*), and several plays. He was also a frequent contributor to the *Democratic Review* and the *American Review*, the two most prominent periodicals in the country at the time. His most important Civil War verse was "The Muster of the North," while "Shane's Head," a ballad about the sixteenth-century Ulster chieftain Shane O'Neill, is one of the most popular in Irish literature. Michael Cavanagh, O'Mahony's secretary, eulogized Savage in his 1892 biography of General Meagher: "During his subsequent career in the United States, where his genius had free scope, John Savage won his meed of fame, as a poet, essayist, dramatist, orator and patriot. He was admired by the public for his acquirements and rectitude, and beloved by his associates for his genial heart and social spirit. Known to men of all classes in the social scale, he made hundreds of personal friends and no personal enemies."

(*Dictionary of National Biography*, *Dictionary of American Biography*, s.v. "Savage, John"; *New York Times*, Oct. 8, 1888, p. 4; Conyngham, *Ireland Past and Present*, pp. 103–104; Savage, *Fenian Heroes and Martyrs*, pp. 48–49, 106–107; Davis, Richard, *Young Ireland Movement*, p. 166; Cavanagh, *Memoirs of General Meagher*, pp. 315–316; Duffy, Charles, *Four Years of Irish History*, p. 597; Daly, *Diary of a Union Lady*, p. 273; D'Arcy, William, *Fenian Movement*, pp. 265, 304, 326, 363; Gibson, *Attitudes of New York Irish*, p. 229; Gordon, *Orange Riots*, p. 51; Moore, *Rebellion Record*, vol. 3, "Poetry and Incidents," pp. 42–44)

## Page 31

**Father Bernard O'Reilly** was born in County Mayo, Ireland, in 1816. (Some sources give County Donegal and 1820 or 1823.) At the age of sixteen he emigrated from his native land and settled in Quebec, Canada, where he attended and was graduated from Laval University. Following his ordination in 1843, he ministered in several parishes in the diocese of Quebec and was among the clergy who attended the plague-stricken Irish immigrants quarantined along the St. Lawrence River in 1847. While still in Canada, he became an ardent supporter of home rule for Ireland and an advocate for Irish colonization in Canada. After entering the Society of Jesus, he was professor of rhetoric at St. John's College, in Fordham, New York City, and, after studying abroad, was assigned to St. Francis Xavier Church in that city. With the outbreak of hostilities between the North and the South, he served as chaplain of the 69th New York State Militia Regiment for a few weeks. He narrowly escaped death during the first battle of Bull Run (July 21, 1861) when his clothing was perforated with bullets as he attended the wounded on the battlefield. After the war he withdrew from the Jesuits and devoted himself to literary pursuits, becoming both a contributor to and a member of the editorial staff of the *New American Cyclopedia*. He subsequently traveled extensively in Europe and contributed a series of letters to the *New York Sun*. While living in France he became the confessor of Napoleon III until the emperor's fall in 1848. O'Reilly was well known to numerous other European personalities of his day, including King Alphonso XIII of Spain, his godson. During his lengthy residence in Rome, O'Reilly made the personal acquaintance of Pope Pius IX and Pope Leo XIII. The latter pontiff selected the Irish priest as his official biographer and appointed him a domestic prelate of the papal throne in 1887. Among O'Reilly's other principal works is a biography of Pius IX. After returning to New York, O'Reilly was made chaplain at the convent of Mount St. Vincent, where he died in 1907. (Bayor and Meagher, *New York Irish*, p. 199; *New York Times*, April 29, 1907, p. 9; *Catholic Encyclopedia, Appleton's Cyclopedia of American Biography*, s.v. "O'Reilly, Bernard")

## Page 32

**Green Flag:** possibly the Prince of Wales Color, the banner presented to the 69th New York State Militia Regiment by Irish citizens of New York City after the regiment refused to march in a parade honoring the heir to the British throne on October 11, 1860. The banner's green field contained a sunburst surrounded by two scrolls containing the memorial words "Presented to the 69th Regiment in Commemoration of the 11th Oct. 1860." (Garcia, "'Fighting' Sixty-Ninth," p. 36)

## Pages 34–35

*From "Our Brave Irish Champions" by Thomas Walsh*

**Nugent:** Robert Nugent (1824–1901), a native of County Down, Ireland, and lieutenant colonel of the 69th New York State Militia Regiment. He later served as colonel of the 69th New York Volunteers and commander of the Irish Brigade after Thomas Meagher's resignation. (Conyngham, *Irish Brigade*, pp. 547–548)

**Granu:** a nickname for Gráinne Ni Mháille (c. 1530–1603), a pirate-queen of Connnaught, Ireland, celebrated in later tradition as a nationalist hero. For forty years she led the resistance to the extension of Tudor power over the west of Ireland. She was known by the English as Grace O'Malley or Granuale (probably an attempted phonetic spelling of her Irish name). *Gráinne* is Irish for the proper noun "Grace." (Boylan, *Dictionary of Irish Biography*, p. 340; Connolly, *Companion to Irish History*, p. 410; Day, *Ireland*, p. 246; Woulfe, *Irish Names*, p. 53)

### Pages 35, 37

**Leonidas:** the king of Sparta whose force of about 8,000 Greeks initially held off a Persian invasion force of 100,000 at Thermopylae, a pass in eastern Greece, in 480 B.C. Most of the Greeks fled, however, when the Persians gained access to the pass. Only 300 Spartans and 700 Thespians under Leonidas fought to the death to defend Thermopylae. (Magill, *Great Events from History*, Ancient and Medieval Series, vol. 1, pp. 237–238) **land of Sarsfield and Shields:** Ireland. Patrick Sarsfield (d. 1693) was a leader in the Irish Catholic resistance (1689–1691) to William III and a supporter of the failed cause of the Stuart king James II. After the Williamite victory in Ireland, Sarsfield and about 12,000 Irishmen went into exile in France. (Lydon, *Making of Ireland*, p. 216) James Shields (1806–1879), a native of County Tyrone, made a reputation for himself as a general in the Mexican War and later as a member of the U.S. Senate from, successively, Illinois, Minnesota, and Missouri. (*Dictionary of American Biography*, s.v. "Shields, James")

### Page 38

**"Patrick's Day":** usually "Saint Patrick's Day," one of several traditional Irish songs by that name. One of them used lyrics written by M. J. Barry:

> Oh! blest be the days when the Green Banner floated,
> Sublime o'er the mountains of free Innisfail,
> When her sons to her glory and freedom devoted,
> Defied the invader to tread her soil.
> When back o'er the main they chased the Dane,
> And gave to religion and learning their spoil,
> When valor and mind, together combined,
> But wherefore lament o'er the glories departed?
> Her star shall shine out with as vivid a ray,
> For ne'er had she children more brave and true-hearted,
> Than those she now sees on St. Patrick's Day.
>
> Her sceptre, alas! passed away to the stranger,
> And treason surrendered what valor had held;
> But true hearts remained amid darkness and danger,
> Which, spite of her tyrants, would not be quelled.
> Oft, oft, through the night flashed gleams of light,
> Which almost the darkness of bondage dispelled;
> But a star now is near, her heaven to cheer,
> Not like the wild gleams which so fitfully darted,
> But long to shine down its hallowing ray,
> On daughters as fair, and sons as true-hearted,
> As Erin beholds on St. Patrick's Day.
>
> Oh! blest be the hour, when begirt by her cannon,
> And hailed as it rose by a nation's applause,
> The flag waved aloft o'er the spire of Dungannon,

Asserting for Irishmen, *Irish Laws*.
Once more shall it wave, o'er hearts as brave,
Despite of the dastards who mock at her cause,
And like brothers agreed, whatever their creed,
Her children, inspired by those glorious departed.
No longer in darkness desponding will stay,
But join in her cause like the brave and true-hearted,
Who rise for their rights on St. Patrick's Day.
(Page, *Irish Songs*, p. 110)

**Green Banner:** a green flag emblazoned with a golden harp, used as a banner of Irish nationalism from at least the early 1640s. (O'Brogain, *Irish Harp Emblem*, p. 17) **Innisfail:** a variant of *Inisfail*, an Irish word meaning "Isle of Destiny," one of many ancient names for Ireland. (MacManus, *Story of the Irish Race*, p. 9) **Dane:** Viking or Norse invaders who were defeated in 1014 by the Irish High King, Brian Bóruma (Boru). (Lydon, *Making of Ireland*, p. 35) **Erin:** a poetic name for Ireland. **Dungannon:** a town in County Tyrone that was the center of the O'Neills until the English seized their lands in the seventeenth century. (Day, *Ireland*, pp. 82, 310)

### Page 38

**"Garry Owen":** an old Irish quickstep which dates from at least 1800 and which was used by several Irish regiments, including the Fifth Royal Lancers. (That regiment was stationed near Garryowen — Gaelic for "Owen's Garden — a suburb of Limerick.) The song's verses sing the glories of drinking and brawling and the camaraderie of Garryowen lancers. (Connell, *Son of the Morning Star*, pp. 293–294)

Let Bacchus's sons be not dismayed,
But join with me, each jovial blade;
Come, drink and sing and lend your aid
To help me with the chorus.

*Chorus*
Instead of spa, we'll drink brown ale,
And pay the reck'ning on the nail,
No man for debt shall go to jail
From Garryowen in glory.

We are the boys that take delight in
Smashing the Limerick lamps when lighting,
Through the streets like sporters fighting,
And tearing all before us.

We'll beat the bailiffs out of fun,
We'll make the mayor and sheriffs run,
We are the boys no man dares dun,
If he regards a whole skin.

Our hearts so stout have got no fame,
For soon 'tis known from whence we came,

Where'er we go they dread the name
Of Garryowen in glory.
(Hoagland, *1,000 Years of Irish Poetry*, p. 264)

### Page 43

*From "Return of Gen. Corcoran, of the Glorious 69th" by William Ferris*
**Broadway:** a fashionable thoroughfare in New York City. On April 23, 1861, the
69th New York State Militia Regiment had marched down Broadway to Pier 4
along the Hudson River and boarded the steamer *James Adger* for the trip south.
(Garcia, "'Fighting' Sixty-Ninth," pp. 37–38) **Bull-Run:** the first battle of Bull Run,
fought in Virginia on July 21, 1861. Colonel Michael Corcoran's 69th New York
State Militia Regiment fought valiantly but suffered heavy losses, about 16 percent of its strength. (Jones, *Irish Brigade*, p. 88) **Fontenoy:** the site in the Austrian
Netherlands (modern Belgium) where the six Irish regiments of the French army
turned the tide for Louis XIV by helping defeat the British and Allied forces on
May 11, 1745. During the battle the Irish regiments numbered 3,870 of the 60,000
French troops and suffered 656 casualties. While smashing through the Allied right
flank, the Irish troops shouted, "Remember Limerick!" — a cry to avenge the surrender of that Irish city to the army of William III in 1691 and the English betrayal
of the subsequent peace terms. (Hennessy, *Wild Geese*, pp. 64–65, 68–69) **Fair Oaks:**
the site of a battle in Virginia on May 31–June 1, 1862. On the second day of the
engagement, General George McClellan ordered the Irish Brigade into action. The
69th and the 88th New York regiments entered the fray with their distinctive battle
cry — half-English, half-Gaelic — while the 63rd New York was dispatched to
guard a bridge and retrieve some field guns. (Jones, *Irish Brigade*, p. 120) **Seven
Pines:** also known as Fair Oaks. The composer may actually mean Seven Days, a
series of engagements in Virginia from June 25–July 1, 1862 (known individually
as Gaines' Mill, Savage Station, Peach Orchard, White Oak Swamp, Glendale, and
Malvern Hill). (Murphy, *Kelly's Heroes*, p. 5) **Cead Maille Failthe:** also *Cead Mile
Failte*, Irish for "a hundred thousand welcomes." (Maclennan, *Dictionary of the
Gaelic Language*) **Erin's Land:** Ireland (from a literary name for the island).

### Page 46

**Father James Dillon and Father Paul Gillen** belonged to the Congregation of the
Holy Cross and had left their posts at Notre Dame College to serve as chaplains in
the war. Gillen was a native of northern Ireland and during the first year of the
war was an unofficial chaplain, ministering to Catholic soldiers wherever he found
them in the Union army. He traveled in a flat-bottomed vehicle pulled by his horse
"Sarsfield" and laden with a few army blankets, some provisions, a chapel tent,
and a folding chair. (When his chapel tent was first "manufactured" in Philadelphia, Gillen and a friend carried the bulky item on their shoulders to the train
station at 11:30 p.m. En route, they were stopped by policemen who at first suspected the pair of burglary.) Gillen later accepted a commission as chaplain in the
170th New York, part of Corcoran's Irish Legion, where he labored until the end
of the war. (Lonn, *Foreigners in the Union Army*, p. 312; Corby, *Chaplain Life*, pp.
307–310)

### Page 51

*From "The Brave Colonel James P. McMahon at Cold Harbor"*
**Longstreet:** James Longstreet (1821–1904), the Confederate general in command

of the Petersburg operations. He was known as Robert E. Lee's "Old War Horse." (Sifakis, *Who Was Who*, pp. 394–395) **Wicklow:** a county on the east coast of Ireland. **town he loved so well:** Lackawanna, New York. McMahon's body was originally buried in Holy Cross Cemetery there, but it was removed to St. Agnes Cemetery in Utica, New York, in 1905. (Boyle, *Party of Mad Fellows*, p. 408) **lake's loud roar:** an allusion to Lake Erie, along whose banks Lackawanna is located.

### Page 53
*From "O! Eri Mo Chroidhe 'Ta M' Intinn Ort"*
**Potomac:** the river separating Maryland and Virginia and on which Washington D.C., is located. **Eire:** Ireland. **Holy Isle of the West:** Ireland.

### Pages 55–58
*From "On Raising a Monument to the Irish Legion" by Charles Graham Halpine*
**th' unshriv'n, unhearsed:** those who died without benefit of confession to a priest ("unshriv'n") and without the proper funeral rites ("unhearsed"). (Simpson and Weiner, *Oxford English Dictionary*) **"sunburst":** a feature of the flags used by many of the Irish regiments in the Union army during the Civil War. The sunburst was a favorite symbol of the Fenians, Irish revolutionaries who sought the establishment of an independent Irish republic. (Kelly, "Green Flags," p. 197) **Lord Clare:** Charles O'Brien (1699–1761), Sixth Viscount Clare, the commander of the Irish troops in the army of Louis XIV at the battle of Fontenoy in 1745. During the battle the Irish Brigade helped defeat the British and Allied forces under the Duke of Cumberland. During the battle the Irish regiments numbered 3,870 of the 60,000 French troops and suffered 656 casualties. While smashing through the Allied right flank, the Irish troops shouted, "Remember Limerick!" — a cry to avenge the surrender of that Irish city to the army of William III in 1691 and the English betrayal of the subsequent peace terms. (Hennessy, *Wild Geese*, pp. 64–65, 68–69) **Cumberland:** the Duke of Cumberland, the son of George II and the commander of the British, Austrian, and Dutch forces against Louis XIV at Fontenoy in 1745. (Hennessy, *Wild Geese*, p. 62) **old green banners:** probably the flags carried by the Irish regiments in the army of Louis XIV. **Limerick's wall:** an allusion to the siege of Limerick by the army of William III in 1691. **our flag ... old green flag:** a green banner emblazoned with a golden harp, used as a symbol of Irish nationalism from at least the early 1640s. (O'Brogain, *Irish Harp Emblem*, p. 17) **yoke of Poland:** an allusion to the fact that during the late eighteenth century part or all of Poland was annexed by Austria, Prussia, and Russia. **kaoine:** a noun from *caoin* (pronounced "cuin"), an Irish verb meaning "weep, lament, mourn." (Maclennan, *Dictionary of the Gaelic Language*) **Meagher's plume of green:** an allusion to the sprig of boxwood worn by General Thomas Meagher at Fredericksburg when the Irish Brigade lacked its customary green regimental flags. **Mat Murphy:** colonel of the 182nd New York Volunteers, a unit in Corcoran's Irish Legion. Murphy commanded the Legion from January 1863 until February 1865, when he was mortally wounded at Hatcher's Run. (Garcia, "'Fighting' Sixty-Ninth," p. 55; Boyle, *Party of Mad Fellows*, 399) **ween:** to think, to suppose. **Green Flag:** not necessarily a particular flag but rather a symbol for the cause of Irish nationalism and independence.

### Chapter 2
**Thomas Meagher, the 69th New York Volunteers, and the Irish Brigade**

**Page 63**
**"Saint Patrick's Day":** See the "Patrick's Day" note on page 310.

**Page 67**
*From "The 69th Brigade"*
**Meagher:** Thomas Francis Meagher (1823–1867) a native of County Waterford, Ireland, and captain of Company K ("Irish Zouaves"), 69th New York State Militia Regiment. He later organized and commanded the Irish Brigade in the Union army during the Civil War. (*Dictionary of American Biography*, s.v. "Meagher, Thomas Francis") **Bull-Run:** the first battle of Bull Run (or Manassas), fought in northeastern Virginia on July 21, 1861. Colonel Michael Corcoran's 69th New York State Militia Regiment fought valiantly but suffered heavy losses (38 killed, 59 wounded, and 95 missing), about 16 percent of its strength. (Jones, *Irish Brigade*, p. 88) **Colonel:** Michael Corcoran (1827–1863), a native of County Sligo, Ireland, and colonel of the 69th New York State Militia Regiment. He was captured at Bull Run on July 21, 1861, and remained a Confederate prisoner for thirteen months. (Conyngham, *Irish Brigade*, pp. 537, 539) **Erin's lovely shore:** Ireland (from a literary name for the island). **landlord's crow-bar brigade:** probably an illusion to the English authorities who evicted Irish tenants from their land during the Great Famine of the mid 1840s. **Queen of England:** Queen Victoria, who visited Ireland in August 1861. (Woodham-Smith, *Queen Victoria*, p. 415)

**Page 68**
*From "Corcoran to His Regiment"*
**Flag . . . Erin's glorious green:** the traditional green banner of Irish nationalism, usually decorated with an embroidered golden Irish harp, with a sunburst above it and a wreath of shamrocks beneath. (Kelly, "Green Flags," p. 195) **Sun-burst:** a favorite symbol of the Fenians, Irish revolutionaries who sought the establishment of an independent Irish republic. (Kelly, "Green Flags," p. 197) **uncrown'd harp:** a golden harp, the predominant feature of the traditional green banner of Irish nationalism. (O'Brogain, *Irish Harp Emblem*, p. 19) **"Remember Limerick":** a cry to avenge the surrender of that Irish city to the army of William III in 1691. (Hennessy, *Wild Geese*, pp. 68–69) **Britain's broken faith:** Britain's failure to observe the generous terms of the Treaty of Limerick (1691) accorded those Irish who surrendered to William III. The chief terms were those guaranteeing to the Irish the possession of their property and the free exercise of their religion. (Lydon, *Making of Ireland*, pp. 216–217) **your Chief:** Colonel Michael Corcoran (1827–1863), a native of County Sligo, Ireland, and colonel of the 69th New York State Militia Regiment. He was captured at the battle of Bull Run in 1861 and remained a Confederate prisoner for thirteen months because he refused to agree never again to take up arms. (Conyngham, *Irish Brigade*, pp. 537, 539) **FAUGH-A-BALLAGH:** Irish for "Clear the Way!" — the rallying cry of the 87th Foot, the Prince's Own Irish Regiment, which served under the Duke of Wellington against Napoleon. (Jones, *Irish Brigade*, pp. 99–100) **Sarsfield:** Patrick Sarsfield (d. 1693), a leader in the Irish Catholic resistance (1689–1691) to William III and a supporter of the failed cause of the Stuart king James II. After the Williamite victory in Ireland, Sarsfield and about 12,000 Irishmen went into exile in France. (Lydon, *Making of Ireland*, p. 216) **O'Neill:** any one of several famous Irish patriots who led the resistance to English rule: Shane O'Neill (c. 1530–1567), whom Elizabeth I recognized as chief-

tain of Tyrone in order to prevent him from becoming a tool of Spanish intriguers against her; Hugh O'Neill, 2nd Earl of Tyrone (c. 1540–1616), who led an unsuccessful Catholic uprising (1595–1603); Owen Roe O'Neill (1590–1649), commander during a major Catholic revolt (1641–1642); and Hugh O'Neill (d. c. 1660), who successfully defended Clonmel against Cromwell. (*New Encyclopaedia Britannica*, Micropaedia, s.v. "O'Neill, Hugh," "O'Neill, Owen Roe," "O'Neill, Shane," "Tyrone, Hugh O'Neill")

### Page 72

**Brian Boru:** an eleventh-century ruler of the provinces of Munster and Leinster in Ireland. In 1013 he was challenged by the Leinstermen and their Norse allies. Brian's forces were victorious at Clontarf the next year, although he himself was killed in the battle. (Lydon, *Making of Ireland*, pp. 31-32, 35) **Wolfe Tone:** Theobald Wolfe Tone (1763–1798), a founder of the United Irishmen movement to create an independent Irish republic. In 1798 he sailed with a French military force to County Donegal but was captured and sentenced to death for treason. He committed suicide in his prison cell. (Newman, *Companion to Irish History*, pp. 196-197) **Edward Fitzgerald:** Lord Edward Fitzgerald (1763–1798), a member of the United Irishmen movement who engaged in negotiations for French military support for Ireland. He was mortally wounded when authorities arrested him for treason in 1798. (*Dictionary of National Biography*, s.v. "Fitzgerald, Lord Edward") **three Irish-born signers:** George Taylor, James Smith, and Matthew Thornton. **earlier Colonel Nugent:** The Nugent to whom Judge Daly referred was Christopher Nugent, a native of County Meath, Ireland, who had been attached to the first troop of Irish horseguards in 1691. After the victory of William III and the capitulation of Limerick, Nugent sailed for France, where James II had taken refuge. Nugent thereafter served in a number of continental campaigns with the French army, first with King James's Horse Guards and then with the Regiment of Sheldon. Nugent was lieutenant colonel of the latter regiment when it shared in the French victory over the Prince of Hesse Cassel's army at Speier on November 15, 1703. At the beginning of the battle, the Imperial (or German) cavalry captured several of the French cannon and turned them upon their foes. Nugent's regiment, which numbered no more than 180 men, initiated a charge and routed two regiments of Imperial Cuirassiers. The Prince of Hesse Cassel lost more than 6,000 troops killed and captured, while the French suffered the loss of only 600 men. During the battle Nugent received seven wounds. Three years later he succeeded to command of Sheldon's Regiment, which he promptly renamed for himself. Over the next decade he and his regiment continued to fight Louis XIII's European battles. To the end a supporter of the Stuarts' claim to the British throne, Nugent accompanied James II's son into Scotland in 1715–16 against the Hanoverian claimant George I. When the British ambassador in Paris complained of Nugent's participation in this military foray, the French government deprived the Irishman of his regiment. This step was taken only out of diplomatic considerations, and in 1718 Nugent was named Major General of Horse. (O'Callaghan, *Irish Brigades*, pp. 153–154, 221) **the Green shall flutter o'er the Red:** a metaphorical way of expressing the hope that some day Ireland (the Green) will triumph over the British (the Red).

### Page 73

**Fontenoy:** the site in the Austrian Netherlands (modern Belgium) where the six Irish regiments of the French army turned the tide for Louis XIV by helping defeat the British and Allied forces on May 11, 1745. During the battle the Irish regiments numbered 3,870 of the 60,000 French troops and suffered 656 casualties. While smashing through the Allied right flank, the Irish troops shouted, "Remember Limerick!" — a cry to avenge the surrender of that Irish city to the army of William III in 1691 and the English betrayal of the subsequent peace terms. (Hennessy, *Wild Geese*, pp. 64–65, 68–69) **Chapultepec:** the name of the fortress defending Mexico City. On September 13, 1847, a force of about 1,000 American soldiers stormed and seized the castle from a garrison of 800 Mexicans. Later that day almost 7,200 U.S. troops captured the capital from its estimated 4,000 to 6,000 defenders. (Shaw, *One Hundred and Seventy-Five Battles*, p. 162; Laffin, *Brassey's Battles*, p. 113)

### Page 74

**Fionn MacCumbal:** also known as Finn MacCool (or MacCumail), the leader of the *Fian* (Fenians), a band of warriors in the service of the high-kings of Ireland. (MacManus, *Story of the Irish Race*, pp. 64–65)

### Page 76

**Captain David Conyngham** was born in County Tipperary, Ireland, in 1825, and for a time he attended Queen's University in Cork. His opposition to the landlord system and to Ireland's political union with Britain led him to join the Young Ireland movement. He took a leadership role in the uprising of 1848, and after its collapse the police placed his name on the list of wanted men. But by the time a grand jury indicted him he had escaped from Ireland. He seems to have fled to the United States at this time, but by 1856 he had returned to Ireland and was contributing articles on political and literary subjects to the *Tipperary Free Press*. When the American civil war began in April 1861, Conyngham sailed for the United States and joined the staff of the *New York Herald*. He apparently was a civilian war correspondent in the early years of the war, but by the battle of Chancellorsville in May 1863 he was a captain attached to the Irish Brigade and an aide-de-camp to General Thomas Meagher. From his experiences with the Irish Brigade, Conyngham began what became the most famous history of that unit, although the work was finished by his friend William O'Meagher, a surgeon attached to the 69th New York. During 1864 and 1865, Conyngham served under General Sherman in Georgia and wrote an account of that officer's march from Atlanta to the sea. (The Irishman distinguished himself at the battle of Resaca de la Palma, where he carried orders under a heavy fire and was wounded in the breast.) His other Civil War work is an unpublished manuscript today known as *Soldiers of the Cross*, an account of the service of various chaplains and nuns during the conflict. After the war he resumed his journalistic career in a succession of posts: editor of a Fenian newspaper known as the *Irish People*, cofounder of the *Staten Island Leader*, part owner of the *Sunday Democrat*, and managing editor of the *New York Tablet*, an Irish nationalist newspaper. He was the author of several novels: *Sarsfield*, about the famous seventeenth-century Irish soldier and exile; *O'Mahony*, about events climaxing in the 1798 rising in Ireland; *Rose Parnell, The Flower of Avondale*, a love story focused on the events of 1798; and *The O'Donnells of Glen Cottage*, about Irish life at the time of the Famine. He also wrote *Lives of the Irish Saints*, *Lives of the Irish Martyrs*, *Ireland: Past and Present* (with J. C. Curtin), and an ecclesiastical history of Ireland (with Father Thomas Walsh). Conyngham died in 1883 and is buried in Calvary Cemetery in Woodside, Queens, Long Island, New York. (Hickey, "Two

Irish-American Writers," pp. 97–98; Fitzgerald, Michael, "From Ballingarry to Fredericksburg," pp. 192–199; Fanning, *Irish Voice in America*, pp. 80–81)

### Page 81

**Knight of Gwynne:** a character in a novel of the same name by Charles Lever. The book is a portrait of an old man who embodies the highest ideal of the word "gentleman." The work also shows that the best elements of the Irish aristocracy opposed the Act of Union (1801) between England and Ireland but were outmaneuvered by the English government, which succeeded in getting the Irish Parliament to vote itself out of existence. (Stevenson, *Dr. Quicksilver*, p. 160; Krans, *Irish Life in Irish Fiction*, p. 291) **Lever and Griffin:** nineteenth-century novelists. Charles Lever was born in Dublin, Ireland, in 1806, although his parents were of English birth or descent. The picaresque protagonists in some of his novels were aristocratic Irishmen. The title character in Lever's *Charles O'Malley, The Irish Dragoon*, for example, studies law in Dublin before joining the army and serving gallantly in Spain against the invader Napoleon. The novels of Gerald Griffin, a native Irishman, faithfully depict the scenery of southern Ireland and the manners of the Irish upper and middle classes. (*Dictionary of National Biography*, s.v. "Lever, Charles James" and "Griffin, Gerald"; Sobczak, *Cyclopedia of Literary Characters*, vol. 1, p. 321) **rock of Cashel:** a steep limestone formation in County Tipperary that served as the seat of ancient chieftains and later the early Munster kings. The rock received its name from the stone fortress (Irish *caiseal*) that most likely occupied the site. (Day, *Ireland*, p. 184) **Burnside:** Ambrose Burnside (1824–1881), the Union commander of the Army of the Potomac until he suffered 12,600 casualties at Fredericksburg, Virginia. (Boatner, *Civil War Dictionary*, pp. 107, 313) **Fredericksburg:** the scene of a disastrous engagement in Virginia on December 13, 1862. During six suicidal charges up Marye's Heights in Fredericksburg, the Irish Brigade lost 46 killed, 416 wounded, and 74 missing out of about 1,250 men led into battle. (O'Brien, "Sprig of Green," p. 69)

### Page 83

**Major James Quinlan:** James Quinlan was born in Clonmel, Ireland, in 1833. After emigrating in 1850, he landed in New York and there studied engineering. In 1853 he joined the National Guard and became a member of the 69th New York State Militia Regiment. A year later he was commissioned a lieutenant and in 1856 was named captain. That same year he married Cecilia Flynn, a native of Ireland, with whom he had three sons and three daughters. Soon after the fall of Fort Sumter, Quinlan left for the South with the 69th as captain of engineers. He was severely wounded at Bull Run. With the creation of the Irish Brigade, he was commissioned major of the 88th New York Infantry. During the Peninsular Campaign, he commanded the regiment in every battle from Gaines' Mill to Malvern Hill. (Mulholland, *Military Order*, p. 111)

### Page 87
#### From "The Green Old Flag"

**Erin's isle:** Ireland, from a literary name for the country. **Clontarf:** the site near Dublin where the forces of Brian Bóruma (Boru), the ruler of the provinces of Munster and Leinster, defeated an army of Leinstermen and their Norse allies in 1014. (Lydon, *Making of Ireland*, pp. 31–32, 35) **Benburb:** the site in northern Ireland where in 1646 Owen Roe O'Neill (c. 1590–1649) routed the Scots under Robert Monroe, the zealous plunderer of many Ulster towns, in what has been described as the greatest Irish victory of the 1640s. (Foster, *Modern Ireland*, p. 80 n; Moody and Martin, *Course of Irish History*, p. 202) **Dunboy:** Dunboy Castle, near Castletownbeare on the Beara Peninsula in southwestern Ireland. Donal O'Sullivan defended the castle until it fell to the English in June 1601. Its fall was followed by O'Sullivan's march with 1,000 persons, including women and children, from Kerry to O'Rourke's castle in Leitrim. Hardly 100 of the refugees reached their destination. (*Ireland*, Michelin Guide, p. 41; Foster, *Modern Ireland*, p. 43 n; Ellis, *Tudor Ireland*, p. 311; MacManus, *Story of the Irish Race*, p. 394) **Fontenoy:** the site in the Austrian Netherlands (modern Belgium) where the six Irish regiments of the French army turned the tide for Louis XIV by helping defeat the British and Allied forces on May 11, 1745. During the battle the Irish regiments numbered 3,870 of the 60,000 French troops and suffered 656 casualties. While smashing through the Allied right flank, the Irish troops shouted, "Remember Limerick!" — a cry to avenge the surrender of that Irish city to the army of William III in 1691 and the English betrayal of the subsequent peace terms. (Hennessy, *Wild Geese*, pp. 64–65, 68–69) **France's fleur-de-lis:** the royal arms of France, showing stylized depictions of three-petaled irises. **Columbia's Stars and Stripes:** the American flag. Columbia is a name formerly used to refer to the United States.

### Page 110

**Fontenoy:** the site in the Austrian Netherlands (modern Belgium) where the six Irish regiments of the French army turned the tide for Louis XIV by helping defeat the British and Allied forces on May 11, 1745. During the battle the Irish regiments numbered 3,870 of the 60,000 French troops and suffered 656 casualties. While smashing through the Allied right flank, the Irish troops shouted, "Remember Limerick!" — a cry to avenge the surrender of that Irish city to the army of William III in 1691 and the English betrayal of the subsequent peace terms. (Hennessy, *Wild Geese*, pp. 64–65, 68–69) **Albuera:** the site in Spain where 23,000 French troops were defeated by an Allied force of 30,000 on May 16, 1811. (Dupuy, *Encyclopedia of Military History*, p. 765) Lawley may have been thinking of the siege of Badajoz, Spain, in 1811, when Napoleon's Irish Legion opposed the Spanish Hibernian Regiment. (Hennessy, *Wild Geese*, p. 137) **Waterloo:** the village in Belgium where Napoleon was finally defeated by a combined force of British and Allied troops on June 18, 1815. More than a third of the Duke of Wellington's victorious British army was Irish. One of the British units at Waterloo was the 87th Foot (the Prince's Own Irish Regiment), whose rallying cry was *Faugh-a-ballagh*, Irish for "Clear the Way!" (Stevens, *Rogue's March*, p. 16; Jones, *Irish Brigade*, pp. 99–100)

### Page 111

**gallant six hundred:** an allusion to Alfred Lord Tennyson's poem "The Charge of the Light Brigade." The poem recounts an episode in 1854 during the Crimean War when a brigade of 673 horsemen under Lord Cardigan made a futile attack against a strongly defended Russian position near Balaclava on the Black Sea. The brigade lost 113 killed and 134 wounded. (Eggenberger, *Dictionary of Battles*, p. 41) **Leonidas:** the king of Sparta whose force of about 8,000 Greeks initially held off a Persian invasion force of 100,000 at Thermopylae, a pass in eastern Greece, in 480 B.C. Most of the Greeks fled, however, when the Persians gained access to the pass. Only 300 Spartans and 700 Thespians under Leonidas fought to the death to defend Thermopylae. (Magill, *Great Events from History*, Ancient and Medieval Series, vol. 1, pp. 237–238)

## Pages 112–113
*From "At Fredericksburg — Dec. 13, 1862" by John Boyle O'Reilly*

**Sumter:** Fort Sumter in Charleston, South Carolina, whose bombardment by the Confederates on April 12, 1861, began the Civil War. **Gorgon fates:** any of three sister-monsters of Greek mythology. They had snakes for hair, and their eyes turned anyone who looked at them into stone. **Burnside's battalions:** Union troops under Ambrose Burnside (1824–1881), the commander of the Army of the Potomac until he suffered 12,600 casualties at Fredericksburg. (Boatner, *Civil War Dictionary*, pp. 107, 313)

## Page 117
*From "Requiem for the Dead of the Irish Brigade" by John Savage*

**Oremus:** Latin for "Let us pray." **Requiem aeternam . . . :** Latin for "Give them eternal rest, O Lord!" **Et lux perpetua . . . :** Latin for "And let perpetual light shine upon them."

## Pages 120–131
*From "Poetical Address Before the Irish Brigade" by Dr. Lawrence Reynolds*

**Columbia:** a name formerly used to refer to the United States. **Yorktown's walls:** Confederate entrenchments at Yorktown, Virginia, the first obstacle in General George McClellan's attempt to seize the Peninsula en route to the capture of Richmond, the Confederate capital. McClellan laid siege to Yorktown from April 16 to May 4, 1862, by which time reports of additional Union troops led the Confederates to abandon their defensive position. (Jones, *Irish Brigade*, pp. 114, 116; Murphy, *Kelly's Heroes*, p. 5) **Irish green:** one of the green banners flown by the regiments of the Irish Brigade. The flag taken into battle by the 69th New York State Volunteers was a deep green and bore in the center an embroidered golden Irish harp, with a sunburst above it and a wreath of shamrocks beneath. (Kelly, "Green Flags," p. 195) **Williamsburg:** the site of an engagement north of Yorktown, Virginia, on May 5, 1862. (Jones, *Irish Brigade*, p. 117) **Fair Oaks:** the site of a battle in Virginia on May 31–June 1, 1862. On the second day of the engagement, General George McClellan ordered the Irish Brigade into action. The 69th and the 88th New York regiments entered the fray with their distinctive battle cry — half-English, half-Gaelic — while the 63rd New York was dispatched to guard a bridge and retrieve some field guns mired in a swamp. (Jones, *Irish Brigade*, p. 120) **Richmond:** the capital of Virginia and the object of McClellan's failed Peninsular Campaign. **McDowell's promised corps:** Although General McClellan demanded that 40,000 men under General Irwin McDowell (1818–1885) be sent from northern Virginia to the Peninsula, McDowell was prevented from doing so because he was busy trying to stop "Stonewall" Jackson's depredations in the Shenandoah Valley. (Jones, *Irish Brigade*, pp. 118, 122) **Green Erin's bold Brigade:** the Irish Brigade. ("Erin" is a literary name for Ireland.) **Mac:** a nickname given to the Union general George McClellan (1826–1885). **Gaines's [sic] Mill:** usually Gaine's Mill or Gaines' Mill, the site of a battle in Virginia on June 27, 1862, during which the Irish Brigade reinforced the collapsing Union line, covered its retreat, and saved the Ninth Massachusetts from being destroyed by Thomas "Stonewall" Jackson. (Athearn, *Thomas Meagher*, pp. 111–112; Conyngham, *Irish Brigade*, p. 186) **Porter's rescued corps:** an allusion to Fitz-John Porter (1822–1910), the Union general who commanded the First Division, Third Corps, Army of the Potomac (March 13–May 18, 1862) and directed the Yorktown siege. (Boatner, *Civil War Dictionary*, p. 661) **Savage Station:** the site of a battle in Virginia on June 29, 1862, when the Irish Brigade was used as a rear guard. The Brigade went into battle "with a roar that might have drowned the musketry" and drove off a group of Virginia artillerymen and their supporting infantry, hauled away and spiked two guns, and chopped the carriages to pieces. (Conyngham, *Irish Brigade*, p. 20) **White Oak Swamp:** the site of a battle in Virginia on June 30, 1862, when the Irish Brigade supported some batteries firing into the enemy position and where General Meagher was seen repeatedly riding a horse up and down the firing line. (Athearn, *Thomas Meagher*, pp. 112–113) **Sumner:** Edwin Vose Sumner (1797–1863), who led the First Division, Second Corps, during the Peninsular Campaign of 1862 and was breveted a major general after the battle of Fair Oaks. On the first day of that battle, he told the Irish Brigade that if they failed the battle was lost. Pointing to his epaulets, he said: "Boys, I stake my position on you. If you run away to-day, I will tear these off and run with you." (Boatner, *Civil War Dictionary*, p. 661; Mulholland, "Irish Brigade," p. 359) **Jackson:** Thomas "Stonewall" Jackson (1824–1863), the famous Confederate officer who received his nickname when General Barnard Bee tried to rally his men at the first battle of Bull Run by pointing out Jackson: "There is Jackson, standing like a stone wall. Let us determine to die here, and we will conquer. Follow me!" (Sifakis, *Who Was Who*, pp. 45, 337) **Lee:** Robert E. Lee (1807–1870), the Confederate commander of the Army of Northern Virginia. **Malvern Hill:** the site of a battle in Virginia on July 1, 1862, when the Irish Brigade's 88th New York Regiment forced the Confederate Louisiana Tigers to retreat. (O'Brien, "Sprig of Green," pp. 73–74) **James's [*sic*] River:** the James River in Virginia. **Titian's coloring:** an allusion to the Italian painter Titian (c. 1477–1576). **Caracchi's [*sic*] power:** an allusion to one or more of the sixteenth-century Italian painters Ludovico, Agostino, and Annibale Carracci. (Turner, *Dictionary of Art*, vol. 5, p. 849) **Magruder:** John Bankhead Magruder (1810–1871), the Confederate officer whose dilatoriness and failure to commit all his men at Malvern Hill (July 1, 1862) contributed to the Union victory. (*American National Biography*, s.v. "Magruder, John Bankhead") **McClellan's skill:** an allusion to the Union commander George McClellan (1826–1885). **that loyal State:** Maryland, so called because it did not join most of the other slave-owning states in seceding from the Union. **arch plotters:** the leaders of the secessionist movement. **South Mountain's pass:** the site of a battle on September 14, 1862, during which Union troops, directed by Major General Ambrose Burnside, seized control of the high ground commanding Turner's Gap through South Mountain near Hagerstown, Maryland. (Boatner, *Civil War Dictionary*, p. 20) **Burnside's rapid horse:** an allusion to Ambrose Burnside (1824–1881), the Union commander of the Army of the Potomac until he suffered 12,600 casualties at Fredericksburg. (Boatner, *Civil War Dictionary*, pp. 107, 313) **clear Antietam:** Antietam Creek, near Sharpsburg, Maryland, the site of the battle of Antietam on September 17, 1862. During this bloodiest of Civil War battles, the Irish Brigade played a conspicuous part in the Union victory by pushing the enemy back to its second line. The Brigade suffered casualties of between 525 and 540 men, 113 of them fatalities. The three New York regiments suffered a casualty rate of about 52 percent. (Jones, *Irish Brigade*, p. 142; Bilby, *Remember Fontenoy!*, p. 60) **Hill:** Ambrose Powell Hill (1825–1865), the Confederate general whose troops late in the day drove back a Union advance at Antietam. (Sifakis, *Who Was Who*, p. 308) **Hooker:**

Joseph Hooker (1814–1879), the Union commander whose troops attacked the Confederates near the Dunker church at Antietam. He was wounded in the foot during the battle. (Foote, *Fort Sumter*, pp. 688, 692) **Harper's [*sic*] Ferry:** Harpers Ferry, a town at the confluence of the Potomac and Shenandoah rivers. Brigadier General Julius White surrendered the town on September 15, 1862, under threat from Confederate forces commanded by "Stonewall" Jackson. The surrender resulted in the capture of 12,000 federal troops. (Faust, *Historical Times*, pp. 340–341) **Bolivar:** actually Bolivar Heights, a Union position west of Harpers Ferry. This Union position was threatened when Confederates placed batteries on School House Ridge opposite. (Robertson, *Stonewall Jackson*, p. 601) **The chief we trusted in:** Major General George McClellan, whom the War Department ordered to Trenton, New Jersey, to await a new assignment. (Jones, *Irish Brigade*, p. 145) **Falmouth:** the site of the Irish Brigade's winter quarters in 1862, located across the Rappahannock River from Fredericksburg, Virginia. **Mary's Hill [*sic*]:** Marye's Heights, the scene of six suicidal charges by the Irish Brigade during an engagement at Fredericksburg, Virginia, on December 13, 1862. The Brigade lost 46 killed, 416 wounded, and 74 missing out of about 1,250 men led into battle. (O'Brien, "Sprig of Green," p. 69) **Fred'ricksburgh [*sic*]:** Fredericksburg. (See the previous entry.) **Irish Ninth:** the Ninth Massachusetts Regiment, rescued by the Irish Brigade from being destroyed by Thomas "Stonewall" Jackson at Gaines' Mill (June 27, 1862). (Athearn, *Thomas Meagher*, pp. 111–112; Conyngham, *Irish Brigade*, p. 186) **Cass:** Colonel Thomas Cass (1821–1862), a native of Ireland who organized and first commanded the Ninth Massachusetts Regiment. He was killed at the battle of Malvern Hill, Virginia. (*National Cyclopedia of American Biography*, s.v. "Cass, Thomas," vol. 9, p. 528) **Thirty-Seventh:** the 37th New York Regiment, also known as the Irish Rifles. (Boyle, *Party of Mad Fellows*, p. 89) **Kearney [*sic*]:** Philip Kearny, the popular Union commander who distinguished himself at Williamsburg and Fair Oaks and during the second Bull Run campaign. He was killed at Chantilly after accidentally riding into enemy lines. (Boatner, *Civil War Dictionary*, p. 449) **Irish Rifles:** the 37th New York Regiment. (Boyle, *Party of Mad Fellows*, p. 89) **Sixty-Ninth:** the 69th Pennsylvania Infantry, named after the more famous 69th New York State Militia Regiment. The 69th Pennsylvania distinguished itself at the battle of Gettysburg by breaking Pickett's charge at the Angle. (McDermott, *69th Regiment Pennsylvania*, pp. 31–32, 82) **Eighty-Eighth:** the 88th New York Regiment, one of the units in the Irish Brigade. **O'Kane:** Colonel Dennis O'Kane of the 69th Pennsylvania Infantry Volunteers. His men pushed back a Confederate attempt to break the Union line at Gettysburg, although he died of wounds to the chest and/or abdomen sustained on July 3, 1862. (Bates, *Pennsylvania Volunteers*, vol. 4, p. 707; Busey, *These Honored Dead*, p. 205) **brave Second:** the Second Corps, First Division, Army of the Potomac. **Glendale:** the site of a battle in Virginia on June 30, 1862. (Murphy, *Kelly's Heroes*, p. 5) **Houston [*sic*]:** probably Lieutenant Colonel James Huston of the 82nd New York Volunteers, who was killed at Gettysburg on July 2, 1863. (Cavanagh, *Memoirs of General Meagher*, pp. 472–473; Phisterer, *New York in the Rebellion*, vol. 4, pp. 2907–2908) **friends of Tammany:** the Democratic political machine organization in New York City. **Hurrah for Joe:** an allusion to General Joseph Hooker (1814–1879), the Union officer to whom Reynolds dedicated this "poetical address." In his dedication Reynolds addressed Hooker as one "who was ever dear to the Irish, from his valor, and under whom they expect that your advance will be a succession of

victories, and that this glorious Union will be preserved now and forever."
(Reynolds, *Poetical Address*, Preface)

**Pages 131–132**
*From "Song of the Irish Brigade"*
**old green flag:** a green flag emblazoned with a golden harp, used as a banner of
Irish nationalism from at least the early 1640s. (O'Brogain, *Irish Harp Emblem*, p.
17) **Liffy's [sic] banks to Shannon's stream:** The Liffey is a river in eastern Ireland (on which Dublin is located); the Shannon is Ireland's principal river, running southwest from northern Ireland to the Atlantic. **pirate rag:** the Confederate
flag. **our gallant leader:** Brigadier General Thomas Meagher. **Stripes and Stars:**
the American flag. **Fair Oaks:** the site of a battle in Virginia on May 31–June 1,
1862. On the second day of the engagement, McClellan ordered the Irish Brigade
into action. The 69th and the 88th New York regiments entered the fray with their
distinctive battle cry — half-English, half-Gaelic — while the 63rd New York was
dispatched to guard a bridge and retrieve some field guns mired in a swamp.
(Jones, *Irish Brigade*, 120) **Frederick's bloody plain:** the scene of a disastrous engagement at Fredericksburg, Virginia, on December 13, 1862. During six suicidal
charges up Marye's Heights, the Brigade lost 46 killed, 416 wounded, and 74 missing out of about 1,250 men led into battle. (O'Brien, "Sprig of Green," p. 69) **our
chieftain:** Brigadier General Thomas Meagher. **Erin:** a literary name for Ireland.
**Columbia's cause:** the Union cause during the Civil War (from "Columbia," a
name formerly used to refer to the United States).

**Page 133**
*From "The Irish Dead on Fredericksburg Heights" by Kate M. Boylan*
**Fredericksburg Heights:** actually Marye's Heights, the scene of a disastrous engagement at Fredericksburg, Virginia, on December 13, 1862. During six suicidal
charges up Marye's Heights, the Brigade lost 46 killed, 416 wounded, and 74 missing out of about 1,250 men led into battle. (O'Brien, "Sprig of Green," p. 69) **Carlow,
Wexford, Tyrone, Wicklow:** counties in Ireland. **Innisbowen:** possibly "Inisbofin,"
the name of islands off the coast of counties Donegal and Galway, Ireland. **Erin's
soil:** Ireland, from a literary name for the island.

**Page 134**
**St. Clair Mulholland:** During the war Mulholland sustained four wounds.
At Fredericksburg, while the 116th Pennsylvania and the other regiments of the
Irish Brigade attempted to storm Marye's Heights, he received a gunshot wound
to the leg. The following spring, after he had been placed in command of the
140th Pennsylvania, he was hit in the ankle at the Wilderness. Only a week later,
in the middle of May, a piece of shell cut his scalp to the bone, and at the battle of
Totopotomoy Creek a sharpshooter's ball struck his groin.

After the war Mulholland was a spokesman for a variety of civic, humanitarian, and fraternal causes. As chief of police of Philadelphia, he reorganized the
police department, introducing mounted patrols in outlying areas and destroying some of the city's worse gangs. For many years he served on the County Board
of Prison Inspectors and used his influence to press for prison reform in his state.
In addition, he was a familiar figure in the American Irish Historical Society, the
Friendly Sons of St. Patrick, and the Hibernian Society of Philadelphia.

At his death Mulholland was eulogized on both sides off the Atlantic. The *Irish News and Belfast Morning News* declared that "on the long and illustrious roll of Irishmen who, by their chivalry, statesmanship, and administrative capacity, have contributed to the upholding of the free institutions of the United States, few deserve a more exalted place than the late General St. Clair Mulholland."

One of the leading Philadelphia journals was far more effusive and eloquent: "And truly may it be said of the great and gallant Irishman who has laid down his sword and gone to rest in his soldier's cloak that he did all a soldier could to live well and die well for the country of his adoption, since he could not offer it for that of his nativity. It was not his lot to fall on the field of his fame, but to rise from the blood-stained soil more than once to take up the task of the soldier-saint, Louis of France, and reveal the tender heart of the woman beating beneath the cuirass of the soldier. To visit the prisons and to bear the message of solace to the despairing victims of a cruel fate was the task which he marked out for himself, and carried out to the very last healthful day of his official career. Many a stout and steadfast heart has 'the black North,' as his native Ulster is erroneously called, brought to the defense and glorification of the American Union, but none surpassing in beautiful qualities that of the quiet and unassuming soldier who now lies in a friendly grave in the land he served, but far from the hills of his native Ulster, the land of the O'Neills and the O'Donnells, and all the representatives of the modern chivalry of 'the Red Branch' — saints like Columbkille and martyrs like Archbishop Plunkett. It is a unique glory that the flag of the American Union owns. She has lured the bravest and the most unselfish from all lands to defend her cause, and she lays the proud tribute of her gratitude and her sorrow on their biers with a hand that knows no discrimination as to authority. The soldier from Antrim who gave his strong right arm, as well as his unselfish heart, to her service was worthy of her, and she of him. And so may it ever be as between America and Ireland. 'Quis separabit?'"

(Kohl, Introduction, *116th Pennsylvania*, pp. xiv–xv, xix, xxiv; Lee, "General St. Clair Mulholland," pp. 502, 504–505)

**Louis of France:** Louis IX, king of France from 1226 to 1270. He was canonized in 1297. (*New Catholic Encyclopedia*, s.v. "Louis IX") **Ulster:** one of the four traditional provinces of Ireland, encompassing what are now Northern Ireland and a portion of the Republic of Ireland. **O'Neills and O'Donnells:** powerful families in Ulster which provided many of the province's kings. (Moody and Martin, *Course of Irish History*, p. 178) **Red Branch:** a fraternity of Celtic knights presided over by Conor MacNessa, a first-century king of Ulster. Their commander was the famous hero Cuchulain. (Joyce, *Short History of Ireland*, p. 36) **Columbkille:** A prince of the O'Neill clan, this sixth-century Irish monk established monasteries throughout Ulster and Scotland. He is also known as Columba. (D'Arcy, Mary, *Saints of Ireland*, p. 73) **Archbishop Plunkett:** Oliver Plunkett (1625–1681), archbishop of Armagh, Ireland, who was falsely charged with complicity in the Popish Plot to murder Protestants and restore Roman Catholicism to England. (D'Arcy, Mary, *Saints of Ireland*, pp. 197, 199) **Antrim:** a county in northern Ireland. **Quis separabit?:** a Latin phrase meaning "Who will separate (them)?"

### Page 138

**Weed, Vincent, and Hazlett:** Union officers either killed or wounded on the second day at Gettysburg in action centered around Little Round Top. General

Stephen Weed was on his way to reinforce Sickles' Third Corps in the Peach Orchard when he was redirected to Little Round Top. While bringing up an artillery battery, he was shot by a rebel sharpshooter. Strong Vincent was mortally wounded while trying to reform his faltering right regiment, the 16th Michigan, en route to Little Round Top. After leading a battery up Little Round Top, Charles Hazlett was killed by sharpshooters as he bent over the mortally wounded Weed. (Sifakis, *Who Was Who*, pp. 190, 428, 444) **Whitworth bolt:** an allusion to the firing of a Whitworth cannon, the best known of which was a 12-pounder with a 2.75-inch bore, which could be fired as either a muzzleloader or a breechloader. (Current, *Encyclopedia of the Confederacy*, vol. 1, p. 102)

### Pages 141–142
#### From "Captain O'Hay" by Michael Scanlon

**Erin:** Ireland, from a literary name for the island. **for his own native land:** Ireland. Rorty was a member of the Fenian Brotherhood, an organization dedicated to the forceful overthrow of British rule in Ireland. Rorty had hoped to return to Ireland as part of a military force of Irish and Irish-American veterans of the Civil War. (Pohanka, "James McKay Rorty," pp. 5, 20–21) **Shannon:** Ireland's principal river, running southwest from northern Ireland to the Atlantic.

### Pages 145–146
#### From "Our Fallen Comrades" by William Collins

**Southern gray . . . Northern blue:** Confederate and Union soldiers, respectively, so called from the color of their uniforms. **Northern blue:** Union soldiers, so called from the color of their uniforms. **Irish Green:** one of the green banners flown by the regiments of the Irish Brigade. **wassail:** a revel characterized by the drinking of healths. **Judgment Roll:** the names of the living and the dead who will be judged by God at the end of the world.

### Pages 146–147
#### From "The Irish Brigade at Gettysburg" by William Geoghegan

**five and twenty years ago:** 1863. **Stonewall Jackson's lips:** an allusion to Thomas "Stonewall" Jackson (1824–1863), the famous Confederate officer who received his nickname when General Barnard Bee tried to rally his men at the first battle of Bull Run by pointing out Jackson: "There is Jackson, standing like a stone wall. Let us determine to die here, and we will conquer. Follow me!" (Sifakis, *Who Was Who*, pp. 45, 337) **damned green flag:** one of the green banners flown by the regiments of the Irish Brigade. The flag taken into battle by the 69th New York State Volunteers was a deep green and bore in the center an embroidered golden Irish harp, with a sunburst above it and a wreath of shamrocks beneath. (Kelly, "Green Flags," p. 195) **Fair Oaks:** the site of a battle in Virginia on May 31–June 1, 1862. On the second day of the engagement, General McClellan ordered the Irish Brigade into action. The 69th and the 88th New York regiments entered the fray with their distinctive battle cry — half-English, half-Gaelic — while the 63rd New York was dispatched to guard a bridge and retrieve some field guns mired in a swamp. (Jones, *Irish Brigade*, p. 120) **Marye's heights:** the scene of six suicidal charges by the Irish Brigade during an engagement at Fredericksburg, Virginia, on December 13, 1862. The Brigade lost 46 killed, 416 wounded, and 74 missing out of about 1,250 men led into battle. (O'Brien, "Sprig of Green," p. 69) **Southland's veterans:**

soldiers from the Southern states. **Killarney's hills:** an area around the town of Killarney in County Kerry, Ireland, known for its surrounding lakes and mountains.

### Pages 148, 150

*From "Father Corby" by James J. Creswell*

**Round Top's crested crown:** probably Little Round Top, a position along Cemetery Ridge on the Gettysburg battlefield. (Murphy, *Kelly's Heroes*, p. 19) **Palmetto tree:** the palm tree emblem on the flag of South Carolina, adopted when it seceded in 1861. **Lee:** Robert E. Lee (1807–1870), the Confederate commander of the Army of Northern Virginia. **Mead [*sic*]:** George Gordon Meade (1815–1872), the commander of the Army of the Potomac, whose troops successfully repulsed the Confederate drive at Gettysburg. He was the great-grandson of Robert Meade, an Irish emigrant who was living in Philadelphia by 1732. (Bache, *Life of General Meade*, p. 2) **Nugent's men:** troops under the command of Robert Nugent (1824–1901), a native of County Down, Ireland, and the colonel of the 69th New York Volunteers. He later served as the commander of the Irish Brigade. (Boyle, *Party of Mad Fellows*, p. 396) **Green of his loved Isle:** one of the green banners flown by the regiments of the Irish Brigade. **soldier-priest:** Father William Corby

### Pages 151–152

*From "A Miracle of War" by Smith Johnson*

**the blue . . . the gray:** Union and Confederate soldiers, respectively. **Hancock's ever-valiant corps:** the Union army's Second Corps, commanded by Major General Winfield Scott Hancock (1824–1886). (Jones, *Irish Brigade*, p. 191) **Meagher's old brigade:** the Irish Brigade. **priest of Meagher's old brigade:** The author means Father William Corby, the chaplain of the 88th New York Infantry, although there were other Catholic chaplains in the Brigade.

### Page 153

**Pantheon . . . Westminster:** allusions to national shrines or memorials to illustrious dead: the Pantheon in Paris and Westminster Abbey in London.

### Page 156

**march of the Fifty-second**: Following the British victory against the French at Talavera, Spain, in July 1809, 3,000 of Robert Craufurd's Light Infantry arrived on the battlefield. These new troops included the first battalions of the 43rd Light Infantry, the 52nd Light Infantry, and the 95th Rifles. They had covered 42 miles in 26 hours. (Glover, *Peninsular War*, p. 112)

### Pages 159–160

*From "The Thousand and Thirty-Seven" by Charles Graham Halpine*

**The Thousand and Thirty-Seven:** an allusion perhaps to the approximate number of enlisted men and officers in the typical regiment. When the 69th New York State Militia Regiment left New York City on April 23, 1861, it numbered in its ranks 16 men and officers on its general staff, 27 company officers, and 996 enlistees (in nine companies). (Conyngham, *Irish Brigade*, pp. 22–23) **April 20, 1864:** the third anniversary of the 69th New York's service as a Civil War unit. **a thousand bayonets . . . the swords were thirty-seven:** an allusion to the 1,000 men and the 37 officers who generally constituted a full regiment.

**Page 164**
*From "Tom Smyth, of the Irish Brigade" by Dr. Lawrence Reynolds*
**Columbia:** a name formerly used to refer to the United States.

**Page 172**
**Asperges me:** one of several parts of the Roman Catholic mass mentioned in Father Corby's description. Each part is known by the beginning word or words of the Latin text: *Asperges me* — "You will sprinkle me, Lord, with hyssop . . ."; *Introibo* — "I will go to the altar of God"; *Credo* — "I believe in God . . ."; *Sanctus! sanctus! sanctus!* — "Holy, holy, holy, Lord God of power and might." **Host:** the bread or wafer consecrated in the celebration of the Eucharist. **words of Consecration:** the words spoken by the priest to transform the bread and wine of the Eucharist into the body and blood of Christ: "This is my body. . . . This is my blood."

**Pages 179–181**
*From "The Ballad of the Sixty-Ninth" by Joseph I. C. Clarke*
**Fates:** the three goddesses of destiny in Greek and Roman mythology. **Yorktown:** the Revolutionary War battlefield in Virginia where the British surrendered on October 19, 1781. **hurtling of a shell:** an allusion to the Confederate bombardment of Fort Sumter in Charleston, South Carolina, on April 12, 1861. **At Lincoln's call:** After the fall of Fort Sumter, President Abraham Lincoln called for 75,000 volunteers for the defense of the nation's capital. **Irish took their stand:** As many as 170,000 Irish-born soldiers fought in the Union army during the Civil War. (Wakin, *Enter the Irish-American*, pp. 120–121) **Corcoran's command:** an allusion to Michael Corcoran (1827–1863), a native of County Sligo, Ireland, and colonel of the 69th New York State Militia Regiment. He was captured at Bull Run on July 21, 1861, and remained a Confederate prisoner for thirteen months because he refused to agree never again to take up arms. (Conyngham, *Irish Brigade*, pp. 537, 539) **Broadway's length:** a fashionable thoroughfare in New York City. On April 23, 1861, the 69th New York State Militia Regiment marched down Broadway to Pier 4 along the Hudson River and boarded the steamer *James Adger* for the trip south. (Garcia, "'Fighting' Sixty-Ninth," pp. 37–38) **Their flag of green:** probably the Prince of Wales Color, presented to the 69th New York State Militia Regiment by Irish citizens of New York City after the regiment refused to march in a parade honoring the heir to the British throne on October 11, 1860. The banner's green field contained a sunburst surrounded by two scrolls containing the memorial words "Presented to the 69th Regiment in Commemoration of the 11th Oct. 1860." (Garcia, "'Fighting' Sixty-Ninth," p. 36) **Old Glory:** the American flag. **Archbishop:** John Hughes (1797–1864), a native of County Tyrone, Ireland, and the first archbishop of New York City. Hughes blessed the troops as he sat in the editorial rooms of the old *Metropolitan Record*, near Houston Street. ("Corcoran of the Sixty-Ninth," pp. 365–367) **Blackburn's Ford:** one of the twelve Civil War battles, campaigns, or engagements mentioned in the poem in which the 69th New York Regiment participated: Blackburn's Ford (July 18, 1861), Bull Run (July 21, 1861), Rappahannock (November 7, 1863), Fair Oaks (May 31–June 1, 1862), Gaines' Mill (June 27, 1862), Malvern Hill (July 1, 1862), Chancellorsville (May 1–5, 1863), Antietam (September 17, 1862), Marye's Heights (Fredericksburg) (December 12–15, 1862), Gettysburg (July 1–3, 1863), Wilderness (May 5–7, 1864), Petersburg (June 16–18, 1864), and Appomattox (April 9, 1865). (Murphy, *Kelly's Heroes*, pp.

5-6) **Nugent:** Robert Nugent (1824–1901), a native of County Down, Ireland, and lieutenant colonel of the 69th New York State Militia Regiment. He later served as colonel of the 69th New York Volunteers and commander of the Irish Brigade. (Boyle, *Party of Mad Fellows*, p. 396) **Meagher:** Thomas Francis Meagher (1823–1867) a native of County Waterford, Ireland, and captain of Company K ("Irish Zouaves"), 69th New York State Militia Regiment. He later organized and commanded the Irish Brigade in the Union army during the Civil War. (*Dictionary of American Biography*, s.v. "Meagher, Thomas Francis") **Cavanagh:** James Cavanagh (1831–1901), a native of County Tipperary, Ireland, and captain of Company C, 69th New York State Militia Regiment. He was severely wounded at Fredericksburg on December 13, 1862. (Conyngham, *Irish Brigade*, pp. 545, 549) **MacMahon [sic]:** James Powers McMahon, originally captain of Company K, 69th New York State Volunteer Regiment, and later colonel of the 164th New York Volunteers, part of Corcoran's Irish Legion. He was killed at Cold Harbor on June 5, 1864. (Phisterer, *New York in the Rebellion*, vol. 3, p. 2704; Conyngham, *Irish Brigade*, p. 553) **Kelly:** Patrick Kelly (?–1864), a native of County Galway, Ireland, and captain of Company E, 69th New York State Militia Regiment. After the Irish Brigade was formed, Kelly became lieutenant colonel of the 88th New York Regiment and succeeded Thomas Meagher as commander of the Irish Brigade. Kelly was killed at Petersburg on June 16, 1864. (Conyngham, *Irish Brigade*, pp. 545, 558) **Haggerty:** James Haggerty, captain of Company A, 69th New York State Militia Regiment. He was killed at the first battle of Bull Run on July 21, 1861. (Phisterer, *New York in the Rebellion*, vol. 1, p. 683) **Clark [sic]:** probably Thomas Clarke, captain of Company D, 69th New York State Militia Regiment. He was wounded at the first battle of Bull Run on July 21, 1861. (Phisterer, *New York in the Rebellion*, vol. 1, p. 680)

### Page 186

**Clare:** Charles O'Brien (1699–1761), Sixth Viscount Clare, the commander of Irish troops in the army of Louis XIV at the battle of Fontenoy in 1745. (*Dictionary of National Biography*, s.v. "O'Brien, Charles"; Hennessy, *Wild Geese*, p. 64) **Dillon:** either Arthur Dillon (1670–1733), one of the "Wild Geese" who went into exile in France and subsequently served as a general in the French army, or his son Colonel James Dillon, who was killed at the battle of Fontenoy in 1745. (*Dictionary of National Biography*, s.v. "Dillon, Arthur") **Sarsfield:** Patrick Sarsfield (d. 1693), a leader in the Irish Catholic resistance (1689–1691) to William III and a supporter of the failed cause of the Stuart king James II. After the Williamite victory in Ireland, Sarsfield and about 12,000 Irishmen went into exile in France. (Lydon, *Making of Ireland*, p. 216) **Landen:** the site in the Austrian Netherlands (modern Belgium) where the French army and its Irish regiments defeated William of Orange (William III of England) in 1693. The Irish exile Patrick Sarsfield was killed during the engagement and was buried on the battlefield. (Hennessy, *Wild Geese*, pp. 35, 42) **Cremona:** the Italian city in which a French garrison of about 4,000 men recovered from a surprise attack by Austrian troops under Prince Eugene of Savoy on February 2, 1702. The garrison included 600 Irish soldiers commanded by Walter Bourke and Daniel Mahoney. The Irish suffered 364 casualties (killed, wounded, and captured). The exploits of Bourke's troops are commemorated in the anonymous poem "The Regiment of Bourke." (O'Callaghan, *Irish Brigades*, pp. 197, 214; *Rhyme With Reason*, pp. 20–21) **Fontenoy:** the site in the Austrian Netherlands (modern Belgium) where the six Irish regiments of the French army turned the tide for Louis XIV by helping defeat the British and Allied forces on May 11, 1745. During the battle the Irish regiments numbered about 3,870 of the 60,000 French troops and suffered 656 casualties. While smashing through the Allied right flank, the Irish troops shouted, "Remember Limerick!" — a cry to avenge the surrender of that Irish city to the army of William III in 1691 and the English betrayal of the subsequent peace terms. (Hennessy, *Wild Geese*, pp. 64–65, 68–69) **Fair Oaks, Malvern Hill, Antietam, and Fredericksburg:** Civil War battles in which the Irish Brigade participated. **five hundred:** closer to 900 (Bilby, *Remember Fontenoy!*, pp. 125, 127)

## Pages 186–189
### *From "Thomas Francis Meagher" by James J. Bourke*

**Montana's tideless wave:** the Missouri River. **nameless grave:** the Missouri River near Fort Benton, Montana, where Meagher presumably drowned on July 1, 1867. **Tribune:** Thomas Meagher, compared to one of the ten Tribunes elected in ancient Rome to protect the interests of the plebeians. **Eire:** Ireland. **Stripes and Stars:** the American flag. **sprigs of green:** sprigs of boxwood worn like ensigns by the soldiers in the Irish Brigade. **"Here comes that damned Green Flag again!":** a comment made by a Confederate officer during the battle of Malvern Hill in Virginia on July 1, 1862. The allusion may be to one of the green banners flown by the regiments of the Irish Brigade, in this case probably the 88th New York Regiment, which at Malvern Hill forced the Confederate Louisiana Tigers to retreat. (Jones, *Irish Brigade*, p. 124; O'Brien, "Sprig of Green" pp. 73–74) **Antietam's day:** September 17, 1862, when Union forces stopped a Confederate advance into Maryland and Pennsylvania. The Irish Brigade played a conspicuous part in the Union victory but suffered casualties of between 525 and 540 men, 113 of them fatalities. The three New York regiments suffered a casualty rate of about 52 percent. (Jones, *Irish Brigade*, p. 142; Bilby, *Remember Fontenoy!*, p. 60) **Fredericksburg's hard foughten field:** the scene of a disastrous engagement at Fredericksburg, Virginia, on December 13, 1862. During six suicidal charges up Marye's Heights, the Brigade lost 46 killed, 416 wounded, and 74 missing out of about 1,250 men led into battle. (O'Brien, "Sprig of Green," p. 69) **the Irish slogan:** perhaps the cry *Faugh-a-Ballagh*, Irish for "Clear the Way!" (Jones, *Irish Brigade*, p. 99) **the Roman chief of old:** possibly Eunus, a Syrian who led a slave revolt in the Roman province of Sicily in 139 B.C. after announcing the gods' blessings for such an undertaking. (Cook, *Roman Republic*, pp. 12–13) **proud city of the Gael:** Dublin, Ireland. **Gael:** used here to refer to the Irish. **Emmet's camping ground:** an allusion to Robert Emmet (1778–1803), an Irish patriot arrested and executed in Dublin for his involvement in an uprising against British rule in 1803. In his speech to the jury he asked that no man write his epitaph until "my country takes her place among the nations of the earth." (Foster, *Modern Ireland*, p. 285; Lydon, *Making of Ireland*, p. 280) **Edward's martyr wound:** the mortal wound sustained by Lord Edward Fitzgerald (1763–1798) during his arrest for treason in 1798. Fitzgerald had joined the United Irishmen movement in its attempt to create an independent Irish republic and had engaged in negotiations for French military support. (*Dictionary of National Biography*, s.v. "Fitzgerald, Lord Edward") **Innisfail:** also *Inisfail*, an Irish word meaning "Isle of Destiny," one of many ancient names for Ireland. (MacManus, *Story of the Irish Race*, p. 9) **Isaiah:** a Hebrew prophet of the eighth century B.C.

**Page 194**

**Emmet:** Robert Emmet (1778–1803), an Irish patriot arrested and executed in Dublin for his involvement in an uprising against British rule in 1803. In his speech to the jury he asked that no man write his epitaph until "my country takes her place among the nations of the earth." (Foster, *Modern Ireland*, p. 285; Lydon, *Making of Ireland*, p. 280) **O'Connell:** Daniel O'Connell (1775–1847), an opponent of the 1801 legislative union of Ireland and England and an advocate of political rights for Irish Catholics, including the right to be elected to Parliament without taking an oath abjuring some of their religious beliefs. In 1828 he was elected to Parliament from County Clare, the first Catholic to contest a parliamentary election since the seventeenth century. His refusal to take the hated oath led the British government to relent, and he was allowed to take his seat after swearing not to subvert the Protestant church establishment. (Lydon, *Making of Ireland*, pp. 283, 287–288)

**Pages 194–196**
*From "A Hosting of the Gael" by Father Charles O'Donnell*

**Emmet:** Robert Emmet (1778–1803), an Irish patriot arrested and executed in Dublin for his involvement in an uprising against British rule in 1803. In his speech to the jury he asked that no man write his epitaph until "my country takes her place among the nations of the earth." (Foster, *Modern Ireland*, p. 285; Lydon, *Making of Ireland*, p. 280) **Donegal, Kerry, Tipperary:** counties in Ireland. **Cathay:** a possible allusion to the Irish and Irish-American soldiers who saw service in China (Cathay) after the Boxer uprising there in 1898. One of the American officers on this mission was Captain Henry Reilly, a native of Ireland and the commander of Battery F of the Fifth U.S. Artillery. On August 15, 1900, his men distinguished themselves by blasting open the first gate into the Chinese capital. Reilly's thirty-eight-year military career was cut short, however, when he was killed by a Chinese bullet as he stood atop the Chien Gate observing his men fire their guns. He was buried the next day on the grounds of the American legation. Reilly's remains were moved to Arlington National Cemetery in Virginia the following April. (MacCloskey, *Reilly's Battery*, pp. 20–21, 173–177) **Belgian battlefields:** a possible allusion to the following episodes. In 1605 Henry O'Neill received from Philip III of Spain command of a regiment of Irishmen in Flanders (modern Belgium, but governed at the time by Spain). In 1692 Irish troops in the service of France helped defeat the troops of William of Orange (William III of England) at Steenkerke in Flanders. The next year the French (and their Irish regiments) again defeated William in Flanders, this time at Landen. The Irish exile Patrick Sarsfield was killed during this last engagement and was buried on the battlefield. (Hennessy, *Wild Geese*, pp. 35, 41–42) **Spain:** a possible allusion to the fact that the three most famous Irish regiments in the Spanish army were the *Hibernia*, the *Ultona* (Ulster), and the *Irlanda*. (Hennessy, *Wild Geese*, p. 131) **Saskatchewan:** a province in Canada. In his allusion to "true sons of Irish blood" from Saskatchewan, the author may have been thinking of James Walsh, a Canadian soldier of Irish descent who saw active service against Fenian raids from the United States in 1866 and 1870. He later became an inspector with the North West Mounted Police and oversaw the construction of Fort Walsh near Cypress Hills, Saskatchewan. (Ross, "Superintendent Walsh," pp. 5, 10–12, 19) **Afric sand:** a possible allusion to the fact that during the French campaigns in Algeria between 1830 and 1856 many Irishmen served as officers in the expeditionary forces. One of them — Patrice MacMahon (1808-

1893) — also served in the Crimean War and the Franco-Prussian War and became the second president (1873-1879) of the French Third Republic. (O'Donnell, Elliot, *Irish Abroad*, pp. 199, 245–246) **Flodden Field:** the site of a battle in northeastern England in which the English defeated the Scots (Gaels) in 1513. **Fontenoy:** the site in the Austrian Netherlands (modern Belgium) where the six Irish regiments of the French army turned the tide for Louis XIV by helping defeat the British and Allied forces on May 11, 1745. During the battle the Irish regiments numbered 3,870 of the 60,000 French troops and suffered 656 casualties. While smashing through the Allied right flank, the Irish troops shouted, "Remember Limerick!" — a cry to avenge the surrender of that Irish city to the army of William III in 1691 and the English betrayal of the subsequent peace terms. (Hennessy, *Wild Geese*, pp. 64–65, 68–69) **Fredericksburg:** the scene of a disastrous engagement in Virginia on December 13, 1862. During six suicidal charges up Marye's Heights in Fredericksburg, the Irish Brigade lost 46 killed, 416 wounded, and 74 missing out of about 1,250 men led into battle. (O'Brien, "Sprig of Green," p. 69) **Who held the heights and threw us back:** The Confederates on Marye's Heights at Fredericksburg were mostly Irish — members of Cobb's Georgia Infantry and Kershaw's South Carolina Infantry. (O'Brien, "Sprig of Green" pp. 65, 68) **Flag of Green:** the flag of the Irish Brigade. **the frayed and faded fold/That was their Cloth of the Field of Gold:** The tattered flag of the Irish Brigade is compared to the gold-threaded cloth which covered the pavilion in which Henry VIII of England and Francis I of France conferred in 1520. The meeting of the two sovereigns took place in an open space near Calais known as the Field of the Cloth of Gold. (Durant, *Reformation*, pp. 526–527)

### Chapter 3
### The 69th New York National Guard Regiment in the Spanish-American War

### Page 201

**"The Wearing of the Green":** a traditional Irish song based on the following poem:

> Oh, Paddy dear, and did ye hear the news that's goin' round?
> The shamrock is forbid by law to grow on Irish ground!
> No more St. Patrick's day we'll keep; his colour can't be seen,
> For there's a cruel law ag'in' the Wearin' o' the Green!
>
> I met with Napper Tandy, and he took me by the hand,
> And he said, "How's poor ould Ireland, and how does she stand?"
> "She's the most distressful country that ever yet was seen,
> For they're hanging men and women there for Wearin' o' the Green.
> An' if the colour we must wear is England's cruel red,
> Let it remind us of the blood that Ireland has shed;
> Then pull the shamrock from your hat, and throw it on the sod,
> An' never fear, 'twill take toot there, though under foot 'tis trod.
>
> When law can stop the blades of grass from growin' as they grow,
> An' when the leaves in summer time their colour dare not show,
> Then I will change the colour, too, I wear in my caubeen;
> But till that day, praise God, I'll stick to the Wearin' o' the Green.
> (Colum, *Anthology of Irish Verse*, p. 100)

*Napper Tandy:* James Napper Tandy (1740–1803), who formed a branch of the radical United Irishmen in Dublin but was soon forced into exile in France. There the French government made him a general and sent him back to Ireland to raise an army against the British. Although he landed off the coast of Donegal in September 1798, he immediately abandoned the venture. While returning to France, he was captured and handed over to the British, who tried and sentenced him to death. At the insistence of Napoleon Bonaparte, however, he was released and ended his days in Bordeaux. (*New Encyclopaedia Britannica*, Micropaedia, s.v. "Tandy, James Napper") *caubeen:* an Irish hat. From the diminutive of *caba*, the Irish word for hat. (Simpson and Weiner, *Oxford English Dictionary*)

### Page 209
*From a poem by Joseph I. C. Clarke*
**role of fame:** list of battles in which the 69th New York participated, particularly during the Civil War: **Antietam:** a battle near Sharpsburg, Maryland, on September 17, 1862. The Irish Brigade played a conspicuous part in the Union victory by pushing the enemy back to its second line. The Brigade suffered casualties of between 525 and 540 men, 113 them fatalities. The three New York regiments suffered a casualty rate of about 52 percent. (Jones, *Irish Brigade*, p. 142; Bilby, *Remember Fontenoy!*, p. 60) **Gettysburg:** a battle fought in Pennsylvania on July 1–3, 1863, during which Confederate forces withdrew after suffering about 28,000 casualties to the Union's 23,000. These casualties included 3,155 Union troops killed and 3,903 Confederates killed. (Boatner, *Civil War Dictionary*, p. 339) **Vaughan's Pass:** probably a three-day engagement in Virginia (February 5–7, 1865) also known as Dabney's Mills and Hatcher's Run. (Boatner, *Civil War Dictionary*, 217, 384–385; Murphy, *Kelly's Heroes*, p. 6) **Petersburg:** a series of engagements near Petersburg, Virginia, on June 16–18, 1864. (Murphy, *Kelly's Heroes*, p. 5) **Mary's Hill [*sic*]:** Marye's Heights, the scene of six suicidal charges by the Irish Brigade during an engagement at Fredericksburg, Virginia, on December 13, 1862. The Brigade lost 46 killed, 416 wounded, and 74 missing out of about 1,250 men led into battle. (O'Brien, "Sprig of Green," p. 69)

### Page 210
**"Garry Owen":** See the "Garry Owen" note on page 311. **"The Wearing of the Green":** See "The Wearing of the Green" note on page 330.

### Chapter 5
### The 69th New York (165th Infantry) Regiment in World War I

### Page 223
**"Garry Owen":** See the "Garry Owen" note on page 311. **Bloody Ford:** perhaps intended to be an allusion to Bloody *Lane*, the sunken road on the battlefield at Antietam, Maryland, where the Irish Brigade suffered casualties of between 525 and 540 men, of whom 113 were fatalities. (Jones, *Irish Brigade*, p. 142; Bilby, *Remember Fontenoy!*, p. 60) **Marye's Heights:** the scene of six suicidal charges by the Irish Brigade during an engagement at Fredericksburg, Virginia, on December 13, 1862. The Brigade lost 46 killed, 416 wounded, and 74 missing out of about 1,250 men led into battle. (O'Brien, "Sprig of Green," p. 69)

## Pages 226

**"The Wearing of the Green":** See "The Wearing of the Green" note on page 330.

## Page 228

**maneen:** probably a neologism meaning "little man," created by adding the Irish suffix *een* ("little") to the word "man." **avic:** from the Gaelic *a mhic-o,* pronounced "a vick oh" and meaning "Oh, son" (used indulgently). (Behan, *Borstal Boy,* p. 367)

## Page 231

**Venite, Adoremus Dominum:** a refrain from the Latin Christmas carol "Adeste, Fideles," known in English as "Oh, Come All Ye Faithful." The phrase is translated as "Come, let us adore the Lord."

## Page 234

**Tommies:** privates in any army, especially the British army. From "Thomas Atkins," a generic name used on military registration forms from at least 1815. (Simpson and Weiner, *Oxford English Dictionary*)

## Page 238

*From "Blaustein of the Irish" by John O'Keefe*

**slainthe:** also "slainte," from *sláinte,* a Gaelic toast meaning "Good health!" (Simpson and Weiner, *Oxford English Dictionary*)

## Pages 239–241

*From "Dawn on the Irish Coast" by John Locke*
*(or "O Ireland, I Bid You the Top of the Morning")*

**TH' ANAM THO' DIAH!:** an Irish phrase possibly translated as "Thou Spirit of God!" (Maclennan, *Dictionary of the Gaelic Language,* pp. 14, 125, 340) **Cliona's shelving strand:** an allusion to Cliodhna (also Clidna), in Irish mythology the goddess of beauty. She was one of the Tuatha de Danaan, the magical divinities subject to the goddess Danu, and ruled the Land of Promise, the Irish afterlife, where death, decay, and violence were unknown. Cliodhna took the form of a sweeping seabird and of a wave, specifically the ninth wave of every series. (That wave was believed to be larger than the preceding eight; for this reason huge waves were called "Clidna's waves.") When she assumed human form, she was called the "shapely one" because of her remarkable beauty. According to legend, Cliodhna fell in love with a mortal named Ciabhan of the Curling Locks. The paramours left the Land of Promise and landed in Glandore, County Cork. When Ciabhan went off to hunt, the goddess remained on the shore until a giant wave swept her back to the Land of Promise. On another occasion Cliodhna seduced the mortal John Fitzjames away from his wife, an argumentative Irish woman named Caitileen Og. Caitileen was the only woman known to berate Cliodhna for playing with human affections and even followed the goddess to the afterlife to demand her husband's return. Although Caitileen's wit almost persuaded the goddess, Cliodhna kept her lover for herself. Tradition says that the bird goddess granted to the Celts the magic of "blarney," the gift of a cajoling tongue. It seems that, when the owner of Blarney Castle in County Cork feared confronting people who were suing him, Cliodhna appeared to him and said, "Kiss the stone you come face to face with in the morning, and the words will pour out of you." To-day Cliodhna is remembered as a fairy queen who rules the sacred hill in Cork known as Carrig Cliodna. (Ann and Imel, *Goddesses*, p. 509; Monaghan, *Goddesses and Heroines*, p. 89) **Kerry:** a county on the west coast of Ireland. **Cove [*sic*]:** Cobh (pronounced "cove"), an Irish port city southeast of Cork. **Shandon's bells:** the carillon of eight bells hung in 1752 in the tower of St. Anne Anglican Church in Cork, Ireland. (*Ireland*, Michelin Guide, p. 67) **asthore machree:** an Irish phrase meaning "(my) treasure, my heart." From *stór* (treasure) and *mo cridhe* (my heart). (Simpson and Weiner, *Oxford English Dictionary*; Maclennan, *Dictionary of the Gaelic Language*, p. 218) **Munster:** one of the four ancient provinces of Ireland, the others being Ulster, Leinster, and Connaught.

## Page 242
*From "Rouge Bouquet" by Joyce Kilmer*
**St. Michael's sword:** an allusion to the archangel Michael, presented in the Book of Daniel as the protector of Israel. In the Book of Revelations (12:7-9), he and other faithful angels cast a dragon (Satan) and his angels out of heaven down to earth. In western Christendom Michael is venerated as the head of the heavenly armies and the patron of soldiers. (*New Catholic Encyclopedia*, s.v. "Michael, archangel") **Patrick, Brigid, Columkill:** the three most famous Irish saints.

## Page 243
**Kathleen ni Houlahan:** a name applied to Ireland personified as a beautiful queen, as was done, for example, by James Mangan, the nineteenth-century Irish romantic poet, in his poem "Kathaleen Ny-Houlahan." (Kraus, *Sean O'Casey*, p. 38; Colum, *Anthology of Irish Verse*, pp. 267–268)

## Page 246
**martyrs of Easter Week:** the fifteen men executed by a British firing squad for their part in an unsuccessful uprising that started in Dublin on Easter Monday 1916. Although the British originally handed down ninety death sentences, all but fifteen were commuted. Of the fifteen men executed, seven had signed the Proclamation of the Irish Republic: Eamonn Ceant, Thomas Clarke, James Connolly, Sean MacDiarmada, Thomas MacDonagh, Padraic Pearse, and Joseph Plunkett. Like Kilmer, the executed MacDonagh, Pearse, and Plunkett were poets. (O'Connor, *The Troubles*, p. 87; Foster, *Modern Ireland*, p. 485)

## Page 261
*From "Joyce Kilmer" by Eleanor Rogers Cox*
**St. Michael-wise:** in the manner of the archangel Michael, venerated in Western Christendom as "St. Michael," the head of the heavenly armies and the patron of soldiers. (*New Catholic Encyclopedia*, s.v. "Michael, archangel") **Eire's lines advancing:** the Irish and Irish-American soldiers in the 165th Infantry. "Eire" is the Irish name for Ireland.

## Page 270
**'Speech on the Sword':** an allusion to an 1846 speech by the Irish nationalist Thomas Francis Meagher in which he refused to forswear for Irishmen the use of physical force in their quest for independence from Britain. In the speech — which earned him the nickname "Meagher of the Sword" — he cited historical examples of how resort to arms had gained political freedom for oppressed peoples.

**Page 276**

*From "When the Sixty-Ninth Comes Back" by Joyce Kilmer*

**The Harp that once through Tara's Halls:** an allusion to a song of the same name by the Irish poet Thomas Moore (1779–1852). (Sears, Minnie, *Song Index*, p. 364) **Potsdam Palace:** Sans-Souci Palace, in Potsdam, Germany, built by King Frederick the Great of Prussia (1740–1786). **Kaiser:** Wilhelm II (1859–1941), the German monarch during World War I. **Border:** the U.S.-Mexican border, where the 69th served from mid July 1916 to mid February 1917 as part of an American force sent to stop incursions by Mexican bandits into the Southwest. **stormy sea:** the Atlantic Ocean. **Marye's Heights, Fredericksburg, Blackburn Ford, Bull Run:** Civil War engagements in which the 69th New York was involved. **Ryan:** possibly Colonel James Ryan or Captain Richard Ryan. Colonel James Ryan was elected to command of the 69th New York State Militia Regiment in 1855. (He was preceded in that command by Colonel Charles S. Roe and was succeeded by Colonel Michael Corcoran.) (Fitzgerald, James, "Sixty-Ninth Regiment," p. 162; "Fighting Sixty-Ninth," *New York World*, March 18, 1877) Captain Richard Ryan was an officer in the 69th New York (165th Infantry) during World War I. He was awarded the Distinguished Service Cross. (Duffy, Francis, *Father Duffy's Story*, Appendix, p. 356) **Roe:** Colonel Charles S. Roe, the first commander of the 69th New York State Militia Regiment after its formation in 1851. (Fitzgerald, James, "Sixty-Ninth Regiment," p. 162) **Corcoran:** Michael Corcoran (1827–1863), a native of County Sligo, Ireland, and colonel of the 69th New York State Militia Regiment. He was captured at Bull Run on July 21, 1861, and remained a Confederate prisoner for thirteen months because he refused to agree never again to take up arms. (Conyngham, *Irish Brigade*, pp. 537, 539) **Colonel Hine:** Charles De Lane Hine (1867–1927), major of U.S. Volunteers in the Spanish-American War and colonel of the 69th New York (165th Infantry) in World War I. (*Who Was Who*)

**Page 284**

*From "The Rainbow's Shepherd" by Father John Kelly*

**Michael's side:** an allusion to the archangel Michael, venerated in Western Christendom as "St. Michael," the head of the heavenly armies and the patron of soldiers. (*New Catholic Encyclopedia*, s.v. "Michael, archangel")

# Citations

## Introduction

1.  Olney, emails, September 12, 2001; December 19, 2001; January 29, 2002.
2.  Ibid., email, September 26, 2001.
3.  Haskell, "New York Guardsman."
4.  Olney, emails, September 17, 2001; September 19, 2001; December 19, 2001. Chivers, "After a War Starts at Home," p. B1.
5.  *New York Times*, December 8, 2001, p. B8.
6.  Flynn, "150th Birthday Commemoration."
7.  Ibid.
8.  Olney, email, December 19, 2001.
9.  Hogan, *Shamrock Battalion*, p. 280.

## Chapter 1
### Michael Corcoran, the 69th New York State Militia, and Corcoran's Irish Legion

1.  Wakin, *Enter the Irish-American*, pp. 120–121.
2.  Coyle, "General Corcoran," p. 109. Foster, *Modern Ireland*, p. 148 n. Lane, "Colonel Corcoran," pp. 13–14.
3.  Lane, "Colonel Corcoran," pp. 4–15.
4.  Ibid., pp. 14–15, 19.
5.  Potter, *To the Golden Door*, p. 557. Lane, "Colonel Corcoran," p. 16. Stallings, *Doughboys*, p. xiv. Fitzgerald, James, "Sixty Ninth Regiment," p. 162. "Fighting Sixty-Ninth," *New York World*, March 18, 1877. Bilby, *Remember Fontenoy!*, p. 3.
6.  Potter, *To the Golden Door*, p. 557. *New York Times*, March 18, 1853, p. 1.
7.  Lane, "Colonel Corcoran," pp. 16, 19–21. *New York Herald*, October 18, 1860, p. 4. Coyle, "General Corcoran," p. 110.
8.  Lane, "Colonel Corcoran," p. 21. Garcia, "'Fighting' Sixty-Ninth," p. 36.
9.  Lane, "Colonel Corcoran," p. 21. Hall, *History of Auburn*, p. 145. Moore, *Rebellion Record*, vol. 2, "Poetry and Incidents," p. 85.
10. Lane, "Colonel Corcoran," p. 21. Conyngham, *Irish Brigade*, p. 20. O'Rourke, *Irish and America*, p. 77. Coyle, "General Corcoran," p. 111. D'Arcy, William, *Fenian Movement*, pp. 11, 37.
11. Moore, *Rebellion Record*, vol. 5, "Poetry and Incidents," p. 63.
12. Garcia, "'Fighting' Sixty-Ninth," pp. 37–38. Conyngham, *Irish Brigade*, pp. 22-23. Corcoran, *Captivity*, pp. 365–366. Jones, *Irish Brigade*, p. 72.
13. Garcia, "'Fighting' Sixty-Ninth," p. 40. Bayor and Meagher, *New York Irish*, p. 199. Maguire, *Irish in America*, p. 562.
14. Lane, "Colonel Corcoran," p. 22. Garcia, "'Fighting' Sixty-Ninth," pp. 41, 43. Bilby, *Remember Fontenoy!*, p. 7.
15. *New York Times*, June 5, 1861, p. 2.
16. Hanchett, *Irish*, p. 34. Halpine, *Life and Adventures*, p. 159.
17. Savage, *Faith and Fancy*, pp. 115–116. Cavanagh, *Memoirs of General Meagher*, p. 383. Conyngham, *Irish Brigade*, p. 2. Johnson and Malone, *Dictionary of*

*American Biography*, s.v. "Savage, John."

18. Savage, *Faith and Fancy*, pp. 9–11.
19. Ibid., pp. 116–117.
20. Moore, *Civil War in Song and Story*, pp. 217–218.
21. Garcia, "'Fighting' Sixty-Ninth," pp. 44–45. Jones, *Irish Brigade*, p. 75.
22. Jones, *Irish Brigade*, pp. 78–81. Meagher, *Last Days of the Sixty Ninth*, p. 5.
23. Jones, *Irish Brigade*, pp. 81–82. Garcia, "'Fighting' Sixty-Ninth," pp. 47–48.
24. Meagher, *Last Days of the Sixty Ninth*, p. 9.
25. Ibid., p. 12.
26. Coyle, "General Corcoran," p. 112. Villard, *Memoirs*, vol. 1, pp. 183–184. Garcia, "'Fighting' Sixty-Ninth," p. 49. Athearn, *Thomas Meagher*, p. 98.
27. Jones, *Irish Brigade*, pp. 84-86. Wakin, *Enter the Irish-American*, pp. 122–123. Garcia, "'Fighting' Sixty-Ninth," p. 50. Conyngham, *Irish Brigade*, p. 36.
28. Cavanagh, *Memoirs of General Meagher*, pp. 397–398. Coyle, "General Corcoran," p. 113. Garcia, "'Fighting' Sixty-Ninth," p. 52. Jones, *Irish Brigade*, p. 88. Athearn, *Thomas Meagher*, p. 98. Daly, *Diary of a Union Lady*, pp. 41, 45.
29. Wright, *Irish Emigrant Ballads*, p. 462.
30. Moore, *Rebellion Record*, vol. 3, "Rumors and Incidents," p. 11. Jones, *Irish Brigade*, p. 89. O'Rourke, *Irish and America*, pp. 78–79. Cavanagh, *Memoirs of General Meagher*, p. 400 n.
31. Conyngham, *Irish Brigade*, pp. 37, 45–46.
32. Photograph, James Haggerty grave, Calvary Cemetery, Woodside, Queens, Long Island, New York. Location: Section 1W, Avenue A, Grave 4/11.
33. Coyle, "General Corcoran," p. 13. Corcoran, *Captivity*, p. 22. The pagination in *The Captivity of General Corcoran* is erratic. The text begins on page 21; page 30 is followed by page 39; page 52, by 61; and page 74, by 85.
34. Corcoran, *Captivity*, pp. 27–30.
35. Ely, *Journal*, pp. 221–222.
36. *New York Herald*, August 28, 1861, p. 1.
37. Corcoran, *Captivity*, pp. 39-43.
38. Ibid., p. 62. Ely, *Journal*, pp. 222–224.
39. Corcoran, *Captivity*, p. 61.
40. Ibid., pp. 50-52, 89. Coyle, "General Corcoran," pp. 116–118.
41. Lane, "Colonel Corcoran," pp. 24–26. Corcoran, *Captivity*, pp. 97–98, 100.
42. *New York Herald*, August 19, 1862, p. 5.
43. Ibid.
44. Ibid., August 22, 1862, p. 1.
45. *New York Times*, August 23, 1862, p. 1.
46. Ibid. Daly, *Diary of a Union Lady*, pp. 167, 180.
47. *New York Times*, August 23, 1862, p. 1. Bayor and Meagher, *New York Irish*, p. 223.
48. Wright, *Irish Emigrant Ballads*, p. 444.
49. *New York Times*, August 23, 1862, pp. 1, 4.
50. Lane, "Colonel Corcoran," p. 28. Garcia, "'Fighting' Sixty-Ninth," pp. 54–55. Daly, *Diary of a Union Lady*, p. 187.
51. Boyle, *Party of Mad Fellows*, p. 172. Bayor and Meagher, *New York Irish*, p. 200. Coyle, "General Corcoran," p. 119. Burton, *Melting Pot Soldiers*, p. 116. Fitzgerald, James, "Sixty Ninth Regiment," p. 168.

52. Burton, *Melting Pot Soldiers*, pp. 116–118.
53. Bayor and Meagher, *New York Irish*, p. 200. Boyle, *Party of Mad Fellows*, pp. 173–174. Fitzgerald, James, "Sixty Ninth Regiment," p. 168. Coyle, "General Corcoran," pp. 119-120.
54. O'Beirne, "Christmas in the Union's Irish Brigades." Lonn, *Foreigners in the Union Army and Navy*, p. 312.
55. Coyle, "General Corcoran," pp. 120–121. Daly, *Diary of a Union Lady*, p. 219. Conyngham, *Irish Brigade*, p. 464.
56. Lane, "Colonel Corcoran," p. 30. *New York Times*, April 20, 1863, p. 1.
57. Fox, *Regimental Losses*, p. 241. O'Beirne, "Recalling the 155th New York."
58. Lane, "Colonel Corcoran," pp. 31–32. Coyle, "General Corcoran," p. 121.
59. *New York Times*, December 28, 1863, p. 8. Garcia, "'Fighting' Sixty-Ninth," p. 55. Coyle, "General Corcoran," p. 122.
60. *New York Times*, January 23, 1864, p. 8.
61. Fox, *Regimental Losses*, pp. 241, 447. Boyle, *Party of Mad Fellows*, pp. 346–347, 381. *War of the Rebellion*, 1st ser., vol. 36, pt. 1, p. 338. Walker, *Second Army Corps*, p. 485.
62. Fox, *Regimental Losses*, pp. 241, 448. *Congressional Medal*, pp. 823, 862. Hewett, *Roster of Union Soldiers*, vol. 9, p. 75.
63. Boyle, *Party of Mad Fellows*, pp. 357–358. Fitzgerald, James, "Sixty Ninth Regiment," p. 170. Fox, *Regimental Losses*, p. 239. O'Beirne, "Recalling the 155th New York." *Congressional Medal*, p. 764.
64. Walker, *Second Army Corps*, p. 513. Fitzgerald, James, "Sixty Ninth Regiment," pp. 170–171.
65. Boyle, *Party of Mad Fellows*, p. 407.
66. *Congressional Medal of Honor*, p. 728. O'Beirne, "Recalling the 155th New York."
67. Conyngham, *Irish Brigade*, pp. 479–481.
68. Cavanagh, *Memoirs of General Meagher*, pp. 407–408.
69. Boyle, *Party of Mad Fellows*, pp. 405–406.
70. Ibid., p. 403.
71. Garcia, "'Fighting' Sixty-Ninth," pp. 54–55. Fox, *Regimental Losses*, p. 239. Boyle, *Party of Mad Fellows*, 399. Photograph, Matthew Murphy grave, Calvary Cemetery, Woodside, Queens, Long Island, New York.
72. Hanchett, *Irish*, p. 176. Halpine, *Poetical Works*, p. 334. Crowley, *Irish Poets and Novelists*, pp. 191–195.
73. *Journal of the American Irish Historical Society* 13 (1914): 108.
74. Photograph, Michael Corcoran grave, Calvary Cemetery, Woodside, Queens, Long Island, New York. Location: Section 4, Range 5, Plot O, Graves 13/16.

## Chapter 2
### Thomas Meagher, the 69th New York Volunteers, and the Irish Brigade

1. *New York Times*, July 28, 1861, p. 1.
2. Ibid.
3. Jones, *Irish Brigade*, p. 93. Athearn, *Thomas Meagher*, pp. 93, 96, 99–100, 106. Conyngham, *Irish Brigade*, pp. 324–325, 547–548.
4. Lonergan, "General Meagher," p. 111–112. Athearn, *Thomas Meagher*, pp. 4–5. Cavanagh, *Memoirs of General Meagher*, p. 65.

5. Cavanagh, *Memoirs of General Meagher*, pp. 71–72.
6. Johnson and Malone, *Dictionary of American Biography*, s.v. "Meagher, Thomas Francis." Maguire, *Irish in America*, p. 550.
7. Athearn, *Thomas Meagher*, p. 92. "America Singing: Nineteenth-Century Song Sheets."
8. *New York Herald*, August 30, 1861, p. 1.
9. "America Singing: Nineteenth-Century Song Sheets."
10. *New York Times*, August 30, 1861, p. 5.
11. Ibid.
12. Athearn, *Thomas Meagher*, p. 102. Lyons, *Brigadier-General Meagher*, pp. 92–94, 102–104, 108–110, 113–115, 118.
13. Daly, *Diary of a Union Lady*, pp. 64, 68, 75. Conyngham, *Irish Brigade*, pp. 51–52.
14. Athearn, *Thomas Meagher*, pp. 106–107. Jones, *Irish Brigade*, pp. 102–103. Maguire, *Irish in America*, p. 549.
15. Jones, *Irish Brigade*, p. 103. *New York Times*, November 19, 1861, p. 8.
16. *New York Times*, November 19, 1861, p. 8.
17. Ibid. Corby, *Chaplain Life*, pp. 295–296.
18. Kelly, "Green Flags," p. 195.
19. Squire, *Celtic Myth*, p. 54. Barker, *Symbols of Sovereignty*, pp. 108–109. O'Brogain, *Irish Harp Emblem*, pp. 17, 22. Kelly, "Green Flags," p. 197. Cavanagh, *Memoirs of General Meagher*, p. 426.
20. Kelly, "Green Flags," p. 194. Conyngham, *Irish Brigade*, pp. 547, 558, 566, 597. Athearn, *Thomas Meagher*, pp. 108–109.
21. Conyngham, *Irish Brigade*, p. 543. Murphy, *Kelly's Heroes*, p. 5.
22. Jones, *Irish Brigade*, p. 110. Johnson and Malone, *Dictionary of American Biography*, s.v. "Corby, William."
23. Corby, *Chaplain Life*, pp. 271–272.
24. Ibid., pp. 291–293.
25. *New York Times*, November 30, 1861, p. 8.
26. Conyngham, *Irish Brigade*, p. 72. Conyngham, *Soldiers of the Cross*, Chapter 12, n.p.
27. Conyngham, *Irish Brigade*, pp. 78, 81–83, 569. Corby, *Chaplain Life*, p. 411.
28. Bilby and O'Neill, "My Sons Were Faithful," p. 114, n. 54. Corby, *Chaplain Life*, pp. 300–301.
29. Cavanagh, *Memoirs of General Meagher*, pp. 433-439.
30. Conyngham, *Irish Brigade*, p. 555. Cavanagh, *Memoirs of General Meagher*, Appendix, pp. 15–16. Jones, *Irish Brigade*, pp. 106–107, 113. Hennessy, *Wild Geese*, p. 114.
31. Lonn, *Foreigners in the Union Army and Navy*, p. 257, n. 22. Conyngham, *Irish Brigade*, pp. 101–102, 564.
32. Jones, *Irish Brigade*, pp. 114, 116–117.
33. Ibid., p. 118. Conyngham, *Irish Brigade*, pp. 146–149. Mulholland, "Irish Brigade," p. 358.
34. Bilby and O'Neill, "My Sons Were Faithful," p. 4. Conyngham, *Irish Brigade*, p. 154. Mulholland, "Irish Brigade," p. 359. Jones, *Irish Brigade*, pp. 120–121. Athearn, *Thomas Meagher*, p. 111.
35. New York Monuments Commission, *Final Report*, vol. 2, p. 495.
36. Bilby, *Remember Fontenoy!*, p. 40.

37. Townsend, *Campaign of a Non-Combatant*, p. 130.
38. Ibid., pp. 129–130.
39. Moore, *Civil War in Song and Story*, p. 412.
40. Conyngham, *Irish Brigade*, pp. 164–165. New York Monuments Commission, *Final Report*, vol. 2, p. 495.
41. Jones, *Irish Brigade*, p. 121. Osborne, *Twenty-Ninth Massachusetts*, pp. 142, 146.
42. Athearn, *Thomas Meagher*, pp. 111–112. Conyngham, *Irish Brigade*, p. 186.
43. Jones, *Irish Brigade*, pp. 122–123. Conyngham, *Irish Brigade*, p. 198. Mulholland, *Military Order*, p. 111.
44. Athearn, *Thomas Meagher*, pp. 112–113. New York Monuments Commission, *Final Report*, vol. 2, p. 498.
45. Conyngham, *Irish Brigade*, pp. 207, 561. Mulholland, "Irish Brigade," p. 368.
46. Athearn, *Thomas Meagher*, pp. 112–114. Bilby and O'Neill, "*My Sons Were Faithful*," p. 4. Jones, *Irish Brigade*, p. 124. O'Brien, "Sprig of Green," p. 73. Cavanagh, *Memoirs of General Meagher*, p. 451. Corby, *Chaplain Life*, p. 306.
47. Mulholland, *Military Order*, pp. 115–116. Bilby, *Remember Fontenoy!*, pp. 45–47. *Congressional Medal*, p. 884. New York Monuments Commission, *Final Report*, vol. 2, p. 511.
48. Conyngham, *Irish Brigade*, pp. 219–220, 237–238. *Congressional Medal*, p. 870.
49. Osborne, *Twenty-Ninth Massachusetts*, p. 170. Headley, *Massachusetts in the Rebellion*, pp. 326–327.
50. Jones, *Irish Brigade*, pp. 125-127. Bilby, *Remember Fontenoy!*, p. 49.
51. Conyngham, *Irish Brigade*, pp. 235–236.
52. *Rhyme With Reason*, p. 84.
53. Corby, *Chaplain Life*, pp. 302–303.
54. Conyngham, *Irish Brigade*, pp. 217, 244–245, 247–248, 251–253. Boyle, *Party of Mad Fellows*, pp. 166–167. Jones, *Irish Brigade*, p. 134. Lane, "Colonel Corcoran," p. 28. Garcia, "'Fighting' Sixty-Ninth," pp. 54–55.
55. Jones, *Irish Brigade*, pp. 135–137.
56. Conyngham, *Irish Brigade*, pp. 293–294.
57. Walker, *Second Army Corps*, pp. 135–136.
58. Jones, *Irish Brigade*, pp. 137–141. Wakin, *Enter the Irish-American*, p. 125. Corby, *Chaplain Life*, pp. 112–113.
59. Jones, *Irish Brigade*, p. 141. Bilby and O'Neill, "*My Sons Were Faithful*," p. 18. O'Brien, "Sprig of Green," p. 75.
60. Bilby and O'Neill, "*My Sons Were Faithful*," p. 19. Bailey, Ronald, *Bloodiest Day*, pp. 99-100. Conyngham, *Irish Brigade*, pp. 305–306, 548.
61. Boyle, *Party of Mad Fellows*, pp. 189–190. Cavanagh, *Memoirs of General Meagher*, p. 462. Wakin, *Enter the Irish-American*, p. 126. O'Brien, "Sprig of Green," p. 76.
62. O'Brien, "Sprig of Green," p. 76. Bilby and O'Neill, "*My Sons Were Faithful*," pp. 25, 28. Jones, *Irish Brigade*, p. 142.
63. Bilby and O'Neill, "*My Sons Were Faithful*," p. 29. Boyle, *Party of Mad Fellows*, pp. 191–192.
64. Bilby, *Remember Fontenoy!*, pp. 57, 244 (n. 16). Conyngham, *Irish Brigade*, p. 560.
65. Jones, *Irish Brigade*, p. 142. Boyle, *Party of Mad Fellows*, p. 193. Bilby, *Remember Fontenoy!*, p. 60.

66. Mulholland, "Irish Brigade," p. 373. Bilby and O'Neill, *"My Sons Were Faithful,"* p. 58.

67. Bilby and O'Neill, *"My Sons Were Faithful,"* pp. 32, 35, 45. Cavanagh, *Memoirs of General Meagher*, p. 462, and Appendix, pp. 18–19.

68. Burton, *Melting Pot Soldiers*, p. 123. Andrews, *North Reports the Civil War*, p. 284. Sears, Stephen, *Landscape Turned Red*, p. 244.

69. Cavanagh, *Memoirs of General Meagher*, Appendix, pp. 16–17.

70. *The Tidings* (Los Angeles), November 7, 1997, p. 7.

71. Photograph, Irish Brigade Monument, Antietam National Battlefield, Sharpsburg, Maryland.

72. Jones, *Irish Brigade*, pp. 143–144. Athearn, *Thomas Meagher*, p. 118. Corby, *Chaplain Life*, p. 118.

73. Jones, *Irish Brigade*, p. 144. Kohl, Introduction, *116th Pennsylvania*, pp. ix–x, xii. Conyngham, *Irish Brigade*, p. 563.

74. Mulholland, *116th Pennsylvania*, pp. 12–13. McCarter, *My Life in the Irish Brigade*, p. 32.

75. McCarter, *My Life in the Irish Brigade*, pp. 15–17.

76. Corby, *Chaplain Life*, p. 29. McCarter, *My Life in the Irish Brigade*, pp. 70–71.

77. Jones, *Irish Brigade*, p. 145. Galwey, *Valiant Hours*, pp. 33–34. Athearn, *Thomas Meagher*, p. 119.

78. Jones, *Irish Brigade*, pp. 147–148. Conyngham, *Irish Brigade*, p. 327.

79. Jones, *Irish Brigade*, p. 162. Galwey, *Valiant Hours*, pp. 74–75.

80. Cavanagh, *Memoirs of General Meagher*, Appendix, pp. 20–21.

81. Pohanka, *James McKay Rorty*, pp. 2, 4–8.

82. Ibid., pp. 8, 16–17, 20.

83. Jones, *Irish Brigade*, p. 148. Boyle, *Party of Mad Fellows*, pp. 206–207.

84. Bilby, *Remember Fontenoy!*, p. 110. Delaney and Tobin, *Dictionary of Catholic Biography*, p. 191. O'Hanlon, "Tribute to a Fallen Irish Hero," p. 22. Spink, "Colonel Richard Byrnes," pp. 119–121.

85. Spink, "Colonel Richard Byrnes," pp. 128, 130, 133–134.

86. McCarter, *My Life in the Irish Brigade*, p. 134.

87. Conyngham, *Irish Brigade*, pp. 330–333, 335–336. Kelly, "Green Flags," p. 200.

88. Jones, *Irish Brigade*, p. 150. McCarter, *My Life in the Irish Brigade*, pp. 43, 249 (n. 5).

89. Walker, *Second Army Corps*, pp. 152–153.

90. Jones, *Irish Brigade*, pp. 151–153. Mulholland, *116th Pennsylvania*, pp. 36, 44. Nugent, "Sixty-Ninth at Fredericksburg," pp. 195–196. O'Brien, "Sprig of Green," p. 62.

91. McCarter, *My Life in the Irish Brigade*, p. 226.

92. Jones, *Irish Brigade*, pp. 153–154. Nugent, "Sixty-Ninth at Fredericksburg," pp. 196–198. O'Brien, "Sprig of Green," pp. 65, 68. Mulholland, *116th Pennsylvania*, p. 57. Galwey, *Valiant Hours*, p. 62.

93. Mulholland, *116th Pennsylvania*, pp. 49–50. McCarter, *My Life in the Irish Brigade*, p. 226.

94. McCarter, *My Life in the Irish Brigade*, pp. 178–180, 182–183. *Congressional Medal*, p. 763.

95. Conyngham, *Irish Brigade*, pp. 343, 346, 348. Kelly, "Green Flags," p. 203.

96. New York Monuments Commission, *Final Report*, vol. 2, p. 489. Mulholland,

"Irish Brigade," pp. 377–378. Woodruff, "Irish Soldier in the Civil War," p. 157. Maguire, *Irish in America*, pp. 578–579.

97. Nugent, "Sixty-Ninth at Fredericksburg," pp. 198–199. Walker, *Second Army Corps*, p. 192. O'Brien, "Sprig of Green," p. 69.

98. New York Monuments Commission, *Final Report*, vol. 2, p. 514. O'Brien, "Sprig of Green," p. 69. Nugent, "Sixty-Ninth at Fredericksburg," p. 199.

99. Conyngham, *Irish Brigade*, pp. 344–345, 350. O'Brien, "Sprig of Green," p. 69.

100. Spink, "Colonel Richard Byrnes," pp. 136, 145–146.

101. Mulholland, *116th Pennsylvania*, pp. 58–59.

102. Donovan, "Battle of Fredericksburg."

103. Galwey, *Valiant Hours*, p. 62. Athearn, *Thomas Meagher*, pp. 120–121. Bagenal, *American Irish*, p. 139. Cavanagh, *Memoirs of General Meagher*, pp. 470–471.

104. Moore, *Rebellion Record*, vol. 6, "Documents," pp. 81–82. Villard, *Memoirs*, vol. 1, p. 371.

105. Mulholland, *116th Pennsylvania*, pp. 61–62.

106. Roche, *John Boyle O'Reilly*, pp. 466–469.

107. Cavanagh, *Memoirs of General Meagher*, pp. 471–473. Mulholland, *116th Pennsylvania*, p. 61. Jones, *Irish Brigade*, pp. 158–159.

108. Kelly, "Green Flags," pp. 206–207.

109. Jones, *Irish Brigade*, p. 161.

110. Conyngham, *Irish Brigade*, p. 347. Mulholland, *116th Pennsylvania*, p. 72.

111. Cavanagh, *Memoirs of General Meagher*, pp. 473–474. *New York Times*, January 17, 1863, pp. 2–3.

112. Savage, *Faith and Fancy*, pp. 31–32

113. Cavanagh, *Memoirs of General Meagher*, pp. 474, 476, and Appendix, p. 34.

114. Ibid., p. 475.

115. Corby, *Chaplain Life*, pp. 136–137.

116. Conyngham, *Irish Brigade*, pp. 366–372. Boyle, *Party of Mad Fellows*, p. 234.

117. Corby, *Chaplain Life*, pp. 140–141. Boyle, *Party of Mad Fellows*, 237. Conyngham, *Irish Brigade*, pp. 373–374, 376, 379–380. Galwey, *Valiant Hours*, pp. 78–79.

118. Reynolds, *Poetical Address*.

119. Conyngham, *Irish Brigade*, pp. 380–382, 562.

120. Ibid., pp. 386–387.

121. McCarter, *My Life in the Irish Brigade*, pp. 232–233.

122. Jones, *Irish Brigade*, pp. 169–175. Athearn, *Thomas Meagher*, p. 125. Corby, *Chaplain Life*, p. 168.

123. Mulholland, *Military Order*, pp. 219–220.

124. Jones, *Irish Brigade*, p. 177. Conyngham, *Irish Brigade*, pp. 406–408, 412–414.

125. Murphy, *Kelly's Heroes*, p. 15. Boyle, *Party of Mad Fellows*, p. 77.

126. Jones, *Irish Brigade*, pp. 185–191. Bache, *General George Meade*, p. 2.

127. Jones, *Irish Brigade*, pp. 190–191. O'Brien, "Irish Brigade," p. 96.

128. Murphy, *Kelly's Heroes*, p. 18. Jones, *Irish Brigade*, pp. 192, 194. O'Brien, "Irish Brigade," pp. 95, 102.

129. O'Brien, "Irish Brigade," pp. 102–103.

130. Mulholland, *116th Pennsylvania*, pp. 407–408.

131. Corby, *Chaplain Life*, p. 184. Stewart, *One Hundred and Fortieth Regiment*, p. 101.

132. Jones, *Irish Brigade*, pp. 194–195. O'Brien, "Sprig of Green," pp. 80–81.
133. O'Brien, "Sprig of Green," p. 81. Mulholland, "Irish Brigade," p. 128. O'Brien, "Irish Brigade," pp. 109, 111.
134. O'Brien, "Irish Brigade," p. 110. Jones, *Irish Brigade*, p. 198. Pohanka, *James McKay Rorty*, pp. 4–5, 8, 15–16, 24.
135. Pohanka, *James McKay Rorty*, pp. 18–19.
136. Ibid., inside front cover.
137. Murphy, *Kelly's Heroes*, pp. 60–61.
138. Photograph, Irish Brigade Monument, Gettysburg National Military Park, Gettysburg, Pennsylvania. Pohanka, *James McKay Rorty*, pp. 5, 8, 15, 24. Murphy, *Kelly's Heroes*, p. 61.
139. Murphy, *Kelly's Heroes*, p. 30. New York Monuments Commission, *Final Report*, vol. 2, p. 482.
140. Corby, *Chaplain Life*, pp. 195–198.
141. Ibid., pp. 199–200.
142. Murphy, *Kelly's Heroes*, pp. 28, 30, 63.
143. Photograph, Army of the Potomac Marker, Gettysburg National Military Park, Gettysburg, Pennsylvania.
144. Murphy, *Kelly's Heroes*, pp. 56, 58–59. Corby, *Chaplain Life*, pp. 401–402.
145. Corby, *Chaplain Life*, pp. 402–404.
146. Mulholland, *116th Pennsylvania*, pp. 120–121.
147. Jones, *Irish Brigade*, pp. 203–205.
148. Ibid.
149. Jones, *Irish Brigade*, p. 205. *New York Times*, July 15, 1863, p. 1; July 16, 1863, p. 1; July 29, 1863, p. 2.
150. *New York Times*, July 18, 1863, p. 1. Jones, *Irish Brigade*, p. 206. Wakin, *Enter the Irish-American*, p. 130.
151. Garraty and Carnes, *American National Biography*, s.v. "Halpin or Halpine, Charles Graham." Stephen and Lee, *Dictionary of National Biography*, s.v. "Halpin or Halpine, Charles Graham."
152. Halpine, *Life and Adventures*, pp. 154–160.
153. Jones, *Irish Brigade*, pp. 211–212. O'Brien, "Sprig of Green," p. 82. Conyngham, *Irish Brigade*, p. 596. *Congressional Medal*, p. 896.
154. Jones, *Irish Brigade*, p. 215. *New York Times*, December 28, 1863, p. 8. Daly, *Diary of a Union Lady*, p. 271.
155. Jones, *Irish Brigade*, pp. 215–216. *New York Times*, January 17, 1864, p. 8. Conyngham, *Irish Brigade*, p. 436.
156. Conyngham, *Irish Brigade*, pp. 430, 432–434.
157. O'Brien, "Sprig of Green," p. 82, 82 n. Conyngham, *Irish Brigade*, pp. 442–444.
158. O'Brien, "Sprig of Green," pp. 82–83. Maull, *Brigadier General Thomas Smyth*, pp. 6–11.
159. Sifakis, *Who Was Who*, p. 609. Maull, *Brigadier General Thomas Smyth*, p. 15.
160. Boyle, *Party of Mad Fellows*, pp. 314–315. Sifakis, *Who Was Who*, p. 609. Conyngham, *Irish Brigade*, pp. 441–442, 542.
161. Hanchett, *Irish*, p. 103. Lounsburg, *Yale Book of American Verse*, pp. 389–390.
162. O'Brien, "Sprig of Green," pp. 83–84. Jones, *Irish Brigade*, pp. 223, 225, 227–228. Mulholland, *116th Pennsylvania*, pp. 186–187. Bilby, *Remember Fontenoy!*, p. 102. Conyngham, *Irish Brigade*, p. 561.

163. Jones, *Irish Brigade*, p. 226. O'Brien, "Sprig of Green," p. 84. Corby, *Chaplain Life*, p. 232.
164. Mulholland, *116th Pennsylvania*, pp. 194–195.
165. Jones, *Irish Brigade*, pp. 227, 230. O'Brien, "Sprig of Green," pp. 84, 84 n, 85. New York Monuments Commission, *Final Report*, vol. 2, p. 504. Maull, *Brigadier General Thomas Smyth*, p. 18.
166. O'Brien, "Sprig of Green," p. 86. Mulholland, *116th Pennsylvania*, p. 222. Conyngham, *Irish Brigade*, pp. 451–453.
167. Spink, "Colonel Richard Byrnes," p. 164. Corby, *Chaplain Life*, pp. 237–238.
168. Conyngham, *Irish Brigade*, p. 542. Maull, *Brigadier General Thomas Smyth*, pp. 17, 19–20. The version of the poem found in Maull is a bit different from and one stanza longer than that found in New York Monuments Commission, *Final Report*, vol. 2, pp. 505–506.
169. O'Brien, "Sprig of Green," pp. 86, 88. Jones, *Irish Brigade*, p. 231.
170. Jones, *Irish Brigade*, p. 231. Spink, "Colonel Richard Byrnes," pp. 171, 173. Corby, *Chaplain Life*, p. 239. Conyngham, *Irish Brigade*, p. 586. Mulholland, *116th Pennsylvania*, p. 256.
171. Photograph, Richard Byrnes grave, Calvary Cemetery, Woodside, Queens, Long Island, New York. Location: Section 3, Range 23, Plot W, Grave 6.
172. O'Brien, "Sprig of Green," pp. 88, 88 (n. 86), 89. Murphy, *Kelly's Heroes*, p. 49.
173. O'Brien, "Sprig of Green," pp. 89–90. Conyngham, *Irish Brigade*, pp. 548, 553, 565, 612. Jones, *Irish Brigade*, p. 234.
174. O'Brien, "Sprig of Green," p. 89. Murphy, *Kelly's Heroes*, p. 51. Conyngham, *Irish Brigade*, p. 558.
175. Photograph, Patrick Kelly grave, Calvary Cemetery, Woodside, Queens, Long Island, New York. Location: Section 4, Range 5, Plot W, Grave 14/16.
176. Mulholland, *116th Pennsylvania*, pp. 270–271.
177. New York Monuments Commission, *Final Report*, vol. 2, pp. 504–505.
178. Conyngham, *Irish Brigade*, pp. 492, 555.
179. Mulholland, *116th Pennsylvania*, p. 279. O'Brien, "Sprig of Green," p. 90.
180. Conyngham, *Irish Brigade*, pp. 465–466, 471–473.
181. Jones, *Irish Brigade*, p. 235. O'Brien, "Sprig of Green," p. 91. Conyngham, *Irish Brigade*, pp. 477–478. Bilby, *Remember Fontenoy!*, p. 117.
182. Corby, *Chaplain Life*, pp. 266–267.
183. Conyngham, *Irish Brigade*, p. 483. Corby, *Chaplain Life*, p. 268.
184. Conyngham, *Irish Brigade*, pp. 484–486.
185. Ibid., pp. 486–488.
186. Boyle, *Party of Mad Fellows*, p. 377. Maull, *Brigadier General Thomas Smyth*, 22–23. The version of the poem found in Maull is a bit different from that in Cavanagh, *Memoirs of General Meagher*, Appendix, p. 22.
187. Maull, *Brigadier General Thomas Smyth*, p. 37.
188. Conyngham, *Irish Brigade*, pp. 495–496, 502–503, 559.
189. Conyngham, *Irish Brigade*, 503–504. O'Brien, "Sprig of Green," p. 92. Bilby, *Remember Fontenoy!*, p. 120–121.
190. O'Brien, "Sprig of Green," pp. 92–93. Conyngham, "Soldiers of the Cross," Chapter 12, n.p.
191. Conyngham, *Irish Brigade*, p. 510. O'Brien, "Sprig of Green," pp. 92–93.
192. Conyngham, *Irish Brigade*, pp. 514–515.
193. Jones, *Irish Brigade*, 245. Conyngham, *Irish Brigade*, pp. 516–517.

194. O'Brien, "Sprig of Green," pp. 93–94. Conyngham, *Irish Brigade*, pp. 522–523. Jones, *Irish Brigade*, p. 248.

195. Maull, *Brigadier General Thomas Smyth*, pp. 42–45. Boyle, *Party of Mad Fellows*, p. 396.

196. Conyngham, *Irish Brigade*, pp. 524, 542, 549. Maull, *Brigadier General Thomas Smyth*, pp. 48–49.

197. Jones, *Irish Brigade*, pp. 249–250. Bilby, *Remember Fontenoy!*, p. 125.

198. Bilby, *Remember Fontenoy!*, pp. 125, 127.

199. Clarke, *Fighting Race*, pp. 26–28.

200. Nugent, "Sixty-Ninth at Fredericksburg," pp. 199–200. Fox, *Regimental Losses*, p. 118. Dyer, *Compendium*, pp. 1259, 1428, 1431, 1440, 1612. Bilby, *Remember Fontenoy!*, p. ix. New York Monuments Commission, *Final Report*, vol. 2, p. 490. Boyle, *Party of Mad Fellows*, pp. 392, 403.

201. Boyle, *Party of Mad Fellows*, p. 387. Moore, *Civil War in Song and Story*, p. 391.

202. Athearn, *Thomas Meagher*, pp. 127–128, 130–132, 142.

203. Ibid., pp. 133, 135–137.

204. Ibid., p. 134.

205. Ibid., pp. 145–146.

206. Ibid., pp. 147–148, 150–151, 153, 155.

207. Ibid., pp. 157–158, 164–165. Lyons, *Brigadier-General Meagher*, pp. 353–356.

208. Cavanagh, *Memoirs of General Meagher*, Appendix, pp. 11–12.

209. Ibid., Appendix, pp. 3–11.

210. Ibid., Appendix, pp. 13–15.

211. Federal Writers' Project, *Montana*, pp. 170, 270–271. Van West, "Montana's Monuments," p. 15. *Helena (Mont.) Independent*, July 7, 1905, p. 1

212. *Helena (Mont.) Independent*, July 7, 1905, p. 1. *Montana Daily Record*, July 4, 1905, p. 8. Hewett, *Roster of Union Soldiers*, vol. 7, p. 288.

213. *Helena (Mont.) Independent*, July 7, 1905, pp. 1, 5. *National Cyclopaedia of American Biography*, vol. 13, p. 324, s.v. "Finerty, John."

214. Photographs, Thomas Meagher Equestrian Statue, State Capitol grounds, Helena, Montana.

215. "Presentation of Meagher's Sword," pp. 320–321, 323–324.

216. Ibid., pp. 324–326.

217. Ibid., pp. 326–327.

218. Ibid., p. 328. O'Donnell, Charles, *Collected Poems*, pp. 71–74.

219. "Presentation of Meagher's Sword," pp. 326–327.

### Chapter 3
### The 69th New York National Guard Regiment in the Spanish-American War

1. Fitzgerald, James, "Sixty Ninth Regiment," pp. 172–173.

2. *New York Times*, April 4, 1898, p. 10; April 5, 1898, p. 11.

3. Fitzgerald, James, "Sixty-Ninth Regiment," pp. 173–175.

4. *New York Times*, May 20, 1898, p. 4.

5. Ibid. Fitzgerald, James, "Sixty-Ninth Regiment," p. 173.

6. Fitzgerald, James, "Sixty-Ninth Regiment," p. 174. *New York Times*, May 25, 1898, p. 3. *New York Herald*, May 25, 1898, p. 6.

7. *New York Times*, May 25, 1898, p. 3. *New York Herald*, May 25, 1898, p. 6.

8. *New York Herald*, May 25, 1898, p. 6.

9.  *New York Times*, May 25, 1898, p. 3; May 27, 1898, p. 2.
10. Fitzgerald, James, "Sixty-Ninth Regiment," p. 175. *New York Times*, June 16, 1898, p. 4.
11. *New York in the Spanish-American War*, vol. 3, p. 3. *New York Times*, August 30, 1898, p. 3.
12. *New York Times*, October 10, 1898, p. 3. Fitzgerald, James, "Sixty-Ninth Regiment," pp. 175–176.
13. *New York Times*, October 10, 1898, p. 3
14. Ibid., October 26, 1898, p. 7.
15. Ibid., December 18, 1898, p. 3.
16. Ibid.
17. Fitzgerald, James, "Sixty-Ninth Regiment," p. 176. *New York Times*, January 11, 1899, p. 3; February 1, 1899, p. 1.
18. *New York Times*, February 1, 1899, p. 1.
19. Ibid.
20. Ibid.
21. Ibid., October 22, 1900, p. 3.
22. Fitzgerald, James, "Sixty-Ninth Regiment," p. 176. *New York Times*, April 24,1904, p. 1.
23. *New York Times*, April 24, 1904, p. 2.
24. Fitzgerald, James, "Sixty-Ninth Regiment," pp. 176–177.
25. *New York Times*, October 14, 1906, p. 24.

**Chapter 4**
**The 69th New York National Guard Regiment in the 1916 Punitive Expedition**

1.  Bailey, Thomas, *Diplomatic History*, pp. 555–560.
2.  Ibid., pp. 560–561. Leckie, *Wars of America*, vol. 2, p. 102. "Fighting 69th in the Mexican Border Campaign."
3.  "Fighting 69th in the Mexican Border Campaign." *New York Times*, July 5, 1916, p. 10.
4.  *New York Times*, July 7, 1916, p. 5; July 9, 1916, p. 5.
5.  Ibid., July 9, 1916, p. 15; July 12, 1916, p. 1.
6.  Ibid., July 13, 1916, p. 1; July 17, 1916, p. 3.
7.  Ibid., July 14, 1916, p. 4; July 15, 1916, p. 3; July 17, 1916, p. 1.
8.  Ibid., July 13, 1916, p. 1.
9.  Ibid.
10. Ibid., July 13, 1916, p. 1; July 14, 1916, p. 4; July 15, 1916, p. 3; July 16, 1916, p. 3.
11. Ibid., July 17, 1916, p. 3.
12. Ibid., July 19, 1916, p. 4.
13. Hughes, "Big Hike," p. 5.
14. Ibid., pp. 6, 24–26, 28.
15. Ibid., pp. 24, 26.
16. "From a National Guardsman," p. 773.
17. *New York Times*, October 13, 1916, p. 13.
18. Ibid.; October 16, 1916, p. 11.
19. Johnson and Malone, *Dictionary of American Biography*, suppl. 1, s.v. "Duffy, Francis Patrick." Garraty and Carnes, *American National Biography*, s.v.

"Duffy, Francis Patrick." Flick, "Father Duffy," p. 385.
20. *New York Times*, February 18, 1917, p. 18; March 7, 1917, p. 5.

## Chapter 5
## The 69th New York (165th Infantry) Regiment in World War I

1. *New York Times*, March 7, 1917, p. 5. Kilmer, "Historical Appendix," p. 331.
2. Kilmer, "Historical Appendix," p. 332. Ettinger and Ettinger, *Doughboy with the 69th*, p. xviii. Duffy, Francis, *Father Duffy's Story*, pp. 14–15.
3. *New York Times*, July 30, 1917, p. 9. Kilmer, "Historical Appendix," pp. 333–334.
4. Tompkins, *Rainbow Division*, pp. 10, 234. Dunlop, *Donovan*, p. 47.
5. Duffy, Francis, *Father Duffy's Story*, pp. 14, 21, 30.
6. Dunlop, *Donovan*, pp. 11–12, 21, 24, 26, 28–29, 44–46, 48–49.
7. *New York Times*, August 21, 1917, p. 3.
8. Ibid.
9. Hogan, *Shamrock Battalion*, pp. 7, 10–11.
10. Kilmer, "Historical Appendix," pp. 334–336. *New York Times*, August 21, 1917, p. 3.
11. Dunlop, *Donovan*, p. 50.
12. Ibid., pp. 50–51.
13. Ettinger and Ettinger, *Doughboy with the 69th*, pp. 7–8.
14. Kemm, "The Literary Legacy of Rupert Hughes." Hughes, *Long Ever Ago*, pp. 19, 87.
15. Ettinger and Ettinger, *Doughboy with the 69th*, pp. 15–16.
16. Kilmer, "Historical Appendix," pp. 338–339. Brown, *Last Hero*, p. 38, 40. Dunlop, *Donovan*, p. 54.
17. Kilmer, "Historical Appendix," pp. 338–339. Hogan, *Shamrock Battalion*, p. 24.
18. Kilmer, "Historical Appendix," pp. 339–340.
19. Ibid., p. 341. Hogan, *Shamrock Battalion*, pp. 28–29.
20. Kilmer, "Historical Appendix," p. 341. *New York Times*, April 20, 1919, sec. 4, p. 1.
21. Dunlop, *Donovan*, pp. 56, 58.
22. Kilmer, "Historical Appendix," p. 342. Hogan, *Shamrock Battalion*, p. 34.
23. Kilmer, "Historical Appendix," p. 342. Hogan, *Shamrock Battalion*, pp. 34–37.
24. Kilmer, "Historical Appendix," pp. 343–344. Dunlop, *Donovan*, p. 61; Hogan, *Shamrock Battalion*, pp. 42–43. *New York Times*, April 20, 1919, sec. 4, p. 1.
25. Kilmer, "Historical Appendix," p. 344. Hogan, *Shamrock Battalion*, pp. 48–50. Duffy, Francis, *Father Duffy's Story*, p. 58.
26. Kilmer, "Historical Appendix," pp. 345–346.
27. Ettinger and Ettinger, *Doughboy with the 69th*, pp. 139, 248.
28. Duffy, Francis, *Father Duffy's Story*, pp. 54–55.
29. Kilmer, "Historical Appendix," pp. 347–349.
30. Hogan, *Shamrock Battalion*, p. 61.
31. Holliday, *Joyce Kilmer*, vol. 2, pp. 14–15.
32. Dunlop, *Donovan*, p. 68. Tompkins, *Rainbow Division*, p. 35.
33. Dunlop, *Donovan*, p. 68. Hogan, *Shamrock Battalion*, pp. 64, 66.

34. Kilmer, "Historical Appendix," p. 350. Dunlop, *Donovan*, pp. 69–70.
35. Dunlop, *Donovan*, p. 70. Kilmer, "Historical Appendix," p. 350. Hogan, *Shamrock Battalion*, p. 73.
36. Reilly, *Americans All*, pp. 133, 139–143.
37. Ettinger and Ettinger, *Doughboy with the 69th*, pp. 47, 243–244. Duffy, Francis, *Father Duffy's Story*, pp. 106, 379.
38. Dunlop, *Donovan*, pp. 71–72.
39. Duffy, Francis, *Father Duffy's Story*, pp. 68–69.
40. Ibid., p. 69. Kyle, *Werner's Readings*, vol. 3, pp. 146–147.
41. Duffy, Francis, *Father Duffy's Story*, p. 69. Kilmer and Campion, *Campion College*, pp. 71–72. Dunlop, *Donovan*, p. 74.
42. Ettinger and Ettinger, *Doughboy with the 69th*, p. 15. Hogan, *Shamrock Battalion*, pp. 75–80.
43. Hogan, *Shamrock Battalion*, pp. 81–82.
44. Kilmer, "Historical Appendix," p. 351.
45. Hogan, *Shamrock Battalion*, pp. 84–86.
46. Kilmer, "Historical Appendix," pp. 351–352.
47. Hogan, *Shamrock Battalion*, pp. 86–87, 92–93.
48. Kilmer, "Historical Appendix," pp. 352–353.
49. *New York Times*, August 18, 1918, p. 8; August 22, 1918, p. 4. Dunlop, *Donovan*, pp. 76, 86. Holliday, *Joyce Kilmer*, vol. 2, p. 141.
50. Holliday, *Joyce Kilmer*, vol. 1, pp. 18, 76; vol. 2, pp. 136–137.
51. *New York Times*, August 22, 1918, p. 4. Duffy, Francis, *Father Duffy's Story*, pp. 14–15.
52. *New York Times*, March 18, 1918, p. 8; April 21, 1918, p. 16.
53. Ibid., April 12, 1918, p. 1.
54. Flick, "Father Duffy," p. 392.
55. Duffy, Francis, *Father Duffy's Story*, pp. 106–107, 109–110.
56. Tompkins, *Rainbow Division*, pp. 36, 38–39. *New York Times*, April 20, 1919, sec. 4, p. 1; July 7, 1918, sec. 9, p. 8.
57. Duffy, Francis, *Father Duffy's Story*, pp. 92–94. Reilly, *Americans All*, pp. 209, 212.
58. Dunlop, *Donovan*, pp. 78–80. Tompkins, *Rainbow Division*, p. vi. Stallings, *Doughboys*, p. 162.
59. Dunlop, *Donovan*, p. 80.
60. *New York Times*, April 20, 1919, sec. 4, p. 1. Dunlop, *Donovan*, pp. 80–81. Hogan, *Shamrock Battalion*, pp. 123–125.
61. Duffy, Francis, *Father Duffy's Story*, pp. 137–138.
62. Hogan, *Shamrock Battalion*, pp. 127–128, 132–133.
63. *New York Times*, April 20, 1919, sec. 4, p. 1.
64. Duffy, Francis, *Father Duffy's Story*, pp. 139–140.
65. *New York Times*, April 27, 1919, sec. 2, p. 1. Dunlop, *Donovan*, pp. 82–83. Brown, *Last Hero*, p. 47. Hogan, *Shamrock Battalion*, pp. 159–160.
66. Duffy, Francis, *Father Duffy's Story*, pp. 216–217.
67. Ibid., p. 286.
68. Brown, *Last Hero*, p. 50. Hogan, *Shamrock Battalion*, pp. 159–164. *New York Times*, July 30, 1918, p. 2. Tompkins, *Rainbow Division*, p. vi.
69. *New York Times*, April 20, 1919, sec. 4, p. 1.
70. Ibid.

71. Dunlop, *Donovan*, pp. 83, 85. Reilly, *Americans All*, pp. 383, 386.
72. "Letters From the Front to the Folks at Home," pp. 231–234.
73. *New York Times*, April 27, 1919, sec. 2, p. 1. Brown, *Last Hero*, pp. 49–50.
74. Brown, *Last Hero*, p. 50. Dunlop, *Donovan*, pp. 83–85.
75. Dunlop, *Donovan*, pp. 51, 62, 64–65, 78, 85–86.
76. *New York Times*, July 6, 1921, p. 2.
77. Ibid. "Sergeant Richard W. O'Neill," p. 222.
78. *New York Times*, July 6, 1921, p. 2.
79. Dunlop, *Donovan*, p. 88. Duffy, Francis, *Father Duffy's Story*, pp. 205–206. *New York Times*, April 27, 1919, sec. 2, p. 1.
80. Dunlop, *Donovan*, p. 88. Brown, *Last Hero*, pp. 54–55. Duffy, Francis, *Father Duffy's Story*, pp. 206–207. Reilly, *Americans All*, p. 383.
81. *New York Times*, August 18, 1918, p. 8; August 22, 1918, pp. 4, 8. Dunlop, *Donovan*, p. 87. Brown, *Last Hero*, p. 52.
82. *New York Times*, August 25, 1918, sec. 4, p. 4. Dunlop, *Donovan*, p. 52.
83. *New York Times*, August 25, 1918, sec. 4, p. 4.
84. Ibid.
85. Ettinger and Ettinger, *Doughboy with the 69th*, pp. 77–78.
86. *New York Times*, April 20, 1919, sec. 4, p. 1; April 22, 1919, p. 7. Ettinger and Ettinger, *Doughboy with the 69th*, p. 142.
87. Dunlop, *Donovan*, p. 89.
88. *New York Times*, September 8, 1918, p. 3; September 9, 1918, p. 10.
89. Duffy, Francis, *Father Duffy's Story*, pp. 230–231.
90. Dunlop, *Donovan*, pp. 89–90, 97–98. *New York Times*, April 27, 1919, sec. 2, p. 1.
91. Dunlop, *Donovan*, p. 98.
92. *New York Times*, April 27, 1919, sec. 2, p. 1. Hogan, *Shamrock Battalion*, pp. 207, 210–211, 216.
93. Brown, *Last Hero*, pp. 57–59.
94. Dunlop, *Donovan*, pp. 99–102. Duffy, Francis, *Father Duffy's Story*, p. 271.
95. Duffy, Francis, *Father Duffy's Story*, pp. 270–271.
96. Dunlop, *Donovan*, pp. 102–104. *New York Times*, April 27, 1919, sec. 2, p. 1. Brown, *Last Hero*, p. 63.
97. *Congressional Medal*, pp. 512–513. *New York Times*, March 8, 1923, p. 18.
98. Reilly, *Americans All*, pp. 697–699.
99. Duffy, Francis, *Father Duffy's Story*, p. 305.
100. *New York Times*, April 27, 1919, sec. 2, p. 1. Duffy, Francis, *Father Duffy's Story*, p. 304.
101. Dunlop, *Donovan*, p. 108. Duffy, Francis, *Father Duffy's Story*, pp. 309, 314.
102. Duffy, Francis, *Father Duffy's Story*, pp. 315–316.
103. Brown, *Last Hero*, pp. 66–69.
104. Ibid., 65, 68. Dunlop, *Donovan*, pp. 106–108. *Congressional Medal*, p. 513.
105. *New York Times*, April 27, 1919, sec. 2, p. 1. Duffy, Francis, *Father Duffy's Story*, pp. 314, 323–324.
106. Duffy, Francis, *Father Duffy's Story*, pp. 325–326. Dunlop, *Donovan*, p. 109.
107. *New York Times*, April 27, 1919, sec. 2, p. 1. Duffy, Francis, *Father Duffy's Story*, p. 355. *New York Times*, April 22, 1919, p. 7.
108. *New York Times*, March 30, 1919, p. 19; March 31, 1919, p. 6; April 3, 1919, p. 2; April 5, 1919, p. 4.

109. *New York Times*, April 20, 1919, sec. 2, p. 12.
110. Ibid., sec. 4, p. 1.
111. Ibid., April 22, 1919, pp. 1, 7; April 24, 1919, p. 6.
112. Ibid., April 22, 1919, p. 7
113. Ibid.
114. Ibid., April 24, 1919, p. 6. Brown, *Last Hero*, p. 71.
115. *New York Times*, April 24, 1919, p. 6.
116. Ibid., April 27, 1919, p. 12.
117. Ibid., April 23, 1919, p. 5. Dunlop, *Donovan*, pp. 111–112.
118. *New York Times*, April 29, 1919, p. 5.
119. Wakin, *Enter the Irish-American*, p. 133. Dunlop, *Donovan*, p. 112. *New York Times*, April 29, 1919, p. 5.
120. Holliday, *Joyce Kilmer*, vol. 1, pp. 110–112.
121. *New York Times*, April 29, 1919, pp. 1, 5. Brown, *Last Hero*, p. 71.
122. Brown, *Last Hero*, p. 71. *New York Times*, April 29, 1919, p. 5.
123. Dunlop, *Donovan*, p. 112. Hogan, *Shamrock Battalion*, pp. 273–274, 280. Duffy, Francis, *Father Duffy's Story*, p. 329.
124. *New York Times*, April 21, 1919, p. 6.
125. Duffy, Francis, *Father Duffy's Story*, pp. 356–358.
126. *New York Times*, April 30, 1919, p. 7. Flick, "Father Duffy," p. 392.
127. *New York Times*, June 27, 1932, pp. 1, 17.
128. Ettinger and Ettinger, *Doughboy with the 69th*, pp. 72–73; Garraty and Carnes, *American National Biography*, s.v. "Duffy, Francis Patrick."
129. *New York Times*, June 27, 1932, pp. 1, 14, 17. *National Cyclopaedia of American Biography*, vol. 30, p. 201, s.v. "Duffy, Francis Patrick."
130. *New York Times*, April 28, 1932, p. 20.
131. Ibid., April 30, 1932, p. 12; April 28, 1932, p. 19.
132. Woollcott, *While Rome Burns*, pp. 49–50.
133. *New York Tmes*, July 2, 1934, p. 17; July 19, 1935, p. 15.
134. Ibid., May 3, 1937, pp. 1, 3; May 2, 1937, sec. 2, p. 1.
135. Ibid., May 3, 1937, p. 3.
136. Ibid., May 2, 1937, sec. 2, p. 3.
137. Ibid., January 25, 1940, p. 23.
138. MacArthur, "Tribute."
139. *New York Times*, January 25, 1940, p. 23.
140. Ibid., January 27, 1940, p. 9.

## Chapter 6
## The 69th New York (165th Infantry) Regiment in World War II

1. Hayes and Faissler, *Modern Times*, p. 444. Schlesinger, *Almanac of American History*, pp. 480–482.
2. "The 165th Infantry in World War II."
3. *New York Times*, October 15, 1940, p. 9; October 16, 1940, pp. 8–9.
4. Ibid., October 21, 1940, p. 17; October 24, 1940, p. 28; November 27, 1943, p. 12.
5. *New York Times*, March 20, 1941, p. 40. "The 165th Infantry in World War II." Ettinger and Ettinger, *Doughboy with the 69th*, p. 275 (n. 5). Love, *27th Infantry*, p. 14.

6. "The 165th Infantry in World War II." Love, *27th Infantry*, pp. 14–17.
7. "The 165th Infantry in World War II." Love, *27th Infantry*, pp. 17–19.
8. Love, *27th Infantry*, pp. 25–26. Morison, *Aleutians, Gilberts and Marshalls*, pp. 121–123.
9. Love, *27th Infantry*, p. 27. Morison, *Aleutians, Gilberts and Marshalls*, pp. 122–123.
10. Morison, *Aleutians, Gilberts and Marshalls*, pp. 124–125.
11. Ibid., p. 126.
12. Ibid., pp. 126, 132. Love, *27th Infantry*, p. 39. *New York Times*, July 17, 1945, p. 2.
13. *New York Times*, November 28, 1943, p. 63.
14. Ibid., November 25, 1943, p. 27; November 27, 1943, p. 12.
15. Love, *27th Infantry*, p. 39. *New York Times*, November 28, 1943, p. 64.
16. Morison, *Aleutians, Gilberts and Marshalls*, pp. 129, 132. Love, *27th Infantry*, pp. 32–33. Spector, *Eagle Against the Sun*, p. 267.
17. *New York Times*, November 28, 1943, p. 65.
18. Spector, *Eagle Against the Sun*, p. 267. Morison, *Aleutians, Gilberts and Marshalls*, pp. 133–134. *New York Times*, November 28, 1943, p. 64.
19. *New York Times*, November 28, 1943, p. 65.
20. Morison, *Aleutians, Gilberts and Marshalls*, p. 134. Love, *27th Infantry*, p. 54.
21. Morison, *Aleutians, Gilberts and Marshalls*, p. 134. Love, *27th Infantry*, p. 55. *New York Times*, April 3, 1944, p. 9.
22. Morison, *Aleutians, Gilberts and Marshalls*, p. 76. *New York Times*, April 19, 1946, p. 31.
23. "The 165th in World War II: The Marianas – Saipan." Snyder, *Historical Guide to World War II*, p. 428. Baudet, *Historical Encyclopedia of World War II*, pp. 424–425.
24. "The 165th in World War II: The Marianas – Saipan." Baudet, *Historical Encyclopedia of World War II*, p. 425. Morrison, *New Guinea and the Marianas*, p. 201.
25. "The 165th in World War II: The Marianas – Saipan." Love, *27th Infantry*, p. 137. Morison, *New Guinea and the Marianas*, p. 206.
26. Morrison, *New Guinea and the Marianas*, pp. 208–209, 330–333. Love, *27th Infantry*, p. 167ff.
27. Morison, *New Guinea and the Marianas*, pp. 330, 334. Love, *27th Infantry*, pp. 226–228, 316–317.
28. Love, *27th Infantry*, pp. 317, 332–333, 339–341, 363, 369, 371.
29. Ibid., p. 369.
30. Morison, *New Guinea and the Marianas*, pp. 334–336.
31. Love, *27th Infantry*, pp. 502–503, 505, 514.
32. Ibid., pp. 515–517.
33. Morison, *New Guinea and the Marianas*, pp. 338–339. Love, *27th Infantry*, p. 519.
34. Parrish, *Encyclopedia of World War II*, p. 457. Love, *27th Infantry*, pp. 551, 563, 567.
35. Love, *27th Infantry*, pp. 567, 569–570.
36. Ibid., pp. 576, 588–590.
37. Ibid., pp. 593–595.
38. Ibid., pp. 596–599.

39.  Ibid., pp. 600, 602.
40.  Ibid., pp. 676–677.
41.  Ibid., pp. 610, 675.

# Works Cited

"America Singing: Nineteenth-Century Song Sheets." Online. Library of Congress. Internet. 7 July 2000. Available: www.lcweb2.loc.gov.

Andrews, J. Cutler. *The North Reports the Civil War*. Pittsburgh: University of Pittsburgh Press, 1985.

Ann, Martha, and Dorothy Myers Imel. *Goddesses in World Mythology*. Santa Barbara: ABC-CLIO, Inc., 1993.

Ardolina, Rosemary Muscarella. *Old Calvary Cemetery: New Yorkers Carved in Stone*. Bowie, Md.: Heritage Books, 1996.

Athearn, Robert G. *Thomas Francis Meagher: An Irish Revolutionary in America*. Boulder: University of Colorado Press, 1949.

Bache, Richard Meade. *Life of General George Gordon Meade*. Philadelphia: Henry T. Coates and Company, 1897.

Bagenal, Philip H. *The American Irish and Their Influence on Irish Politics*. London: Kegan Paul, Trench and Company, 1882.

Bailey, Ronald H. *The Bloodiest Day: The Battle of Antietam*. Alexandria, Va.: Time-Life Books, 1984.

Bailey, Thomas A. *A Diplomatic History of the American People*. 10th ed. Englewood Cliffs, N.J.: Prentice-Hall, Inc., 1980.

Bailyn, Bernard, et al. *The Great Republic: A History of the American People*. 3rd. ed. Lexington, Mass.: D. C. Heath and Company, 1985.

Barker, Brian. *The Symbols of Sovereignty*. North Pomfret, Vt.: David & Charles Inc., 1979.

Bates, Samuel P. *History of Pennsylvania Volunteers, 1861–65*. 14 vols. Harrisburg: B. Singerly (printer), 1869–1871. Reprint, Wilmington, N.C.: Broadfoot Publishing Company, 1993.

Baudet, Marcel, et al., eds. *The Historical Encyclopedia of World War II*. New York: Greenwich House, 1984.

Bayor, Ronald H., and Timothy J. Meagher, eds. *The New York Irish*. Baltimore: The Johns Hopkins University Press, 1996.

Behan, Brendan. *Borstal Boy*. New York: Alfred A. Knopf, 1959.

Bilby, Joseph G. *Remember Fontenoy! The 69th New York and the Irish Brigade in the Civil War*. Hightstown, N.J.: Longstreet House, 1995.

Bilby, Joseph G., and Stephan D. O'Neill, eds. *"My Sons Were Faithful and They Fought." The Irish Brigade at Antietam: An Anthology*. Hightstown, N.J.: Longstreet House, 1997.

Boatner, Mark Mayo. *The Civil War Dictionary*. New York: David McKay Company, Inc., 1959.

Boylan, Henry. *A Dictionary of Irish Biography*. 3rd ed. Niwot, Colo.: Roberts Rinehart Publishers, 1998.

Boyle, Frank A. *A Party of Mad Fellows: The Story of the Irish Regiments in the Army of the Potomac*. Dayton, Ohio: Morningside House, Inc., 1996.

Brady, Anne M., and Brian Cleve. *A Biographical Dictionary of Irish Writers*. New York: St. Martin's Press, 1985.

Brook, Stopford A., and T. W. Rolleston, eds. *A Treasury of Irish Poetry in the English Tongue*. London: Smith, Elder and Company, 1900.

Brown, Anthony Cave. *The Last Hero: Wild Bill Donovan*. New York: Times Books,

1982.

Burton, William L. *Melting Pot Soldiers: The Union's Ethnic Regiments*. Ames: Iowa State University Press, 1988.

Busey, John W. *These Honored Dead: the Union Casualties at Gettysburg*. Hightstown, N.J.: Longstreet Press, 1988.

*Catholic Encyclopedia, The*. New York: The Encyclopedia Press, Inc., 1911.

Cavanagh, Michael. *Memoirs of Gen. Thomas Francis Meagher*. Worcester, Mass.: The Messenger Press, 1892. Reprint, Gaithersburg, Md.: Olde Soldier Books, Inc., n.d.

Chivers, C. J. "After a War Starts at Home, the Guard Prepares to Take It Abroad." *New York Times*, September 18, 2001, p. B1.

Clarke, Joseph I. C. *The Fighting Race and Other Poems and Ballads*. 3rd ed. New York: The American News Company, 1911.

Colum, Padraic, ed. *An Anthology of Irish Verse*. New York: Liveright Publishing Corp., 1948.

*Congressional Medal of Honor, The*. Forest Ranch, Calif.: Sharp & Dunnigan Publications, 1984.

Connell, Evan S. *Son of the Morning Star: Custer and the Little Bighorn*. San Francisco: North Point Press, 1984.

Connolly, S. J., ed. *The Oxford Companion to Irish History*. Oxford: Oxford University Press, 1998.

Conyngham, David Power. *Ireland Past and Present*. New York: James Sheehy, 1884.

———. *The Irish Brigade and Its Campaigns*. New York: William McSorley & Company, 1867.

———. "Soldiers of the Cross." Typed manuscript, University of Notre Dame.

Cook, S. A., et al. *The Roman Republic 133–44 B.C.* Vol. 9 of *The Cambridge Ancient History*. Cambridge: Cambridge University Press, 1951.

Corby, William. *Memoirs of Chaplain Life: Three Years with the Irish Brigade in the Army of the Potomac*. Edited by Lawrence Frederick Kohl. New York: Fordham University Press, 1992.

Corcoran, Michael. *The Captivity of General Corcoran*. Philadelphia: Barclay and Company, 1864.

"Corcoran of the Sixty-Ninth." *The Journal of the American Irish Historical Society* 10 (1911): 365–367.

Corkery, Daniel. *The Hidden Ireland: A Study of Gaelic Munster in the Eighteenth Century*. Dublin: M. H. Gill and Son., Ltd., 1925.

Coyle, John G. "General Michael Corcoran." *The Journal of the American Irish Historical Society* 13 (1914): 109–126.

Crimmins, John D. *Irish-American Historical Miscellany*. N.p.: John D. Crimmins, 1905.

Crowley, D. O. *Irish Poets and Novelists*. 3rd ed. San Francisco: n.p., 1893.

Current, Richard N., ed. *Encyclopedia of the Confederacy*. 4 vols. New York: Simon & Schuster, 1993.

Daly, Maria Lydig. *A Diary of a Union Lady 1861–1865*. Edited by Harold Earl Hammond. New York: Funk & Wagnalls Company, Inc., 1962.

D'Arcy, Mary Ryan. *The Saints of Ireland: A Chronological Account of the Lives and Works of Ireland's Saints and Missionaries at Home and Abroad*. St. Paul, Minn.: The Irish American Cultural Institute, 1974.

D'Arcy, William. *The Fenian Movement in the United States 1858–1886*. Washington,

D.C.: The Catholic University of America Press, 1947.

Davis, Richard. *The Young Ireland Movement*. Dublin: Gill and Macmillan, 1987.

Day, Catharina. *Ireland*. London: Cadogan Books, 1991.

Delaney, John J., and James Edward Tobin. *Dictionary of Catholic Biography*. Garden City, N.Y.: Doubleday and Company, Inc., 1961.

Donovan, John. "Details of the Battle of Fredericksburg." Online. Internet. 2 July 2000. Available: www.geocities.com.

Duffy, Charles Gavan. *Four Years of Irish History 1845–1849*. Melbourne: George Robertson, 1883.

Duffy, Francis. *Father Duffy's Story: A Tale of Humor and Heroism, of Life and Death with the Fighting Sixty-Ninth*. With a historical appendix by Joyce Kilmer. New York: George H. Doran Company, 1919.

Dunlop, Richard. *Donovan: America's Master Spy*. Chicago: Rand McNally & Company, 1982.

Dupuy, R. Ernest, and Trevor N. Dupuy. *The Encyclopedia of Military History*. 2nd rev. ed. New York: Harper & Row, 1986.

Durant, Will and Ariel. *The Reformation*. Vol. 6 of *The Story of Civilization*. New York: Simon and Schuster, 1957.

Dyer, Frederick H. *A Compendium of the War of the Rebellion*. 3 vols. New York: Thomas Yoseloff, 1959.

Eggenberger, David. *A Dictionary of Battles*. New York: Thomas Y. Crowell Company, 1967.

Ellis, Steven G. *Tudor Ireland: Crown, Community and Conflict of Cultures, 1470–1603*. London: Longman Group Ltd., 1985.

Ely, Alfred. *Journal of Alfred Ely, A Prisoner of War in Richmond*. Edited by Charles Lanman. New York: D. Appleton and Company, 1862.

*Encyclopaedia Britannica, The*. 29 vols. New York: Encyclopaedia Britannica Company, 1910-1911.

Ettinger, Albert M., and A. Churchill Ettinger. *A Doughboy with the Fighting 69th: A Remembrance of World War I*. Shippensburg, Pa.: White Mane Publishing Company, Inc., 1992.

Fanning, Charles. *The Irish Voice in America: Irish-American Fiction from the 1760s to the 1890s*. Lexington, Ky.: The University Press of Kentucky, 1990.

Faust, Patricia L. *Historical Times Illustrated Encyclopedia of the Civil War*. New York: Harper & Row, 1986.

Federal Writers' Project of the Work Projects Administration. *Montana: A State Guide Book*. American Guide Series. New York: Hastings House, 1939.

Ferguson, Gary Lynn. *Song Finder: A Title Index to 32,000 Popular Songs in Collections, 1854–1992*. Westport, Conn.: Greenwich Press, 1995.

"Fighting Sixty-Ninth, The." *New York World*, March 18, 1877.

"Fighting 69th in the Mexican Border Campaign, The." Online. Internet. 2 July 2000. Available: www.hourigan.com.

Fitzgerald, James. "The Sixty-Ninth Regiment, New York City." *The Journal of the American Irish Historical Society* 9 (1910): 161–182.

Fitzgerald, Michael. "From Ballingarry to Fredericksburg: David Power Conyngham (1825–1883)." *Tipperary Historical Journal* (1988): 192–200.

Flick, Ella M. E. "Father Duffy." *The Catholic World* 137 (July 1933): 385–394.

Flynn, Sean Michael. "69th's 150th Birthday Commemoration." Online. Internet. 3 March 2002. Available: www.fighting69th.com/69th's_150th.htm.

Foote, Shelby. *Fort Sumter to Perryville*. Vol. 1 of *The Civil War: A Narrative*. New York: Random House, 1958.

Foster, R. F. *Modern Ireland 1600–1972*. London: The Penguin Press, 1988.

Fox, William F. *Regimental Losses in the American Civil War 1861–1865*. Albany: Albany Publishing Company, 1889.

"From a National Guardsman." *Outlook* 113 (August 2, 1916): 773.

Galwey, Thomas Francis. *The Valiant Hours: Narrative of "Captain Brevet," an Irish-American in the Army of the Potomac*. Edited by W. S. Nye. Harrisburg, Pa.: The Stackpole Company, 1961.

Garcia, Christopher-Michael. "The 'Fighting' Sixty-Ninth New York State Militia at Bull Run." In *The History of the Irish Brigade: A Collection of Historical Essays*. Fredericksburg, Va.: Sergeant Kirkland's Museum and Historical Society, Inc., 1997.

Garraty, John A., and Mark C. Carnes, eds. *American National Biography*. 24 vols. New York: Oxford University Press, 1999.

Gibson, Florence E. *The Attitudes of the New York Irish Toward State and National Affairs 1848–1892*. New York: Columbia University Press, 1951.

Glover, Michael. *The Peninsular War 1807–1814*. Hamden, Conn.: Archon Books, 1974.

Gordon, Michael. *The Orange Riots: Irish Political Violence in New York City 1870 and 1871*. Ithaca, N.Y.: Cornell University Press, 1993.

Hall, Henry. *History of Auburn, New York*. Auburn, N.Y.: Dennis Brothers and Company, 1869.

Halpine, Charles Graham. *The Life and Adventures, Songs, Services, and Speeches of Private Miles O'Reilly*. New York: n.p., 1864.

————. *The Poetical Works of Charles G. Halpine*. New York: Harper & Brothers, 1869.

Hanchett, William. *Irish: Charles G. Halpine in Civil War America*. Syracuse: Syracuse University Press, 1970.

Haskell, Bob. "New York Guardsman Conveys Patriotism, Anger in Recovery Effort." Army LINK News. Online. Internet. 3 December 2001. Available: www.dtic.mil/armylink/news/Sep2001/a20010928ngready.html.

Hayes, Carlton J. H., and James H. Hanscom. *Ancient Civilizations: Prehistory to the Fall of Rome*. New York: Macmillan Publishing Company, Inc., 1968.

Hayes, Carlton J. H., and Margareta Faissler. *Modern Times: The French Revolution to the Present*. New York: Macmillan Publishing Company, Inc., 1966.

Headley, Phineas. *Massachusetts in the Rebellion*. Boston: Walker, Fuller, and Company, 1866.

*Helena (Mont.) Independent*.

Hennessy, Maurice. *The Wild Geese: The Irish Soldier in Exile*. Old Greenwich, Conn.: The Devin-Adair Company, c. 1973.

Hewett, Janet B., ed. *The Roster of Union Soldiers, 1861–1865*. Wilmington, N.C.: Broadfoot Publishing Company, 1998.

Hickey, D. J., and J. E. Doherty. *A Dictionary of Irish History Since 1800*. Totowa, N.J.: Barnes & Noble Books, 1981.

Hickey, W. "Two Irish-American Writers." *The Irish Book Lover* (January 1914): 97–98.

Hoagland, Kathleen, ed. *1,000 Years of Irish Poetry*. New York: The Devin-Adair Company, 1947.

Hogan, Martin J. *The Shamrock Battalion of the Rainbow: A Story of the "Fighting Sixty-Ninth."* New York: D. Appleton and Company, 1919.

Holliday, Robert Cortes, ed. *Joyce Kilmer.* 2 vols. Vol. 1, *Memoirs and Poems.* New York: George H. Doran Company, c. 1918. Vol. 2, *Prose Works.* Garden City, N.Y.: Doubleday, Doran & Company, Inc., 1929.

Hughes, Rupert. "The Big Hike." *Collier's Weekly* 58 (November 11, 1916): 5–6.

———. *Long Ever Ago.* New York: Harper and Brothers, 1918.

*Ireland,* Michelin Guide, 1992 ed.

Johnson, Allen, et al., eds. *Dictionary of American Biography.* 28 vols. New York: C. Scribner's Sons, 1928–1988.

Jones, Paul. *The Irish Brigade.* Washington, D.C.: Robert B. Luce, Inc., 1969.

Joyce, P. W. *A Short History of Ireland.* London: Longmans, Green, and Company, 1895.

Kelly, Barney. "The Green Flags of the Irish Brigade." In *The History of the Irish Brigade: A Collection of Historical Essays.* Fredericksburg, Va.: Sergeant Kirkland's Museum and Historical Society, Inc., 1997.

Kemm, James O. "The Literary Legacy of Rupert Hughes." Online. University of Iowa Special Collections. *Books at Iowa* 42 (April 1985). Internet. 18 September 2001. Available: www.lib.uiowa.edu.

Keneally, Thomas. *The Great Shame and the Triumph of the Irish in the English-Speaking World.* New York: Doubleday, 1998.

Kilmer, Joyce. "Historical Appendix." In *Father Duffy's Story: A Tale of Humor and Heroism, of Life and Death with the Fighting Sixty-Ninth.* New York: George H. Doran Company, 1919.

*Kilmer and Campion.* Prairie du Chien, Wisc.: Campion College, n.d.

Kohl, Lawrence Frederick. Introduction to *The Story of the 116th Pennsylvania Volunteers in the War of the Rebellion,* by St. Clair Mulholland. New York: Fordham University Press, 1996.

Krans, Horatio Sheafe. *Irish Life in Irish Fiction.* New York: Columbia University Press, 1903.

Kraus, David. *Sean O'Casey: The Man and His Work.* New York: The Macmillan Company, 1960.

Kyle, George, and Mary Kyle Dallas. *Werner's Readings and Recitations.* 57 vols. New York: Edgar S. Werner & Company, 1891.

Laffin, John. *Brassey's Battles: 3500 Years of Conflict, Campaigns and Wars.* London: Brassey's Defence Publishers, 1986.

Lane, Phyllis. "Colonel Michael Corcoran, Fighting Irishman." In *The History of the Irish Brigade: A Collection of Historical Essays.* Fredericksburg, Va.: Sergeant Kirkland's Museum and Historical Society, Inc., 1997.

Leckie, Robert. *The Wars of America.* 2 vols. New York: Harper and Row, 1968.

Lee, Thomas Zanslaur. "General St. Clair Mulholland." *The Journal of the American Irish Historical Society* 9 (1910): 501–505.

"Letters From the Front to the Folks at Home." *The Journal of the American Irish Historical Society* 17 (1917): 231–234.

Lonergan, Thomas S. "General Thomas Francis Meagher." *The Journal of the American Irish Historical Society* 12 (1912–13): 111–126.

Lonn, Ella. *Foreigners in the Union Army and Navy.* Baton Rouge: Louisiana State University Press, 1951.

Lounsburg, Thomas R. *Yale Book of American Verse.* New Haven: Yale University

Press, 1912.

Love, Edmund G. *The 27th Infantry Division in World War II*. Washington, D.C.: Infantry Journal Press, 1949.

Lydon, James. *The Making of Ireland*. London: Routledge, 1998.

Lyons, W. F. *Brigadier-General Thomas Francis Meagher: His Political and Military Career with Selections from His Speeches and Writings*. New York: D. & J. Sadlier and Company, 1886. Reprint, Danbury, Conn.: Archer Press, 1975.

MacArthur, Douglas. "Tribute to the Fighting 69th and Father Duffy." Online. Internet. 11 July 2000. Available: www.thewildgeese.com.

Maclennan, Malcolm. *A Pronouncing and Etymological Dictionary of the Gaelic Language*. Aberdeen: Acair and Aberdeen University Press, 1979.

MacCloskey, Monro. *Reilly's Battery: A Story of the Boxer Rebellion*. New York: Richard Rosen Press, Inc., 1969.

MacManus, Seumas. *The Story of the Irish Race*. Rev. ed. New York: The Devin-Adair Company, 1968.

Magill, Frank N., ed. *Great Events from History*. Ancient and Medieval Series. 3 vols. Englewood Cliffs, N.J.: Salem Press, Inc., 1972.

Maguire, John Francis. *The Irish in America*. London: Longmans, Green, 1868.

Maull, D. W. *The Life and Military Services of the Late Brigadier General Thomas A. Smyth*. Wilmington, Del.: H. & E. F. James, 1870.

McCarter, William. *My Life in the Irish Brigade: The Civil War Memoirs of Private William McCarter, 116th Pennsylvania Infantry*. Edited by Kevin E. O'Brien. Campbell, Calif.: Savas Publishing Company, 1996.

McDermott, Anthony W. *A Brief History of the 69th Regiment Pennsylvania Volunteers*. Philadelphia: D. J. Gallagher & Co., 1889.

Meagher, Thomas Francis. *The Last Days of the Sixty Ninth in Virginia*. New York: *Irish American*, 1861.

Monaghan, Patricia. *The New Book of Goddesses and Heroines*. St. Paul, Minn.: Llewellyn Publications, 1998.

*Montana Daily Record*.

Moody, T. W. and F. X. Martin, eds. *The Course of Irish History*. Niwot, Colo.: Roberts Rinehart Publishers, 1995.

Moore, Frank, ed. *The Civil War in Song and Story 1860–1865*. New York: P. F. Collier, 1882.

———, ed. *The Rebellion Record*. 11 vols. New York: G. P. Putnam, 1862–1864.

Morison, Samuel Eliot. *Aleutians, Gilberts and Marshalls, June 1942–April 1944*. Vol. 7 of *History of United States Naval Operations in World War II*. Boston: Little, Brown and Company, 1975.

———. *New Guinea and the Marianas, March 1944–August 1944*. Vol. 8 of *History of United States Naval Operations in World War II*. Boston: Little, Brown and Company, 1975.

Mulholland, St. Clair A. "The Irish Brigade in the War for the Union." In *Memoirs of Chaplain Life: Three Years with the Irish Brigade in the Army of the Potomac* by Father William Corby. Edited by Lawrence Frederick Kohl. New York: Fordham University Press, 1992.

———. *Military Order: Congress Medal of Honor Legion of the United States*. Philadelphia: n.p., 1905.

———. *The Story of the 116th Pennsylvania Volunteers in the War of the Rebellion*. Edited by Lawrence Frederick Kohl. New York: Fordham University Press,

1996.

Murphy, T. L. *Kelly's Heroes: The Irish Brigade at Gettysburg*. Gettysburg: Farnsworth House Military Impressions, 1997.

*National Cyclopaedia of American Biography, The*. 63 vols. New York: James T. White and Company, 1893–1984.

Neilson, William Allan, ed. *Webster's New International Dictionary of the English Language*. 2nd ed. Springfield, Mass.: G. & C. Merriam Company, 1957.

*New Catholic Encyclopedia*. 17 vols. New York: McGraw-Hill, 1967–1979.

*New Encyclopaedia Britannica, The*. 32 vols. Chicago: Encyclopaedia Britannica, c. 1998.

*New York Herald*.

*New York in the Spanish-American War 1898*. 3 vols. Albany: James B. Lyon (printer), 1900.

*New York Irish History* 5 (1990–91): 28.

New York Monuments Commission for the Battlefields of Gettysburg and Chattanooga. *Final Report on the Battlefield of Gettysburg*. [*New York at Gettysburg*]. 3 vols. Albany: J. B. Lyon Company, 1900.

*New York Times*.

Newman, Peter. *Companion to Irish History from the Submission of Tyrone to Partition 1603–1921*. Oxford: Facts on File, 1991.

Nugent, Robert. "The Sixty-Ninth Regiment at Fredericksburg." *The Journal of the American Irish Historical Society* 15 (1916): 191–200.

O'Beirne, Kevin. "Christmas in the Union's Irish Brigades." Online. Internet. 1 July 2000. Available: www.thewildgeese.com.

———. "Recalling the 155th New York." Online. Internet. 2 July 2000. Available: www.thewildgeese.com.

O'Brien, Kevin E. "The Irish Brigade in the Wheatfield." In *The History of the Irish Brigade: A Collection of Historical Essays*. Fredericksburg, Va.: Sergeant Kirkland's Museum and Historical Society, Inc., 1997.

———. "Sprig of Green: The Irish Brigade." In *The History of the Irish Brigade: A Collection of Historical Essays*. Fredericksburg, Va.: Sergeant Kirkland's Museum and Historical Society, Inc., 1997.

O'Brogain, Seamus. *The Wolfhound Guide to the Irish Harp Emblem*. Dublin: Wolfhound Press Ltd., 1998.

O'Callaghan, John Cornelius. *History of the Irish Brigades in the Service of France*. New York: P. O'Shea, 1887.

O'Connor, Ulick. *The Troubles: Ireland 1912–1922*. Indianapolis: The Bobbs-Merrill Company, Inc., 1975.

O Dónaill, Niall, ed. *Foclóir Gaeilige-Béarla* [Irish-English Dictionary]. Baile Atha Cliath [Dublin]: Oifig an tSoláthair [Supply Office], 1977.

O'Donnell, Charles. *Collected Poems*. Notre Dame, Ind.: Notre Dame University Press, 1942.

O'Donnell, Elliot. *The Irish Abroad: A Record of the Achievements of Wanderers from Ireland*. New York: E. P. Dutton and Company, n.d.

O'Donoghue, D. J. *The Poets of Ireland: A Biographical and Bibliographical Dictionary of Irish Writers of English Verse*. Dublin: Hodges, Figgis and Company, Ltd., 1912. Reprint, Detroit: Gale Research Company, 1968.

O'Hanlon, Ray. "Tribute to a Fallen Irish Hero." *Irish Echo*. May 25–31, 1994.

Olney, Victor. Emails to the author.

"165th Infantry in World War II, The." Online. Internet. 2 July 2000. Available: www.hourigan.com.

"1656th Infantry in World War II: The Marianas – Saipan." Online. Internet. 3 December 2001. Available: www.hourigan.com.

O'Rourke, Kevin. *Currier and Ives: The Irish and America*. New York: Henry N. Abrams, Inc., 1995.

Osborne, William H. *The History of the Twenty-Ninth Regiment of Massachusetts Volunteer Infantry in the Late War of the Rebellion*. Boston: Albert J. Wright (printer), 1877.

Page, N. Clifford, ed. *Irish Songs: A Collection of Airs Old and New*. Boston: Oliver Ditson Company, 1907.

Parrish, Thomas, ed. *The Simon and Schuster Encyclopedia of World War II*. New York: Simon and Schuster, 1978.

Phisterer, Frederick. *New York in the War of the Rebellion 1861–1865*. 5 vols. 3rd ed. Albany: J. B. Ryan Company, 1912.

Pohanka, Brian C. "James McKay Rorty: An Appreciation." A monograph written for the unveiling of a memorial to Rorty at First Calvary Cemetery, Queens, New York, May 29, 1993.

Potter, George. *To the Golden Door: The Story of the Irish in Ireland and America*. Boston: Little, Brown and Company, 1960.

"Presentation of the Sword of General Meagher to the University of Notre Dame, March 4, 1914." *The Journal of the American Irish Historical Society* 13 (1914): 320–331.

Reilly, Henry J. *Americans All. The Rainbow at War: Official History of the 42nd Rainbow Division in the World War*. Columbus: The F. J. Heer Publishing Company, 1936.

Reynolds, Lawrence. *Poetical Address Before the Irish Brigade*. Albany: Michael O'Sullivan, 1863.

*Rhyme With Reason: A Garland of Irish Shamrocks. Many of Them Grown in America*. Chicago: P. G. Smyth, 1911.

Robertson, James, Jr. *Stonewall Jackson: The Man, the Soldier, the Legend*. New York: Simon & Schuster Macmillan, 1997.

Roche, James Jeffrey. *Life of John Boyle O'Reilly*. Chicago: J. S. Hyland & Company, 1891.

Ross, David. "Superintendent James Morrow Walsh." An interpretative and biographical study prepared for Fort Walsh National Historic Site, Canadian Heritage, December 1996.

Savage, John. *Faith and Fancy*. New York: James B. Kirker, 1864.

———. *Fenian Heroes and Martyrs*. Boston: Patrick Donahoe, 1868.

Schlesinger, Arthur M., Jr., ed. *The Almanac of American History*. New York: Bramhall House, 1986.

Seagrave, Pia Seija, ed. *The History of the Irish Brigade: A Collection of Historical Essays*. Fredericksburg, Va.: Sergeant Kirkland's Museum and Historical Society, Inc., 1997.

Sears, Minnie Earl, ed. *Song Index: An Index to More Than 12,000 Songs in 177 Song Collections Comprising 262 Volumes and Supplement*. New York: The H. W. Wilson Company, 1926. Reprint, North Haven, Conn.: The Shoe String Press, Inc., 1966.

Sears, Stephen W. *Landscape Turned Red: The Battle of Antietam*. New Haven: Ticknor

& Fields, 1983.

"Sergeant Richard W. O'Neill." *The Journal of the American Irish Historical Society* 24 (1925): 222.

Shaw, Roger. *One Hundred and Seventy-Five Battles*. Harrisburg, Pa.: The Military Service Publishing Company, 1937.

Sifakis, Stewart. *Who Was Who in the Civil War*. New York: Facts on File Publications, 1988.

Simpson, J. A., and E. S. C. Weiner, eds. *The Oxford English Dictionary*. 2nd ed. Oxford: Clarendon Press, 1989.

"69th Brigade, The." Online. Library of Congress. Internet. 2 July 2000. Available: www.lcweb2.loc.gov.

Snyder, Louis L. *Louis L. Snyder's Historical Guide to World War II*. Westport, Conn.: Greenwood Press, 1982.

Sobczak, A. J., ed. *Cyclopedia of Literary Characters*. Rev. ed. 5 vols. Pasadena, Calif.: Salem Press, Inc., c. 1998.

Spector, Ronald H. *Eagle Against the Sun: The American War with Japan*. New York: The Free Press, 1985.

Spink, Barry. "Colonel Richard Byrnes: Irish Brigade Leader." In *The History of the Irish Brigade: A Collection of Historical Essays*. Fredericksburg, Va.: Sergeant Kirkland's Museum and Historical Society, Inc., 1997.

Squire, Charles. *Celtic Myth & Legend*. London: Gresham Publishing, Inc., n.d. Reprint, Van Nuys, Calif.: Newcastle Publishing Company, Inc., 1975.

Stallings, Laurence. *The Doughboys: The Story of the AEF, 1917–1918*. New York: Harper and Row, 1963.

Stephen, Leslie, and Sidney Lee, eds. *Dictionary of National Biography*. 66 vols. London: Smith, Elden, & Company, 1885–1901.

Stevens, Peter F. *The Rogue's March: John Riley and the St. Patrick's Battalion*. Washington, D.C.: Brassey's, 1999.

Stevenson, Lionel. *Dr. Quicksilver: The Life of Charles Lever*. London: Chapman & Hall, Ltd., 1939.

Stewart, Robert Laird. *History of the One Hundred and Fortieth Regiment, Pennsylvania Volunteers*. Philadelphia: Regimental Association, 1912.

Thomason, John W., Jr. *Jeb Stuart*. New York: Charles Scribner's Sons, c. 1958.

*Tidings* (Los Angeles).

Tompkins, Raymond S. *The Story of the Rainbow Division*. New York: Boni and Liveright, 1919.

Townsend, George Alfred. *Campaign of a Non-Combatant and His Romaunt Abroad During the War*. New York: Blelock & Company, 1866. Reprint, Alexandria, Va.: Time-Life Books, 1982.

Turner, Jane, ed. *The Dictionary of Art*. 34 vols. London: Macmillan Publishing Ltd., 1996.

U.S. War Department. *The War of the Rebellion: A Compilation of the Official Records of the Union and Confederate Armies*. 70 vols. in 128 parts. Washington, D.C.: Government Printing Office, 1880–1901.

Van West, Carroll. "Montana's Monuments: History in the Making." *Montana: The Magazine of Western History* 40 (No. 4, 1990): 12–25.

Villard, Henry. *Memoirs*. 2 vols. Boston: Houghton, Mifflin and Company, 1904.

Wakin, Edward. *Enter the Irish-American*. New York: Thomas Y. Crowell Company, 1976.

Walker, Francis A. *History of the Second Army Corps in the Army of the Potomac*. New York: Charles Scribner's Sons, 1887.

*Who Was Who in America*. Vol. 1 (1897–1942). Chicago: Marquis–Who's Who, 1968.

Wilson, James Grant, and John Fiske. *Appleton's Cyclopaedia of American Biography*. New York: D. Appleton and Company, 1888.

Wittke, Carl. *The Irish in America*. Baton Rouge: Louisiana State University Press, 1956.

Woodham-Smith, Cecil. *Queen Victoria*. New York: Alfred A. Knopf, 1972.

Woodruff, Charles A. "The Irish Soldier in the Civil War." *The Journal of the American Irish Historical Society* 11 (1912): 154-159.

Woollcott, Alexander. *While Rome Burns*. New York: The Viking Press, 1934.

Woulfe, Patrick. *Irish Names and Surnames*. Rev. ed. Kansas City: Irish Genealogical Foundation, 1992.

Wright, Robert L., ed. *Irish Emigrant Ballads and Songs*. Bowling Green, Ky.: Bowling Green University Popular Press, 1975.

# Index